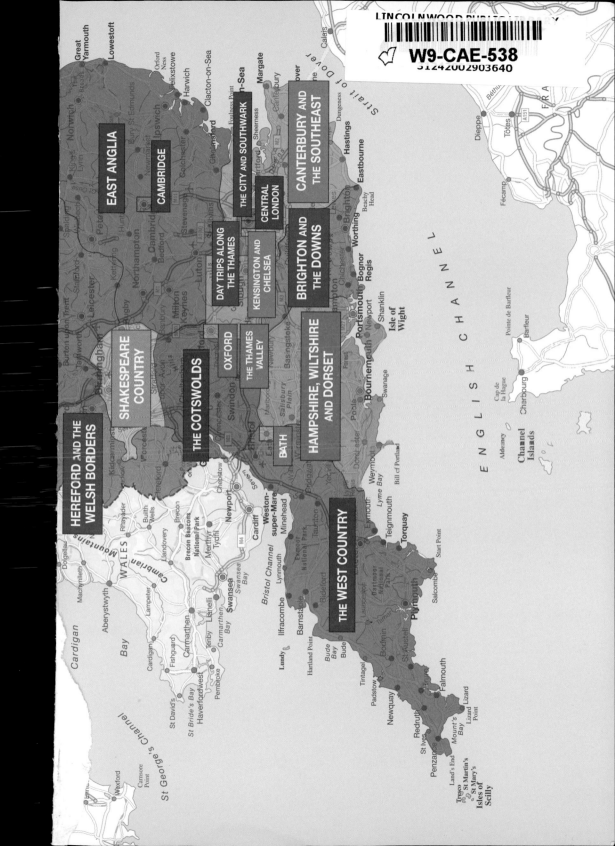

EAST ANGLIA

CAMBRIDGE

THE CITY AND SOUTHWARK

CENTRAL LONDON

CANTERBURY AND THE SOUTHEAST

DAY TRIPS ALONG THE THAMES

KENSINGTON AND CHELSEA

BRIGHTON AND THE DOWNS

SHAKESPEARE COUNTRY

OXFORD

THE THAMES VALLEY

THE COTSWOLDS

BATH

HAMPSHIRE, WILTSHIRE AND DORSET

HEREFORD AND THE WELSH BORDERS

THE WEST COUNTRY

ENGLISH CHANNEL

Cardigan Bay

St George's Channel

Bristol Channel

WALES

Cambrian Mountains

Brecon Beacons National Park

Exmoor National Park

Dartmoor National Park

Isle of Wight

Channel Islands

Strait of Dover

FRANCE

INSIGHT ○ GUIDES

ENGLAND

PLAN & BOOK
YOUR TAILOR-MADE TRIP

BRAZIL · **CHILE** · **ECUADOR**

TAILOR-MADE TRIPS & UNIQUE EXPERIENCES CREATED BY LOCAL TRAVEL EXPERTS AT INSIGHTGUIDES.COM/HOLIDAYS

Insight Guides has been inspiring travellers with high-quality travel content for over 45 years. As well as our popular guidebooks, we now offer the opportunity to book tailor-made private trips completely personalised to your needs and interests. By connecting with one of our local experts, you will directly benefit from their expertise and local know-how, helping you create memories that will last a lifetime.

HOW INSIGHTGUIDES.COM/HOLIDAYS WORKS

STEP 1

Pick your dream destination and submit an enquiry, or modify an existing itinerary if you prefer.

STEP 2

Fill in a short form, sharing details of your travel plans and preferences with a local expert.

STEP 3

Your local expert will create your personalised itinerary, which you can amend until you are completely satisfied.

STEP 4

Book securely online. Pack your bags and enjoy your holiday! Your local expert will be available to answer questions during your trip.

BENEFITS OF PLANNING & BOOKING AT
INSIGHTGUIDES.COM/HOLIDAYS

PLANNED BY LOCAL EXPERTS

The Insight Guides local experts are hand-picked, based on their experience in the travel industry and their impeccable standards of customer service.

SAVE TIME & MONEY

When a local expert plans your trip, you save time and money when you book, even during high season. You won't be charged for using a credit card either.

TAILOR-MADE TRIPS

Book with Insight Guides, and you will be in complete control of the planning process, from the initial selections to amending your final itinerary.

BOOK & TRAVEL STRESS-FREE

Enjoy stress-free travel when you use the Insight Guides secure online booking platform. All bookings come with a money-back guarantee.

WHAT OTHER TRAVELLERS THINK ABOUT TRIPS BOOKED AT
INSIGHTGUIDES.COM/HOLIDAYS

Trip to Portugal

Every step of the planning process and the trip itself was effortless and exceptional. Our special interests, preferences and requests were accommodated resulting in a trip that exceeded our expectations.

Corinne, USA ★★★★★

Trip to Vietnam

The organization was superb, the drivers professional, and accommodation quite comfortable. I was well taken care of! My thanks to your colleagues who helped make my trip to Vietnam such a great experience. My only regret is that I couldn't spend more time in the country.

Heather ★★★★★

DON'T MISS OUT
BOOK NOW AT
INSIGHTGUIDES.COM/HOLIDAYS

CONTENTS

Travel tips

TRANSPORT

A – Z

FURTHER READING

Maps
Inside front cover England
Inside back cover London Underground &
Central London

LEGEND
🔎 Insight on
📷 Photo story

THE BEST OF ENGLAND: TOP ATTRACTIONS

△ **Tower of London**. With a colourful history dating back to 1078, this historic site now houses the crown jewels. Queens were beheaded here, princes murdered and traitors tortured. Once a place to be avoided, it is now one of London's top visitor attractions. See page 108.

△ **Cornish beaches**. Surfers head to Cornwall for some of England's finest beaches, especially to the north coast to ride the Atlantic rollers. Towering cliffs and stretches of pristine sands bring walkers and family holidaymakers, too. See page 258.

▽ **The Eden Project**. An award-winning eco-friendly garden paradise contained within huge geodesic biome domes. See page 255.

△ **Stratford-upon-Avon**. William Shakespeare's picturesque birthplace is a good base from which to explore the beautiful and historic Warwickshire countryside. See page 165.

▷ **York Minster**. One of the finest Gothic cathedrals in the world, with elaborate pinnacles and an impressive collection of medieval stained glass. See page 323.

△ **Durham Cathedral**. Probably the finest Norman building in the country, perched dramatically above the River Wear. See page 348.

△ **Chatsworth House**. Britain's most impressive aristocratic estate. This vast Palladian mansion has an Arcadian setting in landscaped gardens and deer park. See page 287.

▽ **Stonehenge**. Find England's most famous prehistoric monument on Salisbury Plain. It consists of an outer ring and inner horseshoe of sarsen stone brought from South Wales. The mysterious circle's purpose is unknown, though the tumuli around the site hint at ancient funerary significance. Some scholars suggest a link with astronomy. See page 227.

▽ **The Lake District**. A striking landscape of deep lakes and steep-sided valleys. See page 311.

▷ **Oxford**. One of Europe's most renowned centres of learning since the 12th century, this university city is steeped in history and culture. See page 145.

THE BEST OF ENGLAND: EDITOR'S CHOICE

Castle Howard in North Yorkshire.

TOP ATTRACTIONS FOR FAMILIES

Alton Towers, Staffordshire. Britain's best-known theme park has wild white-knuckle rides and other thrills. See page 271.

Beamish, County Durham. This open-air museum in 300 acres (121 hectares) tells the social history of the northeast, with tram rides, a working farm and collier village. See page 348.

Ironbridge Gorge Museums, Telford. Series of museums on the River Severn celebrating the birthplace of the Industrial Revolution. See page 269.

Jorvik Viking Centre, York. Take an underground ride into the world of Vikings – splendidly revamped after the disastrous 2015 flood. See page 326.

Legoland, Windsor. Rides, shows and multiple attractions within easy reach of the capital. See page 137.

Longleat Safari Park. The first safari park outside Africa in the grounds of a stately home. See page 228.

National Maritime Museum, Greenwich. Recalling when Britain ruled the waves. See page 126.

SS *Great Britain*, Bristol. A brilliant re-enactment of life on the world's first iron-hulled ship with a screw propeller. See page 245.

Falconry display at Hampton Court Palace.

THE FINEST ROYAL AND STATELY HOMES

Windsor Castle. The Queen's official residence, a day trip from London. See page 136.

Buckingham Palace. Her Majesty's London base, famous for the Changing of the Guard. See page 90.

Hampton Court Palace, Surrey. Henry VIII's magnificent palace has wonderful gardens. See page 131.

Brighton Pavilion. Outrageously extravagant seaside palace built for the Prince Regent in the 1810s. See page 210.

Sandringham House. Norfolk retreat for the royals at Christmas. See page 183.

Alnwick Castle. Home of the Dukes of Northumberland; Harry Potter flew around here in the movies. See page 353.

Apsley House. "No. 1, London" has been the London home of the Dukes of Wellington for 200 years. See page 122.

Blenheim Palace, Oxfordshire. This vast, English Baroque pile is the family home of the Dukes of Marlborough; Winston Churchill was born here in 1874. See page 153.

Burghley House, Lincolnshire. Glorious Elizabethan mansion set in a deer park on the outskirts of the pretty town of Stamford. See page 278.

Castle Howard, Yorkshire. One of England's grandest stately homes, with formal gardens and sandstone follies. See page 338.

ENTHRALLING MUSEUMS

The Mallard at the National Railway Museum, York.

Ashmolean, Oxford. Renowned museum of art and archaeology collected by scholars from around the world. See page 151.

British Museum, London. This world-class institution charts the history of civilisation. See page 100.

Merseyside Maritime Museum. Slavery and emigration are the abiding themes in this evocative museum in Liverpool. See page 301.

National Media Museum, Bradford. Covers the history of film, television and photography. See page 333.

National Motor Museum, Hampshire. Beaulieu Abbey, home of the aristocratic Montagu family, puts veteran cars on show. See page 225.

National Railway Museum, York. Explore over 300 years of railway history. See page 326.

Science Museum, London. London's engrossing displays of inventions, with over 10,000 exhibits – and plenty to amuse the children. See page 120.

THE BEST GARDENS

RHS Gardens, Wisley. The Royal Horticultural Society's showcase garden with its stunning glasshouse. See page 215.

Royal Botanic Gardens, Kew. Fine day out from central London to magnificent gardens first planted in 1759. See page 129.

Sissinghurst Castle, Kent. Beautiful gardens designed by Vita Sackville-West. See page 200.

Tresco Abbey Gardens, Isles of Scilly. Subtropical gardens set around the 12th-century Priory of St Nicholas. See page 257.

The Palm House at Kew Gardens.

In the garden at the Barbara Hepworth Museum, St Ives.

TOP ART GALLERIES

Baltic Centre for Contemporary Art, Gateshead. The largest contemporary-arts venue outside London. See page 350.

Barbara Hepworth, St Ives. The sculptor's home in an attractive Cornish fishing village. See page 259.

Constable Country, Suffolk. Follow the trail of Britain's great landscape painter. See page 189.

1853 Gallery in Salts Mill, Saltaire. David Hockney has a permanent gallery in this splendid old mill in his native Bradford. See page 333.

The Lowry, Salford, Manchester. Stylish gallery named after the local painter famed for his depictions of industrial townscapes. See page 307.

National Gallery, London. Treasures from the Renaissance to the Impressionists – and it's free. See page 86.

Tate Modern, London. Hugely popular gallery in a former power station. See page 111.

The Walker, Liverpool. Wonderful collection of Victorian and Pre-Raphaelite paintings. See page 302.

River Eye, Gloucestershire.

Camber Sands in Kent.

Bamburgh Castle,
Northumberland.

THIS ENGLAND

England has a fascinating and colourful history, a rich culture, great cities and varied landscapes, yet it's also small and compact – perfect for a rewarding visit.

All dressed up for Notting Hill Carnival.

Everyone has their own idea of England – "this blessed plot, this earth, this realm, this England" (a quote from Shakespeare, of course). Many think of red double-decker buses, thatched cottages and country houses, village pubs and cream teas, cheery Liverpudlians and eccentric aristocrats. Others focus on England's fast-moving contemporary art scene, its world-class football teams or its passion for shopping (Napoleon memorably referred to England as a "nation of shop-keepers"). Most visitors will admit at least to being intrigued about the cult of the Royal Family in England – while a few seem almost obsessed by it. Certainly, among her own heterogeneous subjects the Queen remains an almost mythical figure and a popular institution.

In reality, there's some truth to most of the popular images of England. The steel-and-glass offices of the City of London do seem to reek of money just like in the newsreels. Meanwhile, if you go looking for it, you really can find the grey tower blocks and rusting factories of post-indus-trial decay. Then again, the green valleys and romantic vistas of the Lake District do match the impossibly perfect picture-postcards, and some of the country's beach resorts really do seem to be stuck in a 1950s time warp, or go further back where the stately homes are redolent of the life depicted in television's *Downton Abbey*.

Corpus Christi College.

Whatever your expectations, as a visitor you are unlikely to be disap-pointed. There really is something to cater to every taste and person-ality crammed into this small country. Even so, perhaps some will be surprised to find that there is no longer smog in London, that it doesn't rain as much as they had expected and that Indian restaurants far out-number fish-and-chip shops. On the other hand, most visitors will be delighted to find that the countryside often does look remarkably green and enticing, and that in spite of motorway madness and urban sprawl, there are still corners that match up to the most fanciful of idylls.

Catching up with the news in Wells-next-the-Sea.

THE ENGLISH CHARACTER

Some see this restless island race as tolerant, charming and funny, while others find them aloof, insular and hypocritical. But what are the English really like?

Summing up national character is fraught with difficulties. Seemingly every generalisation can be written off as, at best, cliché, and at worse, ill-informed prejudice. Nevertheless, as the saying goes, there's a kernel of truth in every lie, and if you ask the English themselves what they're like you'll find broad consensus on many features. A survey by a market research company found that the characteristics most popularly associated with Englishness by the English themselves were: drinking tea, talking about the weather, queuing, speaking English when abroad, keeping a stiff upper lip and moaning. This may seem a trivial list and rather stereotypical, but most visitors who spend any length of time in the country will come to recognise quite a few of them.

At the same time, visitors are often surprised by the variety they encounter on so small an island. Take a pin and put it down on a map of England and you will find a different experience each time: different people, different houses, different scenery, different accents, different values and different views. Together they make up an astonishing island race; a character that is the sum of so many parts.

THE CONTRADICTORY ENGLISH

Perhaps the heterogeneity of the English relates, at least in part, to their gift for ambiguity – or some might say hypocrisy. As a character in Alan Bennett's play *The Old Country* puts it, "When we say we don't mean what we say, only then are we entirely serious." If that seems contradictory, there's more to come. The British continue to embrace marriage, yet their divorce rate is one of the highest in Europe. They laud family life, yet the traditional practice of the upper classes is to pack their children off to boarding school as soon

Bure Valley Railway.

⊘ ENGLISH ECCENTRICS

In *English Eccentrics*, poet Edith Sitwell (1887–1964) stated that the English were prone to eccentricity because of "that peculiar and satisfactory knowledge of infallibility that is the hallmark and the birthright of the British nation". The aristocracy has provided several eccentrics, such as the 8th Earl of Bridgewater, who organised banquets for dogs, or the 5th Earl of Portland, who liked to live underground. Today's British eccentrics include fashion designer Vivienne Westwood, with her enduring disregard of the establishment, and Prime Minister Boris Johnson, whose bumbling approach gets him out of scrapes that would sink other politicians.

as possible, and many feel they have no choice but to park their aged parents in old people's homes. They pride themselves on their solidarity in war, yet cling to a divisive class system in peacetime.

They are also famed for their tolerance and sense of humour, yet, as the writer Paul Gallico observed, "No one can be as calculatedly rude as the British, which amazes Americans, who do not understand studied insult and can only offer abuse as a substitute." Britain's nearest neighbours can be just as amazed as Americans. André Maurois advised his fellow country-

Enjoying a drink in Grosvenor Square, Mayfair.

men, "In France it is rude to let a conversation drop; in England it is rash to keep it up. No one there will blame you for silence. When you have not opened your mouth for three years, they will think, 'This Frenchman is a nice quiet fellow.'"

The truth, as always, is more complicated. If Maurois had been in Liverpool or Leeds, he might not have got a word in. The Englishman who has "all the qualities of a poker except its occasional warmth" probably lives in the overcrowded south-east, where standoffishness is a way of protecting precious privacy.

But certain generalisations can be made. Because Britain is an island, it remains deeply individualistic and often seems aloof and more reserved when compared to its more volatile

European neighbours. You'll find on the one hand keen upholders of tradition, revellers in royal pageantry and proud followers of their athletes; on the other hand as innovators, embracers of modern technology and keen partakers of foreign cuisines.

ACCENTS

When, in *Pygmalion* (later to be reborn as *My Fair Lady*), George Bernard Shaw set Professor Henry Higgins the task of passing off Eliza Doolittle, a common Cockney flower seller, as a duchess at an ambassador's dinner party, there was no question about Higgins's first priority: he had to change her accent. Then, as now, a person's origins, class as well as locality, could be identified by the way he or she speaks and, as Shaw wisely observed, "It is impossible for an Englishman to open his mouth without making another Englishman despise or hate him."

It is remarkable – given these social pressures, the small size of Britain and the homogenising influence of television – that a vast variety of regional accents continue to flourish. Yet they do: two Britons, one with a strong West Country accent and the other from Newcastle upon Tyne, might struggle to understand each other.

With Asian and West Indian immigrants having added to the variety of speech patterns in Britain, consensus about what constitutes "proper English speech" has become even more elusive. Pity the manufacturers of digitised voice generators: who in Glasgow wants their cooker to inform them in a Surrey accent that their roast is ready, or what Oxfordshire driver wants his car to tell him in a Norfolk accent to fasten his seat-belt? The same unsatisfactory solution again presents itself and machines embrace Received Pronunciation.

SOCIAL CLASS

A newspaper cartoon cunningly caught the British confusion over its social attitudes. "I don't believe in class differences," its well-heeled gentleman was explaining, "but luckily my butler disagrees with me."

The implication is that the lower classes, far from being revolutionaries, are as keen as anyone to maintain the status quo, and that they still embody the attitude to the upper classes

"Mark my words," warned playwright Alan Bennett, "when a society has to resort to the lavatory for its humour, the writing is on the wall."

parodied more than a century ago by W.S. Gilbert in the comic opera *Iolanthe*:

Bow, bow, ye lower middle classes!
Bow, bow, ye tradesmen, bow, ye masses!

From time to time, the class rigidity seems set to crumble, but the promise is never quite fulfilled, mainly because the British have a genius for absorbing dissenters into "the system" as surely as a spider lures a fly into a web. The 1960s promoted a new egalitarianism; but it wasn't long before such former threats to civilised society as rock star Mick Jagger were consorting with the Royal Family. In the 1980s, the consensus among classes seemed again to be threatened, this time by Thatcherism, whose economic policies created stark inequalities between the regions and swelled the ranks of the disgruntled unemployed; worried about their election prospects, the Conservative Party replaced Mrs Thatcher in mid-term with the more emollient John Major.

Mr Major's humble origins suggested that any working-class boy who applied himself diligently could become prime minister – surely a threat to the power of the upper classes? And what about the supposedly left-wing traditions that nurtured Tony Blair and Gordon Brown? In reality, however, the true aristocrat is unperturbed by such irrelevancies, regarding a prime minister as the nation's equivalent to his butler. David Cameron tried to cross the boundaries, as a member of the old boy set, an old Etonian Tory, while insisting on being a modern man of the people and even quoting "lots of people call me Dave".

The monarchy cements the social hierarchy; fringe aristocrats define their social standing in relation to their closeness to royalty, and the elaborate system of honours – from peerages and knighthoods to Companionships of the British Empire – transform achievement into much sought-after feudal rank because the titles (even though generally decided by the politicians of the day) are bestowed in person by the monarch.

The ruling class is a pragmatic coalition of middle- and upper-class members. Generally, "they" (the people who seem to make all the decisions) remain strangely amorphous; common speech refers constantly to the fact that "they" have built an inadequate new motorway or that "they" have allowed some hideous glass skyscraper to be placed next to a Gothic cathedral – a peculiar dissociation from power in an avowedly democratic soci-

Market stall, Great Yarmouth.

ety. But "they" have certain characteristics in common: they tend to have been educated at any one of a dozen public schools and then to have progressed to either Oxford or Cambridge universities. From then on, the network is firmly in place and, with the help of dinner parties, country-house weekends and college reunions, the bush telegraph of power keeps lines of communications open. The "old school tie" has a durable knot.

Despite the traditional dominance of the established set in politics, a wave of "anti-establishment" voices are beginning to join the chorus. Mirroring a global trend, with US President Trump the most notable anti-establishment politician on the world stage, British politicians like Labour's Jeremy Corbyn and Nigel Farage, leader of the Brexit party, have captured the public imagination. Like him or loathe him, Farage has perfected his "man of the people" persona, defining himself in opposition to the established order.

THE OBSESSION WITH SPORT

The English are rightly renowned for their love of sports, and a good many of the world's most popular games were indeed invented in England. Nowadays, however, despite undying enthusiasm for watching and playing such sports as cricket, rugby and football, the English have to accept that they are routinely defeated by many of the countries to which they originally exported these games. All the same, it is, as they say, playing the game rather than winning that is important, and the writer Vita Sackville-West put it well when she wrote, "The Englishman is seen at his best the moment that another man starts throwing a ball at him." By this token, being a good loser is viewed as a sign of maturity – except by a

Revellers at Jack in the Green Festival, Hastings.

⊘ THE ENGLISH AS SEEN BY STATISTICIANS

Although it has the highest proportion of agricultural land in Europe (71 percent), England has the lowest proportion of employment in farming. Most of England's 55.6 million people live in cities, yet countryside causes win widespread allegiance: the Royal Society for the Protection of Birds has over 1 million paid-up members and the National Trust has more than 4 million. The population density of London is the highest of any area of England, with 5,490 people per square kilometre, and the southwest has the lowest density with 220 people per square kilometre.

Women outnumber men but earn less on average (£471 per week for women compared to £567 for men). For a small country, there are wide discrepancies: the highest life expectancy for men is in the prosperous southeast (83.3 years) and the lowest is in the less prosperous northeast (79.8); for women, the southeast and southwest seems to offer the promise of the longest life (86.7).

Immigrants from the old British Empire did not distribute themselves evenly around the country, and nor have recent migrants. Almost 37 percent of Londoners were born outside the UK, a figure that rises to 42 percent in inner London. Outside London, that figure averages 12 percent, with fewest migrants gravitating to the northeast (5 percent). The population of England is projected to rise to 60 million by 2027.

minority of football hooligans – and is in many ways the essence of Englishness.

The same casual approach was brought to bear when choosing a national patron saint. St George, a 3rd-century Christian martyr, never set foot in England. Tales of his exploits – most notably, rescuing a maiden from a fire-belching dragon – must have struck a chord in medieval society when related by soldiers returning from the Crusades. St George's Day, on 23 April, has traditionally passed almost unnoticed and only recently has the English flag (a red cross on a white background) been waved at football matches to spur on Eng-land's hard-pressed players.

ENGLAND ON ITS OWN

Nationalism in England is a particularly fraught issue. Patriotism seems embarrass-ing to many, partly as a result of the nation's problematic colonial past, and is only brought out on special occasions such as international football matches and royal weddings. There is no English national dress and no English national anthem either. (The closest anyone ever gets is a rousing rendition of William Blake's *Jerusalem*).

> "When two Englishmen meet, their first talk is of the weather," said the lexicographer Dr Samuel Johnson (1709–84). The reason is no doubt its great changeability.

In the past it's been easy for the English to take their nationality for granted, but in recent years cause has arisen to revise this attitude. Scotland and Wales now have a measure of autonomy in the form of separate legislative assemblies in Edinburgh and Cardiff. Yet there is no assembly for England, and there is some disquiet that Scottish and Welsh MPs can vote on matters that affect England but not their own constituents. All this came to a head in the "neck and neck" Scottish referendum on inde-pendence in September 2014. This somewhat unnerved the English public and though the final count proved a little less close and Scots voted to stay within the United Kingdom by 55

to 45 percent it showed that many Scots – and to perhaps a lesser extent the Welsh – are keen to stand alone. With further Scottish devolution on the cards and maybe another referendum in the future, the English may finally be forced to define their own nationality as distinct from the "Britishness" of the past.

England's complex relationship with nationalism came to a head more recently in the Brexit referendum of 2016, when the UK narrowly voted to leave the European Union. The Brexit debate, still yet to be concluded

Blooming bargains at Columbia Road market, London.

as the UK chaotically tries to negotiate its departure from the Union, has exposed deep divides across England and rest of the UK. "Leave" supporters feel the UK would be bet-ter off alone; "Remainers" wish to stay closer aligned with their European kin. Many hard-line Brexiteers see themselves as national-ists, while many Remainers would rather view themselves as European. On which side of the Brexit divide one sits often comes down to the question of identity.

For any visitor to England armed with a ste-reotypical image of the reserved, stiff upper-lipped, class-conscious resident, there is the converse where there's a friendly welcome from people proud of their green and pleasant land.

DECISIVE DATES

PREHISTORY

500 000 BC

Boxgrove Man, from West Sussex, the first known human in England.

2000 BC

Stonehenge erected.

700 BC

Celts arrive from Central Europe.

ROMAN OCCUPATION (55 BC–AD 410)

55 BC

Julius Caesar heads first Roman invasion.

AD 61

Rebellion of Boadicea, Queen of the Iceni, is crushed.

ANGLO-SAXON AND DANISH KINGS (449–1066)

449–550

Arrival of Jutes, Angles and Saxons.

897

Alfred the Great, King of Wessex, defeats the Vikings.

980–1016

Viking invasions are renewed.

THE NORMANS (1066–1154)

1066

Conquest of England by William, Duke of Normandy.

1067

The Tower of London is begun.

William the Conqueror's invasion of Britain, from the 12th-century Bayeux Tapestry.

1086

The Domesday Book, a complete inventory of England, is made.

THE PLANTAGENETS (1154–1399)

1154

Henry II becomes king.

1215

King John signs the Magna Carta at Runnymede.

1348–9

The Black Death kills between a third and half of the population.

1381

Peasants' Revolt takes over London. The leader, Wat Tyler, is beheaded at Tower Hill.

1387

Geoffrey Chaucer's *Canterbury Tales* is published.

HOUSES OF LANCASTER AND YORK (1399–1485)

1455–85

Wars of the Roses between the competing Houses of York and Lancaster.

1476

William Caxton sets up England's first printing press.

THE TUDORS (1485–1603)

1485

Henry VII is crowned king after defeating Richard III.

1497

John Cabot explores the North American coast.

1534

Henry VIII abolishes papal authority in England and becomes Supreme Head of the Church of England.

1536

Act of Union joins England and Wales.

1558

Elizabeth I begins her 45-year reign.

1580

Sir Francis Drake completes his circumnavigation of the world.

1588

The Spanish Armada is defeated.

THE STUARTS (1603–1714)

1603

James VI of Scotland is crowned James I of England.

1605

Guy Fawkes fails to blow up Parliament.

1620

The Pilgrim Fathers set sail for America.

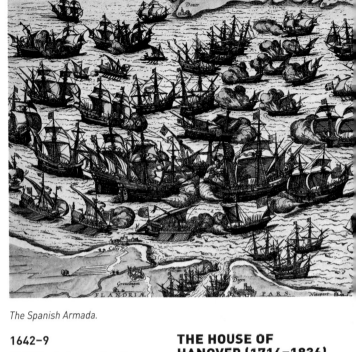

The Spanish Armada.

1642–9

Civil War between Royalists and republican Roundheads. The monarchists are defeated and Charles I is beheaded.

1666

The Great Fire of London.

The Great Fire of London, 1666.

THE HOUSE OF HANOVER (1714–1836)

1714

George I of Hanover takes the British throne.

1721

Sir Robert Walpole becomes Britain's first prime minister.

1769

Captain Cook makes first voyage to Australia.

1775

James Watt patents the first steam engine.

1805

Admiral Lord Nelson is killed at Battle of Trafalgar.

THE VICTORIAN AGE (1837–1901)

1837

Victoria becomes queen, at the age of 18.

1851

London hosts the Great Exhibition to show off advances in technology and industry.

1863

The first section of the London Underground railway is built.

1876

The Queen becomes Empress of India.

THE EDWARDIAN ERA AND THE GREAT WAR (1901–18)

1912

The *Titanic* sinks.

1914–18

World War I. More than 1 million Britons and Allies die.

HOUSE OF WINDSOR (1918–PRESENT)

1919

Nancy Astor is Britain's first woman MP.

The Great Exhibition in Hyde Park, 1851.

1926

A General Strike by workers paralyses the nation.

1936

Edward VIII abdicates to marry an American divorcee, Mrs Wallis Simpson.

1939–45

World War II. Many civilians die in heavy bombing.

1946

National Health Service is established by the Labour government.

1953

Coronation of Queen Elizabeth II in Westminster Abbey.

1966

England hosts football World Cup and wins.

1973

Britain joins the European Community.

1979

Margaret Thatcher becomes Britain's first woman prime minister.

1994

First trains run through the Channel Tunnel.

1997

Tony Blair and the Labour Party win the general election. Diana, Princess of Wales, dies in a car crash in Paris.

British and French engineers at the breakthough point in the Channel Tunnel.

Queen Elizabeth II on her Diamond Jubilee tour.

2005
Suicide bomb attacks in London.

2008
The economic boom comes to an abrupt halt as banks collapse and confidence plummets.

2010
The general election results in a coalition government of Conservatives and Liberal Democrats.

2012
The Queen's Jubilee celebrates a reign of 60 years. London hosts the Olympic Games.

2014
Scotland votes to stay within the United Kingdom.

2015
David Cameron and the Conservative Party win the general election.

2016
The UK narrowly votes to leave the European Union in a nationwide referendum. Former Home Secretary Theresa May becomes Prime Minister.

2017
Three terror attacks shake England, in Manchester (22 dead), Westminster (5 dead) and London Bridge (8 dead). UK triggers Article 50 (the UK-EU divorce negotiations).

2019
Theresa May resigns as Prime Minister and is succeeded by Boris Johnson.

Boris Johnson outside No. 10 Downing Street.

CONQUEST AND CONFLICT

The Romans made their mark, Christianity was established, the Normans conquered, warfare mired the country for centuries, and Henry VIII broke with Rome to establish the Church of England.

While the first Roman invasion of Britain occurred in 55 BC under the leadership of Julius Caesar, permanent settlement by the Romans was only established after the more comprehensive expedition of AD 43. Even then, it required ongoing effort for the Romans to maintain control of their new Celtic subjects. In AD 61, the Celtic Queen Boadicea (Boudicca) led a rebellion which, before it was finally crushed, succeeded in destroying the new Roman capital, Londinium. In AD 122, the emperor Hadrian had a wall built across the north of England to keep the marauding Picts at bay; much of the wall remains even today, running from Carlisle to Newcastle.

In all, Roman control lasted nearly 400 years, leaving behind a series of walled towns – London, York and Chester among them – linked by a network of roads so well constructed that they survived for centuries. The remains of Roman baths, amphitheatres and villas have also survived and can be seen in towns such as Bath and Colchester. The Romans also introduced Christianity, literacy and the use of Latin – though when they left, their influence faded surprisingly fast.

ANGLO-SAXONS AND VIKINGS

The next wave of invaders – Angles and Saxons – pushed the native Celts westwards into Wales and north into Scotland, and established their own kingdoms. In the mid-9th century the Danes (Vikings) gave up raiding and decided to settle. Alfred of Wessex, "Alfred the Great", agreed that they would control the north and east ("the Danelaw"), while he ruled the rest.

The Anglo-Saxons introduced their Teutonic religion, which was closely related to the Old Norse theology, and Christianity fell into

Henry VIII, who brought about the English Reformation.

abeyance in much of England – and only gained ascendancy again in the 7th and 8th centuries. Irish monks brought Celtic Christianity to northern and middle England, and at Lindisfarne, in Northumberland, a monk named Aidan established a monastery where beautifully illustrated Gospels, now kept in the British Museum, were produced. At the end of the 6th century Augustine was sent on a Christian mission from Rome and became the first archbishop of Canterbury. The Synod of Whitby in 664 established Roman Christianity as the dominant form in England.

THE NORMAN CONQUEST

After Alfred's death Canute, the Danish leader, became king and ruled well, but left no strong successor. The crown later passed to Edward "the Confessor", a pious man who built Westminster Abbey. On his death in 1066, Harold, his nominated successor, became king. William of Normandy came to claim the throne allegedly promised him by Edward, and defeated Harold on Senlac Hill near Hastings. The Norman Conquest is the best-known event in English history.

> Today, the Domesday Book is kept in the National Archives, Kew, and is a fascinating document of early social history. An online version is available at www.nationalarchives.gov.uk.

William was crowned in Westminster Abbey and set out to consolidate his kingdom. Faced with rebellion in the north, he took brutal action, devastating the countryside, and then building a string of defensive castles. In order to collect taxes, William had a land and property record compiled: the survey was called the Domesday Book, because it seemed to the English not unlike the Book of Doom to be used by the greatest feudal lord of all on Judgement Day, and was completed in 1006.

After William's son Henry died in 1135, civil war broke out between the followers of his daughter, Matilda, and those of her cousin, Stephen. Eventually Matilda's son by Geoffrey of Anjou, Henry, became king in 1154.

MONASTERIES AND MYTHS

During this period the monasteries became centres of power. Canterbury, Westminster and Winchester were the most active in the south, Fountains Abbey and Rievaulx in the north. Benedictine orders were a vital part of the feudal system, while the more spiritual Cistercians founded the wool trade, which became England's main source of wealth. Both provided hospitality to a stream of pilgrims, such as those in Chaucer's The Canterbury Tales, written in the 14th century.

Chaucer's Knight also demonstrates the medieval courtly tradition that engendered the Arthurian myth. Arthur probably existed, but it was Geoffrey of Monmouth, a 12th-century

historian, who popularised the legends, his magical sword Excalibur and the wizard Merlin, and designated Tintagel Castle in Cornwall as Arthur's birthplace.

SHAKESPEARE'S KINGS

William Shakespeare drew on the lives of the Plantagenet and Tudor kings who ruled from 1154 to 1547, around whom he wove fanciful plots and heroic tales. But he did not tackle the first Plantagenet king, Henry II: that was left for T.S. Eliot, in Murder in the Cathedral.

An engraving of Queen Boadicea leading an uprising of tribes against the Romans.

Relations between Church and State became increasingly strained during Henry's reign. Archbishop Thomas Becket resisted the king's interference in clerical matters and when Henry articulated his wish that someone would "rid me of this turbulent priest", four knights took him literally and murdered Becket on the altar steps of Canterbury Cathedral (1170).

Henry's son Richard I, known as Coeur de Lion (Lionheart), came to the throne in 1189. He spent most of his time in the Holy Land fighting Crusades. At home his prolonged absence and expensive exploits plunged the country into chaos. This tumultuous period, presided over by Richard's brother and successor John, gave rise to the legendary Nottingham outlaw Robin Hood, who is imagined to have preyed on the rich to give to the poor.

> In the mid-14th century, the Black Death, transmitted by rat fleas along merchant routes from China, reduced the world population from around 450 million to around 350 million.

King John signing the Magna Carta.

⊙ THE HUNDRED YEARS' WAR

The Hundred Years War (1337–1453) began when Edward III claimed the French throne. At the best-known battle, Crécy, more than 30,000 French troops were killed, but by 1371 the English had lost most of their French possessions. After a lull, Edward's claim was revived by his great-grandson, Henry V. With very few English casualties and the help of Welsh longbowmen, Henry defeated the French at Agincourt and made a strategic marriage to a French princess. It is said that the English "V" sign, an insulting hand gesture, comes from archers at Agincourt waving the two fingers used on their bows at the French. By the time he died in 1422, Henry controlled all of northern France.

THE MAGNA CARTA

King John is generally considered a bad king. He quarrelled with the Pope, upset the barons and imposed high taxes. The barons presented him with a series of demands on behalf of the people, which became the Magna Carta (Great Charter), signed at Runnymede near Windsor in 1215. Although history sees the Charter as a milestone, it brought no immediate solution.

John's son, Henry III, proved little better, filling his court with foreign favourites and embarking on a disastrous war with France. The

The War of the Roses, as imagined by a painter in 1850.

barons, under Simon de Montfort, rebelled and in 1265 de Montfort summoned a Parliament, which has been called the first House of Commons. Under Edward I, Henry's son, Wales was conquered, and Edward's newborn son became Prince of Wales, a title held by the heir to the throne ever since.

PLAGUE AND POLL TAX

The reign of Edward II had little to commend it. He lost Gascony, upset his barons and was deposed by Parliament in 1327, before being brutally murdered in Berkeley Castle. His son, Edward III, spent most of his reign fighting the Hundred Years War (see box). On the domestic front, times were hard. The Black Death, which reached England in 1348, killed nearly a third of the population. By leaving so much land untended and making labour scarce, it gave surviving peasants a better bargaining position. After a poll tax was clumsily introduced in 1381, the peasants of Kent and East Anglia rose in rebellion against the 14-year-old King Richard II. The Peasants' Revolt was brutally suppressed, but it did precipitate the end of the feudal system.

THE WARS OF THE ROSES

Scarcely had the Hundred Years War ended when aristocratic rivalries for the throne led to the Wars of the Roses. This name is a convenient shorthand for the battles between the House of York, symbolised by the white rose, and that of Lancaster, symbolised by the red. Henry IV deposed his cousin Richard II in 1399 and in so doing became the first member of the House of Lancaster to ascend the throne. Dynastic wars continued intermittently for much of the next century, reaching a particularly gruesome climax in 1483 when the 12-year-old Edward V and his brother Richard were apparently murdered in the Tower of London to make way for their uncle, Richard III. Richard was subsequently killed in 1485 at the Battle of Bosworth, in Leicestershire, where Shakespeare, portraying him as a hunchback, had him offering his kingdom for a horse.

The wars of succession finally ended – though there were later attempts to rekindle them – with the marriage of the Lancastrian Henry VII (1485–1509) to Elizabeth of York. This united the opposing factions and put the country under the rule of the Tudors.

THE BREAK FROM ROME

Henry VII refilled the royal coffers, but most of the money was squandered on a series of French wars by his son, Henry VIII – best remembered as the gluttonous and licentious ruler who married six times, divorced twice and beheaded two of his wives (see box). He also brought about the Reformation in England – for political rather than religious reasons, when the Pope refused to annul his marriage to Catherine of Aragon.

When Henry died in 1547, he was succeeded by his only male heir, Edward, a sickly 10-year-old who died six years later. His half-sister Mary then came to the throne and won the nickname "Bloody Mary". A devout Catholic, she restored the Old Religion and had some 300 Protestants burned as heretics. Mary is also remembered as the monarch who lost the French port of Calais, the last British possession on the Continent, during a renewed war with France. More remorseful about this than the loss of so many lives, she declared that when she died the word "Calais" would be found engraved on her heart.

The Battle of Agincourt in 1415.

⦿ HENRY VIII

Henry VIII is famed for two things: his six marriages and the English Reformation. The two were, of course, closely linked. Henry's first wife, Catherine of Aragon, failed to produce a male heir, and when Henry became infatuated with Anne Boleyn, he sought a divorce. However, Henry's Lord Chancellor, Cardinal Wolsey, failed to persuade the Pope to grant an annulment and was subsequently charged with treason. In the end, Henry bypassed Rome and declared himself Supreme Head of the Church in England in 1534. Between 1536 and 1541, Henry's Reformation went on to dissolve the monasteries, plunder shrines and transfer a fifth of England's landed wealth into new hands.

FROM ELIZABETH TO EMPIRE

Religious upheaval, civil war, a commonwealth followed by a restoration, industrial revolution, the establishment of a parliamentary system and the growth of an empire transformed the country.

The Elizabethan Age has a swashbuckling ring to it: the Virgin Queen and her dashing courtiers, the defeat of the Spanish Armada and the exploits of the great "sea dogs", Frobisher and Hawkins. Sir Walter Raleigh brought tobacco back from Virginia; Sir Francis Drake circumnavigated the world. Even the great poets Sir Philip Sidney and John Donne spent time before the mast – although William Shakespeare stayed at home, entertaining crowds at the Globe Theatre in London.

Elizabeth I was the daughter of Henry VIII and Anne Boleyn, and re-established Protestantism in England after the harsh reign of her Catholic half-sister, Mary. Elizabeth ruled from 1558 to 1603 and spent much of the first three decades resisting Catholic attempts to dethrone or assassinate her. The Pope declared her illegitimate and conspiracies continually rallied round the enigmatic Mary, Queen of Scots, as an alternative, Catholic pretender to the throne. The execution of Mary in 1587 finally removed this threat, and the defeat of the Spanish Armada the year after provided a long-sought sense of security.

Elizabeth never married, and indeed cultivated the cult of the "Virgin Queen". She was succeeded – quite peacefully – by Mary's son, James I (VI of Scotland), the first of the Stuarts. His reign, however, was no less bedevilled by religious controversy. Puritans called for a purer form of worship and Catholics engineered a number of plots, one of which resulted in Sir Walter Raleigh's 13-year imprisonment in the Tower of London.

The most famous of the conspiracies was the Gunpowder Plot of 1605, when Guy Fawkes attempted to blow up the Houses of Parliament, an event still commemorated on 5 November, when Fawkes is burned in effigy throughout the land. Puritan protests were more peaceful, but

English ships and the Spanish Armada.

James had little sympathy. Some left the country: a small group who became known as the Pilgrim Fathers set sail in the *Mayflower* in 1620 and founded New Plymouth in North America.

CIVIL WAR

The Stuart period was one of conflict between Crown and Parliament, and under Charles I relations with Parliament went from bad to dreadful. King and Commons were constantly at each other's throats, and in 1641 discontented Irish Catholics took advantage of their disarray to attack the settlers who had taken their land during the reign of James I. Thousands were massacred and the subsequent outcry in England precipitated the Civil War.

Opposition to the royalists was led by Oliver Cromwell, whose troops' short-cropped hair led them to be called Roundheads. Most of Cromwell's followers were Puritans or Presbyterians and adopted a Reformed theology, simplicity of dress and an earnestness of attitude. They also pursued the virtues of hard work and egalitarianism, and came to form a kind of middle class.

Eventually, the Roundheads prevailed, and in early 1649 Charles I was led to his execution on a scaffold erected outside Inigo Jones's Banqueting House in Whitehall. He reputedly wore two shirts, so he would not shiver in the January cold and cause people to think he was afraid.

In Scotland, Charles's son and namesake was crowned king at Scone in 1651. He marched into England where he was defeated at Worcester, and eventually escaped to France. Meanwhile, Cromwell and "the Rump" – the Parliamentary members who had voted for Charles's execution – declared England a commonwealth. In 1653 Cromwell dissolved Parliament, formed a Protectorate with himself as Lord Protector and ruled alone until his death in 1658. Without him republicanism faltered, and in 1660 Charles II was crowned king in Westminster.

Charles II's reign (the "Restoration") is often characterised in the history books as being a time of relaxation and hedonism after the austere rule of Cromwell and the Puritans. Charles himself had a fondness for high living, kept a string of mistresses and fathered at least a dozen illegitimate offspring. Even so, the Restoration period was not without its religious troubles. In 1678 an agitator, one Titus Oates, disclosed a bogus "Popish Plot" to assassinate the king. Thousands of Catholics were imprisoned and no Catholic was allowed to sit in the House of Commons – a law that was not repealed for more than 150 years.

WHIGS AND TORIES

Fear of the monarchy ever again becoming too powerful led to the emergence of the first political parties, both known by nicknames: Whigs, a derogatory name for cattle drivers, and Tories, an Irish word meaning outlaws. Loosely speaking, Whigs opposed absolute monarchy and supported religious freedom, while Tories were upholders of Church and Crown.

In 1685 Charles was succeeded by his brother, James II (1685–8), who imposed illegal taxation and tried to bring back absolute monarchy and Catholicism. Rebellions were savagely put down, with hundreds hanged and many more sold into slavery. Whigs and Tories allied against him and

> *Defeating the Spanish Armada in 1588 gave England naval supremacy, which laid the foundations for a future of flourishing trade, expansionism and colonisation.*

Elizabeth I, the "Virgin Queen".

in 1688 offered the crown to James's daughter, Mary, and her husband, the Dutch prince William of Orange. This move became known as the Glorious Revolution because Parliament had proved more powerful than the Crown – a power spelled out in a Bill of Rights, which severely limited the monarch's freedom of action.

William landed in England and James fled to France. Backed by the French, he arrived in Ireland in 1689 where Irish Catholics lent him support, but with disastrous results for both sides. At Londonderry 30,000 Protestants survived a 15-week siege but were finally defeated. In 1690, William's troops trounced James at the Battle of the Boyne, and he fled to France, dying in 1701. Protestant victory was complete.

War with France dragged on, becoming, in Queen Anne's reign, the War of the Spanish Succession. Her commander-in-chief, John Churchill, Duke of Marlborough, won a famous victory at Blenheim in 1704, for which he was rewarded with Blenheim Palace, near Oxford. During Anne's reign the name Great Britain came into being when, in 1707, the Act of Union united England and Scotland.

> *The English Civil War of 1642–9 has become romanticised, and today a society flourishes which re-enacts the principal battles for fun.*

HANOVERIAN BRITAIN

On Anne's death, a reliable Protestant monarch was needed. George of Hanover, great-grandson of James I on his mother's side, but with a Hanoverian father, and German in language and outlook, was invited to Britain. He never learned to speak fluent English, and had no great liking for his subjects.

The Hanoverian dynasty, under the four Georges, spanned a period of nearly 115 years. It was a time of wars with France and Spain, of expanding empire (although America was lost after the War of Independence in 1776), industrialisation and growing demands for political reform.

THE GROWTH OF LONDON

When George and his queen, Sophia, arrived from Hanover in 1714 the city's population stood at 550,000 despite the ravages of the Great Plague of 1665 which had killed 100,000 Londoners. This was due largely to migrants from rural areas who came in search of work.

London had been partially rebuilt after the Great Fire of 1666, which started in a baker's shop in Pudding Lane and destroyed two-thirds of the timber-built city. But the subsequent elegant buildings designed by Sir Christopher Wren (1632–1723), such as St Paul's Cathedral, were a far cry from the overcrowded and insanitary slums in which most people lived.

In the more affluent areas, some streets were widened to allow carriages to pass and rudimentary street lighting was introduced in the early 19th century. Westminster Bridge was illuminated by gaslight for the first time in 1813. Theatres, concert halls and newly fashionable coffee houses sprang up.

Royalty spent their time at Buckingham House, Kensington Palace and Hampton Court. George III bought Buckingham House and George IV had it redesigned by John Nash into a Palace, though Queen Victoria was the first monarch to take up residence. Parliament met at Westminster, although not in the present building, which was built after a fire destroyed its predecessor in 1834.

Slums depicted by Hogarth in Gin Lane.

⊘ THE GREAT PRETENDERS

The Hanoverian period saw the last violent attempts to overthrow the monarchy in the shape of the two Jacobite rebellions in support of the "Pretenders", descendants of James II. The first rebellion, in 1715, in support of his son James, the "Old Pretender", was quashed near Stirling and its leaders fled to France. Thirty years later his grandson Charles, the "Young Pretender", known as Bonnie Prince Charlie, raised a huge army in Scotland but was savagely defeated in battle at Culloden by the Duke of Cumberland. No more "Pretenders" arose. From then on power struggles would be political ones, for it was with politicians and Parliament that real power lay.

COLONIAL POWER

The treaty signed at the end of the Seven Years War with France in 1763 allowed Britain to keep all its overseas colonies, making it the leading world power. The empire had been growing since 1607 when Virginia, an English colony in America, had been established. In 1620 English Puritans had settled in Massachusetts, and other settlements were made later in the century. By 1700 most were governed by a Crown official and incorporated into Britain's Atlantic Empire.

Throughout the 17th century the demand for goods – furs, silk, tobacco, sugar – led to a series of wars with the Dutch and the French from which Britain emerged in control of much of West Africa, Newfoundland and Nova Scotia and some of the Caribbean islands. The French and English battled for supremacy in Canada and India during the 18th century. By 1760 England had proved the clear winner. Colonial trade, unfortunately, went hand in hand with slavery. It was not until 1807 that the tireless efforts of William Wilberforce helped make the trade illegal and another 27 years before slavery was abolished in all British colonies.

AGRICULTURE AND INDUSTRY

Radical changes took place in the English countryside in the late 18th century: the narrow-strip system of farming which had prevailed since Saxon times ended when a series of Enclosure Acts empowered wealthier landowners to seize land and divide it into enclosed fields. This explains the patchwork quality of much of Britain's countryside. Arable farming became more efficient and profitable, but for the evicted tenants it was a disaster. The dispossessed farmers left their homes to look for work in the towns, which soon became impossibly overcrowded.

The first steam engine was devised by an Englishman at the end of the 17th century but it was the Scottish inventor James Watt (1736–1819) who modified the design in the 1770s and made steam an efficient source of energy, which would power trains and ships as well as factory machinery. Steam pumps allowed speculators to drain deep coalmines, which vastly increased coal production. Abraham Darby's method of smelting iron with coke instead of charcoal hugely increased the production of iron which was used for machinery, railways and shipping. In 1779,

the world's first cast-iron bridge was built in Coalbrookdale, Shropshire, and can still be seen today. Textiles had long been a vital part of Britain's economy, and James Hargreaves's invention

> By the end of the 19th century, goods from Britain's colonies were flooding into the wharves of East London, and the docklands came to be known as the "warehouse of the world".

John Churchill, Duke of Marlborough.

☉ THE GREAT EXHIBITION OF 1851

In 1851, Queen Victoria opened the Great Exhibition of the Works of all Nations in Hyde Park in London. Its magnificent glass building – dubbed the "Crystal Palace" – showed off Britain's skills and achievements to the world and attracted some 6 million visitors. With the profits of £186,000, Prince Albert, Queen Victoria's German-born husband, realised his great ambition of establishing a centre of learning. Temples to the arts and sciences blossomed in Kensington's gardens, nicknamed "Albertopolis". What was later named the Victoria and Albert Museum opened in 1857, followed by the Royal Albert Hall in 1871, the Albert Memorial in 1872 and the Natural History Museum in 1881.

of the Spinning Jenny in the 1770s opened the way to mass production. As in agriculture, mechanisation destroyed the livelihood of many.

Goods and materials needed improved transportation to reach a market, and the 18th century saw massive outlay on canal-building. By 1830 all the main industrial areas were linked by waterways, although most of these would fall into disuse when the new railways proved faster and more efficient (today, cleared out and cleaned up, they provide thousands of miles of leisure boating, with more miles of canal in Birmingham than there

Drawing of the Manchester & Liverpool Railway, 1825.

are in Venice). New roads were built, too. By the early 19th century, men such as Thomas Telford and John Macadam, who gave us the road surface called "tarmac", had created a road network totalling some 125,000 miles (200,000km).

Above all, this was the age of the railways, when iron and steam combined to change the face of the country, and were romanticised in such paintings as *Rain, Steam and Speed* by J.M.W. Turner. Cornishman Richard Trevithick built the first steam locomotive, and the Stockton and Darlington Line was the first railway line to open, in 1825, with George Stephenson's *Locomotion*. Isambard Kingdom Brunel, who designed the elegant Clifton Suspension Bridge across the Avon Gorge, laid down the Great Western Railway.

THE FEAR OF REVOLUTION

The two events that most alarmed the British ruling classes in the late 18th century were the American War of Independence and the French Revolution – a fear exacerbated by wars with France and Spain and the dissatisfaction provoked by heavy taxes and the loss of trade they caused. Known as the Napoleonic Wars, these hostilities began around 1799 and rumbled on until 1815, giving Britain two of its greatest heroes, Admiral Lord Nelson (1758–1805) and the Duke of Wellington (1769–1852).

However, political change in England was to come not through revolution but through gradual reform. Between 1832 and 1884 three parliamentary Reform Bills were passed, extending the enfranchisement of the populace.

The 1829 Emancipation Act, which allowed Catholics to sit in Parliament, was another measure that frightened the old school. And the Repeal of the Corn Laws – heavy taxes on imported corn which were crippling trade and starving the poor – split the ruling Conservative Party. The "Peelite" faction, followers of the pro-Repeal Sir Robert Peel, joined with Whigs to form the Liberal Party.

GEORGIAN GIVES WAY TO VICTORIAN

From 1811, King George III was too ill to rule, and so his son, also called George, ruled as his proxy as the Prince Regent, until the father's death in 1820 and the son's succession. The so-called Regency period bridged the transition from Georgian to Victorian, and came to be associated with distinctive styles in the fields of fashion, architecture and design.

⊙ THE PRE-RAPHAELITES

John Ruskin (1819–1900) was one of the founders of the Pre-Raphaelite Brotherhood of painters and writers which flourished in the final years of the 19th century. William Morris (1834–96), who devoted himself to the revival of medieval arts and crafts, shared Ruskin's ideals. Examples of his decoration and furnishings can be seen at Kelmscott Manor, near Oxford, for a time the centre of the Brotherhood's activities, and also at the Red House in Bexleyheath. The latter contains fine stained glass by Edward Burne-Jones, whose work, along with that of fellow Pre-Raphaelites John Millais and Dante Gabriel Rossetti, is spread through galleries in London, Birmingham, Manchester and Liverpool.

One of the chief characteristics of the Regency style was opulence. The Prince Regent himself lived a thoroughly decadent life and much of the aristocracy followed suit – reckless behaviour considering that the French Revolution was still within living memory. As well as accumulating large debts, numerous mistresses and various illegitimate children, the Prince Regent grossly overate and drank, making him not only obese, but also chronically ill. His profligacy extended to the places he frequented, which were rebuilt in grand style, with fine architecture and extravagant interior decoration. London's Buckingham Palace and Regent's Park, and the Royal Pavilion in Brighton, are his lasting legacy.

George IV died in 1830 and was succeeded by his younger brother, William IV. He in turn was succeeded by Victoria, his 18-year-old niece, who would go on to have a longer reign (1837–1901) than any other previous British monarch. It proved to be a time of extraordinary progress in industry and engineering – as celebrated in the Great Exhibition of 1851, organised by her technology-loving husband, Prince Albert. Victoria's reign also saw the expansion of the Empire, with vast territorial gains in Africa and Asia. After the Indian Rebellion of 1857, the Subcontinent came under direct British control; much of East Africa was acquired in the following decades, and economies from China to Argentina came heavily under Britain's sway.

THE AGE OF DICKENS

While the vast wealth brought back from the Empire paid for showpiece projects such as the London Underground, social deprivation retained a conspicuous presence in England. In London, the squalor and crime that Charles Dickens (1812–70) portrayed so evocatively in his novels were all too real. Fortunately, change – albeit slow – was on the way. After a cholera epidemic in 1832 measures were taken to provide drainage and clean water. The police force that Sir Robert Peel established in 1829, and which took the nickname "Bobbies" from him, was helping combat crime. Peel also abolished the death penalty for many petty crimes, influenced by the ideas of the utilitarian thinker Jeremy Bentham, who founded University College, London.

Working-class people, on the whole, were not attracted by revolutionary struggle and preferred to pursue their aims through trade-union organisation and representation in Parliament. The first working-class Member of Parliament, in 1892, was John Keir Hardie, the Scottish miners' leader, and 14 years later the British Labour Party won its first parliamentary seats. Although Karl Marx (1818–83) lived and worked in London for much of his life – his tomb can be seen in London's Highgate Cemetery – his ideas were shared only by a relatively small group of middle-class intellectuals.

Middle-class life was comfortable and pleasant. Improved transport – including the world's first underground railway, opened in London in 1863 – enabled people to work in towns but live in leafy suburbs.

Four generations of royalty: Victoria with future monarchs George V, Edward VII and Edward VIII.

SHAW AND WILDE

At the theatre, audiences were being entertained by the plays of two Anglo-Irish writers: George Bernard Shaw (1856–1950), who believed in combining education with entertainment, introduced radical politics into his work; and Oscar Wilde (1854–1900), who was to end his glittering career in a prison cell on charges of homosexuality, poked sophisticated fun at London's high society.

All in all, Britain was feeling pleased with itself by the time of Queen Victoria's Diamond Jubilee in 1897. The jubilee saluted 60 years of rule for the woman who had spent much of her reign as a black-clad widow, who had given her name to the age, and who ruled over the biggest empire in the world.

MODERN TIMES

Following the ravages of two world wars and the end of its imperial adventure, England was forced to redefine its relationship with the rest of Europe – an issue that has come full circle since then.

World War I claimed over a million British casualties, most of them under the age of 25. But had the sacrifice been worth it? Men who had fought in France and been promised a "land fit for heroes" were disillusioned when they found unemployment and poor housing awaited them at the war's end in 1918. Women who had worked in factories while the men were away were not prepared to give up any of their independence.

There were strikes on the railways and in the mines and political unrest led to four general elections in just over five years, including one which brought the Labour Party to power for the first time. In 1926 a general strike paralysed the country, but the unions' demands were not met and the men returned to work, much disgruntled and worse off than before.

THE ROARING TWENTIES

There was another side to life, of course. For some, unaffected by gloomy financial reality, these were the roaring twenties. Women with cropped hair and short dresses drank cocktails and danced to the new music, jazz, which had crossed the ocean from America. Silent films, another US import, were the wonder of the age.

The New York Stock Market crash of 1929 looked as if it would bring the party to an end. The effects soon spread throughout Europe, and by 1931 England was entering the Great Depression. The principal victims of the recession were in the industrial areas of northern England, south Wales, and Clydeside in Scotland. Three million people lost their jobs and suffered real misery with only the "dole", a limited state benefit, to keep them from starvation and homelessness. British cinema thrived as people sought an escape from reality.

A policeman directs the traffic in Northampton, 1930.

The scale of the carnage in World War I shocked even such patriots as the writer Rudyard Kipling (1865–1936), who had been firmly committed to the aims of the war: he lost his only son.

In the south of England and the Midlands, the depression hit less hard and recovery was faster, mainly due to the rapid growth of the motor, electrical and light engineering industries. The bold, geometric designs of Art Deco, which began in Paris in 1925, could soon be seen adorning the spanking new factories lining the main roads.

WORLD WAR II

With memories of the "war to end all wars" still fresh in people's minds, there was great reluctance to enter another conflict. But by 1939 the policy of appeasement of German aggression was no longer tenable. Although Britain's island status saved it from invasion, the war involved civilians in an unprecedented way. German bombing raids tore the heart out of many ports and cities. Much of the modern building in British towns, not always blending too harmoniously, has been erected on former bomb sites.

Many London families spent their nights in the Underground stations, the safest places during an attack, and a lot of people from cities and industrial areas were evacuated to the countryside during the worst of the Blitz. For children, sent to live with strangers while their parents remained behind, it was both a time of great loneliness and the first glimpse many of them had ever had of green fields and woodlands. For some of the country families on whom they were billeted, it may have been their first glimpse of the effects of urban deprivation.

Sir Winston Churchill (1874–1965) had received massive popular support as an inspirational war leader, and is still regarded by many people as Britain's greatest prime minister. But when hostilities ended in 1945 the electorate declined to re-elect him and voted overwhelmingly for a Labour government: the war effort had fostered egalitarianism and many returning servicemen felt that electing a Conservative government again would simply resuscitate the old class differences.

The problems of the war-torn country proved intractable, but the Labour government strove to keep its promises. The basis of the welfare state was laid, providing free medical care for everyone and financial help for the old, the sick and the unemployed. The Bank of England, coalmines, railways and steelworks were nationalised. These were hard and joyless years, however, and wartime rationing of food, clothing and fuel continued into the early 1950s.

THE END OF EMPIRE

One of the most far-reaching consequences of the war was that it hastened the end of Britain's empire. Starting with India's independence in 1947, the colonies one after another achieved autonomy during the next two decades. Jamaica and Trinidad did not gain independence until 1962, but they were two islands whose people were among the first black immigrants to Britain in the early 1950s, when work was plentiful and immigrants were officially welcomed to fill the labour gap. Newcomers from the Caribbean settled mainly in London at first, while later immigrants from the Indian Subcontinent made their homes in the Midlands, where textiles and the motor industry offered employment.

Tube stations became wartime bomb shelters.

⊘ THE ABDICATION CRISIS

In 1936, following the death of George V, the country was rocked by an unprecedented crisis. Edward VIII succeeded his father but was obliged to abdicate when family, Church and government united in their refusal to let him marry a twice-divorced American, Mrs Wallis Simpson. The couple married in France and remained in permanent exile as the Duke and Duchess of Windsor. Edward's brother came to the throne and, as George VI, became a popular monarch, not least for the solidarity which he and his Queen showed to their subjects during the Blitz. The story became the subject of a major film, *The King's Speech*, starring Colin Firth.

The post-war years were ones of uneasy peace. Britain joined the war against North Korea in 1950 and its troops, still a conscripted army, fought there for four years. In 1956, following Egyptian nationalisation of the Suez Canal, British and French forces conspired to attack Egypt, pleading bogus provocation. The action was widely condemned both at home and particularly in the United States, representing an ignominious end to Britain's imperial ambitions.

These were also the years of the Cold War between the Soviet Union and the West, which

Churchill appeals to the electorate in 1945.

prompted Britain to become a nuclear power. The first British hydrogen bomb was tested in 1957, after the world's first nuclear power station had opened in Cumberland (now Cumbria). The Campaign for Nuclear Disarmament (CND) was born in response and organised large protest marches.

A NEW ELIZABETHAN AGE

All was not gloom and doom. In 1951 the Festival of Britain was held in the newly built Royal Festival Hall on London's South Bank – the National Theatre was added to the concrete complex in 1964.

The Festival was designed to commemorate the Great Exhibition 100 years earlier and

strongly signalled the beginning of the end of post-war austerity. In 1953, a new Elizabethan Age began as Elizabeth II was crowned in Westminster Abbey. Britain's Television Age began in earnest that day too, as millions watched the coronation live on tiny flickering screens.

By the latter half of the decade things were definitely looking up. Harold Macmillan, the Conservative prime minister, declared in a famous speech that people had "never had it so good". New universities were built, with the aim of making higher education a possibility for more than just the privileged elite. Most people had two weeks' paid holiday a year and, alongside the traditional seaside resorts, holiday camps blossomed, offering cheap family vacations.

Social attitudes were changing too, reflected in the rise of a group of writers known as "angry young men", including John Osborne and Arnold Wesker, whose plays challenged conventional values.

THE 1960S AND 1970S

The 1960s saw an explosion of new talent, much of it from the north of England. Alan Sillitoe and Stan Barstow wrote about working-class life in a way no one had done before. Northern actors, such as Albert Finney and Tom Courteney, achieved huge success, and, in the cinema, directors Lindsay Anderson and Karel Reisz made British films popular box-office attractions. Pop music, as it was now called, underwent a revolution when a group from Liverpool, The Beatles, became world celebrities and turned their hometown into a place of pilgrimage.

The introduction of the contraceptive pill prompted a revolution in sexual attitudes, and the laws relating to abortion, homosexuality and censorship were liberalised. It was a decade of optimism and national self-confidence was infectious: in 1966 England's footballers even beat West Germany to win the World Cup.

It was during the winter of 1973, when an oil embargo and a miners' strike provoked a State of Emergency and brought down Edward Heath's Conservative government, that the self-confidence collapsed. In the same year, with mixed feelings, Britain finally became a full member of the Common Market (now the

European Union). Rising oil prices pushed up the cost of living, high inflation took its toll and unemployment soared.

Oil was discovered in the North Sea. But, although building oil rigs provided jobs, the oil revenues were largely soaked up in payments to the jobless. There was no economic miracle.

To deepen the gloom, English cities were again bombed. This time the perpetrators were the IRA, who were fighting to end British rule in Northern Ireland. By 1979, unemployment had reached 3.5 million and a wave of strikes plunged the country into what was called "the winter of discontent" – the media has a tendency to quote Shakespeare in times of crisis. An election returned the Conservatives to office under their new leader, Margaret Thatcher.

THATCHER'S BRITAIN

The impact of the West's first woman prime minister was enormous, but her personal popularity soon began to fade as the economy remained weak. Her political stock was dramatically strengthened in 1982 by the Falklands War when an invading Argentinian force was beaten off these South Atlantic islands, remnants of the empire.

For many, the 1980s meant increased prosperity. The most ambitious development was the renewal of London's derelict docklands area into a new commercial centre, with its own airport and light railway system, and prestige housing for young urban professionals. Docklands' Canary Wharf development was dubbed Chicago-on-Thames.

For others, however, the Thatcher years were associated with ruthless de-industrialisation – especially in the north of England. State-run industries were privatised in a move which former Conservative prime minister, Harold Macmillan, likened to "selling the family silver". Steelworks, shipyards and coalmines were closed down. The miners' strike of 1984–5 was a particularly bitter episode, leading to the break-up of whole communities and the end of a way of life.

Eventually, after 11 years of Thatcherite rule, people began to tire of the Iron Lady's uncompromising style and she was finally voted out in November 1990 – not by the electorate, but by her own party who believed she had lost touch with the country. She was replaced by a less combative leader, John Major, whose period of rule was dominated by economic recession and the issue of Britain's position within Europe: did Britain really feel European enough to be part of a full monetary union – perhaps even, one day, a political union?

INTO THE NEW MILLENNIUM

Two events in 1997 shook the nation out of its dreary complacency. In a general elec-

Captain Bobby Moore surrounded by members of the England team after their victory at Wembley in 1966.

tion the Conservative Party was swept from power as the Labour Party roared in with an unassailable majority in the House of Commons. The Conservatives were left without a single seat in either Scotland or Wales, both of which voted in subsequent referendums for a greater degree of self-rule; devolution took effect in 1999 with the setting up of new assemblies in Edinburgh and Cardiff.

The second defining event in 1997 was the death in a car crash in Paris of Diana, Princess of Wales. The wave of grief that swept the country took everyone by surprise. Some attacked the Royal Family for failing to display sufficient anguish.

But Tony Blair's new government soon disappointed many by abandoning its socialist roots, promoting unexpectedly conservative economic policies with evangelical fervour. The crucial question of whether Britain should embrace the single European currency, the euro, was put on the back burner.

THE END OF NEW LABOUR

Tony Blair's popularity continued largely intact until 2003, when he decided to go against public opinion by making Britain a full coalition part-

Lord Coe, Jonathan Edwards and Dame Kelly Holmes take part in the London 2012 Cultural Olympiad.

ner with George W. Bush's administration in the invasion of Iraq. More than a million British citizens marched in protest. The subsequent failure of the invading forces to find the much-touted weapons of mass destruction in Iraq compounded the damage to Blair's reputation.

Blair finally resigned in 2007, and his Chancellor, Gordon Brown, took over as Prime Minister. Sadly, for him, the "honeymoon period" did not last long before the credit crunch of 2008 plunged the country into economic crisis. Several of Britain's largest banks became insolvent, property prices collapsed and a deep recession took hold. Fortunately, decisive action was taken: the government bailed out the insolvent banks, the central bank slashed interest rates and printed hundreds of billions of pounds (causing the currency to devalue), and a programme of public spending cuts was begun.

AN INSECURE SOCIETY

Understandably, though, the electorate had had enough, and support for the Labour Party slumped at the general election of 2010. Yet no clear winner emerged, and it was left for David Cameron's Conservatives to form a coalition government with Nick Clegg's Liberal Democrats. The focus of Coalition policy was the reduction of Britain's mountain of public debt with austerity the watchword at all levels of government and gradually the economy was set on the road to a modest recovery.

In 2011, the grey mood was somewhat relieved by the long-anticipated wedding of Prince William to Catherine Middleton (now the Duchess of Cambridge). Tensions, however, were bubbling beneath the surface with serious rioting and looting on the streets of London and cities throughout England. Public sympathy was scant, the rioting blamed on a breakdown of social morality and gang culture. Things looked up in 2012 with the Queen's Diamond Jubilee and the Olympic Games galvanising public spiritedness and national unity.

Westminster, and to an extent the country at large, underwent a decided lack of confidence during the Scottish referendum of September 2014. After a close-fought campaign the Scots marginally voted to stay in the United Kingdom. However, the high levels of support for Scottish independence, further devolution and the ongoing popularity of the pro-independence Scottish National Party (SNP) were clear signs that parts of the UK were beginning to seriously question the status quo and their national identity. Thorny issues over the UK's future were not just confined to Scotland.

For several years, there had been rumblings over the future of Britain in the EU. Having promised a public referendum on the subject as an election pledge, Cameron was obliged to deliver and on 23 June 2016, the country went to the polls. Despite the Prime Minister's campaigning for a "remain" vote and warnings of the likely economic impact of leaving the EU, long-stagnating concerns over

British sovereignty and immigration tipped the balance and 52 percent of voters opted for "Brexit". The results depicted a polarised nation: Scotland and Northern Ireland backed a remain vote, while Wales and England voted in favour of Brexit – although most of the major English cities bucked the trend (London, Bristol, Liverpool and Manchester voted overwhelmingly to remain). Cameron resigned the next day and former Home Secretary Theresa May subsequently became the country's second female Prime Minister.

The following year, England was left reeling after a spate of terror attacks. On 22 March 2017, a terrorist drove into pedestrians on Westminster Bridge, killing four people, before fatally stabbing a policeman outside the Houses of Parliament. Two months later, the Manchester Arena bombing killed 22 concertgoers at an Ariana Grande gig and, on 3 June, London was delivered another devastating blow when terrorists killed eight and injured 48 others in and around Borough Market. During this time of turmoil, Theresa May praised Britain's resolve and commended the bravery of the emergency services, but the nation's spirits were low. A catastrophic fire at Grenfell Tower in London, largely spread by the building's cladding, compounded the disasters of 2017, killing 72. While the bravery of London fire fighters was praised, the government response was heavily criticised for its poor co-ordination and lack of leadership, with charities and volunteers taking the initiative in relief efforts; Theresa May cut a distant figure when she visited Grenfell Tower the day after the fire, where she chose not to meet with survivors.

In between these distressing events, May triggered Article 50 (UK-EU divorce negotiations); called a snap election and lost her Conservative majority; and quickly agreed a deal with Northern Ireland's Democratic Unionist Party (DUP) to have its support in key votes. Some light relief came in 2018 with a flurry of royal news: the Duchess of Cambridge gave birth to Prince Louis on 23 April, while Prince Harry and *Suits* actress Meghan Markle got married in Windsor Castle on 19 May. The couple – now the Duke and Duchess of Sussex – celebrated the birth of Archie Harrison Mountbatten-Windsor just under one year later on 6 May 2019.

Brexit divorce negotiations, meanwhile, have so far proved fruitless and chaotic. Theresa May resigned in May 2019 after failing to push her Brexit deal through Parliament (having had her deal rejected no less than three times), departing on 7 June. She was succeeded by Boris Johnson, who took the reins amid continuing political deadlock. Boris immediately ramped up plans and funds for a no-deal Brexit, an option that is looking increasingly likely. The outcome and effects of the UK's decision to leave the EU hang delicately in the balance.

Theresa May on the campaign trail in 2017.

⊘ THE PRESS

A major component of political life in England since World War II has been the newspaper industry. Britain's belief in a free press unencumbered by privacy laws – together with the dominance of a handful of national newspaper titles – has made politicians increasingly beholden to the favour of media barons. And the ownership of the mainstream media is concentrated in very few hands. Newspapers have continually set the political agenda, and the chances of winning an election without wide press support are considered something the parties would consider far too risky to contemplate.

STATELY HOMES

England's grand stately homes reflect more than privileged lives. They also illustrate centuries of social history, and of great artistic and architectural achievement.

England's stately homes have a fascination that attracts millions of visitors every year. Many have embraced the tourist theme enthusiastically, with added incentives such as safari parks, transport museums, historical re-enactments and adventure playgrounds, but at the heart of them all lies a house with a story. A palace crammed with works of art may tell of great political achievements; a rambling manor house may reflect centuries at the heart of a close-knit agricultural community; a great house may even show how the servants and estate workers went about their daily duties.

A house that may appear to be pure 18th-century neoclassical may well be hiding a medieval core and perhaps a Tudor fireplace where Elizabeth I once warmed her toes. Victorian high-flyers often confused the issue by building fanciful yet somehow convincing medieval-style castles, complete with every convenience that Industrial Revolution technology provided.

The short Edwardian era saw both the carefree heyday of the country-house party and the onset of World War I, which marked the demise of stately homes in their traditional role. Maintaining them became ever more costly, and an ingenious solution was provided in 1953 when the 13th Duke of Bedford, faced with huge death duties when he succeeded his father, confronted the prospect of donating Woburn Abbey in Bedfordshire to the National Trust. Instead, he opened it to the public, charging them to view the 12th-century building and its contents. He later added a safari park to its grounds. Then a golf club and antiques centre, plus wedding and conference facilities were added to the menu. Initially, many fellow aristocrats condemned the Duke's ideas as crass commercialism, but some soon followed his example.

Castle Howard in Yorkshire was built between 1699 and 1712 for the 3rd Earl of Carlisle.

Blenheim Palace is one of Britain's largest private houses. The palace is an orgy of Baroque style, with Doric and Corinthian columns, frescoed ceilings, and extravagant fountains in the grounds.

Queen Victoria dined at Chatsworth House on numerous occasions as the guest of the 6th Duke of Devonshire.

Coughton Court, ancestral stately home of the Throckmorton family in Warwickshire, England.

The power of the past

The National Trust (www.nationaltrust.org.uk), founded in 1895, is a registered charity and receives no state grant. Covering England, as well as Wales and Northern Ireland, it initially protected open spaces and threatened buildings, but soon it began preserving places of historic interest or natural beauty for the enjoyment of future generations.

It now cares for ancient monuments, historic houses and gardens, industrial sites, coastline and countryside. Many country houses and gardens were donated to it by their owners who could no longer afford to maintain them or to pay death duties. Broadening its heritage ambitions, it even acquired the childhood homes of John Lennon and Paul McCartney. The Trust is funded entirely by membership subscriptions and donations from its 4 million members, by legacies and by admission charges.

Another organisation, English Heritage (www.english-heritage.org.uk), which became a registered charity in 2015, cares for historic buildings and monuments such as Stonehenge. It also advises on the preservation of the historic environment. Both organisations have paid membership schemes, which allow members free access to the properties they administer.

Knole in Kent, birthplace of the writer Vita Sackville-West, was built by an Archbishop of Canterbury in 1456–86 and is surrounded by a 1,000-acre (400-hectare) deer park.

Highclere Castle in Hampshire – used in the hit television drama Downton Abbey – was designed by Sir Charles Barry, who was also responsible for the Houses of Parliament in Westminster.

The statues, figurines, iron benches and sundials that grace the gardens of stately homes have not escaped the attention of professional thieves, who have been known to peruse Country Life magazine to identify opportunities.

A performance of Guys and Dolls at the Minack Theatre, Cornwall.

THEATRE

"Plays make mankind no better and no worse," claimed Lord Byron. But for visitors, they do provide many a memorable night's entertainment in glorious historic surroundings.

From the moment you arrive in Stratford-upon-Avon you know you are in the Birthplace of the Bard. From the Shakespeare Tour buses to the T-shirts proclaiming "Will Power", from Anne Hathaway's Cottage to the site of New Place (where the great man spent his later years), this pretty little town is dedicated to the Shakespeare industry.

What it is all based on are the plays, performed by the Royal Shakespeare Company in the theatre beside the Avon, as they are in theatres throughout the world. By some rare gift this 16th century writer was able to encapsulate emotions, to universalise petty jealousies and major tragedies, in words that still ring fresh and now, with humour that seems to work even when translated into Japanese.

Shakespeare is part of the national heritage, revered even by those who rarely, if ever, visit a theatre. Lines from his plays are part of the language, most actors express a wish to play Hamlet at some time in their career, and there are few classical directors who don't itch to stage their own interpretation of these great works.

Outside Stratford-upon-Avon, the best place to see Shakespeare is in London, where both commercial theatres and subsidised venues such as the National Theatre regularly stage star-led productions. In summer, Shakespeare's Globe, a replica of the 16th-century theatre-in-the-round where some of these plays were first performed, stages the plays in a setting on London's Bankside. But you could probably see a Shakespeare play, professional or amateur, somewhere in the country on most nights of the year.

MORE THAN JUST SHAKESPEARE

London's theatrical history goes back to a playhouse opened at Shoreditch in 1576 by James

A banner marking the 400th anniversary of Shakespeare's death in 2016.

Burbage, the son of a carpenter and travelling player, and its development encompasses a strong tradition of taking side-swipes at social issues. In the *Roaring Girl* of 1611, for example, playwright Thomas Dekker dwelt at some length on London's traffic jams.

In modern times, live theatre was supposed to succumb first to movies then to television, yet it is still one of those essential attractions that every visitor to London is supposed to experience. Outside the capital, there are groundbreaking repertory theatres in most major cities, and amateur dramatics fill countless halls around the country (why the supposedly reserved English are so keen on dressing up and making fools of themselves in broad farces is worthy of a psychological dissertation).

Critics bemoan the fact that lavish musicals have come to dominate London's mainstream theatre. Once, no one would have guessed that the West End would hijack the genre from Broadway. Yet it happened with surprising speed. First, Tim Rice and Andrew Lloyd Webber demonstrated the possibilities of the cunningly crafted rock-musical form with *Jesus Christ Superstar* and *Evita*. Then, leaving Rice to indulge his passion for cricket and aptitude for writing Oscar-

The Royal Shakespeare Theatre in Stratford-upon-Avon.

> *Unsold tickets for London theatres are sold daily at a discount at the "TKTS" booth in Leicester Square. Noticeboards display what is available that day, and many tickets are half-price. It is open Mon–Sat 10am–7pm, Sun 11am–4.30pm.*

winning tunes for Disney cartoons, Lloyd Webber focused his fanaticism for the stage musical by composing *Cats* (based on the poetry of T.S. Eliot), *Phantom of the Opera, Starlight Express, Sunset Boulevard* and *The Lady in White*.

Traditionalists claim that the mania for musicals has squeezed out new drama productions.

Yet a glance at the theatre listings online doesn't entirely bear out this claim. New writing is still staged at the Royal Court and the Bush, and hit plays such as Jez Butterworth's *Jerusalem* and *The River* have subsequently transferred to the West End and then Broadway. Experimental work and alternative comedy is continually being mounted at fringe theatres, and playwrights such as David Hare, Tom Stoppard and Alan Bennett do not lack an audience. Moreover, classics continue to be staged at the National Theatre, the Old Vic, the Young Vic and the Donmar Warehouse.

THE HOLLYWOOD TOUCH

Since the 1990s, London's West End theatres have regularly attracted film stars to tread the boards. Many – including Michael Gambon, Ian McKellen, Maggie Smith, Diana Rigg, Helen Mirren and Ralph Fiennes – are locally grown stars and this represents their triumphant return. Others – including Nicole Kidman, Danny DeVito, Zach Braff and Christian Slater – are established Hollywood names, and have attracted new audiences to old theatres. Recent stars of the screen that have also graced London's stages are *Game of Thrones* sensation Kit Harington, *Downton Abbey* star Lily James and *Avengers* draw Tom Hiddleston. Claire Foy and Matt Smith, who starred together in hit Netflix series *The Crown*, are also set to make their debuts in Duncan Macmillan's *Lungs* at the Old Vic theatre in the 2019–20 season. Another theatre with TV and film-business connections is the Donmar Warehouse, a not-for-profit enterprise based in a stylish venue in Covent Garden. Sam Mendes was previously its artistic director, and stars that have featured in its productions include Jude Law and Kenneth Branagh.

FRINGE VENUES

In addition to the well-known central theatres, there are many recognised fringe venues in the capital, while theatres outside the centre, in Hampstead, Richmond and Wimbledon, are used as proving grounds for West End runs. Fringe productions range from standard Shakespeare on a low budget to the latest shows by minority groups keen to put across political or social messages, though much of the new young writing is dark and funny and well observed.

Established fringe venues include the Young Vic (on The Cut, near the Old Vic), the Almeida (in Islington) and the Half Moon (in the East End).

Lively pub theatres include the King's Head in Islington and the Gate Theatre at Notting Hill Gate.

In summer there is open-air theatre in Regent's Park (often a Shakespeare play and a musical) and also in Holland Park in West London, which produces around six operas a season.

NATIONAL COMPANIES

Among the most important features of the London theatre scene are the two major subsidised companies: the National Theatre and the Royal Shakespeare Company.

The National, with three auditoria on the South Bank, has the advantage of being a modern building (though its fierce concrete design isn't to everyone's taste) and its technology is impressive – revolving stages are only the start of it. A backstage tour offers a good mixture of information and anecdote. Another attraction is the fact that some seats for each production are available for just £15 each, courtesy of business sponsorship. Plays of particular note first produced at the National, which went on to be box office hits at the cinema, have been Alan Bennett's *The History Boys* and Michael Morpurgo's stunning *War Horse*, subsequently made into a film directed by Stephen Spielberg. Both also played on Broadway. Nicholas Hytner, the artistic director who guided these plays to success, left the theatre in 2015 and teamed up with Nick Starr, former executive director at the National, to launch the £12-million Bridge Theatre. The London Bridge venue opened with well-received performances of *Young Marx* and *Julius Caesar*.

In contrast to the National, the RSC gave up its London home in the Barbican Centre some years ago, and now stages seasons at various West End theatres. This has made it less visible in the capital, though the company does still attract big names from stage and screen to try their hands at the classics.

REGIONAL THEATRE

Although Londoners find it hard to believe, theatre is flourishing in many English cities apart from the capital, and the best regional productions regularly make their way to the West End. Among the repertory theatres in the UK are the Royal Exchange in Manchester, the Everyman in Liverpool, the West Yorkshire Playhouse in Leeds, the Theatre Royal in Newcastle, the Crucible in Sheffield, the Nottingham Playhouse, and the Theatre Royal in

Plymouth. Despite constant financial pressures, many of these theatres maintain high artistic standards, and have in the past provided training grounds for many of England's greatest actors.

> *In summer Shakespeare's plays can be seen on the spot where they were first performed, in a replica of the Globe Theatre on the South Bank of the River Thames.*

Buxton Opera House in Derbyshire.

⊘ DRAMA FESTIVALS

Bath Fringe Festival (tel: www.bathfringe.co.uk) late-May to early June, coinciding with the Bath International Music Festival, tel: 01225-463 362 for both events.

Brighton Festival (www.brightonfestival.org) mid-May, drama, comedy and music staged in numerous venues, tel: 01273-709 709.

Cambridge Shakespeare Festival (www.cambridgeshakespeare.com) July and August, open-air productions in college gardens, tel: 07955-218 824.

Minack Theatre Summer Season (www.minack.com) April to September – outdoor theatre built into a cliff facing the sea, tel: 01736-810 181.

PAINTING THE LANDSCAPE

The English countryside has long been a source of inspiration to artists, and two painters in particular changed the way we see it for ever.

England's major contribution to European art is in landscape painting. And in this genre, two figures – James Mallord William Turner, the son of a Covent Garden barber, and John Constable, whose father was a Suffolk miller – were supreme.

England did not share Europe's earlier tradition of art based on Christianity. Church property was destroyed or seized under Henry VIII in 1535, and the Puritans who ousted the monarchy in the mid-17th century rid the Church of all signs of idolatry. For longer than any Englishman can remember, paintings and icons in church have been frowned upon.

BACK TO NATURE

The English not only turned against what they saw as the vanity and pomp of Rome; they also failed to take much interest in the established Anglican Church of England. "There is no religion in England," noted the French philosopher Montesquieu in 1730. "If anyone mentions religion people begin to laugh." The great religious houses were in ruins, but Shakespeare's "ruined choirs that once so sweetly sang" inspired a piety among Romantics in the back-to-nature Age of Reason.

In England, poets such as William Wordsworth (1770–1850), bard of the Lake District and scourge of the prevailing Industrial Revolution, extolled the simple beauty of nature, an idea that soon became fashionable: walking was a habit taken up by intellectuals, and the "English garden" overturned the convention of formal Italianate gardens in favour of more informal plantings. The word "picturesque" entered the language, meaning a view of a landscape that suggested a painting.

J.M.W. Turner had no education but from time to time he was moved to write poetry, and his early paintings – *Tintern Abbey* (1794) and *Buttermere*

The lake poet William Wordsworth.

(1798) – were also subjects of Wordsworth's poems. Turner went on the first of numerous tours of the country when he was 14, in 1789, the same year he began to study at the Royal Academy school. His tireless pens and brushes made him one of England's most prolific painters. He made jottings wherever he went, and many parts of England can lay claim to his attention. "Turner seats" have been put up in the Yorkshire Dales so visitors can admire the scenes he painted. Around the south coast, in Hastings and elsewhere, he depicted stormy seas, influenced by Dutch maritime painting. And at Petworth House in West Sussex, where he was given a studio, he painted English parklands. The Turner Gallery at the Tate Britain gallery in London holds some of the finest examples of his works.

TURNER'S METHODS

He worked in watercolour (at the time considered merely a medium for colouring prints) and, from 1796, in oils. That same year he had his first exhibited oil painting at the Royal Academy, *Fisherman at Sea off the Needles*, depicting a small boat on a perilously stormy moonlit night. He always lived near water, never far from the Thames, and he took houses near the sea to watch the effects of the sun on the water.

He was a small, industrious figure, who wished to be left alone to get on with his work. Constable

Born six years after the poet, in 1776, Constable never lost sight of his Suffolk roots. Unlike Turner, Constable never strayed far from home. He never

> *Examples of Constable's works can be seen at the National Gallery and Victoria and Albert Museum in London, as well as on his home turf in Suffolk – in the Wolsey Art Gallery at Christchurch Mansion in Ipswich (see page 187).*

Turner's Rain, Steam and Speed (1844).

sat at the same dining table at the Royal Academy, but they were not friends and they never spoke to each other about their work. In the 1840s, living with his mistress in Chelsea, Turner was known to his neighbours as Mr Booth and was thought to be a retired admiral. His lack of education and rough manner may have cost him the presidency of the Royal Academy that he deserved.

CONSTABLE'S COUNTRY

Turner had been elected a full member of the Academy in 1802, the year John Constable first exhibited there. Four years later, Constable met Wordsworth in the Lake District. They had much in common: a desire for the simple rural life and no time for any luxury or grandeur their fame might have brought.

went abroad and most of his work was done in the south of England. His father owned Dedham and Flatford mills in the Stour Valley, which can be identified in some of his paintings, as can many parts of the river. Even in his day it was known as "Constable country". But pressure of work obliged him to live nearer London, at least for half the year, and he bought a house in Hampstead, which looks down over the city. The flat East Anglian landscapes had begun his obsession with skies, but it was here that he began to collect and classify them, writing down the time and date he had observed them. Clouds were, he believed, the chief organ of sentiment.

Constable brought a freshness of light and colour to his large canvases, such as *The Hay Wain* (1821, National Gallery, London), which has become almost a cliché of English art, and still tops popularity polls. His brush strokes were so fevered, so light and dashing that his works were called "sketches", for they were often more like impressions of what he saw. Later he might work a sketch up into a more formal, composed painting. Critics dismissed the sketches as being lesser works, and complained about his "whitewash" and "snow", the strokes of white that lightened his subjects. In 1824 *The Hay Wain* won a gold medal at the Paris Salon. Turner's work, described by Constable as "airy visions, painted with tinted steam", also had a great influence abroad.

Turner's impressionistic works such as *The Fighting Temeraire* (1838) or *Rain, Steam and Speed* (1844), both now housed at London's National Gallery, were as far from mainstream European art in their day as Picasso's *Les Demoiselles d'Avignon* (1907) was in his. Turner came to be emulated both in Britain and abroad. In Britain he was never surpassed. And it would be many more years before a French painter, Claude Monet, exhibited in the Salon a painting of a glimpse of a sunrise on water, *Impression: Soleil Levant* (1872), which inspired a French critic to describe him, dismissively, as an *Impressioniste*.

The Hay Wain (1821), painted by Constable.

⊘ SCHOOLS AND STYLES

Medieval art Found its greatest expression in illuminated manuscripts, such as the Lindisfarne Gospels.

Renaissance England's Renaissance produced notable portraiture, such as the School of Miniatures.

Baroque Portraiture by Van Dyck; classical scenes, such Rubens's ceiling in the Banqueting House in Whitehall.

Grand Manners and Conversation Pieces 18th-century studies of the wealthy. Principally Joshua Reynolds and Thomas Gainsborough; George Stubbs, renowned animal painter, earned more by painting portraits of horses.

Romantics Landscape paintings by John Constable and J.M.W. Turner; also paintings depicting fear at the changes of the Industrial Revolution, by artists such as John Martin.

Pre-Raphaelites Established in 1848 by Dante Gabriel Rossetti, Holman Hunt and John Millais; longed for a return to the medieval golden age. William Morris, founder of the Arts and Crafts Movement, was also a Pre-Raphaelite.

Camden Town Set Walter Sickert and associates responded to the French Post-Impressionists.

St Ives Not so much a school, more a 1920s West Country retreat for Barbara Hepworth, Ben Nicholson and others.

Pop Art David Hockney and Pauline Boty were important innovators in the Pop Art movement of the 1960s.

Britart A new crop of Young British Artists (YBA) – Damien Hirst, Rachel Whiteread, Tracey Emin – brings shock and irreverence to the stuffy art world.

FOOD AND DRINK

A burgeoning enthusiasm for food, combined with the influences of a multicultural society, means that eating in England has never been so varied and exciting.

English food and drink has come a long way over the past 50 years. Once upon a time, meat and two veg was the norm (with the meat always well done, and the vegetables boiled for hours), and you couldn't get a glass of wine in many restaurants, or a cup of coffee in many pubs. The situation couldn't be more different today: diners have embraced a wide range of cuisines from across the world, the English now drink more wine than beer, and connoisseurship of blends of coffee has become a daily ritual.

While many of the old criticisms were well deserved, that isn't to say that England's indigenous cuisine is without merit. Regional specialities abound, and the quality can be world-class. The joys of freshly caught crabs in Cromer, shrimps in Morecambe Bay or smoked fish in Craster should not be overlooked. Neither should spicy local sausages in Cumbria or new-season lamb from the Romney Marshes. And even English wines – particularly sparkling whites – are starting to hold their own against their Continental competitors.

Among the reasons for the renaissance in English food and drink are higher expectations fostered by foreign holidays, the availability of ingredients from across the globe and the increasingly multicultural nature of British society. Another factor that shouldn't be ignored is the influence of the numerous television chefs. In their different ways, Keith Floyd, Gordon Ramsay, Jamie Oliver, Hugh Fearnley-Whittingstall, Angela Hartnett and Mary Berry have all had an incalculable impact over the last couple of decades, paving the way for a new generation of boundary-breaking chefs such as Michelin-starred Jason Atherton, the multi-award-winning Tom Aikens, and James Lowe of Michelin-starred Lyle's.

Fine dining at L'Enclume in the Lake District.

A BREAK WITH TRADITION

Traditional eating patterns have undergone a gradual change: few people regularly cook at home the "full English breakfast" of fried eggs, sausages, bacon and mushrooms – colloquially known as "the heart attack special". But it is still on offer in most hotels and bed-and-breakfast establishments.

The typical English tea – sandwiches, cakes and pots of tea – survives in country tearooms and high-end hotels – but has disappeared from most households, because people usually aren't at home at "teatime".

Fish and chips are still popular and, in seaside towns in particular, can be delicious. Overfishing, however, has made white fish such as cod relatively scarce and expensive, so it is no longer a cheap alternative to meat. In many places fish-and-chip shops have closed down, to be replaced with restaurants selling takeaway tandoori or fried chicken.

The huge growth in Chinese and Indian restaurants, ranging from the cheap takeaway to the high-quality establishment, reflects the influence of England's immigrant communities on the daily diet. Curry in particular remains hugely popular – although much of it is an anglicised version that would be unrecognisable in India or Pakistan: consider chicken tikka masala or Birmingham baltis, for example. However in recent years other cuisines have come to the fore, with Thai, Vietnamese and Japanese flavours gaining in popularity. Indian chefs have responded by highlighting more healthy versions of the stereotypical masalas and showcasing regional Indian dishes.

Italian food, too, has become so ubiquitous that there is a whole generation of English people who could not imagine a world where pizza or lasagne was not readily available.

A fine selection of cheese at London's Borough Market.

Chef Tom Aikens dishes up.

⊘ TEA – THE NATION'S FAVOURITE DRINK

Tea has always been regarded as a British institution and the nation's most popular drink. However change is in the air and tea drinking is in decline, having dropped by almost a quarter since the 1970s, and coffee, with all its specialities, is overtaking as the nation's favourite beverage. No longer tea and biscuits but fancy coffees and pastries. However, there has been a big jump in the sale of specialised teas such as fruit, herbal and green. Alongside the lattes and cappuccinos are camomile, peppermint and raspberry leaf.

The history of tea is fascinating. Diarist Samuel Pepys found his first cup of China tea such a novelty in 1660 that he gave it a special entry. In its early days, it was so expensive that it was locked away in caddies to stop the servants helping themselves.

The habit of afternoon tea with cakes was started around 1840 by the Duchess of Bedford. This is a ritual that can still be enjoyed in many upmarket hotels and countless tearooms and cafés across the country. Some of the most elaborate "high teas", as they are known, are to be had at luxurious London hotels such as the Berkeley, the Ritz and the Savoy. Be sure to book in advance, and dress smartly (no jeans or trainers, and jackets and ties for men). So despite its apparent demise tea will continue to be served in its evolving forms and may yet give the coffee buffs a run for their money.

Vegetarianism has long been popular. It is no longer regarded as a rather odd fad that was probably not very good for you, but is now well respected, and in addition to thriving vegetarian restaurants, most other eating establishments

> At the time of writing, England has five restaurants with three Michelin stars, 18 with two stars and 125 with one star.

Fresh fish at London's Borough Market.

also offer a range of vegetarian dishes. There's been an explosion in the vegan food scene in recent years, particularly in major cities where everything from takeaway junk-food haunts to Michelin-starred restaurants specialise in plant-based menus. There has also been a trend towards catering for food intolerances, such as serving gluten-free alternatives.

The streets of London and other major cities are lined with restaurants and cafés offering a fusion of culinary styles, as might be expected, but what is more surprising is that this wide choice of food has radiated to provincial towns and rural communities. Many village pubs will have menus that range from warm goat's cheese salad to roast beef, from Thai fish cakes to *moules marinière*.

CULINARY GAINS AND LOSSES

English cheeses have made a comeback in recent years. When soft cheeses from the Continent first became widely available, indigenous varieties such as Cheddar, Wensleydale and Stilton fell out of fashion. But their worth has now been recognised once more – as has that of Somerset-made varieties of soft cheeses such as Brie and Camembert, and regional cheeses such as Cornish Yarg, Lincolnshire Poacher and Dorset Blue Vinney.

Many small grocers' shops and delicatessens sell regional cheeses, and there are specialist shops where the variety is almost overwhelming. At Christmas, Stilton, recognised as the queen of English cheeses, is sold in discreetly decorated gift boxes by superior stores such as Harrods and Fortnum & Mason. It is traditionally consumed with a glass of port.

Despite the huge range of exotic fruits and vegetables on offer in the supermarkets, it can be hard to find a true crunchy English apple, except in apple-growing areas, where you can buy them at roadside stalls and farm shops. Cob nuts and cherries from Kent are also increasingly hard to find. However, farmers' markets, where fresh produce is sold direct from the growers, are a good source of the old varieties, many of which are seeing a comeback. One of the most famous is Borough Market in London, though there are countless examples across England (see www.lfm.org.uk and http://hampshirefarmersmarkets.co.uk, for example).

One thing the English are still traditional about is their puddings, also known as desserts. Passion-fruit sorbet is all very well, and there are those who think that profiteroles represent the height of French achievement, but a strong body of opinion holds that treacle tart, syrup sponge pudding or apple pie are the only civilised way to finish a meal, with lashings of custard, of course. Catering to this demand, many otherwise adventurous restaurants put such comfort foods on their menus. There is even a Pudding Club (www.puddingclub.com), whose members meet regularly for meals consisting only of traditional puddings, such as Spotted Dick and Sussex Pond pudding (which has a whole lemon in the centre).

The English pub is accepted as an institution, offering real ale, good company and a warm welcome to all. That's the tradition. But what's the reality?

The word "pub" is merely a shortened form of "public house", an indication that the earliest ale houses were simply private homes where the occupant brewed beer and sold it at the front door or across a table in the living room. To indicate that the house sold ale, the owner would hang out a sign, not saying "Ale" – as the average Saxon peasant never graduated to literacy – but a pole topped with a bough of evergreen.

There is no shortage of claimants to be the "Oldest Pub in Britain", but one with a stronger case than most is the Trip to Jerusalem, in Nottingham – certainly in business at the time of the Crusades, hence its name. Like so much else in British life, the institution of the pub reached its zenith in Victorian times, and the country is still rich in opulent pub interiors from that period, despite all the efforts of philistine pub-owning corporations to rip them out in the name of "modernisation".

So, what makes a good traditional pub? The English beer-drinker's Bible, the annual *Good Beer Guide*, offers a few guidelines that resonate: "In a good pub, the greatest attention is given to the drink, and in particular to the beer. Sociability, on both sides of the bar, comes a close second... A good pub has a caring, responsive landlord... there is always one bar (and preferably two) to accommodate those people who simply want to drink and chat without the distraction or inhibition induced by overbearing decor, noisy entertainment, or intrusive dining." That's certainly a popular – and traditional – vision of the local pub, but over the last few decades many examples have adapted to changing customer preferences.

THE 21ST-CENTURY PUB

Nowadays, more and more pubs serve good food. Tea and coffee are often on offer, and families are being made more welcome. While most pubs still ring a bell for "last orders" at 11pm and then expect you to drink up and depart by 11.30pm, since 2003, pub landlords have been able to apply for extended opening hours, up to 24 hours a day, seven days a week. A smoking ban has also changed the character of English pubs, and undoubtedly freshened up the atmosphere.

Since the turn of the millennium, pubs have suffered amid changing drinking habits and economic downturn. They have often had to adapt, or at worst, close. The last ten years or so has seen the rise of the gastropub, where the emphasis is on food rather than drink. When it is done well, the gastropub can be very good. Places such as the Anchor and Hope in London's Southwark, the Hind's Head at Bray in the Thames Valley or the Drunken Duck at Ambleside in the Lake District all combine excellent food and drink with an informal atmosphere and plenty of character. Meanwhile, a growing crop of

The Nutshell, Britain's second-smallest pub.

independent brewery taprooms are springing up, offering brewery tours and tastings of craft beers and house ales, from local favourite Beavertown in Tottenham Hale to award-winning Wylam in Newcastle upon Tyne.

In villages and small towns, many pubs still retain their historic function as overnight stopping-off places. Some of the grander examples (the George at Stamford, for instance) are former coaching inns; others are much simpler, with just a few bedrooms upstairs. The Campaign for Real Ale (www.camra.org.uk) publishes the aforementioned *Good Beer Guide*, with its lists of the best inns. These often present good value for money, and, seeing as they remain the social hubs of their communities, they almost always guarantee a warm welcome and an authentically English experience.

📷 ENGLISH CHEESES

In recent decades the English have become the "big cheeses" of the cheese-making world, giving the *grands fromages* across the Channel a run for their money.

According to the British Cheese Board (www.brit-ishcheese.com) there are over 700 named cheeses produced in the UK. Many of these are quite recent inventions, produced in an "artisanal" fashion in small quantities, but to an extremely high quality. The impetus for this cheese-making renaissance is often ascribed to consumers' growing appreciation of local farm produce, sustainable methods of manufacture and the Slow Food movement (www.slowfood.org.uk).

Among the most celebrated of the newer varieties of English cheese is Stinking Bishop, a soft cheese from Gloucestershire that is immersed in perry (pear cider) made from the Stinking Bishop pear every four weeks until it has matured. Another great favourite with the cheese-eating public is Cornish Yarg, which is based on a recipe found in a book in a farmer's attic; the farmer's name was Mr Gray – "Yarg" spelt backwards. After it comes out of the cheese press, this semi-hard cow's-milk cheese is wrapped in nettle leaves, forming an edible rind. The nettle leaves not only help preserve the cheese, but they also impart a distinctive mushroomy flavour.

Many of the better-known English cheeses have much longer histories. Cheshire cheese, for example, dates back to Roman times, and is even mentioned in the Domesday Book. Cheddar is named after the Cheddar Gorge Caves in Somerset, where the cheese was stored as it ripened. Crumbly Wensleydale cheese – beloved of cartoon characters Wallace and Gromit – was first made by French Cistercian monks who had come from the Roquefort region to settle in North Yorkshire.

The official Wallace and Gromit Wensleydale cheese on display.

Participants in the Cheese Rolling Festival at Cooper's Hill, Gloucestershire, race down the steep slope.

Competitors participate in the annual event of Cheese Rolling in the village of Stilton, held every May Day Bank Holiday. This sees teams of four compete against each other to be crowned the "Stilton Cheese Rolling Champions".

Traditional English Cheddar cheese maturing in Cheddar Gorge Caves, Somerset.

Stilton

This smelly, blue-veined, creamy cheese has long been a stalwart of English cuisine, and is traditionally eaten at Christmas accompanied by a glass of port.

The cheese was first discovered in the 1730s by an innkeeper in the village of Stilton, which is not far from Huntingdon in the north of Cambridgeshire. The inn was on a stagecoach route between London and the north of England, and this enabled the reputation of the cheese to spread rapidly across the country. Some decades later, a cheese-maker from Wymondham across the county border in Leicestershire established the cheese's quality and shape standards along lines we would recognise today. Stilton has since been trademarked and given Protected Designation of Origin status (PDO) such that only licensed dairies in the counties of Derbyshire, Leicestershire and Nottinghamshire can produce it, and then only to strict guidelines. Among other rules, the cheese must be made in its traditional cylindrical form, must not be pressed, and must be allowed to form its own crust.

George Orwell's essay "In Defence of English Cooking" names Stilton "the best cheese of its type in the world".

Cornish Yarg cheese, with its distinctive rind.

Cheese-makers produce authentic Wensleydale cheese, stamped with a seal of authenticity, at the company's creamery in Hawes, nestling in the Yorkshire Dales.

WALKING IN ENGLAND

"If I could not walk far and fast, I think I should just explode and perish," said Charles Dickens, summing up how many feel about this English pastime.

Despite the pressures of cramming 64 million inhabitants together on one island, Britain has managed to retain many areas of unspoilt countryside. An important part of such conservation efforts is the system of National Parks and National Trails. These were established in the decades after World War II to help offset the effects of an ambitious programme of new towns and housing estates. At the same time, motorways were laid out across the countryside and – much to the regret of many – the rural railway network was slashed, following the notorious Beeching Report.

There are currently 10 National Parks in England (www.nationalparks.gov.uk). These include the Lake District, the Norfolk Broads and the most recent, the South Downs. In addition to these, there are 14 National Trails in England (www.nationaltrail.co.uk) – including the Offa's Dyke Path, which runs along the border with Wales. The Pennine Bridleway (205 miles/330km), the South Downs Way (100 miles/160km) and large sections of several other trails can also be navigated by horse riders and cyclists.

Borrowdale Valley, Lake District National Park.

Long-distance paths are signposted and marked with an acorn symbol, public footpaths with a yellow arrow and public bridleways (walkers and horse riders) with a blue arrow.

AROUND THE COAST

If you want to be really ambitious, you can, of course, walk around Britain's entire coastline – but this 4,000-odd-mile (6,437km) jaunt is not for the faint-hearted. Fortunately, there are shorter (and well-signposted) sections of coast that make

spectacular walks. There's the 93-mile (150km) North Norfolk Coast Path, which takes in miles of white sand and some of the country's finest bird sanctuaries. Then you could try sections of the 630-mile (1,014km) South West Coast Path around Dorset, Devon and Cornwall, which takes in the fossil cliffs of Chesil Beach, the most southwesterly point of the British mainland at Land's End, and Exmoor National Park, famous for its herds of wild horses.

THE LAKE DISTRICT

For walking with the ideal combination of water and mountain, rock and vegetation, head up to the northwest of England to the Lake District. The central part of the Lakes is a national park (www.lakedistrict.gov.uk), and encompasses all of the land in England higher than 3,000ft (914 metres) including Scafell Pike, England's highest mountain at 3,209ft (978 metres). It also contains towards 100 lakes – although only one, Bassenthwaite Lake, is officially named a lake, the others being meres, waters or tarns.

The aesthetic perfection of the Lakes has long been admired. The so-called Lake Poets – Wordsworth, Coleridge and Southey – took inspiration from the landscape for their romantic conception of man's place in nature. The artist and critic John Ruskin (1819–1900), who championed the cause of naturalism in art, lived in a house facing Coniston

COAST TO COAST

Another popular route devised by Wainwright is the Coast to Coast Walk, a 192-mile (309km) path that begins in the Lake District and stretches across to Robin Hood's Bay in North Yorkshire. Walkers are supposed to dip their feet in the Irish Sea at the start and the North Sea at the end. In between, they pass through three national parks: the Lake District, the Yorkshire Dales and the North York Moors. The walk splits conveniently into manageable sections and, with overnight stays at guesthouses along the way, the entire route can be fitted into a two-week holiday.

Approaching Carbis Bay, Cornwall.

Water, and some time later, Beatrix Potter bought a farm near Ambleside, where she continued working on her beautifully illustrated animal tales.

In more recent times, close observation of the Lakeland landscape has yielded the extraordinary work of Alfred Wainwright (1907–91). His guidebooks detailing the best routes up the fells are reproductions of his own manuscripts, with beautiful pen-and-ink drawings and immaculate handwriting. Seven volumes cover 214 of the fells, which are now often collectively referred to as "the Wainwrights", and conquering the complete set of peaks is a popular challenge among walking enthusiasts. Wainwright himself considered the "finest half-dozen" fells to be Scafell Pike, Bowfell, Pillar, Great Gable, Blencathra and Crinkle Crags.

⊘ NATIONAL CYCLE NETWORK

The National Cycle Network (www.sustrans.org.uk) comprises 14,000 miles (2,2531km) of cycle paths. The routes aim to minimise contact with motor traffic, and although some are on minor roads, many others are on disused railway lines, canal towpaths and bridleways. The network is signposted using a white bicycle symbol on a blue background, with a white route number in an inset box. In addition, there is the National Byway (www.thenationalbyway.org), a 3,200-mile (5,150km) cycling route that runs along quiet roads around England and parts of Scotland and Wales. These circular routes range in length from 16 miles (26km) to 50 miles (80km). Signposts have white writing on a brown background.

Leanne Kiernan playing for West Ham United during the Women's FA Cup Final at Wembley, 2019.

SPORTING PASSIOI S

Whether you like watching or playing, are into boxing or bowls, England's obsession with sport means you'll find something to suit your sporting needs.

The English have often been portrayed as preferring sport to art and culture. It's probably true, though it's not something you'll find many people apologising for. The English are responsible for inventing – or at least playing a crucial role in developing – a wide range of sports that are popular now around the world. Football, rugby (both Union and League versions), cricket, tennis, boxing and snooker all trace their histories back to these shores. And although England nationals may no longer dominate the first ranks of many of these sports, the country does still host some of the world's most prestigious tournaments.

FOOTBALL

In the last few decades, association football (soccer) has undergone a remarkable transformation in Britain. Even 25 years ago, its fan base was largely male, stadiums offered standing room only (with no toilet facilities for women), and match days were plagued with pitched battles between gangs of hooligans. Things are very different today, in large part because of the enormous cash injection from satellite television fees. Premier League clubs can now afford the best players in the world, most grounds have been completely revamped with seating and modern amenities, and the fan base is far wider and more family-orientated. But although hooliganism is largely a thing of the past, the passion of the crowd and the quality of their singing and swearing is as robust as ever.

RUGBY

Rugby is said to have been invented when one of the pupils of Rugby public school picked up the ball and ran in a game of football early in the 19th century. It is a national institution today, with two types: Union, played in Scotland, Wales

Saracens take on Wasps in the European Rugby Champions Cup semi-final.

Rugby, it has been said, is a thug's game played by gentlemen, while football is a gentleman's game played by thugs.

and predominantly the south of England; and League, played in the north of England.

Rugby Union, formerly for amateurs only, is now professional. The season runs from September to May, with international matches played at Twickenham. One of the highlights of the season is the Six Nations Championship, a competition between England, Ireland, Scotland, Wales, France and

Italy. Rugby League, which is broadly speaking more an institution of northern England, has long been professional and culminates in the Super League final at Old Trafford in October.

CRICKET

Silly mid-off, LBW, googly, square leg and golden duck: cricket is a funny old game, with arcane terminology and matches up to five days long. Those in the know, however, swear that once you understand the basics, it's an engrossing sport that will have you rejoicing in the sound of leather on willow (or, to the uninitiated, ball on bat). As with a number of traditional British sports, cricket is also played in many of the Commonwealth countries. Over the last 100 years, several of these – India, Australia and South Africa, for example – have outdone the former colonial power in developing their fan bases and often in the skill of their teams too. Nevertheless, the England team has proved strong in recent years, winning the ICC Cricket World Cup in 2019, beating New Zealand in a show-stopping final that resulted in a tie and an unprecedented Super

Lewis Hamilton celebrates winning the British Grand Prix at Silverstone.

⊘ ENGLAND'S QUIRKIEST SPORTS

Sport is a field in which the English have traditionally enjoyed exercising their eccentricity. At the mildly puzzling end of the spectrum are the annual **Thames Punting Championships**, held at Maidenhead (see www. maidenheadrc.org.uk). It's a gentlemanly affair, and speeds attained never exceed sedate. More bizarre is the annual **Mud Race** at Maldon, Essex (www.maldonmudrace.com), which involves a couple of hundred people wading across the River Blackwater at low tide. And the annual **Cheese-Rolling** at Cooper's Hill in Gloucestershire (www. officialcheeserolling.com) is downright eccentric. A round of Double Gloucester cheese is rolled down the hill for competitors to chase.

Over tiebreak (which was also drawn). In the end, the match was decided by boundary count.

Purists assert that the "Test" series is the most sublime version of the game. It consists of five matches lasting five days each played between different national teams. The most famous of such contests is the Ashes series between England and Australia. It is played every other year, with each country taking turns to host the event.

Alongside the international matches, Britain has its own domestic competitions: a league of 18 counties play each other in matches that consist of "limited overs". Between 20 and 50 overs (an over consists of six balls) are bowled by each side so that a match can usually be completed in one day. Each county has its own home ground.

HORSERACING

Horseracing in Britain is either flat racing – unobstructed runs over varying distances – or National Hunt (steeplechase) racing, where the horses have to jump over hurdles or fences along the course. There are race courses all over the country and race meetings throughout the year, which make an enjoyable, family-friendly day out. Perhaps the most famous course is Newmarket, which is also a centre for stud farms and horse training, and is home to the National Horseracing Museum.

Among the biggest events in the racing calendar are Royal Ascot, a five-day race meeting attended by the Queen in the third week of June; the Cheltenham Festival, a four-day National Hunt meeting in mid-March; the Grand National at Aintree in April, the longest and most gruelling National Hunt race in the calendar; and the richest flat race, the Derby, held at Epsom in early June. The dress codes enforced at the stand or "enclosure" areas, which offer the best views, are all part of the entertainment, especially on Ladies' Day. On-course betting is a part of the experience, and is conducted in hard cash only.

MOTOR RACING

The heart of motor racing worldwide, Britain has produced a number of World Champions, from Mike Hawthorn and Jim Clark to James Hunt, Nigel Mansell, Damon Hill, Jenson Button and Lewis Hamilton. The British Grand Prix, the highlight of the British motor-racing calendar, is traditionally held at Silverstone in Northamptonshire. It usually takes place on the second weekend in July. Tickets for the race itself are very expensive, but there is a wide range of types of race at Silverstone at other times in the year. Britain's other race tracks (most notably Brands Hatch and Donington) also host race meetings, specialising in everything from touring cars to powerful single seaters. Rallying is also very popular.

ROWING

The major rowing competitions in Britain are popular spectator events. Over the first weekend of July, Henley Royal Regatta offers five days of "head-to-head" races on the Thames, where two crews compete side by side in each round of a knockout tournament. Henley is also a major social event, where spectators dress for show.

Perhaps the most famous rowing fixture in the world is the annual Oxford and Cambridge Boat Race, held on a Saturday or Sunday in late March

or early April. The competitors are all students at Oxford and Cambridge universities, though the large number of international oarsmen has given rise to suspicions that many crew members are admitted to their university on account of their rowing abilities alone. The race runs from Putney to Chiswick Bridge, and spectators can watch for free from many vantage points along the course.

TENNIS

The Wimbledon fortnight is one of Britain's best-loved sporting highlights, attracting nearly 400,000

England's Ben Stokes during the ICC Cricket World Cup Final against New Zealand in 2019.

spectators in person and millions of television viewers worldwide. It takes place at the end of June and early July on the immaculate grass courts at the All England Club in Wimbledon, southwest London.

After a crushing defeat to Roger Federer in the 2012 final, Andy Murray came back stronger in 2013 to beat Novak Djokovic in the final and become the first British male singles winner since Fred Perry in 1936. He claimed the title for a second time in 2016, after which he was honoured with a knighthood in 2017. In 2019, Murray announced his intention to retire from tennis, partly due to a hip injury, but at the time of writing he was still competing.

THE ROYAL FAMILY

The Royal Family play an essential part in England's image around the world. Nowhere else in the world is there a monarchy so steeped in history or so grand.

"Her Majesty's speech delivered upon the reassembling of Parliament was, as usual, insipid and uninstructive. Its preferred topic was Her Majesty's approaching marriage, a matter of little importance or interest to the country, except as it may thereby be burdened with additional and unnecessary expense." That curt dismissal of Queen Victoria was written by a correspondent of *The Times* a century and a half ago. Since then the English have become noticeably more democratic, more pluralistic, more educated, more informed and far more reverential to the family whose historic role they continue to acknowledge.

THE ROLE OF THE MONARCHY

Her Majesty Queen Elizabeth II is given millions of pounds a year by the state, earns millions more from her own investments, has the run of a string of palaces and is custodian of the world's largest private collection of art. Conscious of public perception, in the 1990s she finally began to pay tax on her private earnings, and many "lesser" royals were removed from the Civil List, which provides public money towards their expenses. All the same, every so often there is an outcry if "lesser" royals are seen to be living off the fat without putting in time on what can be an arduous stream of official engagements.

But the British still – for the most part – regard the monarchy as a useful and desirable institution. By its very age it is a potent symbol of national identity; by being above party politics and not subject to election, it provides the state with a sense of last-bastion hope against the incompetence of often uninspiring politicians; and not least it is a darned good show. Unlike Queen Victoria, who tried to interfere with her

Queen Elizabeth II on her way to Westminster for the State Opening of Parliament.

democratically elected prime ministers and became so disenchanted with the whole business of politics that she seriously considered packing her bags and ruling the Empire from Australia, her descendants who have reigned this century have been adept at keeping clear of the political arena.

ROYALS IN THE 21ST CENTURY

Queen Elizabeth II passed retiring age in 1986, but there is no sign yet of her standing back from her duties. In 2007 she became the oldest monarch to have sat on the English throne (beating George III, who died aged 81 years, 7 months and 24 days). In 2012, she celebrated her Diamond Jubilee, marking 60 years on the throne – with events that included a pageant on the Thames, a concert at Buckingham Palace and the lighting of beacons throughout the United Kingdom. On 9 September 2015 she finally eclipsed Queen Victoria's record-breaking reign of 63 years 216 days.

The opinion polls show, too, that she retains broad support. Her son and heir, Charles, Prince of Wales, is somewhat less popular and can seem ill at ease in public – although he has successfully carved out a role for himself in promoting charitable causes and ethical and cultural values. And the opinion polls also show that the public is warming to his consort, Camilla, Duchess of Cornwall – a far cry from Camilla Parker-Bowles's (as she was) long portrayal as the third person in the marriage of Charles and Diana, Princess of Wales. There are still occasional calls that Charles should stand aside in favour of his more paparazzi-friendly eldest son, Prince William, but they are less fervent than in the past.

Following Diana's tragic death, there has been more forgiveness of the royals' fallibility. Nobody wants them to return to being the remote figureheads they were until the 1960s; Diana's overwhelming popularity stemmed from her rejection of formal protocol and willingness to express her emotions as well as from her glamour. This seems to be the attraction with William, whose wedding in 2011 to Catherine Middleton, now Duchess of Cambridge, has helped to boost the royal family's popularity.

⊙ THE OPENING OF PARLIAMENT

If you are visiting London between October and December, you may get the opportunity to see the Queen – as Head of State – opening the new session of Parliament. She travels from Buckingham Palace in a magnificent state coach to Westminster, with the Imperial State Crown being conveyed in its own carriage ahead of the Queen. Spectators can watch the procession as it travels down the Mall and along Whitehall. On arrival, the Queen puts on the crown and her parliamentary robe, and enters the House of Lords. No monarch has set foot in the House of Commons (where the MPs sit) since the ill-fated Charles I in 1642.

William's understated approach, coupled with the Duchess's "commoner" background, helps to show that the young generation of royals is

> Her Majesty Queen Elizabeth II is a descendant of both King Egbert of Wessex (AD 827–39) and King McAlpin of Scotland (1057–93), and is related to all the half-dozen remaining monarchs of Europe.

The Queen's 90th birthday celebrations at Windsor Castle in 2016.

more in touch with the public than the critics might like to argue. The birth of Prince George in 2013, Princess Charlotte in 2015 and Prince Louis in 2018 has further endeared the royals to the public.

Prince Harry has also modernised the monarchy, working with his brother to raise awareness of mental-health issues and bucking traditions through his relationship with American *Suits* actress Meghan Markle. Harry married Meghan in a star-studded wedding at Windsor Castle in May 2018 and the couple – now the Duke and Duchess of Sussex – celebrated the birth of Archie Harrison Mountbatten-Windsor a year later.

A view of the Seven Sisters, Sussex, from Seaford Head.

Malvern Hills panorama.

Tower Bridge, London at sunset.

Sunny Port Isaac, Cornwall.

INTRODUCTION

A detailed guide to the country, with principal sights clearly cross-referenced by number to the maps.

Holmfirth, Yorkshire.

For all the fuss it has made in history, and despite the fact that its language has been exported around the world, England is a rather small place. The largest of the four constituent elements that make up the United Kingdom, it covers 50,331 sq miles (130,357 sq km) – about the same size as New York State or one of New Zealand's islands. But its population of over 55.6 million is over two and a half times New York State's, and over 15 times both New Zealand's islands.

By far the greater portion of the population lives in the south. The large northern towns, Liverpool, Manchester and Newcastle, grew vast on the Industrial Revolution, and though they suffered during the de-industrialisation of the 1970s and 80s, they have recently undergone something of a renaissance and are now proud regional centres. Birmingham, Britain's second city, has benefited from its more central location and remains a hub of industry, services and transport.

The country is divided into counties, the old English shires, where sheriffs transacted local business. They have provided titles for the nation's nobility and though their names and boundaries have been tinkered with twice in post-war years, they are redolent of the country's past and continue to inspire local pride.

At the start of the third millennium, England, owing to post-war migrations, is a less homogenised nation than ever before – all nations of the world can be found in London. Local accents and dialects that not long ago were thick on the ground are now waning, but new cultures, traditions and accents have been added by incoming populations.

Half-timbered houses, Lavenham, Suffolk.

England's ever-changing landscape provides incomparable scenery. The Lake District has England's highest mountains and deepest lakes, while Yorkshire offers windswept moors and lush green dales. The South Downs possess gentler, chalky undulations, and the Fenlands of East Anglia are as flat as a pancake, with soil that's almost black. Every part of the country has its own distinctive architecture too – from West Country thatch to Cotswold stone, weatherboarded Kent to half-timbered East Anglia, black-slated Cumbria, and the sandstones, red and yellow, of Cumbria and York. It doesn't take much effort in England, and not many miles, to feel that you have travelled a long way.

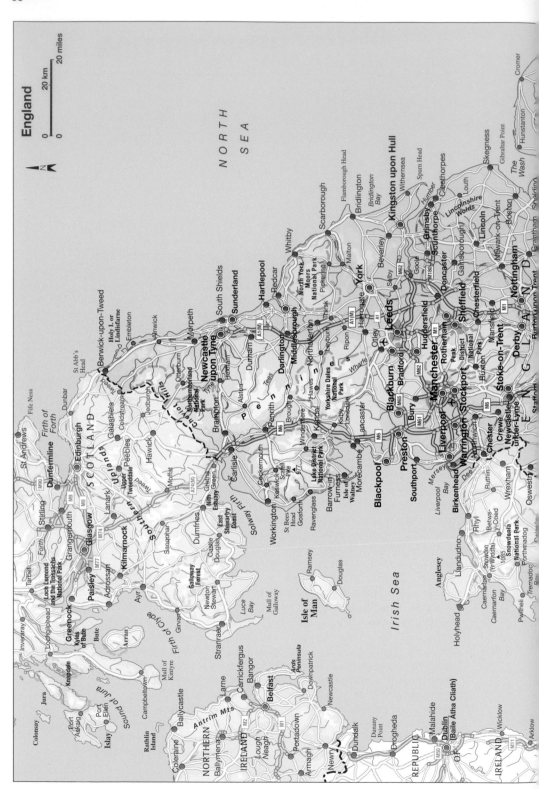

England

Central London

0   500 m
0   500 yds

N

FINSBURY

Sadler's Wells Theatre

The City University

SHOREDITCH

Hoxton Sq.

Calvert Ave

Queen Elizabeth Olympic Park

CLERKENWELL

Old Street

Bethnal Green Road

Sclater St

Shoreditch High Street Station

SPITALFIELDS

Clerkenwell Road

Worship Street

Dennis Severs' House 54

Chancery Lane

Exhibition Halls

Chiswell St

Old Spitalfields Market 53

Brushfield St

18 Staple Inn

Farringdon

Farringdon Station

Barbican

Arts Centre

Beech St

Barbican

St Giles 35

Moorgate

Liverpool Street Station

Petticoat Lane Market

Aldgate East Fotografiska

Chancery Lane

Smithfield Market

St Bartholomew-the-Great

Museum of London 36

London Wall

Liverpool Street

London Wall

Houndsditch

Aldgate

31 Dr Johnson's House

City Thameslink Station

Stock Exchange

Guildhall 37

Tower 42

33 St Mary Axe (The Gherkin)

Aldgate High St

Minories

Holborn Circus

Paternoster Sq.

St Paul's

Bank of England 38

Royal Exchange

Lloyd's 39

Leadenhall Market

Fenchurch Street Station

Tower Gateway

34 St Paul's Cathedral

One New Change

Poultry

Mansion House

Bank

Leadenhall Street

30 St Bride's (Crypt Museum)

Mansion House

Fenchurch

Corn Exchange

Trinity House

Tower Hill

29 Middle Temple

Inner Temple Hall

INNER TEMPLE GARDENS

Blackfriars

Cannon Street

Cannon Street Station

Monument 40 Monument

Tower Hill

41 Tower of London

Victoria Embankment

Upper Thames

St Katharine Docks 52

HQS Wellington

IIMC President

Blackfriars Station

Millennium Bridge

Bankside Pier

Southwark Bridge

Swan Lane Pier

Thames

Tower Pier

HMS Belfast

V London Studios

OXO Tower

Tate Modern 47

46

Shakespeare's Globe Theatre & Exhibition

Clink Prison Museum

Golden Hinde

London Bridge City Pier

Tower Bridge Experience 42

Gabriel's Wharf

SOUTHWARK

Southwark St

45

Southwark Cathedral

Hay's Galleria

City Hall

LONDON BR. CITY PARK

Tower Bridge

Upper Ground

Stamford Street

Borough Market

London Bridge

London Bridge Station

Bridge Theatre

Butler's Wharf

Waterloo East Station

Southwark

Union Street

View from The Shard

The Shard 44

Tooley Street

Tooley St

Southwark

Union St

Guy's Hospital

St Thomas St

Crucifix Lane

Greenwich

Lambeth North

Borough

Long Lane

43 Fashion & Textile Museum

Bermondsey St

Westminster Br. Rd

TABARD GARDENS

BOROUGH

Long Lane

Jamaica Rd

Lambeth

George's Road

Dover Street

BERMONDSEY

Abbey Street

51 Imperial War Museum

Elephant & Castle

Tower Bridge Rd

Elephant & Castle Station

New Kent Road

NEWINGTON

THE NATIONAL GALLERY

CENTRAL LONDON

Each year London attracts millions of visitors, who are enticed by this multi-faceted metropolis, where you never know what you'll find round the next corner.

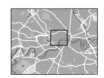

No one has captured in words the excitement of London as well as Samuel Johnson, the doctor who had a literary cure for just about everything: "When a man is tired of London he is tired of life, for there is in London all that life can afford." Today, some 240 years later, Johnson's words still ring true. London's variety is inexhaustible.

A good starting point is **Trafalgar Square ❶**. One of the most impressive public squares in the world, it was laid out in the 1830s and 1840s by Sir Charles Barry and dedicated to the memory of Admiral Lord Nelson and his decisive victory over Napoleon's fleet off Cape Trafalgar in 1805. The square is a paragon of the classical style, enclosed by graceful white facades and dominated by the 162ft (50-metre) **Nelson's Column** and four sculpted bronze lions. The fourth plinth, in the northwest corner of the square, showcases temporary works by contemporary artists; past commissions have included Antony Gormley, Rachel Whiteread and Marc Quinn. Trafalgar Square is the strategic centre of London: the statue of **Charles I** occupies the spot from where all distances to/from London are measured. The financial wizards of the City of London work to the east; the main shopping centres are to the west; the entertainment

empire of the West End lies directly to the north; and the government palaces of Whitehall and Westminster stretch to the south along the River Thames.

The square has long been the site of public gatherings, political demonstrations and New Year celebrations. Every Christmas a 70ft (20-metre) Norwegian spruce is erected in the square, a gift from the city of Oslo in recognition of the protection given by Britain to members of the Norwegian Royal Family in World War II.

❂ Main attractions
Trafalgar Square
Covent Garden
Buckingham Palace
Westminster Abbey
Houses of Parliament
Regent's Park
Bloomsbury
British Museum
Hampstead

Map on page 82

Buckingham Palace.

> **Tip**

Look out for candlelit concerts held in St Martin-in-the-Fields – and try out the café in the crypt where excellent coffee and reasonably priced meals are served. It is a popular eating place for office workers and tourists alike, so expect it to be busy.

THE NATIONAL GALLERY

Running along the north flank of Trafalgar Square is the **National Gallery** ➋ (www.nationalgallery.org.uk; daily 10am–6pm, Fri until 9pm; charge for some exhibitions). Founded in 1824, the gallery has grown into one of the most outstanding and comprehensive collections in the world, with a list of masters ranging from Leonardo and Rembrandt to El Greco and Van Gogh. The collection is arranged chronologically, from the 13th century to the end of the 19th century. The modern Sainsbury Wing, designed by Robert Venturi, houses the rich Renaissance collection.

Around the corner, established in 1856, is the **National Portrait Gallery** (www.npg.org.uk; daily 10am–6pm, Fri until 9pm; charge for some exhibitions). Presenting an illustrated British history, it contains the faces of the nation's illustrious men and women executed by a wide range of artists and photographers. Only a fraction of the collection's paintings, drawings, sculptures and photographs is on display at any given time. The rooftop Portrait

An old-fashioned tobacconist in Covent Garden.

Restaurant affords spectacular views over London.

To the right of the National Gallery is the church of **St Martin-in-the-Fields** (www.stmartin-in-the-fields.org; Mon–Fri 8.30am–6pm, Sat–Sun 9am–6pm, with exceptions; free), the oldest surviving structure on Trafalgar Square, built along simple but elegant lines by James Gibbs in 1722–6. The church became well known during World War II, when its crypt was a refuge from the Blitz. St Martin's is still the parish church for Buckingham Palace, with royal boxes at the east end.

COVENT GARDEN

Northeast of Trafalgar Square begins the maze of narrow streets and tiny alleys called **Covent Garden** ➌. There has been some type of market on this spot for more than 300 years, but the name actually derives from the convent garden that occupied the area until Henry VIII's Dissolution. At the centre of Covent Garden lies a cobblestone piazza, designed by Inigo Jones, and superb steel-and-glass market

> **FACT FILE**

Situation On roughly the same latitude as Berlin and Vancouver, 40 miles (64km) from the North Sea.

Size 115 sq miles (300 sq km).

Population 8.6 million.

Transport system Underground (Tube) and buses. Oyster smartcards generally offer the cheapest travel option. Paris is 2 hours 15 minutes by Eurostar train from St Pancras International. Boat trips on the Thames from Charing Cross pier.

Tallest building The Shard, by London Bridge Station.

Liveliest festival Notting Hill Carnival.

Best produce market Borough Market.

Oldest pubs Prospect of Whitby (1520), Wapping (East London); The George Inn (1676), Borough High Street (South London) – London's only galleried coaching inn.

Biggest attractions British Museum and National Gallery.

Finest building Westminster Abbey.

Best for roast beef Simpson's on the Strand, Rules on Maiden Lane.

Best views of the city Waterloo Bridge for panoramas day and night; unbeatable vistas from the London Eye.

pavilions constructed in the 1830s to house flower, fruit and vegetable stalls. The market was moved to new quarters south of the river at Nine Elms in 1974, and in the early 1980s Covent Garden was refurbished into an area of restaurants, shops and cafés. It's also a favourite venue for street entertainers.

The market and boutique-lined streets are popular for shopping, especially cobbled **Neal Street**, which is mostly shoes and fashion. Off Earlham Street is **Neal's Yard**, with an apothecary, cheese shop and other natural food shops surrounding a tiny square full of potted trees. This colourful corner is also home to artisanal coffee shops and lovely little deli-wine bars. The covered **Jubilee Market** (what most Londoners think of simply as Covent Garden Market) shelters an appealing medley of fashion boutiques, gift stores, arts and crafts stalls, restaurants, street performers, the occasional puppet show and, on Mondays, an antiques market. Nearby is **Stanfords** at 12–14 Long Acre (off Covent Garden, to the north of the piazza), a specialist map and travel bookshop.

Covent Garden is also busy in the evenings, offering a plethora of places to drink and eat, many of which offer pre- and post-theatre menus. Those with a taste for English tradition might imbibe at one of the many ancient pubs in the area such as the **Lamb and Flag** (on Rose Street, off Floral Street), a 17th-century pub once frequented by prizefighters and known as the "Bucket of Blood".

Used as a backdrop for the movie *My Fair Lady* in 1964, Covent Garden is also synonymous with British theatre. Dominating the west end of the piazza, **St Paul's Church** (1633), by Inigo Jones, is known locally as the "actor's church". On the second Sunday in May a service commemorates the Punch and Judy puppet tradition, first noted here in 1662 by diarist Samuel Pepys. There's a brass-band procession of Mr Punches around the area at 11am and puppetry performances in the afternoon.

The **Theatre Royal** was established on Drury Lane in 1663 and is still a showcase for musicals. In 1733, another theatre was built nearby, on the site now occupied by the majestic

A street entertainer performs in Covent Garden.

Trafalgar Square.

The grand facade of the Royal Opera House.

Flags line the Mall.

Royal Opera House (box office tel: 020-7304 4000; www.roh.org.uk), home of both The Royal Opera and The Royal Ballet. Inside, the magnificent Floral Hall (now known as the Paul Hamlyn Hall) houses a bar and restaurant.

The old flower market, in the south-eastern corner of the square, is now home to the impressive **London Transport Museum,** which has a big collection of horse-drawn coaches, buses, trams, trains, rail carriages and some working displays (www.ltmuseum.co.uk; daily 10am–6pm). It effectively traces the social history of modern London, whose growth was powered by transport, and deals intelligently with issues such as congestion and pollution. Facilities for children are good: there are extensive play areas, simulators to allow them to "drive" a Tube train, and an indoor picnic area where you can eat your own packed lunch.

CHARING CROSS ROAD

Bibliophiles usually make haste for **Charing Cross Road**, which is dotted with bookshops, though there are far fewer here than was once the case. Most notable is **Foyles**, said to be the largest bookstore in London.

Charing Cross Road is on the east side of **Leicester Square** , where the city's main multiplex cinemas stage celebrity-filled film premieres. Look out, too, for the statue of London-born Charlie Chaplin as *The Little Tramp*, a Shakespeare fountain and the half-price tickets booth (see page 52).

SOMERSET HOUSE

To the south of Covent Garden lies the Strand, a broad thoroughfare that links Trafalgar Square with the City of London in the east. Here, by Waterloo Bridge, is the neoclassical **Somerset House** (www.somersethouse.org.uk), built in 1770–1835. It now houses the **Courtauld Institute of Art** (www.courtauld.ac.uk; daily 10am–6pm), which is particularly noted for its collection of paintings by Van Gogh, Gauguin and Cézanne. The gallery is currently closed for redevelopment and is expected to reopen in late 2020; however, more than 20 artworks from its collection are on display at the

◉ CLUB LAND

Each of London's clubs has its own character and attracts a certain type of person. It is said that bishops and Fellows of the Royal Society join the Athenaeum, the foremost academic club, while actors and publishers opt for the Garrick or Savile Club. Diplomats, politicians and spies prefer Brooks's, the Travellers, Boodle's or White's, while the media set gather at the Groucho Club in Soho. The novelist Jules Verne used the Reform Club (Pall Mall), the leading liberal club, as the setting for Phileas Fogg's wager that he could travel around the world in 80 days.

The majority of London's clubs are the near-exclusive preserve of men. Their continuing influence in the social, commercial and political life of the capital should not be underestimated.

National Gallery over this period. In the winter, the courtyard of Somerset House is the setting for a temporary ice rink; in summer, rows of fountains play out here, and in the evenings there are sometimes outdoor film screenings. At the rear of the building (to the south) is the splendid River Terrace, which in summer has outdoor seating for the café with great river views and, sometimes, showcases artworks.

ST JAMES'S PALACE

A far different atmosphere is found in **Pall Mall ❼**, which runs through the heart of the St James's district on the west side of Trafalgar Square. This is London's "Club Land" – the grand buildings lining the road are the exclusive gathering places of the Great and Good. The street takes its name from *paille maille*, a French lawn game imported to England in the 17th century and played by Charles I on a long green which once occupied this site.

Wedged between the wood-panelled halls of Pall Mall and the leafy landscape of Green Park are a number of stately homes. The most impressive of these, built by Henry VIII in the 1530s, is **St James's Palace ❽**, now occupied by royal offices. Nearby is **Clarence House** (tel: 0303-123 7321; www.royalcollection. org.uk; closed until August 2020 for maintenance work), the London residence of Prince Charles.

THE MALL

The Mall is London's impressive ceremonial way, a broad avenue that runs from Buckingham Palace to Admiralty Arch, by Trafalgar Square. The spectacular Trooping the Colour takes place on the Mall each June, as Queen Elizabeth II rides sedately down the avenue in a horse-drawn carriage with an escort of Household Cavalry as part of a 300-year-old ceremony to mark the official birthday of the monarch. The legions mass on **Horse Guards Parade**, a huge open space behind Whitehall, where a royal unit troops its regimental flags to the tune of marching music and thundering drums.

The Household Cavalry participate in the **Changing the Guard** ceremony,

The statue of Shakespeare in Leicester Square.

⊙ Tip

In mid–late September each year, Open House weekend (www.londonopenhouse.org) allows the public to see inside some of the capital's more architecturally interesting buildings. Some of them are grand government offices; others may be private homes. As many as 700 buildings of all kinds are open, and all for free.

which takes place outside Buckingham Palace (see www.changing-guard.com for details); you can also catch the soldiers making their way from Buckingham Palace via The Mall and Whitehall during Changing the Guard.

On the Mall is the **Institute of Contemporary Arts** ❾ (www.ica.art; Tue–Thu, Sun noon–11pm, Fri–Sat until midnight), offering a programme of cutting-edge modern painting, sculpture and performing arts as well as art-house movies and documentaries.

BUCKINGHAM PALACE

Londoners have a love-hate relationship with **Buckingham Palace** ❿. To some, the Queen's home is one of the ugliest buildings in the capital, but it's also held in esteem as the symbol of Britain's royalty. The palace arose within a mulberry grove in the early 18th century as a mansion for the powerful Duke of Buckingham. It was purchased in 1762 by George III (who preferred to live in St James's Palace). However, it wasn't grand enough for George IV (the Prince Regent), and soon after the building

Crowds gather outside Buckingham Palace.

came under his control in 1820, he commissioned his favourite architect, John Nash, to rebuild it on a more magnificent scale. Despite costly alterations, the palace wasn't occupied until Victoria became queen in 1837 and made it the official royal residence in London. (She famously complained that it had too few bedrooms, and had another wing built.) If the flag is flying above the palace, it means that the Queen is in residence. Visitors today can see the **State Rooms** (www.royalcollection.org.uk/visit/buckinghampalace; late July–Aug daily 9.30am–7.30pm, last admission 5.15pm; Sept until 6.30pm, last admission 4.15pm), which are open when the Queen is in residence at Balmoral in Scotland. Other areas that can be visited include the **Royal Mews** (Apr–Oct daily 10am–5pm, Feb–Mar, Nov Mon–Sat 10am–4pm, last admission 45 mins before closing), which contain royal vehicles from horse-drawn coaches to Rolls-Royces, and the **Queen's Gallery** (daily 10am–5.30pm, late July–Sept 9.30am–5.30pm), which displays artworks from the Royal Collection.

In front of the palace, the **Queen Victoria Memorial**, built in 1901 (the year of Victoria's death), encompasses symbolic figures glorifying the achievements of the British Empire and its builders.

Bounding Buckingham Palace on the north and east are two of London's renowned green spaces – the arboreal tracts of St James's Park and Green Park. **St James's** ⑪ in particular has lush vegetation and a tranquil lake. Indeed, the park provides a haven for a multitude of water birds, office workers on their lunch breaks and pram-pushing mums. The wooden footbridge across the lake gives a superb view of Buckingham Palace.

The more rugged **Green Park** ⑫ is where Charles II used to take his daily stroll in the 17th century, and has deck-chairs for hire in the summer months.

WESTMINSTER ABBEY

A short walk from the southeast corner of St James's Park is **Westminster**, the seat of English government for some 750 years. Westminster is also a holy place – the burial ground

of English monarchs, the site of one of the greatest monasteries of the Middle Ages and a showcase for some of the most inspiring Gothic architecture in London. The area was a marshy wasteland inhabited by lepers until the 11th-century reign of Edward the Confessor, who built both a great church and a palace upon the reclaimed land.

Westminster Abbey ⑬ (www.westminster-abbey.org; Mon–Fri 9.30am–3.30pm, Wed until 6pm but closed 3.30–4.30pm, Sat 9.30am–1pm) was founded by Edward the Confessor, who is buried in front of the high altar. In December 1066, the ill-fated Harold (soon to lose his throne to William the Conqueror) was crowned as the new king in the Abbey. Since that day, all but two English monarchs have been crowned here.

Little remains of Edward's Saxon abbey; it was completely rebuilt under the Normans and then redesigned in flamboyant French Gothic style 200 years later. The **Henry VII Chapel** is a 16th-century masterpiece of fan-vaulted stone ceilings, decked out in colourful medieval banners. **Poets'**

St James's Palace.

Westminster Abbey.

The Jewel Tower.

The Houses of Parliament.

Corner contains the graves of Chaucer, Tennyson and Dryden, plus monuments to Shakespeare, Milton, Keats, Wilde and many others. The abbey also houses the **English Coronation Chair**, built in 1300 for Edward I and still used for the installation of new monarchs. High above the nave, the abbey's medieval triforium was opened to the public in 2018 for the first time in 700 years. The **Queen's Diamond Jubilee Galleries** display the abbey's fine collection of treasures, as well as offering excellent views into the church.

THE HOUSES OF PARLIAMENT

On the river side of Westminster Abbey rise the **Houses of Parliament ⑭**, an elaborate Gothic structure designed in the 1830s by Charles Barry and August Pugin to replace the old Westminster Palace built by Edward the Confessor. The building is one of the triumphs of Victorian England: 940ft (280 metres) long with 2 miles (3km) of passages and more than 1,000 rooms.

At the south end is **Victoria Tower**, from which a Union flag flies whenever Parliament is in session, while on the north flank rises the Elizabeth Tower, renamed in honour of the Queen in 2012, but commonly known as **Big Ben** after the massive bell, cast in 1858, that strikes the hours. (Big Ben fell silent in 2017 due to major repair work, which is expected to last until 2021.) Facing Big Ben is **Portcullis House**, a modern office block for Members of Parliament.

Within Parliament convene the two governing bodies of Great Britain, the House of Commons and the House of Lords, which moved into the old Palace of Westminster after Henry VIII vacated the premises in the 16th century. The Commons, comprised of the elected representatives of various political parties, is the scene of lively debate. You can watch proceedings from the safety of the **Visitors' Gallery**; see website for details (www.parliament.uk).

One of the few relics of the old Westminster Palace to withstand a devastating fire in 1834 is **Westminster Hall**, a 240ft (72-metre) long room built in 1099 with a hammer-beam roof of ancient oak. The hall has seen some of English history's most dramatic moments, from the trial of Sir Thomas More in 1535 to the investiture of Oliver Cromwell as Lord Protector in 1653.

Whitehall is the avenue that runs north from the Houses of Parliament to Trafalgar Square. It is the location of numerous government ministries, as well as the prime minister's residence at **No. 10 Downing Street**, just off Whitehall and blocked by security gates.

At the end of King Charles Street, down Clive Steps, a small wall of sandbags identifies the **Churchill War Rooms** ⑮ (www.iwm.org.uk/visits/churchill-war-rooms; daily 9.30am–6pm), the underground nerve-centre from which Winston Churchill directed Britain's war effort. Using old photographs for reference, the rooms have been meticulously restored to their 1940s appearance.

On the other side of Whitehall is **Banqueting House** (tel: 020-3166 6155; daily 10am–5pm), a remnant of the old Whitehall Palace and a masterpiece of the English Baroque. Inigo Jones built the hall in 1622 at the request of James

I. A decade later Peter Paul Rubens added the allegorical ceiling.

ALONG MILLBANK

The rather uninspiring **Victoria Street**, peppered with chain stores and lunch stops that serve the office workers in the modern blocks that dominate this traffic-clogged road, runs southwest from Parliament Square. Set back from the street is the terracotta **Westminster Cathedral** ⑯, England's most important Roman Catholic church, built in the 1890s in a bizarre Italo-Byzantine style, with a lavish interior of multicoloured marble and an exterior in alternating red and white bricks. The **Campanile Tower** (Mon–Fri 9.30am–5pm, with exceptions) offers superb views.

Millbank follows the gentle curve of the Thames to the south of Parliament Square, first passing the **Victoria Tower Gardens** (home of Rodin's *The Burghers of Calais*) before sweeping round to the neoclassical home of **Tate Britain** ⑰ (www.tate.org.uk; daily 10am–6pm, later for selected exhibitions; free except for special exhibitions), in

Westminster Abbey.

An iconic view of Big Ben and the Houses of Parliament at Westminster.

HOW PARLIAMENT WORKS

Widely known as the mother of parliaments, the British Parliament has been a model for democracies all over the world.

The Houses of Parliament comprise the House of Commons and the House of Lords. The Commons, the House of locally elected Members of Parliament (MPs), known as the Lower House, wields virtually all the power but inhabits only half the building. Jutting out towards Parliament Square is Westminster Hall, with the offices, dining rooms and libraries of the Commons; in the centre is the Commons' debating chamber. To the right of Westminster Hall is the domain of the Lords, whose role is to examine and sometimes block bills proposed by the Lower House (although a bill can be reintroduced). Until recently, most lords governed by birthright, but the voting rights of most hereditary peers have now been abolished and the upper

The state opening of Parliament in the opulent House of Lords.

house is now the preserve of life (ie non-hereditary) peers, ennobled for services to the nation.

There are 650 elected MPs, yet the Commons seats only about 450. This is not usually a problem since MPs attend sessions when they wish (and indeed there are proposals to reduce the number of MPs to 600). The governing party sits on one side, facing the opposition. Cabinet ministers sit on the front bench, opposite the "Shadow Cabinet" (the leading members of the opposition). The Cabinet, consisting of up to two dozen ministers, and chaired by the prime minister, meets at 10 Downing Street weekly to review major issues.

PARLIAMENTARY PROCEDURE

Major parties represented are the Conservatives, Labour and the Scottish Nationalists; the Liberal Democrats secured just eight seats at the 2015 General Election, although this rose to 12 seats in the 2017 General Election. General elections are run on the basis of local (constituency) rather than proportional representation, and it is therefore possible for a party to gain a majority of seats (usually required to push through its bills) without having won the majority of votes from the electorate nationally. This is often referred to as the "first past the post" system. The procedure of lawmaking is so complex that a bill usually takes more than six months to be enacted. If it is still incomplete at the end of the parliamentary year, it is dropped.

Parliament meets from October to July. In November, the government's plans for the year are announced in the Queen's Speech at the State Opening of Parliament, held in the chamber of the Lords. From the Visitors' Gallery (formerly known as the Strangers' Gallery), the public can watch the House of Commons at work, though seats are limited and security precautions have become stricter since a flour-filled condom thrown from the gallery hit Tony Blair in 2004. The weekly Prime Minister's Question Time usually attracts a full house. Sessions are chaired by the Speaker, who keeps order and calls on MPs to speak. The cry of "Order, Order" is frequently heard above the parliamentary babble. The Speaker is also responsible for the rules governing MPs' behaviour.

an area of London called Pimlico. The Tate, founded in 1897 by Henry Tate, of the Tate & Lyle sugar empire, holds the national collection of British art (and has a sister venue on the south bank, Tate Modern, see page 111). Among the outstanding British paintings are portraits by Thomas Gainsborough (1727–88), evocative views of the English countryside by John Constable (1776–1837), and dramatic and impressionistic seascapes and landscapes by the prolific J.M.W. Turner (1775–1851), which are housed in the Clore Gallery. These are the paintings Turner bequeathed to the nation on his death, with the stipulation that they should all be hung in one place, and should be available for the public to see, without charge.

OXFORD STREET

Just three stops on the tube from Pimlico Station is Oxford Circus and London's busiest shopping street, **Oxford Street** ⑱, which marks the boundary between Marylebone and the exclusive district of Mayfair. The western half of Oxford Street contains most of London's top department stores, including the capacious and stylish **Selfridges** and beloved stalwart John Lewis; the eastern end is less upmarket and accommodates a mixture of souvenir shops and chain stores, especially as you get towards **Tottenham Court Road**, a centre for electronics stores, a 10-minute walk east from the major crossroads at Oxford Circus.

MARYLEBONE

To the north of Oxford Street is the district of **Marylebone** (pronounced *marly-bone*), which continues up to the southern edge of Regent's Park. The area's cultural highlight is the **Wallace Collection** ⑲ (www.wallacecollection.org; daily 10am–5pm; free, except certain special exhibitions), in Manchester Square. This treasure trove of 17th- and 18th-century fine and decorative arts includes Sèvres porcelain, French furniture and works by Titian, Rubens and Holbein.

Infamous in the 18th century for its taverns, boxing matches and

Westminster Cathedral, the foremost English Catholic church.

At the Cabinet War Rooms.

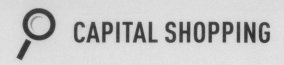

CAPITAL SHOPPING

London is a great place to shop, and there are retail opportunities to suit all budgets and tastes.

WEST END

The principal shopping streets are Oxford Street and Regent Street, which bisect at Oxford Circus. The smarter end of **Oxford Street** is around Bond Street station and at its intersection with Regent Street. As well as dozens of menswear and women's fashion shops, there are large department stores, including Marks & Spencer, Selfridges and John Lewis. **Regent Street** itself is more upmarket, and perhaps its finest landmark is the half-timbered headquarters of Liberty, purveyors of classic fabrics and homeware. Nearby are Hamleys multi-storey toy store and Burberry, and. at No. 235, the stunning Apple flagship store. North of the West End, the Thomas Heatherwick-designed **Coal Drops Yard** is a high-end shopping enclave set in con-verted Victorian viaducts, which opened in 2018 as part of the King's Cross regeneration.

BOND STREET AND ST JAMES'S

New Bond Street and Old Bond Street are the smart end of town. Designer fashion houses mingle with art galler-ies (including Sotheby's auction house) and nearby

Liberty on Great Marlborough Street is a local landmark.

Burlington Arcade offers bijou gems for the rich. **Savile Row**, parallel to Old Bond Street, is where shirts and suits are elegantly tailored – at a price. On the other side of Piccadilly is **St James's**, designed originally for the court hangers-on; everything here is bespoke. Old-fashioned barbers and cigarette and cigar shops give a nod to bygone days. Fortnum & Mason, established in 1707, is at 181 Piccadilly and sells the best of British foods. It is renowned for its luxury picnic hampers.

COVENT GARDEN

One of the first, and one of the most successful, developments from old market to new, London's former fruit and vegetable traders' stalls are now bijou shops. Paul Smith is in Floral Street. **Long Acre** is lined with fashion labels. Stanford's, the renowned travel bookshop, is on Mercer Walk.The best shops for books, antiquarian, second-hand and new, are round the corner in **Charing Cross Road**. On the north side of Covent Garden are boutiques in Earlham Street, Shelton Street and Shorts Gardens.

KENSINGTON AND CHELSEA

West London led the fashion stakes in the Swinging Sixties. Now rich patrons remain. In **Knightsbridge** Harvey Nichols and Harrods hold sway. Sloane Street, with a clutch of elegant fashion and jewellery design-ers, leads to Peter Jones department store on Sloane Square and the **King's Road**, where fashion shops begin. **High Street Kensington**, where the famous Biba store once flourished, has a number of fashion bou-tiques. Adjoining it is **Kensington Church Street**, for genuine, and genuinely expensive, antiques.

MARKETS

London has over 100 street markets, which carry on a tradition going back to the Middle Ages. **Borough Market** is the premier farmers' market and offers organic and gourmet products from Wednesday to Saturday. **Spitalfields**, just nearby, is popular with tour-ists looking for craft gifts. **Portobello Road** near Notting Hill Gate is a lively street dealing in antiques, though dedicated hunters will also head to **Bermondsey Square Antiques Market** on Friday. Younger browsers visit **Camden Lock Market,** which has stalls selling streetwear, old records and speciality foods.

cockfights, Marylebone is now best known for its high street, which is lined with chic (and pricey) boutiques and excellent cafés and restaurants. The renaissance in this part of town started with the opening of a branch of the Conran Shop – the store, housed in a former stables, is at the top (northern) end of the street.

On the northern edge of Marylebone is the very popular tourist attraction **Madame Tussauds** ❷⓪ (www.madametussauds.co.uk; daily 9am–5.30pm, with exceptions). It was first established in 1802 by Marie Tussaud, who learned her craft in post-Revolution Paris, making wax effigies of the heads of guillotine victims. Today's waxworks are of celebrities, from pop stars to sports heroes – though anyone who fades from the headlines is soon melted down.

On Baker Street itself, at No. 221b, is the **Sherlock Holmes Museum** (www.sherlock-holmes.co.uk; daily 9.30am–6pm), which celebrates Arthur Conan Doyle's fictitious detective, who supposedly lived here. The museum recreates Victorian rooms and has waxwork tableaux.

REGENT'S PARK

Regent's Park ❷① is a vast green space with a long and chequered history. Henry VIII established a royal hunting ground here on land seized from the Abbess of Barking. Later, in the early 19th century, the park became part of the Prince Regent's (later George IV) great scheme for a huge processional thoroughfare and palace complex to stretch from Pall Mall to Primrose Hill. The prince commissioned John Nash to design and develop the scheme, but the dream got only as far as the famed Regency terraces on the southern fringe of the park, which represent Nash at his best.

London Zoo (www.zsl.org; daily late Mar–early Sept 10am–6pm, early Sept–late Oct until 5pm, late Oct–mid-Feb until 4pm, late Feb–late Mar until 5.30pm)

was founded in Regent's Park in 1826 by Sir Stamford Raffles, who also founded Singapore. Among the zoo's features are an aviary designed by Lord Snowdon, a glass pavilion housing the ecologically oriented Web of Life exhibition, the spectacular Land of the Lions and Penguin Beach, the spacious home for the zoo's ever-popular aquatic birds.

MAYFAIR AND PICCADILLY

Exclusive **Mayfair** is home to many of Britain's wealthiest residents. By the mid-18th century, the powerful Grosvenor family had purchased the land here and developed Mayfair into an elegant Georgian housing estate. This enticed the wealthy of dreary inner London to move out and settle in one of the city's first suburbs.

Today, the area is known for its expensive designer shops; the main thoroughfare, **Bond Street** ❷❷, is lined with names such as Chanel, Gucci, Bulgari, Mulberry, Prada and many others. Mayfair is also renowned as a centre of the European art market. It is home to all of the country's top

The Sherlock Holmes Museum on Baker Street.

The Burlington Arcade.

The winged statue of Eros in Piccadilly Circus.

Ronnie Scott's jazz club.

antiques dealers as well as numerous private art galleries, around Cork Street, and the top auction houses, including Sotheby's (New Bond Street) and Christie's (King Street). It's worth looking out, too, for **Savile Row**, the traditional home of bespoke tailoring, and lined with smart shops bearing venerable names.

Among all these upmarket retail opportunities is **Handel and Hendrix in London** (25 Brook Street; www.handelhendrix.org; Mon–Sat 11am–6pm), located in the former home (from 1723 to 1759) of the composer of the *Messiah*, where legendary guitarist Jimi Hendrix also once lived next door. The Hendrix Flat is now open to the public and the exhibition reflects his music and life in 1960s London.

Piccadilly is the bustling road that runs due west from Piccadilly Circus towards Hyde Park Corner. Along it are many smart shops, such as high-class grocer Fortnum & Mason and several attractive Victorian arcades – covered shopping streets of which Burlington Arcade with its uniformed doormen

is the most famous. Just south of Piccadilly is Jermyn Street, which is dotted with traditional men's outfitters – especially shirt-makers, shoe-makers and the occasional hatter.

A few doors from Burlington Arcade is the prestigious **Royal Academy of Arts** ㉓ (www.royalacademy.org.uk; daily 10am–6pm, Fri until 10pm), which stages blockbuster exhibitions of major artists. A suite of galleries for temporary art exhibitions was added to the recently renovated Burlington Gardens building in 2018, along with a studio-view walkway connecting to Burlington House. In addition, you can now enter this arts complex from a new Mayfair entrance.

At the eastern end of Piccadilly is **Piccadilly Circus** ㉔, a busy junction crowded with black cabs, red buses and awestruck tourists. At its centre stands what is known as the Statue of Eros: this is, though, a misnomer as it is strictly a fountain and was originally entitled *The Angel of Christian Charity* in honour of the philanthropist Lord Shaftesbury.

⊘ A NIGHT ON THE TOWN

Soho entertains a real cross-section of Londoners and some of London's best-known clubs are here, ranging from Ronnie Scott's jazz club on Frith Street to Club 49 on Greek Street. Old Compton Street is the centre of the LGBTQ scene, with pubs such as the Admiral Duncan and Comptons drawing big crowds.

Nearby Leicester Square and Covent Garden are also popular nightspots, though they cater more for tourists and younger clubbers from out of town. Most of the so-called "super-clubs" around Leicester Square have now closed down and the area is undergoing a much-needed revamp – though the big cinemas there remain open for business.

With the new late-licensing laws many bars stay open until at least 3am, which has removed much of the 11pm rush towards neighbourhood clubs. Some bars can be difficult to get into, but this tends to be because of capacity rather than the dress codes of old. Many of the cafés also stay open into the small hours.

To the northeast of the City of London are Hoxton and Shoreditch, which in recent decades have developed into London's epicentre of gritty urban cool. However, slicker venues and workers from the City are now moving in and the atmosphere is changing again. Even so, clubs such as Cargo and DJ bars such as Plastic People remain perennially popular.

Nearby is the porticoed London Pavilion, which houses **Body Worlds London** (bodyworlds.com; Sun–Thu 9.30am–7pm, Fri–Sat until 9pm), the first permanent museum for Gunther von Hagens' interesting and mildly macabre touring exhibition of plastinated dead bodies, designed to uncover the workings of the human body.

Running northwest from Piccadilly Circus, and dividing Mayfair from Soho, is John Nash's curving **Regent Street**, home to classy shops from Liberty to Hamleys and an Apple Store, as well as a scattering of more standard chain stores.

1960s as a centre for avant-garde fashions; nowadays, its fashion stores are distinctly less ground-breaking. The southern part of the district – to the south of Shaftesbury Avenue, around Gerrard Street and Lisle Street – is known as **Chinatown**, and is packed with Chinese (and some Japanese and Vietnamese) restaurants.

In the heart of Soho is **Berwick Street**, the site of a fruit-and-vegetable market. Karl Marx lived around the corner on **Dean Street** in the building now inhabited by the Quo Vadis restaurant.

Greek busts at the British Museum.

SOHO

The district of **Soho** was long known for its low-life bars and sex clubs, but the sleazy side has largely gone, with only a few strip shows remaining. Instead, the area is a now a fashionable quarter for restaurants, bars and media companies, and the immediate vicinity of Old Compton Street is popular with the trendy London LGBTQ crowd. Just off Regent Street is the pedestrianised Carnaby Street, famous in the

BLOOMSBURY

A short stroll away but a complete change of scene is **Bloomsbury**, the intellectual and scholastic heart of the city. Many University of London colleges have buildings in this area, including the **School of Oriental and African Studies**, and **University College** in Gower Street. Bloomsbury was the address of such intellectual figures as John Maynard Keynes (1883–1946) and Virginia Woolf (1882–1941).

The upmarket Fortnum & Mason department store.

Adults are only allowed into Coram's Fields if accompanied by a child.

Taking a break on Lincoln's Inn Fields.

The novelist Charles Dickens was another Bloomsbury resident. He lived with his family at 48 Doughty Street in the late 1830s, during which time he wrote parts of *Oliver Twist* and *The Pickwick Papers*. His home, now the **Charles Dickens Museum** 25 (www.dickensmuseum.com; Tue–Sun 10am–5pm), is filled with his portraits, letters, furniture and other personal effects.

Bloomsbury's main visitor attraction, however, is the **British Museum** 26 (www.britishmuseum.org; daily 10am–5.30pm, Fri until 8.30pm; charge for special exhibitions), one of the world's greatest collections of art and archaeology. The museum was founded in 1753 to house the vast collection of 71,000 items that the physician and naturalist Sir Hans Sloane had amassed during his lifetime. Sloane (remembered today in place names such as Sloane Square) left his eclectic mix of antiquities, manuscripts, medals and prints to the nation. Originally housed in a 17th-century mansion, the museum opened to the public in 1759.

The British Museum is both a priceless art collection and a monument to human civilisation, encompassing antiquities from almost every period and every part of the world – Egyptian, Assyrian, Greek, Roman, Indian, Chinese, Islamic and Anglo-Saxon. Among its multiple treasures are the Rosetta Stone from Egypt (the key that unlocked the secrets of hieroglyphic script), the great 7th-century Anglo-Saxon Sutton Hoo treasures, the Nimrud friezes from Mesopotamia, the Portland Vase (a striking cameo-glass vase) and the Elgin Marbles, the remarkable figures that once graced the Parthenon in Athens. There are coins from ancient Rome, Babylonian statues, carved Native American pipes and jade from Imperial China. One of the most extraordinary sights is that of Lindow Man, the preserved body of an Iron Age man that was found in a peat bog in Cheshire. Discovered in 1984, he died a violent death – possibly a ritual killing. Scientists have established that his last meal was of unleavened bread, made from wheat and barley. More than 50,000 of the 6.5 million objects owned by the museum are on display at any one time, so don't expect to see everything in one day.

At the centre of the museum complex is the Great Court, a large glazed plaza containing the majestic Lion of Knidos and an Easter Island statue – and also a shop, café and restaurant. The museum also holds major exhibitions here in the old rotunda Reading Room in the middle of plaza. The core of the British Library used to occupy this space (and, famously, Karl Marx wrote *Das Kapital* at one of its desks). In 1997, the library's entire collection of more than 9 million books – including a Gutenberg Bible, Magna Carta and manuscripts relating to Dickens and many other writers – relocated to new premises on Euston Road.

Not far away, to the northeast of Russell Square, at 40 Brunswick Square, is the **Foundling Museum** 27 (www.foundlingmuseum.org.uk; Tue–Sat 10am–5pm,

Sun 11am–5pm), home to a fine art collection built up by a philanthropic sea captain Thomas Coram, who started a hospital and school for foundlings and encouraged artists, including William Hogarth, to donate works to raise funds. Other artists featured include Gainsborough and Reynolds, and there is a collection of artefacts relating to the composer George Frideric Handel. Adjacent is **Coram's Fields**, a children's playground where adults may enter only if accompanied by a youngster.

HOLBORN

To the south of Bloomsbury is **Holborn**, which centres on the busy street and Tube station of the same name. This is London's legal district, where you can find the historic Inns of Court. **Staple Inn** ㉘, a timber-framed Elizabethan structure that once served as a hostel for wool merchants, survived the Great Fire of London. It shows how much of the city must have looked before the 1666 fire devastated it. There were originally 12 inns, founded in the 14th century for the lodging and education of lawyers on "neutral" ground between the merchants of the City and the monarchs of Westminster. Today only four remain, and barristers in England and Wales must belong to one of them in order to practise.

Gray's Inn has a garden designed by Francis Bacon in 1606 – a haven of plane trees and smooth lawns that provides a tranquil lunchtime retreat. **Lincoln's Inn**, north of Fleet Street, is perhaps the most impressive inn, with a medieval hall and a 17th-century chapel by Inigo Jones. Outside is the leafy expanse called **Lincoln's Inn Fields**, once a notorious venue for duels and executions, but nowadays a magnet for summer picnickers and sunbathers.

On the north side of the park square is the **Sir John Soane's Museum** (13 Lincoln's Inn Fields; www.soane.org; Wed–Sun 10am–5pm; free), an eccentric townhouse that is a sort of British Museum in miniature. Soane (1753–1857), a celebrated architect, lived here and built up a remarkable collection of antiquities and paintings, which all remain *in situ* for visitors to enjoy. A highlight of its art

Sir John Soane's Museum is full of paintings, drawings and models of his projects.

The British Museum's Great Court.

Along Fleet Street.

Dog-walker on Hampstead Heath.

gallery is Hogarth's satirical *Rake's Progress*. On the first Tuesday of the month the museum stays open late and is lit by candelight, which makes for a wonderfully atmospheric visit.

The most fascinating of the inns is the twin complex of the **Inner** and **Middle Temples** ㉙. The name derives from the Knights Templar, a medieval religious fraternity that occupied this site until the early 14th century. The temple has changed little: it is still a precinct of vaulted chambers, hammerbeam roofs and lush wood panelling. In the 16th-century Middle Temple Hall, Shakespeare's own company once performed *Twelfth Night* for the Elizabethan court.

The 12th-century **Temple Church** is one of only four "round churches" left in England. It contains a number of knights' tombs and a tiny punishment cell.

FLEET STREET

In **Fleet Street**, centre of the national newspaper industry until the 1980s, **St Bride's** ㉚ is still the parish church of journalists. It is an impressive 17th-century church by Sir Christopher Wren, and its crypt contains remnants of Roman and Saxon London. At 17 Fleet Street, **Prince Henry's Room** (www.cityoflondon.gov.uk; not open to the public) is one of the few houses to survive the Great Fire of 1666.

Just north of Fleet Street at 17 Gough Square is **Dr Johnson's House** ㉛ (www.drjohnsonshouse.org; Mon–Sat May–Sept 11am–5.30pm, Oct–Apr until 5pm), where the great man of letters and compiler of the first English dictionary, Samuel Johnson, lived from 1748 to 1759.

NORTH LONDON

Full of pretty houses on leafy groves, **Hampstead** ㉜ seems the quintessence of an English village. In reality, it is not so much rural idyll as exclusive suburb, but a haven in a hectic city nevertheless. Until not so long ago, Hampstead was the home of artists, writers and anyone of a liberal disposition. At the last count, the suburb had over 90 blue plaques commemorating such famous residents as John Constable, George Orwell, Florence Nightingale and Sigmund Freud. Now, you only need to have deep pockets

to live here: its pretty alleys, leafy streets and expansive heath make this suburb a desirable address.

On Keats Grove is **Keats House** (www.cityoflondon.gov.uk; Mar–Oct Wed–Sun 11am–5pm, Nov–Feb Fri–Sun only 11am–5pm), the Regency villa where the consumptive poet lodged before departing for Rome, where he died a year later, in 1821, aged just 25. Under a plum tree in the garden he penned one of his best-loved poems, *Ode to a Nightingale*.

Nearby is 2 Willow Road (www.national trust.org.uk/2-willow-road; Mar–Oct Wed–Sun 11am–5pm), a modernist house designed by Erno Goldfinger (after whom the James Bond baddie was named) for himself. Inside is his art collection, with works by Henry Moore, Bridget Riley, Max Ernst and Marcel Duchamp.

Sigmund Freud briefly lived here too, after fleeing the Nazis in 1938; the **Freud Museum** preserves his house at 20 Maresfield Gardens much as he and his daughter Anna left it (www.freud.org.uk; Wed–Sun noon–5pm).

Despite the encroachment of suburbia, the area retains a village atmosphere, aided by the proximity of 790-acre (310-hectare) **Hampstead Heath**. An 18th-century decree forbade building on the Heath, thus preserving a rambling tract of dark woods and lush meadows where the only large structure is **Kenwood House** (www.english-heritage.org.uk; daily 10am–5pm; free). This mansion houses the art collection of brewing magnate Edward Guinness, and includes some well-known works by Rembrandt, Vermeer and Turner. There are also fine Robert Adam interiors.

Haverstock Hill runs from Hampstead into Camden Town, where weekend crowds flock to markets. Since 1972, **Camden Lock Market** ⱬ has featured antiques, crafts, vintage clothes – and talented buskers. The Dingwalls music venue is sited here, and a traditional canal boat runs trips from the West Yard area along the Regent's Canal to Little Venice (www.londonwaterbus.com). Meanwhile, Camden High Street is full of bars, pubs and small-scale music venues such as the Dublin Castle and the Jazz Café.

Camden Lock Market.

The Shard.

THE CITY AND SOUTHWARK

The City is the oldest part of London, where Britain's financial institutions are tightly packed. Across the river, Southwark has revived its ancient role as an entertainments centre.

Fleet Street sweeps from London's theatreland into Ludgate Hill and the **City of London**, a history-packed square mile that sits atop the remains of both Roman and medieval towns. "The City", as it is generally known, was for centuries the domain of merchants and craftsmen, a powerful coalition of men who helped force democracy upon the English monarchy and then built the world's largest mercantile empire.

Despite the encroachment of modern office blocks, the area retains something of its medieval ways: the square mile is still governed separately from the rest of London, by the ancient City Corporation and its Court of Common Council – relics of the medieval trade and craft guilds. Outside the jurisdiction of London's popularly elected mayor, it has its own separately elected Lord Mayor, who rides through the City each November in a golden coach.

WREN'S MASTERPIECE

Sitting at the top of Ludgate Hill and dominating the skyline is **St Paul's Cathedral** ❸❹ (www.stpauls.co.uk; Mon–Sat 8.30am–4.30pm, until 5.30pm in summer), its massive dome punching upwards through the forest of high-rises that has come to surround it since World War II.

After the Norman St Paul's was destroyed in the Great Fire of 1666,

Charles II asked the architect Christopher Wren to design a new cathedral to befit the status of London. Wren's first plan was rejected as too radical, but he responded with a blend of Italian Baroque and classical influences – a huge cruciform building, whose stone cupola takes it to a height of 365ft (111 metres), second only to that of St Peter's in Rome.

St Paul's arose in 1675–1710 as the first cathedral built and dedicated to the Protestant faith. It played host to Queen Victoria's Diamond Jubilee

⊘ Main attractions
St Paul's Cathedral
The Monument
The Shard
The Tower of London and the Crown Jewels
Southwark Cathedral
Shakespeare's Globe
Tate Modern
London Eye

Map on page 82

The Tower of London.

⏱ **Fact**

The Lord Mayor's Show begins at the Mansion House, the official residence of the Lord Mayor, each November, as the newly elected mayor rides through the City in a golden coach. Thousands of spectators line the route to watch the colourful procession, a combination of traditional pageantry and elements of carnival.

ceremonies in 1897, Winston Churchill's funeral in 1965 and the wedding of Prince Charles and Lady Diana Spencer in 1981. The cathedral miraculously survived the Blitz, though the neighbourhood around it was destroyed by German bombs and missiles.

St Paul's is a notable burial place; among those entombed within are Wellington, Nelson, Reynolds, Turner and Wren himself. Its interior displays the work of the finest artists and craftsmen of the late 17th century: iron grillework of Tijou, wooden choir stalls by Grinling Gibbons and the murals inside the dome by Sir James Thornhill.

The cathedral's appearance is deceptive. The famous dome viewed from afar would look overly large if seen from inside the building. The dome you look up at from within is in fact a much smaller dome, on top of which is built a brick cone. The cone's purpose is to support the massive weight of the external Portland stone dome, which weighs more than 50,000 tons.

Around the inside of the dome stretches the **Whispering Gallery**, so called because you can easily comprehend the voices of anyone standing on the opposite side of the void. A winding stairway leads to the outside of the dome, where there are panoramic views of London.

A chapel behind the High Altar, damaged during the Blitz, was restored as the American Chapel, with a book of remembrance paying tribute to the 28,000 American citizens based in the UK who died in World War II.

THE BARBICAN

To the north of St Paul's is the **Barbican Centre** ㉟ (www.barbican.org.uk), its 1960s Brutalist architecture contrasting starkly with the stately form of the cathedral. This urban renewal project arose from the rubble of an old neighbourhood that had been destroyed in the 1940–41 Blitz. Within the complex is the Barbican Arts Centre, accommodating an art gallery, a theatre, a cinema and a concert hall; the complex also houses a large number of apartments and a library, and is home to the London Symphony Orchestra. In September 2017, Banksy painted two murals on the walls of the Barbican, in a nod to the then-forthcoming Basquiat: Boom for Real exhibition. One appears to be the anonymous street artist's take on Jean-Michel Basquiat's 1982 *Boy and Dog in a Johnnypump*; the other shows a Ferris wheel with crowns in place of passenger carts.

Nearby, on London Wall, is the fascinating **Museum of London** ㊱ (www.museumoflondon.org.uk; daily 10am–6pm; free), which charts the history of the city. There are models of old buildings, reconstructed shopfronts, interactive exhibits, special exhibitions (such as on town criers and street photography), a reference library, antique vehicles and a number of historic artefacts such as the Lord Mayor's state coach.

Also in this neighbourhood is **St Bartholomew-the-Great**, a Norman church that has also served as a stable,

The entrance to St Paul's Cathedral.

factory, wine cellar, coal store and even as Benjamin Franklin's London printworks during its 1,000-year history.

THE GUILDHALL

In the shadows of the Barbican's skyscrapers is the **Guildhall** ㉗ (Gresham Street; tel: 020-7332 1313; www.guildhall.cityoflondon.gov.uk; opening times vary; free), one of the few buildings to survive the Great Fire and now the home of the City government and the setting for glittering banquets and corporate events. This ornate Gothic structure was built in 1411 with funds donated by various livery companies, the medieval trade and craft guilds that held sway over the City. Inside the Guildhall is the **Great Hall**, decorated with the colourful banners of the 12 livery companies and the shields of all 92 guilds.

BRITAIN'S FINANCIAL HEARTLAND

A short walk east along Gresham Street brings you to a bustling intersection dominated by the bulk of the neoclassical **Bank of England** ㉘. The Bank still prints and mints all British money, administers to the national debt and also sets interest rates.

Around the corner on Bartholomew Lane is the entrance to the **Bank of England Museum** (www.bankofengland.co.uk; Mon–Fri 10am–5pm; free), where visitors are even allowed to pick up a gold bar.

Nearby stands the old London **Stock Exchange**, founded in 1773. The trading floor is no longer used, as shares are now traded electronically. This computerisation brought demands for office buildings purpose-built for modern communications. One of the first, and most dramatic, is the 1986 **Lloyd's of London** building in Lime Street, designed for the insurance group by Richard Rogers. Another impressive piece of architecture is **30 St Mary Axe**, a 40-storey tapering glass tower designed by Lord Foster and known affectionately as "The Gherkin". The slightly taller **Tower 42** (25 Old

Broad Street), named after the number of floors, also soars up at this point – the bulk of the building is given over to offices, but those with a head for heights can enjoy drinks at **Vertigo 42**, the sky-high champagne bar (tel: 020-7877 7842; www.vertigo42.co.uk). Book ahead and ask for the seats nearest the lift to ensure the best view.

This area is seeing an escalation of skyscrapers that have been given nicknames relating to their unusual shapes: the Leadenhall Building, AKA the "Cheesegrater" because of its wedge shape; the "Walkie Talkie", or 20 Fenchurch Street, topped by the glass-domed Sky Garden, a three-floor, foliage-filled space that's home to a bar, restaurant and open terraces; and The Scalpel, named because of its angular design.

Close to these modern icons of architecture, down Gracechurch Street, is **Leadenhall Market** ㉙. Once the wholesale market for poultry and game, the magnificent Victorian structure has been converted into a handsome commercial centre, with a collection of

A view of St Paul's from the roof terrace of the shopping plaza, One New Change.

The Lloyd's of London building has a highly distinctive exterior.

⊙ Fact

Miraculously, only half a dozen people died in the Great Fire of London, which destroyed most of the medieval city. Samuel Pepys, the diarist, and first person to inform the king about the fire, dug a pit in his garden to save his wine and "Parmazan" cheese.

restaurants, cafés, fashion boutiques, and book and gift shops that attract City workers at breakfast and lunchtime.

The City of London's other steel-and-glass Victorian constructions – the railway stations – were also given facelifts during the 1980s building boom. **Liverpool Street** was overhauled and Fenchurch Street acquired a 1930s Manhattan-style office block, **1 America Square**, over its railway lines. **Broadgate**, a complex of office blocks around three squares, includes a food and drink hub and a voluptuous sculpture, Fernando Botero's *Broadgate Venus*.

Gracechurch Street leads further south to London Bridge and the Thames. Just before you reach the river, a huge fluted column peers over the helter-skelter of rooftops: the 202ft (60-metre) **Monument** ⓵ (www.the monument.info; daily 9.30am–6pm, Oct–Mar until 5.30pm). This is Sir Christopher Wren's memorial to the Great Fire of 1666, which destroyed more than 13,000 houses. You can climb 311 steps to a small platform, from which there is an impressive view.

Southwark Cathedral.

THE TOWER OF LONDON

Lower Thames Street traces the medieval banks of the river past the old Billingsgate Fish Market and the elegant Custom House. A medieval fortress commands this southeast corner of the City: the **Tower of London** ⓸ (www.hrp. org.uk; Tue–Sat 9am–5.30pm, Sun–Mon 10am–5.30pm, closes 4.30pm in winter). The Tower has served, over the centuries, as fortress, palace, prison and museum, as well as arsenal, archive, menagerie and treasury. William the Conqueror built the inner keep (the **White Tower**) as both a military stronghold and a means of impressing his new subjects in England. Constructed between 1078 and 1098, it was the largest building in Britain and soon symbolised royal domination. It remained a royal residence until the 16th century, when the court moved to more comfortable quarters in Westminster. The Tower then became the storehouse for the Crown Jewels and the most infamous prison and execution ground in London. After 1747 it became the Royal Mint, Archive and Menagerie – although wild animals had been kept there since the reign of Henry III in the 13th century. German spies were executed here in both world wars.

The White Tower houses the diminutive **St John's Chapel**, built in 1080 and now the oldest church in London. Beneath Waterloo Barracks is a vault containing the **Crown Jewels**, including the Imperial State Crown, which sparkles with 3,000 stones, and the **Royal Sceptre**, which centres around a 530-carat diamond called the Star of Africa. A moving walkway ensures that visitors cannot linger long over the principal exhibits.

Also worth seeing are the **Coins and Kings** exhibition, exploring the history of the Royal Mint, and the permanent display of weapons from the mid-17th to mid-19th century in the **Royal Fusiliers Museum**.

The Tower is protected by the Yeomen Warders or Beefeaters, so called not because of their carnivorous habits but because they were founded in the 16th century as the *buffetiers* or guardians of the king's buffet.

Outside again, there are magnificent views of **Tower Bridge** 42, London's most iconic river crossing. This striking Gothic structure looks deceptively old – in actual fact, it opened in 1894. Its bascules still rise frequently – four or five times on some days – to let tall vessels through. The **Tower Bridge Exhibition** (www.towerbridge.org.uk; daily 9.30am–5.30pm) offers a tour of the inside of the bridge, as well as superb views.

BANKSIDE

On the south side of Tower Bridge is the restaurant-lined **Butler's Wharf**, the former shipping wharf and warehousing area, which now houses luxury flats in the upper floors. A few minutes' walk west along the river takes you to the new **Bridge Theatre** (www.bridgetheatre.co.uk), opened in 2017 by Nicholas Hytner and Nick Starr, impresario duo of National Theatre fame. Since opening, the venue has had several

acclaimed productions including *My Name is Lucy Barton*, a one-woman show starring Laura Linney, and *A German Life* with a spectacular performance by Maggie Smith from *Downton Abbey*.

The riverside walk between Tower Bridge and London Bridge passes by the World War II battleship **HMS *Belfast*** (www.iwm.org.uk; daily Mar–Oct 10am–6pm, Nov–Feb 10am–5pm). A tour takes you round the cramped accommodation endured by its 950-man crew.

Continuing past more renovated warehouses towards London Bridge, cut through **Hay's Galleria**, a small shopping mall carved out of a former tea wharf, to reach Tooley Street.

Nearby, at 83 Bermondsey Street, is the unmissable pink-and-orange **Fashion and Textile Museum** 43 (www.ftmlondon.org; Tue–Sat 11am–6pm, Thu until 8pm, Sun 11am–5pm), created by Zandra Rhodes to honour 1950s British designers and to teach students.

Further along the street, at No. 144–152, is White Cube (www.whitecube.com; Tue–Sat 10am–6pm, Sun noon–6pm),

The Gherkin and Church of St Andrew Undershaft.

Beefeaters at the Tower of London.

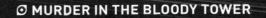

⊘ MURDER IN THE BLOODY TOWER

For hundreds of years Beauchamp Tower in the Tower of London was England's most prestigious jail, reserved for enemies of the state. Henry VI and Richard II were among royal prisoners, and in 1483 Edward IV's heirs, Prince Edward, aged 12, and Prince Richard, 10, were murdered in what came to be called the Bloody Tower (they are done to death off-stage in Shakespeare's *Richard III*). The executioner's axe came down on Tower Hill behind the castle, but the privileged lost their lives on the block inside the tower's grounds, among them two wives of Henry VIII: Anne Boleyn and Catherine Howard.

The Duke of Orleans, captured at the Battle of Agincourt in 1485, composed verse and contemplated his fate here for 25 years. The most eloquent prisoners were Sir Thomas More and Sir Walter Raleigh. More, author of *Utopia*, refused to recognise Henry VIII as Head of the Church, and before his execution he wrote *Dialogue of Comfort against Tribulation*. Raleigh, the Elizabethan buccaneer, wrote *The History of the World* during his 12-year incarceration with his family, and even managed to grow tobacco on Tower Green.

One of Shakespeare's patrons, the Earl of Southampton, kept his cat in his cell for company: legend has it that the cat climbed into the tower and down a chimney to find him.

> **Tip**

There's always something to see and do free at the South Bank (www.southbanklondon.com): lunchtime concerts; live music, including jazz, blues and folk; the National Theatre pre-performance recitations and exhibitions at the Hayward Gallery; plus street entertainers and great views from the restaurants.

the largest of the celebrity gallery owner Jay Jopling's sites.

At the end of the street, and on Friday mornings only, is Bermondsey Square Antiques Market, which has successfully shed its bad reputation. Arrive early if you are after a bargain and for the best choice, as the hundreds of traders start gathering at 4am.

LONDON BRIDGE AND SOUTHWARK CATHEDRAL

Looking up from London Bridge, you can't miss the **The Shard** ㊹, the tallest building in Western Europe, at 1,016ft (310 metres) high, housing offices, a hotel, restaurants and apartments. Book in advance to take the lift up to level 72 for unobstructed views of the city from the open-air viewing gallery (www.theviewfromtheshard.com; Apr–Oct daily 10am–10pm, Nov–Mar Sun–Wed 10am–8pm, with exceptions). Below, level 69 offers interactive touch-screen telescopes.

Just to the south of London Bridge is the imposing **Southwark Cathedral** ㊺ (www.cathedral.southwark.anglican.org),

where Shakespeare was a parishioner. Augustinian canons erected the original church in the 13th century, but the cathedral has been much altered since then, and now has a sensitively designed refectory, library, conference centre and shop. It holds free organ recitals on Mondays at 1.10–1.40pm (except Aug and Dec) and free classical concerts on Tuesdays (3.15–4pm).

Adjacent is **Borough Market**, a wholesale fruit-and-vegetable market whose history dates back 1,000 years. The full market is held on Wednesday and Thursday (10am–5pm), Friday (10am–6pm) and Saturday (8am–5pm), offering a wide range of gourmet and organic products and hot meals from across the globe, in addition to fruit and veg. A smaller number of stalls are set up on Monday and Tuesday (10am–5pm).

Beyond the cathedral, by the Thames in the St Mary Overie Dock, is a full-size copy of Sir Francis Drake's galleon, the *Golden Hinde* (www.goldenhinde.com; daily 10am–6pm, Nov–Mar until 5pm). The original circumnavigated the globe in 1577.

The Tate Modern's impressive building.

Just to the west, the **Clink Prison Museum** (www.clink.co.uk; daily 10am–6pm, with exceptions) features old armour and torture instruments.

SHAKESPEARE'S GLOBE

Continue westwards along the river to reach a replica of the 1599 **Shakespeare's Globe** ⑯ (tel: 020-7401 9919 for performances; www.shakespearesglobe.com). This open-roofed theatre-in-the-round stages the Bard's plays close to where they were first performed (guided tours daily every hour 9.30am–5pm). The season runs mid-Apr to mid-Oct but plays can also be seen year-round at the indoor Sam Wanamaker Playhouse.

TATE MODERN

Next door to the Globe is a towering brick chimney that identifies **Tate Modern** ⑰ (www.tate.org.uk; Sun–Thu 10am–6pm, Fri–Sat 10am–10pm; free, charge for special exhibitions). This iconic former power station houses the national collection of international modern and contemporary art (Tate Britain houses British art; see page 93). The massive turbine hall gives temporary, large-scale installations room to breathe. With the addition of a new building – the Switch House (now known as the Blavatnik Building) – behind the original power station in 2016, the ever-expanding gallery features over 250 artists from around 50 countries, mixing the work of artists such as Picasso, Bacon, Pollock, Rothko and Warhol.

Tate Modern is linked to St Paul's across the river by the **Millennium Bridge**, a slender footbridge designed by Sir Norman Foster.

THE SOUTH BANK

Further west along the river is the **National Theatre** (www.nationaltheatre.org.uk) – actually three theatres under one roof. For a peek behind the scenes, you can book a backstage tour (tel: 020-7452 3000). Adjacent is the **Southbank Centre** ⑱ (tel: 020-7960 4200; www.southbankcentre.co.uk), London's largest arts complex. The **Royal Festival Hall** plays host to orchestral concerts, while next door are the **Queen Elizabeth Hall** and the **Purcell Room**, used for smaller-scale

Olives for sale at Borough Market.

events, from chamber music to poetry readings. There are often free performances at lunchtime and in summer.

On the upper level of the complex is the **Hayward Gallery**, which has changing exhibitions of contemporary art. **BFI Southbank**, in the shadow of Waterloo Bridge, presents a repertory of vintage and foreign-language films as well as the London Film Festival each November. The British Film Institute also runs the **IMAX Cinema**, which has the largest screen in Britain, and rises like a behemoth from the roundabout at the south end of Waterloo Bridge.

THE LONDON EYE

Continuing westwards, you come to the 450ft (135-metre) high **London Eye** ❹⑨ (tel: 0871-781 3000; www.londoneye. com; Jan–Mar and Sept–Dec Mon–Fri 11am–6pm, Sat–Sun 10am–8.30pm, Apr–Aug daily 10am–8.30pm, July–Aug Sat–Sun until 9.30pm), an observation wheel erected for the millennium. The 32 enclosed capsules take 30 minutes to make a full revolution, and on a clear day, you can see for 25 miles (40km).

Spitalfields Market.

Next to it is the majestic **County Hall**, built between 1909 and 1933 and until 1986 the seat of the Greater London Council. It now contains two hotels, as well as the **London Sea Life Aquarium** (www2.visitsealife.com; Mon–Fri & Sun 10am–6pm, Sat 9.30–7pm), which accommodates underwater species from sharks to stingrays. Also here is the **London Dungeon** (www.thedungeons. com/london/en; daily 10am–5pm, Sat until 6pm, with exceptions), which provides a gruesome, actor-led account of London's history, including the Black Death, the Great Fire and the grisly deeds of Sweeney Todd and Jack the Ripper. The complex also houses Shrek's Adventure (www.shreksadventure.com); the interactive attraction allows you to meet animated characters from the famous movie.

Upriver from the South Bank complex, beyond Westminster Bridge, is **Lambeth Palace** ❺⓪, which has been the London residence of the Archbishop of Canterbury for nearly 800 years (pre-booked tours only; www. archbishopofcanterbury.org). The garden and deconsecrated church of St Mary

ⓞ EAST LONDON'S ART SCENE

The East End is home to some of the capital's best contemporary art galleries, both public and commercial. The major public art space here is the **Whitechapel Art Gallery** (77–82 Whitechapel High Street; tel: 020-7522 7888; www.whitechapel.org; Tue–Sun 11am–6pm, Thu until 9pm), founded by a local vicar and his wife in 1897. The building, designed by the Arts and Crafts architect Charles Harrison Townsend, today hosts important exhibitions of contemporary art. Just to the east, at No. 10 Whitechapel Road, **Fotografiska** opened in 2019, becoming London's largest permanent photography gallery, with seven exhibition spaces sprawled across 89,000 sq ft (8,2700 sqna metres). Also of note is **Rivington Place** (Rivington Street; www. rivingtonplace.org; Tue–Fri 11am–6pm, Thu until 9pm, Sat noon–6pm; free), devoted to cultural diversity, with both art exhibitions and film screenings.

Close to Rivington Place, at 82 Kingsland Road is Flowers (www.flowersgallery.com; Tue–Sat 10am–6pm). The creation of Angela Flowers, this much-admired gallery showcases work from more than 40 established and emerging artists, including Patrick Hughes, Derek Hirst and Nicola Hicks.

Other notable commercial galleries include **Victoria Miro** (16 Wharf Road, N1; www.victoria-miro.com), while smaller galleries line Hackney's **Broadway Market** and **Vyner Street** – the latter has less established galleries run on tiny budgets in old shops and post-industrial buildings.

nearby are home to the lovely **Garden Museum** (www.gardenmuseum.org.uk).

Just south, in Lambeth, is the tasteful Newport Street Gallery (www.newportstreetgallery.com), owned by artist Damien Hirst to showcase his own work alongside other artists from his collection.

THE IMPERIAL WAR MUSEUM

Another landmark south of the river is the **Imperial War Museum** ⑤ (www.iwm.org.uk; daily 10am–6pm; free, charge for special exhibitions), situated on Lambeth Road. Perhaps it is no accident that the grand structure in which it is housed was once Bethlem, a hospital (opened in 1815) for the care of the insane (from which the word "bedlam" comes), for the Imperial War Museum does a marvellous job of conveying the madness of war. The Imperial War Museum has dedicated itself to living history rather than dusty cases of artefacts: you can go and sit in a replica of a bomb shelter and listen to the neighbours argue. There are also changing exhibitions covering different aspects of war.

EAST LONDON

Back on the north bank of the river, downstream from Tower Bridge lie **St Katharine Docks** ㊾. Built in 1828 as a shipment point for wool and wine, the docks were renovated in the early 1980s and have become a posh residential and commercial district. The complex contains a shopping arcade, a yacht harbour, a pub, a hotel and several old warehouses (such as the Ivory House) now converted into modern offices and flats. It is the most successful of the docklands developments that extend east from here to the Isle of Dogs, home to the cluster of skyscrapers known as Canary Wharf. The development is testimony to the continuing ambition of the City's financiers. A branch of the Museum of London, the **Museum of London Docklands** (West India Quay; www.museumoflondon.org.uk/Docklands; daily 10am–6pm; free) documents the city's history as a port and hosts excellent events for young children. The skyscraper generally referred to as "Canary Wharf", unmissable for its pointy hat and visible from across London, is actually

A bird's-eye view from the London Eye.

One Canada Square. It was long the UK's tallest building, although The Shard at London Bridge has overtaken it. Below it is a shopping centre, with fashion and food stores.

Northeast of the Tower is the warren of narrow streets that marks the start of the **East End**, traditionally London's working-class district. For centuries, the East End has been the place where newly arrived immigrants have settled. Huguenots, Jews, Bangladeshis and Somalis have all made their mark on the area, and it is one of the most culturally exciting parts of the capital.

On Commercial Road is **Old Spitalfields Market** ❸ (www.oldspital fieldsmarket.com), a former wholesale fruit-and-vegetable market that now has clothes and crafts stalls. In the streets around are many interesting boutiques, including along Hanbury Street, the northern part of Brick Lane and (to the west) Commercial Street. A short walk south, around Middlesex and Wentworth streets, is **Petticoat Lane Market** (Mon–Fri 10am–4.30pm and greatly expanded Sun 9am–2pm), a chromatic jumble of clothes, bric-a-brac and food.

Two streets beyond Spitalfields Market, at 18 Folgate Street, is the 18th-century time warp of **Dennis Severs' House** ❹ (www.dennissevershouse.co.uk; check website for tour dates and times). In 1967, Severs moved from his native California and bought this former silk weaver's house. Living with no electricity or modern appliances, he recreated its 18th-century state. It is now as if the original family have just left the room, leaving a half-eaten scone and a smouldering fire.

At the northern end of Brick Lane are Shoreditch and Hoxton, which were badly damaged by bombing during World War II and remained somewhat run-down for a long time afterwards. It was only in the 1990s that the area started to regenerate, as artists and nightclubs moved in, attracted by the relatively low cost of accommodation. Today, despite retaining a gritty feel, the area is no longer cheap, but a large number of bars, restaurants (especially Vietnamese on Kingsland Road) and nightclubs remain.

The Imperial War Museum.

VISITING THE OLYMPIC PARK

The 2012 Olympic Games were held in London, with the focus of attention on the Olympic Park in Stratford, in the east of the city.

Numerous other venues were also used – both across the capital and across the country. Equestrian events were held in the picturesque confines of Greenwich Park, beach volleyball on Horse Guards Parade in Westminster, football matches at Old Trafford in Manchester and rowing races at Eton Dorney.

THE OLYMPIC LEGACY

Following on from the Games, the Olympic Park has been preserved as a vast, open green space known as Queen Elizabeth Olympic Park (www.queeneliza betholympicpark.co.uk), a fine tribute to the Olympics' legacy. Sitting alongside waterways, walking and cycling trails, gardens and wildlife, most of the major venues remain, and can still be visited for sports or just to view the architecture and design.

The centrepiece is the 80,000-capacity Olympic Stadium in the south of the Olympic Park, which was originally used for the main track events, but has now been upgraded to become a multi-purpose space and is also home to West Ham United Football Club.

Sweeping away from the stadium are gardens that celebrate the tradition of British horticulture, featuring over 250 species of plant. In the park's southeast corner is the Aquatics Centre, designed by the late architect Zaha Hadid, and already an iconic building. Another architectural feat is the Velodrome at the northern end of the site; this eco-friendly structure is clad in wood, and is 100 percent naturally ventilated. Also notable is the Copper Box Arena, used for handball and fencing, among other events, during the Games.

Another engineering curiosity is the ArcelorMittal Orbit (www.arcelormittalorbit.com; book tickets online), a huge sculpture that towers 72ft (22 metres), higher than New York's Statue of Liberty. Designed by artist Anish Kapoor, it is made up of over 1,400 tons of steel and cost almost £20 million. It's no wonder therefore that it is named after one of London's richest residents and was sponsored by his steel company. Visitors can ascend to the flying-saucer-style viewing platform and enjoy spectacular views over the Olympic Park and the city beyond. For a dramatic descent, visitors can take the helter-skelter-type slide right to the bottom.

FAMILY FUN

There is a lot for the whole family to do, including playgrounds featuring sand pits, tree houses, slides, oversized swings and rocks to climb. Another favourite with children is the Waterworks Fountain, with 195 jets of computer-controlled water; it is guaranteed to give them a soaking; the fountain is illuminated at night with colourful neon lights.

Visitors can travel to Queen Elizabeth Olympic Park from Central London by public transport: overground trains run from London Liverpool Street to Stratford as do Tube trains on the Jubilee and Central lines.

EATING OUT IN THE OLYMPIC PARK

There are a number of cafés and restaurants within the Olympic Park, but the neighbouring Westfield Stratford City shopping centre has about 70 dining outlets

The ArcelorMittal Orbit sculpture.

A brightly painted mews house in Chelsea.

KENSINGTON AND CHELSEA

Home to some of Britain's best and brightest – and wealthiest – the royal borough of Kensington and Chelsea offers the visitor fine museums, lovely streets to stroll along and chichi shopping.

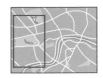

In the 19th century Chelsea was a mildly bohemian "village" just outside the sprawl of Central London. Among its more famous residents were Oscar Wilde, John Singer Sargent, J.M.W. Turner and Mark Twain. In the 20th century it has been home to T.S. Eliot, J. Paul Getty, Mick Jagger and Keith Richards. Its main artery is the **King's Road ❶**, which was once a tranquil country lane but was later widened into a private carriage road from St James's Palace to Hampton Court on the order of King Charles II. It rose to its pinnacle of fame in the 1960s, when designers Mary Quant and Ossie Clark set up shop here, and it was in its boutiques that the miniskirt first made its revolutionary appearance. In the 1970s Vivienne Westwood and Malcolm McLaren took up the avant-garde baton, dominating the punk scene with their boutique, Sex. Today the street attracts a well-heeled crowd and is far more mainstream. Alongside the fashion stores, it is now is the location of the **Saatchi Gallery** (www.saatchigallery.com; daily 10am–6pm; free), housed in a former army barracks set back from the King's Road on Duke of York Square. The gallery showcases contemporary art in changing exhibitions alongside immersive installations by emerging artists.

The Royal Albert Hall.

CHELSEA GARDENS AND PENSIONERS

Running parallel with the King's Road, down by the river, is Royal Hospital Road, home to the **Chelsea Royal Hospital ❷** (www.chelsea-pensioners.co.uk; Mon–Sun 10am–5pm; free, charge for tours, book in advance), Sir Christopher Wren's masterpiece of the English Baroque style, opened as a home for invalid and veteran soldiers in 1682. A few hundred army pensioners still reside here, and parade in their scarlet frockcoats on Founder's Day every

◎ **Main attractions**
Saatchi Gallery
Chelsea Physic Garden
Harrods
Victoria and Albert Museum
Natural History Museum
Science Museum
Kensington Palace

Map on page 118

June. Visitors can see the Great Hall, the Octagon, the Chapel, the museum and Ranelagh Gardens, the site of the Chelsea Flower Show since 1862.

On Royal Hospital Road, tracing the history of the British military from the 15th century is the **National Army Museum** (www.nam.ac.uk; daily 10am–5.30pm, first Wed of month until 8pm; free). Further along the same street is the entrance to the **Chelsea Physic Garden** (www.chelseaphysicgarden.co.uk; Apr–Oct Mon–Fri, Sun 11am–6pm, Nov–Mar Mon–Fri 10am–dusk), a botanical laboratory founded in 1676. It's a pretty place for a stroll and afternoon tea.

At the end of Royal Hospital Road is Flood Street, where Margaret and Denis Thatcher once lived at No. 19,

and continuing on to the banks of the river, you soon find yourself on Cheyne Walk, one of London's most exclusive streets. Past residents include George Eliot, J.M.W. Turner, Dante Gabriel Rossetti and, more recently, Mick Jagger. On the south bank of the river, opposite here, is **Battersea Park** ③, with gardens designed as part of the Festival of Britain in 1951, and the Buddhist Peace Pagoda, commemorating the 1985 Year of Peace. Alongside, the area around Battersea Power Station is undergoing an exciting £9-billion revamp; the Power Station itself is being redeveloped to house a mixture of über-luxury apartments, restaurants and shops. Several restaurants and shops are already open, although, the Power Station itself won't open its

doors to the public until 2020, when a new tube station will make this historic building more accessible than ever.

Just off Cheyne Walk is Cheyne Row, and at No. 24, time stands still in **Carlyle's House** (www.nationaltrust.org. uk/carlyles-house; Mar–Oct Wed–Sun 11am–5.30pm). The Scottish historian and philosopher Thomas Carlyle brought his wife Jane to live in this elegant Queen Anne house in 1834. Their home was turned into a museum in 1896 and remains a time capsule of Victorian life, with papered-over panelling and books, furniture and pictures just as the Carlyles left them.

BELGRAVIA

East of Sloane Square is the exclusive district of **Belgravia**, originally grazing land until Thomas Cubitt developed it as a town estate for aristocrats in the early 19th century. The neighbourhood retains this exclusive quality as the home of diplomats, senior civil servants, celebrities and the occasional duke or baron.

North of Belgravia via Sloane Street is **Knightsbridge**. Another upmarket part

of London, it is the home of **Harrods ④** (see page 120), the city's most famous department store, owned by the Qatari royal family. At night, its light-spangled facade resembles an enormous Victorian birthday cake. Inside, the tiled food halls are especially impressive.

VICTORIA AND ALBERT MUSEUM

At the end of the Brompton Road is the district of South Kensington, noted for its large museums (all free). The **Victoria and Albert Museum ⑤** (V&A; www.vam.ac.uk; daily 10am–5.45pm, Fri until 10pm; free) on Cromwell Road is the most famous of these. Its 7 miles (11km) of galleries house more than 5 million items of fine and applied arts, with exhibits ranging from exquisite Persian miniatures to a whole room designed by Frank Lloyd Wright. One minute one can be admiring the 1515–16 Raphael cartoons drawn for the tapestries in the Sistine Chapel, and the next examining E.H. Shepard's illustrations for *Winnie-the-Pooh* or appreciating a plaster cast of Michelangelo's

Shopping on the King's Road.

Chelsea Pensioners at the Royal Hospital.

The Victoria and Albert Museum.

David. Other highlights include an outstanding collection of Indian art in the Nehru Gallery, fashion from the 17th century to the present day in the Fashion Galleries, and the British Galleries, which trace the country's tastes from 1500 to 1900. The latest addition to the line up is the Photography Centre, opened in 2018, which displays artworks and artefacts tracing photography from its invention to the present day. The museum has the particularly pleasant Garden Café, as well as a smaller one in a beautiful vaulted room designed by William Morris. Sitting alongside the Henry Cole Wing, the new Exhibition Road quarter opened in 2017. The £48-million extension, designed by Stirling Prize-winning architect Amanda Levete, includes the grand porticoed Blavatnik Hall entrance, the subterranean Sainsbury Gallery and the porcelain-tiled Sackler Courtyard and café.

NATURAL HISTORY MUSEUM

If any of London's museums encapsulates the Victorians' quest for knowledge and passion for cataloguing data, it's the **Natural History Museum** ❻ (Cromwell Road; www.nhm. ac.uk; daily 10am–5.50pm; free), just across the road from the V&A. Occupying an extravagant Gothic-Romanesque building, it has one of the best dinosaur and prehistoric lizard collections anywhere in the world. The highlight is a full-scale animatronic T-Rex that roars and twists, while other popular exhibits include a life-size model of a blue whale and a simulated earthquake machine. A subterranean cloister, wildlife garden and public square are set to be added to the museum's entrance space by 2020.

SCIENCE MUSEUM

Adjacent to the Natural History Museum, with its entrance on Exhibition Road, is the **Science Museum** ❼ (www.science museum.org.uk; daily 10am–6pm; free). It has more than 10,000 exhibits, plus attractions such as an IMAX theatre and interactive galleries. Highlights include the world's oldest surviving steam locomotive, the Apollo 10 command module (1969), the huge Spacelab 2 X-ray

Harrods at night.

⊘ HARRODS

London's most famous department store employs more than 5,000 staff and has over 330 departments – a far cry from its humble beginnings as a grocery store with two assistants. It famously claims to be able to source any item, and then send the purchase to its customer anywhere in the world. Under this remarkable policy, Noël Coward was bought an alligator for Christmas, and former US president Ronald Reagan was given a baby elephant. In reality customers are more likely to come away with teddy bears, toiletries and other items bearing the bottle-green Harrods logo. At night the store's exterior is lit up with 11,500 energy-efficient light bulbs. Its millions of annual visitors are subject to a rather vague dress code. Doormen are on hand to enforce these house rules.

telescope – the actual instrument flown on the Space Shuttle – and full-size models of the Huygens Titan probe and Beagle 2 Mars Lander.

ROYAL ALBERT HALL

On the northern fringe of South Kensington is the **Royal Albert Hall ❽** (tickets and tours, tel: 020-7589 8212; www.royalalberthall.com). Queen Victoria laid the foundation stone for the concert hall in 1867 in memory of her late husband, Prince Albert, a highly cultured man who was responsible for founding many South Kensington institutions. The circular 8,000-seat auditorium stages a varied programme from pop concerts to the BBC-sponsored summer Promenade Concerts – the Proms – an annual showcase of mostly classical music.

Across Kensington Gore sits the **Albert Memorial ❾**, an extravagant Gothic monument that rises suddenly from the plane trees of Kensington Gardens and Hyde Park. Prince Albert sits under a lavishly gilded canopy, forever reading the catalogue from the 1851 Great Exhibition. Marble figures on the lower corners of the steps depict America, Asia, Africa and Europe.

PALACES AND GARDENS

A short walk westwards through the park brings you to **Kensington Palace ❿** (www.hrp.org.uk; daily Mar–Oct 10am–6pm, Nov–Feb 10am–5pm). Christopher Wren refurbished the mansion for William and Mary in the 1690s, and for nearly 100 years it served as the principal royal residence in London. Princess Diana once lived here, and an apartment, formerly the residence of Princess Margaret, has been refurbished for Diana's son, Prince William, who now resides there with his wife, the Duchess of Cambridge, and his children. Many of the first-floor State Apartments can be viewed, as well as the royal dress collection, with exhibits dating from the 18th century to the present day, including some of Diana's gowns.

To the north of the palace is the **Diana, Princess of Wales Memorial Playground**, where children can let off steam.

A hippopotamus at the Natural History Museum.

In the Natural History Museum's Hintze Hall.

The Albert Memorial.

Kensington Palace's gardens.

Also in Kensington Gardens is the **Serpentine Gallery** (www.serpentinegallery.org; Tue–Sun 10am–6pm; free), a small art museum that stages adventurous exhibitions of modern and contemporary art. The museum added the Serpentine Sackler Gallery, in 2013, in a Grade II-listed building ("The Magazine") just northeast of the original gallery, to showcase "the stars of tomorrow" in the visual arts.

To the east, Kensington Gardens merges into Hyde Park. At the southeast corner is **Apsley House** (149 Piccadilly; www.english-heritage.org.uk; Apr–Oct Wed–Sun 11am–5pm, Nov–Mar Sat–Sun 10am–4pm), which was formerly the home of the Duke of Wellington, who defeated Napoleon at Waterloo in 1815. The mansion displays a fine collection of furniture, silver, porcelain and paintings.

In the northeast corner of Hyde Park is **Speakers' Corner**, where orators and idiots passionately defend their beliefs. This tradition began when the Tyburn gallows stood here (1388–1783), and felons were allowed to make a final unexpurgated speech to the crowds before being hanged.

LEIGHTON HOUSE

Holland Park, just west of Kensington Palace via Kensington High Street, incorporates large areas of woodland, a Japanese garden and an adventure playground. In summer an open-air theatre stages opera and drama.

At 12 Holland Park Road is **Leighton House** (Wed–Mon 10am–5.30pm), the home of the Victorian artist Lord Frederic Leighton from 1866 until he died in 1896. The *pièce de résistance* is the Arab Hall, inspired by a Moorish palace in Palermo. Almost next door is the Commonweath Institute, which since late 2016 has housed the **Design Museum** (www.designmuseum.org; check website for opening times), which presents exhibitions related to architectural, industrial, fashion, graphic and product design.

NOTTING HILL AND SHEPHERD'S BUSH

North of Holland Park (and northwest of Kensington Gardens) is **Notting Hill,**

one of London's most highly sought-after residential districts, with handsome white-stucco Victorian terraces and villas. On the last Sunday and Monday of August the narrow streets explode with music and colour as the city's West Indian population stages Europe's largest street carnival here.

The district's other famous attraction is the **Portobello Road Market** ⑯ (Mon–Wed 9am–6pm, Thu 9am–1pm, Fri–Sat 9am–7pm). By far the busiest day is Saturday, when the street becomes jammed, as people browse the antiques and bric-a-brac. There is also a more fashion-forward market, with original-designer along with second-hand clothes, jewellery and ephemera stalls underneath the Westway flyover further along Portobello.

To the west of Notting Hill and Holland Park is the residential district of Shepherd's Bush, now visited by tourists largely for its shopping centre, the Westfield. It is smaller than its sister-centre in Stratford in the east, but is vast nevertheless.

LITTLE VENICE AND ST JOHN'S WOOD

The posh residential district of **Little Venice** lies at the junction of the Grand Union, Regent's and Paddington canals, and residential moorings for barges here are much sought after. Refurbished canal barges operated by the **London Waterbus Company** (www.londonwaterbus.co.uk; tel: 020-3763 9981) run east from Little Venice to Regent's Park through another exclusive residential neighbourhood, **St John's Wood**. At its heart is **Lord's Cricket Ground** ⑰. The **Cricket Museum** here (entrance on St John's Wood Road; www.lords.org; tel: 020-7616 8595; tours daily, except match days) is filled with two centuries of memorabilia but can only be visited during the Lord's tour.

Also in St John's Wood are the Abbey Road recording studios, with the zebra crossing the Beatles made so famous, and the **London Central Mosque**, completed in 1977, incorporating an Islamic Cultural Centre.

Regent's Canal runs for 14km (9 miles) linking the Grand Union Canal with the Thames.

Shopping at Portobello Market.

An aerial view of the O2, formerly the Millennium Dome, on the Greenwich Peninsula.

DAY TRIPS ALONG THE THAMES

The Thames has played a central role in London's history. You can travel by boat to a variety of fascinating places along its banks, including Greenwich, Kew Gardens and Hampton Court.

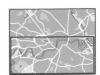

London's riverside areas can be reached by local London transport including river taxis, as well as by privately run riverboats. Eastwards is elegant historic Greenwich and London's Docklands – the latter greatly developed since the 1980s but rather lacking in tourist attractions apart from a few historic riverside pubs. To the west are the upmarket suburban areas of Kew, Richmond and Twickenham, and Hampton Court, further beyond. The western stretch of the river is very much a focus of pleasure: in summer, oarsmen and yachtsmen pit their wits against its tides and people stroll along its tow paths, laze at its bankside pubs or cruise about in their "gin palaces" (motor yachts).

ROYAL GREENWICH

There have long been settlements at **Greenwich ❶**. In the 11th century Vikings pulled their longboats ashore, slew Archbishop St Alfege and ravaged London. In 1427 Bella Court Palace was built on the riverside and became a royal retreat. Henry VI made it his favourite residence, and subsequent Tudor monarchs – Henry VIII, Elizabeth I and Mary – were all born at Greenwich. It was here that Sir Walter Raleigh is supposed to have laid his cloak over a

pool of mud, so that Queen Elizabeth would not get her feet wet. Nowadays cruisers (www.thamesriverservices.co.uk) bring tourists from Westminster via Greenwich all the way to the **Thames Barrier** (see page 127).

James I had the old palace in Greenwich demolished and commissioned Inigo Jones to build a new private residence for Queen Anne. The result was the **Queen's House**, completed in 1637, a masterpiece of the Palladian style and perhaps the finest piece of Stuart architecture in England.

Main attractions

National Maritime
 Museum and Royal
 Observatory
The O2
Thames Barrier
Kew Gardens
Hampton Court Palace

Map on page 126

Boats at Westminster Pier.

Greenwich has been associated with British sea power for the past 500 years, and next door is the **National Maritime Museum** (www.rmg.co.uk/national-maritime-museum; daily 10am–5pm; free, charge for special exhibitions only), showcasing an excellent seafaring collection. Here, the 1805 Battle of Trafalgar is relived and the glory of the nation's maritime tradition unfolds, with boats, paintings and memorabilia from heroic voyages. The Sammy Ofer Wing houses a permanent gallery Voyagers: Britons and the Sea as well as a large and child-friendly restaurant.

A short walk up the hill is the **Royal Observatory** (www.rmg.co.uk/royal-observatory; daily 10am–5pm), constructed at Greenwich by Charles II in 1675 in order to perfect the arts of navigation and astronomy. Since that time, the globe's longitude and time zones have been measured from the Greenwich Meridian, which cuts right through the middle of Flamsteed House, today a museum of astronomical instruments and timepieces and, in a separate building, is a planetarium.

By the waterfront (on dry land) is one of England's most famous ships. The ***Cutty Sark*** (www.rmg.co.uk/cuttysark; daily 10am–5pm), built in 1869, was the last of the great China clippers – a speedy square-rigger that once ran tea from the Orient to Europe. The ship was preserved for the nation in 1922 and has been in dry dock by the Thames in naval Greenwich since 1954. Following a devastating fire in May 2007, this London landmark has been impressively restored to its former glory. Raised above its dry dock, visitors can now view the ship from underneath as well as walk the decks above. Also restored, the ships figurehead depicts the witch who pursued Tam O'Shanter in the eponymous poem by Robert Burns, getting so close that she pulled off his horse's tail. The Scots name "cutty sark" relates to the cut-down shift that the witch is wearing.

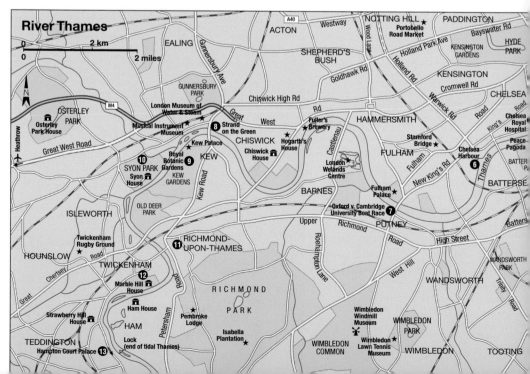

TO THE THAMES BARRIER

The other main highlight of Greenwich is its crafts and antique markets, especially the covered one at the heart of the town centre. Full markets are held at weekends, although some stalls set up in the week as well (www.greenwichmarket-london.com; daily 10am–5.30pm, with exceptions). There are also several outdoor markets at the weekend, one on Greenwich High Road, between the cinema and the clock tower, focusing on vintage and retro items.

From Greenwich, you can take riverboats further downstream. Sights en route include the **O2 concert arena ❷** (North Greenwich Tube Station; bookings tel: 0844-856 0202; www.theo2.co.uk), built on a bend in the river. This huge entertainment centre hosts top rock concerts and sports events, and features several restaurants inside. From here you can board the Emirates Air Line (www.emiratesairline.co.uk), for panoramic views over the city while being transported across the Thames. Further

The Thames Barrier.

downstream still is the **Thames Barrier ❸**, which is used to regulate the level of the river and protect Central London from tidal floods.

Also downstream from Greenwich is the Royal Navy's **Historic Dockyard** at Chatham (see page 195), which flourished under Henry VIII and Elizabeth I. In the late 17th century, Sir Christopher Wren built the **Royal**

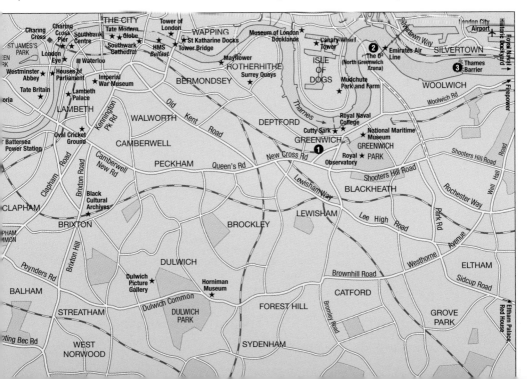

Hospital for Seamen at Greenwich, an elegant complex in the Baroque style that became the **Royal Naval College**. Its highly decorated chapel and elaborate Baroque Painted Hall, decorated in the early 18th century by Sir James Thornhill and freshly restored in 2019, are open to the public (www.ornc.org; daily 10am–5pm; free). The new Sackler Gallery, set in the vaulted Sir King William Undercroft, was also added in 2019 and tells the history of Thornhill's masterpiece.

UPSTREAM: GARDENS AND GRAND HOUSES

Riverboats (www.wpsa.co.uk) go upstream from Westminster, past Chelsea, all the way to Kew, Richmond and Hampton Court. Alternatively, visitors can take the District Tube Line, which extends westwards as far as Richmond, or the overground trains which run from Waterloo.

As you travel upstream from Chelsea Bridge, on the south bank is the Peace Pagoda in **Battersea Park** ❹, erected by Japanese Buddhists for the 1985 Year of Peace, while on the opposite bank is Sir Christopher Wren's **Chelsea Royal Hospital** ❺ and, beyond, the upmarket development at **Chelsea Harbour** ❻. But the leafy riverbank does not really begin until **Putney** ❼, the starting point for the boat race between Oxford and Cambridge universities each March or April.

Beyond is Hammersmith Bridge. The Piccadilly and District Tube lines go to Hammersmith, the starting point of a riverside walk that leads to Chiswick and harbours a number of historic taverns along the way, including the 18th-century Dove on Upper Mall, where the words of *Rule, Britannia* are supposed to have been written by James Thomson. **Strand on the Green** ❽, just beyond, has pretty Georgian houses and charming fishermen's cottages. After your walk, try one of the riverside pubs, including the Bull's Head and the City Barge, both nearly 400 years old.

A further diversion at Chiswick is **Hogarth's House** (williamhogarthtrust.

The Cutty Sark at Greenwich.

org.uk; tel: 020-8994 6757; Tue–Sun noon–5pm; free), a 17th-century mansion now filled with engravings and personal relics of one of England's most famous artists. **Chiswick House**, an early 18th-century Palladian villa designed by the third Earl of Burlington, is even more delightful (overground train from Waterloo to Chiswick, or District or Piccadilly Tube Line to Turnham Green; www.chgt.org.uk; Apr–Oct Mon & Wed 11am–3pm, Sat–Sun until 4pm).

KEW GARDENS

Kew, a quiet suburb upstream and across the Thames from Chiswick, is home to the 300-acre (120-hectare) Royal Botanic Gardens – generally known simply as **Kew Gardens ⑨** (www.kew.org; daily 10am–5.30pm, with exceptions). The gardens were first planted in 1759 under the direction of Princess Augusta, who was then living on the site. In 1772, George III put Kew in the hands of botanist Sir Joseph Banks, who had just returned from a round-the-world expedition to collect plant specimens

with Captain Cook, and the collection grew and grew. There are special areas given over to redwoods, orchids, roses, rhododendrons, and alpine and desert plants. Kew is now a Unesco World Heritage Site.

The most famous of Kew's nurseries is the **Palm House**, a vast Victorian pavilion of steel and glass that contains hundreds of tropical plants. The ecologically correct and energy-saving **Princess of Wales Conservatory**, opened in 1987, has 10 climatic zones, ranging from arid to moist tropical, under one roof.

In addition to the glasshouses there are various temples and other follies dating back to the period of royal ownership of the gardens in the 18th and early 19th centuries. The **Chinese pagoda**, built in 1762, reflects the fashion for chinoiserie in English garden design in the mid-18th century. The classically styled, Grade I-listed Orangery, dating from 1761, too dark to house citrus trees as was intended, is now a pleasant café-restaurant.

The tree-top walk at Kew Gardens.

The Royal Naval College.

⊙ Fact

The walk up Richmond Hill to Richmond Park leads past views over the Thames and London; in the foreground you may see cows grazing on Petersham Meadows. This view is the only one in England to be protected by an Act of Parliament, passed in 1902.

Kew's newest addition is the **Children's Garden**, which opened in May 2019. It includes a jasmine-draped tunnel, 13ft (4-metre) -high canopy walk wrapped around a 200-year-old English oak, and different educational zones exploring everything that a plant needs to grow.

Across the Thames from Kew is another famous botanical centre, **Syon Park ⑩** (District Line to Gunnersbury, then the 237 or 267 bus to "Brentlea Gate"). The Dukes of Northumberland built a great mansion here in the 16th century, while the lush gardens were added by the great English landscape gardener, "Capability" Brown (see page 219). **Syon House** (www.syonpark.co.uk; house: Mar–Oct Wed–Thu, Sun 11am–5pm; gardens: daily mid-Mar–Oct 10.30am–5pm), a neoclassical building remodelled in the 18th century by Robert Adam, has a lavish Baroque interior and impressive conservatory.

RICHMOND-UPON-THAMES

Reachable by train from Waterloo or via the District Tube Line, Richmond-upon-Thames ⑪ retains its village atmosphere with its cluster of book and antiques shops, upmarket fashion boutiques, tea salons and charming riverside pubs, such as the White Cross. The Victorian-style **Richmond Theatre** sits on the edge of the green and is a showcase for productions on their way to the West End. **Richmond Park** was enclosed by Charles I as a royal hunting estate and is now the only royal park that keeps a large stock of deer. On the way to the park, a walk up Richmond Hill from the centre of town leads to a magnificent view west over the Thames.

Bus 371 from Richmond will take you to the flamboyant 17th-century **Ham House**, an annexe of the Victoria and Albert Museum (www.nationaltrust.org.uk/ham-house-and-garden; house: Mar–mid-Oct daily noon–4am (rest of year tours only on certain days, tel: 020-8940 1950); garden: daily 11am–5pm). The house contains a rich collection of paintings (including works by Reynolds and Van Dyck),

Cows grazing on Petersham Meadows.

⊙ THE THAMES PATH

Starting at the Thames Barrier in the east and ending at the river's source in the Cotswolds 180 miles (290km) away, the Thames Path (www.nationaltrail.co.uk) provides some of the best views of the city and beyond. It is a trail that can be walked by people of all ages. From Putney in West London the path takes on a rural aspect, passing the London Wetlands Centre in Barnes, the grand riverside houses of Chiswick and the pretty cottages of Strand on the Green. After Kew Bridge, the path skirts round Kew Gardens, with Syon Park across the river. At Richmond, with Petersham Meadows on your left and the river ahead of you, it's hard to believe the city is within spitting distance. Along this stretch you'll see Marble Hill House and Ham House.

tapestries, furniture, carpets and clothing.

Richmond Bridge leads across to **Twickenham**, the home of English rugby (international games are staged in winter at the huge Twickenham Rugby Football Ground). The 18th-century **Marble Hill House** ⑫ (www.english-heritage.org.uk; tel: 020-8892 5115; house: guided tours only Apr–Oct Sat–Sun; park: year-round 6.30am–dusk) on Richmond Road is a Palladian-style dwelling that has long provided a retreat for the secret affairs of the Crown. Both George II and George IV kept their mistresses in this mansion. Today the house contains a fine picture gallery and a lovely garden, the setting for outdoor Shakespeare productions and concerts in summer.

HAMPTON COURT PALACE

Above Twickenham is Teddington, the lock that marks the end of the tidal Thames, and then **Hampton Court Palace** ⑬ (www.hrp.org.uk; daily 10am–6pm, Nov–Mar until 4.30pm). Its two distinctive architectural styles make it both the paragon of the Tudor style and the self-proclaimed English version of Versailles. In the early 16th century, Hampton Court was built by Cardinal Wolsey as the finest and most flamboyant residence in the realm. When Wolsey fell from grace, he gave the palace to Henry VIII in a futile attempt to regain favour. The king instantly fell in love with it and moved there with Anne Boleyn. He ordered the construction of the Great Hall, the Clock Court and the Library, and enlarged the gardens. It is said that Elizabeth I used Hampton Court as an illicit love nest away from the prying eyes of Westminster. She also planted the gardens with exotic trees and flowers brought to England from the New World by Sir Francis Drake and Sir Walter Raleigh.

In the 1690s, the sumptuous **State Apartments** were designed by Wren for William and Mary, who also commissioned the Maze. Today the 1,000 rooms are filled with paintings, tapestries and furnishings from the past 450 years.

> **◯ Tip**
>
> A foot ferry (Mar–Oct; charge) crosses the Thames between Ham House on the south bank of the Thames and Marble Hill Park on the north bank.

Hampton Court.

Windsor Castle.

The Changing of the Guard at Windsor Castle.

THE THAMES VALLEY

Winding its way across the western Home Counties of Buckinghamshire, Berkshire and Oxfordshire, the Thames crosses some of the gentlest and most quintessentially English of landscapes.

The banks of this historic waterway have seen civilisations come and go. On the twin hills of Sinodun (*dun* means fort in Celtic), south of Dorchester-on-Thames, the early Britons built a major camp as early as 1500 BC. After the arrival of Julius Caesar, the Romans did the same, and the remains of both settlements can be seen today. The Thames is a river of plenty and has made its valley a fertile farmland. In the Middle Ages the river was so thick with salmon that even the poor ate it as a staple. Great abbeys and monasteries flourished here, and kings and queens have made it their home.

RUNNYMEDE

To fly-fishermen, the Thames Valley begins at Bell Weir Lock just a mile north of **Staines-upon-Thames**, south of the M4 beside the orbital M25. On the west side of the motorway is Egham and the riverside meadow at **Runnymede ❶** where, on 15 June 1215, King John signed Magna Carta. Tradition maintains that the barons encamped on one side of the Thames while the king's forces occupied the other. Magna Carta Island, the larger of the two river islands, was the neutral ground on which they met. Above is **Cooper's Hill**, which affords a panoramic view of Windsor Castle to the north.

At the bottom of the hill lies the Magna Carta Memorial, a domed

neoclassical structure presented by the American Bar Association in recognition of the charter's influence on the American Constitution. Nearby is the John F. Kennedy Memorial, standing in the plush acre that, in 1965, the Queen gave to the United States in perpetuity.

A pleasant diversion from Runnymede follows the riverside road from Staines to **Datchet**. This was once the Datchet Lane, mentioned in Shakespeare's comedy *The Merry Wives of Windsor*, along which Sir John Falstaff

⦿ Main attractions
Runnymede
Windsor Castle
Legoland
Stanley Spencer Gallery, Cookham
River and Rowing Museum, Henley-on-Thames

Map on page 137

On the river at Marlow.

Tip

Weather permitting, the Changing of the Guard at Windsor takes place at 11am on alternate days; check www.windsor.gov.uk for specific dates. A band usually accompanies the guard. Many find it more splendid than the Buckingham Palace ceremony.

was carried in a basket of dirty linen to be ducked in the Thames.

WINDSOR'S ROYAL CASTLE

England's most famous castle lies across the river from Datchet at **Windsor ②** (daily Mar–Oct 10am–5.15pm, Nov–Feb 10am–4.15pm, last admission year-round 1 hour 15 mins before closing, also closed for state visits). The town is 30 miles (48km) west of London, 55 minutes by train from London's Waterloo (direct) or about 30 minutes from Paddington (change at Slough from the latter).

Since the reign of Henry I in the 12th century, Windsor Castle has been the chief residence of English and British sovereigns. William the Conqueror founded the original structure, a wooden building that consisted most probably of a motte and two large baileys enclosed by palisades. The stone fortifications were built in the 12th and 13th centuries. Rising dramatically on a chalk cliff, the castle you see today incorporates additions by nearly every sovereign since. In the 19th century, George IV and Queen

Historic Windsor Castle.

Victoria spent almost £1 million on additions. The late 20th century saw great restoration of the interior, in particular of **St George's Chapel** (closed Sun except for worship), the worst casualty of a disastrous fire in 1992.

EXPLORING THE CASTLE

Part of the Lower Ward, St George's Chapel is one of the finest examples of Perpendicular architecture in England (rivalled only by King's College Chapel at Cambridge and the Henry VII Chapel at Westminster). Dedicated to the patron saint of the Order of the Garter, the chapel displays the swords, helmets, mantles and banners of the respective knights in the choir stalls.

In the Upper Ward are the **State Apartments**. These serve as accommodation for visiting foreign sovereigns and are occasionally closed to the public. Lavishly furnished, they include many important paintings from the royal collection, including works by Rubens, Van Dyck, Canaletto and Reynolds. There are also drawings by Holbein, Michelangelo, Leonardo and Raphael.

⊙ FACT FILE

Largest town Reading.

Communications Accessible via the M25 orbital motorway; Windsor is a 55-minute train journey from London Waterloo (direct) and 30 minutes from Paddington (change at Slough). There are also riverboat services running between April and September from Runnymede, Windsor, Henley-on-Thames and Marlow.

Historical data Dorchester-on-Thames began as a Roman fortress, known as Durocina; Windsor Castle was founded in the 1070s by William the Conqueror; Magna Carta was signed at Runnymede in 1215.

Major attractions Windsor Castle – main residence of the royal family; Cliveden – once the home of the Astor family and now a luxury hotel; Cookham – picturesque village and birthplace of eccentric artist Stanley Spencer; Henley-on-Thames – famous for the June/July regatta; Sonning – the prettiest of the Thames villages; Dorchester-on-Thames – an ancient Roman town.

For the children Legoland theme park at Windsor (www.legoland.co.uk). Direct train and/or coach connections from London.

Interesting diversions St Albans, with a medieval cathedral and the remains of the Roman city of Verulamium; the Gardens of the Rose, which grow the white rose of York and the red rose of Lancaster.

The Round Tower is what everyone thinks of as Windsor Castle. Climb the 220 steps for the wide valley view, but you won't be able to see the east side of the Upper Ward, which houses the Queen's private apartments. Instead, venture outside and south of the castle to the **Great Park**, more than 4,800 acres (1,920 hectares) of lush greenery. The **Savill Garden**, created in the 1930s by Sir Eric Savill, is renowned for its rhododendrons, and incorporates a landscaped garden created to mark the Queen's Golden Jubilee and a Rose Garden by Andrew Wilson.

LEGOLAND

Some 2 miles (3km) from Windsor town centre on the B3022 Windsor–Ascot road is **Legoland Windsor** (www.legoland.co.uk; mid-Mar–Oct daily 10am–5pm, Sat–Sun until 6pm, with exceptions), a popular theme park aimed at 3- to 12-year-olds and based around the children's building blocks – millions of them. Its 150 acres (60 hectares) of wooded landscape include rides – such as the underwater Atlantis Submarine Voyage – shows

and workshops. Lego is a contraction of two Danish words, *leg godt*, meaning "play well", and the park puts a worthy emphasis on learning as well as having fun. (Shuttle buses run from Windsor; Greenline coaches run from London Victoria, tel: 0844-801 7261.)

ETON

Across the river from Windsor is **Eton College** (not open to the public), that most famous of English public schools, founded in 1440 by the 18-year-old Henry VI. The original set of buildings included a collegiate church, an attached grammar school and an almshouse. It was Henry's intention that the church and school become a place of pilgrimage and devotion to the Virgin. The Wars of the Roses cut him short. He was murdered in the Tower of London, and every year on the anniversary of his death an Etonian lays a wreath of lilies in the cell in which he died.

Eton is a cluster of red-brick Tudor buildings with little towers and hulking chimneys. The **School Yard** (the outer quadrangle), the **Long Chamber** and

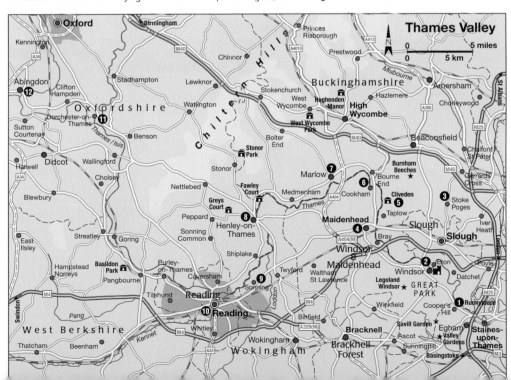

⊙ Where

Driving around the M25 northeast of Stoke Poges, you soon come to the exit for the town of **St Albans**. This was once the Roman settlement of Verulamium, and remains of its walls are still visible. The **Verulamium Museum** (www.stalbansmuseums.org. uk; Mon–Sat 10am–5pm, Sun 2–5pm) has a wonderful collection of mosaics, and remains of a Roman bath house and theatre can also be seen. Nearby **St Alban's Cathedral** (daily 8.30am– 5.45pm; donations welcomed) was founded in 793 and is named after the first English Christian martyr, who was beheaded by the Romans early in the 3rd century.

the **Lower School** all date from the 15th century. The chapel, in Perpendicular style, has 15th-century wall paintings depicting the miracles and legends of the Virgin. Most of the windows were damaged in World War II, but some of the modern installations are interesting. The cloisters dating from the 1440s are stunning; beyond them stretch the fields on which, according to the Duke of Wellington, the Battle of Waterloo was won.

Stoke Poges ❸, north of Eton and beyond the commuter town of **Slough** (damned by critics from Sir John Betjeman to Ricky Gervais), is the final resting place of the poet Thomas Gray and the inspiration for his *Elegy Written in a Country Churchyard*. The monument erected in 1799 commemorates him with a maudlin inscription, but the sheer beauty of the churchyard – its old lych gates, its rose bushes and its garden of remembrance – is what attracts visitors.

MAIDENHEAD

Half a dozen miles (10km) upriver from Eton lies **Maidenhead ❹**, the starting point of some of the most beautiful

Eton College.

countryside in the valley. Known in medieval times as Maydenhythe – one suggested meaning being maidens' landing place – its bridges are its most interesting feature: the 128ft (38-metre) arches of Brunel's railway bridge are thought to be the largest brick spans ever constructed.

From Maidenhead, the A4130 goes 8 miles (13km) directly to Henley, but there are several picturesque villages and towns clustered on either side of the river nearby. **Bray**, nestled in a bend in the Thames just south of Maidenhead, has a lovely church that dates from 1293. The **Jesus Hospital**, founded in 1627, is also interesting, and still cares for 26 older citizens from a trust set up by its originator. A more contemporary claim to fame is as a mecca for foodies, thanks to its having a pair of three-Michelin-starred restaurants: Heston Blumenthal's Fat Duck and Alain Roux's Waterside Inn.

Taplow is another pretty village, on the north side of the Thames opposite Maidenhead. From here, a road runs through Burnham to **Burnham Beeches**, a pastoral stretch of 375 wooded acres (150 hectares), especially attractive in autumn.

Upstream from Maidenhead is **Cliveden Reach**, another wooded tract, this one owned by the National Trust. The Italianate house, called **Cliveden ❺**, once the home of a Prince of Wales, several dukes and the Astor family, is poised dramatically above cliffs. Before World War II Nancy Astor turned it into a meeting place for politicians and celebrities, and in the 1960s it became notorious as the place where Secretary of State for War John Profumo and alleged call-girl Christine Keeler met.

Today, Cliveden is leased out from the National Trust and run as a luxury hotel (www.clivedenhouse.co.uk). The main rooms are viewable part of the year (Apr–Oct Mon, Tue & Thu 11am– 1pm). The gardens are open to the public and are decorated with Roman

fountains, temples and topiary (daily mid-Feb–Oct 10am–5.30pm, Nov–Dec 10am–4pm). Maps, available at the entrance, show suggested walks through the woodland, with spectacular views of the Thames.

COOKHAM

Cookham ❻ is yet another picturesque riverside village, though it is best known as the home of the artist Stanley Spencer (1891–1959). Spencer's painting of Cookham Bridge hangs in London's Tate Britain (see page 93). The **Stanley Spencer Gallery**, dedicated to his work, is housed in The King's Hall, on the High Street, where he attended Sunday school (http://stanleyspencer.org.uk; Easter–Oct daily 10.30am–5.30pm, Nov–Easter Thu–Sun 11am–4pm).

A copy of his painting of *The Last Supper* hangs in **Holy Trinity Church**, parts of which date from the 12th century. The 15th-century tower is unusual: it is one of the few church towers with both a clock and a sundial.

Six miles (9km) upriver is **Marlow ❼**, the market town where Mary Shelley wrote *Frankenstein*. In 1817 she lived in West Street ("Poets' Row") with her husband, the poet Percy Bysshe Shelley, while he was writing the poem *The Revolt of Islam*. In Saxon times, Marlow was known as Merelaw, but what you see today is comparatively new: the suspension bridge and **All Saints Church** date from the 1830s. The rustic walks along the river below Marlow Lock are refreshing, as is **Quarry Wood**, 25,000 acres (10,000 hectares) of beech woods on the Berkshire bank.

HENLEY-ON-THAMES

Henley-on-Thames ❽, a small market town with many old buildings, has been known for its rowing since 1839, when it hosted the world's first river regatta. The five-day Henley Royal Regatta, usually held at the end of June beginning of July, attracts rowers from all over the globe; it's also a major social event, where spectators dress for show and overindulge in champagne. More minor regattas are held at weekends throughout the summer.

A view of the River Thames from the gardens at Cliveden.

Cliveden house.

As its name implies, the **River and Rowing Museum** in Mill Meadows (http://rrm.co.uk; daily 10am–5pm) casts its net wider than just rowing to include a re-creation of *The Wind in the Willows*, Kenneth Grahame's much-loved children's classic, published in 1908. The building itself is set on stilts to protect it against flooding from the Thames.

There are several stately homes around Henley, but the most exquisite is the National Trust's **Greys Court** (Mar–Oct daily 1–5pm, Nov–Feb until 3pm). To the west of Henley, this well-preserved Tudor house has remains of an earlier manor house dating from the 14th century. There is a crenellated tower, a huge wheel once used for drawing water using donkey-power, and a maze.

Shiplake is a sprawling village notable for its church, rebuilt in 1689, but housing lovely 15th-century stained glass from the abbey church of St-Bertin in St-Omer, France. The poet Alfred, Lord Tennyson (1809–92) was married here to Emily Sellwood in 1850.

The Cox Seat exhibit in the Rowing Gallery at the River and Rowing Museum in Henley.

READING AND AROUND

Shiplake is en route to **Sonning** ❾, considered by many to be the prettiest of Thames villages. The little islands that rise here in the river make the views especially pastoral. By contrast, in the lower valley is the industrial town of **Reading** ❿: an important traffic hub and retail centre and known for its annual rock festival, but generally regarded as a somewhat uninspiring place. The playwright Oscar Wilde (1854–1900) was broken by two years' hard labour in the town's red-brick jail. On his release in 1897 he wrote *The Ballad of Reading Gaol*.

Streatley and **Goring**, 10 miles (16km) north of the A329, face each other on either side of the river. Streatley is the prettier of the two villages, situated at the foot of the Berkshire Downs. Five miles (8km) northwest is **Blewbury**, a lovely town with thatched cottages, watercress beds and winding lanes.

Located upriver about 8 miles (13km) away is **Dorchester-on-Thames** ⓫.

⊘ LITERARY CONNECTIONS

For a relatively small area, the Thames Valley has a surprisingly high number of literary connections.

Kenneth Grahame, author of the children's classic *The Wind in the Willows*, lived in the area for much of his life – at Cookham Dean as a child and in his later years in Pangbourne.

In Marlow's West Street, also known as Poets' Row, Mary Shelley completed *Frankenstein*. In 1817 she and her husband, the poet Percy Bysshe Shelley, settled here for a short time. While here he wrote a series of pamphlets under the pseudonym of The Hermit of Marlow, and composed and published the poem *The Revolt of Islam*.

Thomas Gray completed his *Elegy Written in a Country Churchyard* while living in Stoke Poges in 1751.

This ancient village was, at different times, a Roman fort (Durocina) and a cathedral city. The abbey church (www.dorchester-abbey.org.uk; daily 8am–6pm, or until dusk in winter) was spared demolition at the Dissolution by a local resident who bought it from the Crown for £140. The stained glass in the nave dates from the 14th century. In the chancel is a Jesse Window in which Jesse, Christ's ancestor, lies on the sill with a fruit vine springing from his belly. The High Street, which follows the line of the Roman road to Silchester, is lined with timber-framed buildings.

Sutton Courtenay and **Clifton Hampden** are picturesque riverside villages with lush willow trees hanging low over the banks. There's good swimming here in summer. Sutton Courtenay is especially interesting, with a well-preserved Norman church and a cluster of medieval houses nearby. In the graveyard is the resting place of Eric Blair (1903–50), better known as the writer George Orwell.

ABINGDON

After Sutton Courtenay the river turns north, on its way to **Abingdon** ⑫, on the doorstep of Oxford. This old town sprang up in the 7th century around a powerful Benedictine mitred abbey (St Mary's). In the 14th century the townspeople led a bloody uprising against the monks, though it was not until the Dissolution that the abbey lost its power. Most of the ecclesiastical buildings were destroyed – don't be fooled by the 19th-century artificial ruins (follies) in the abbey grounds. But some authentic buildings remain, including the abbey **Gateway**, the 13th-century **Checker** (with its idiosyncratic chimney), whose name – similar to "exchequer" – is thought to reflect its former use for accounting, and the 15th–16th-century **Long Gallery**.

Dating from 1682, Abingdon's County Hall, of the open-ground-floor type, was built by Sir Christopher Wren's mason, the same man responsible for the dome of St Paul's Cathedral in London. East Saint Helen's, with the church at the foot, is perhaps the prettiest street.

Abingdon's County Hall.

Spectators line the Royal Regatta route at Henley.

THE ENGLISH SEASON

The Season is when high society is on display. The events are mostly sporting, but a sense of style is more important than a sense of fair play.

The English Season was originally invented by upper-crust Londoners in the 18th century as a series of mid-summer amusements. This was the time when young girls "came out" at society balls, at which eligible young men would be waiting to make a suitable match; the presence of royalty was always an important endorsement of social cachet. This annual rigmarole thrived during the 19th century and only declined in importance in the mid-20th century. Nowadays, its legacy is a series of sporting and cultural events, in which the Royal Family continue to take a keen interest.

Cynics claim, however, that the events themselves are insignificant compared to their importance as social gatherings. People who care nothing for rowing attend Henley Regatta at the end of June or beginning of July; philistine amateurs flock to the Royal Academy's Summer Exhibition; the musically challenged die for a ticket to Glyndebourne's opera season and ill-informed people queueing for tickets to Wimbledon seem to think it's the only tennis tournament in the world.

Cowes Week, held off the south coast in August, the peak of the sailing season.

Life's a picnic at the Henley Regatta, held in the Oxfordshire town, late June/early July. Some people even take an occasional break to watch the rowing championships.

Russian model Natalia Kapchuk at Ascot, 2017.

Looking out over Glastonbury Festival.

The alternative season

Muddy fields and dripping campsites don't dampen the spirits of those attending the "alternative" season – the annual round of music festivals. The larger ones attract the best bands from around the world, and you don't have to be a hippie, crustie or a member of a youth tribe to attend. Many people take a tent to the large weekend events.

The largest rock event, the Glastonbury Festival in Somerset, takes place at the end of June. More than 1,000 performances are given on 18 main stages by more than 500 bands, and it attracts big names from Beyoncé and Coldplay to Florence & the Machine. Tickets sell out quickly (and you must register in advance of the release).

If you can't get to Glastonbury, try the four-day Lakefest, which takes place in early August at Eastnor Castle in the rolling Herefordshire hills. This is a family-oriented event, with all sorts of fun activities vying with a wide variety of music – from the Charlatans to Kaiser Chiefs.

The best world music festival is WOMAD, held in Malmesbury, Wiltshire, in late July. The Reading Festival in late August attracts some of the best US rock groups, and the Cambridge Folk Festival takes place in July or August.

International Polo Day is held at the Guards Polo Club, Windsor Great Park, in July. Cartier's sponsorship sets the tone.

Being a tennis umpire at Wimbledon at the end of June/ early July can take nerves of steel as the players fight it out in the game's top championship.

Glyndebourne, a summer opera location set on the South Downs near Brighton, is renowned as much for its lavish picnic hampers as it is for the performances of its star singers.

Bicycles on Broad Street.

OXFORD

England's first mass-production car factory was built here, but it is the legendary "dreaming spires" of Oxford's colleges that draw in students and tourists in their thousands.

The seat of England's oldest university, **Oxford** (www.ox.ac.uk), "the city of dreaming spires", was also the site of the first Morris Motors car factory and since World War II has been an industrial city as much as an academic one – something that is easy to forget when touring the colleges and museums. A good starting point is **Carfax** (the name derives from the Latin, *quadrifurcus*, "four-forked", or French *Quatre Voies*, "four ways"), where the four main streets – Cornmarket, High Street, Queen Street and St Aldate's – meet. **Carfax Tower ⓐ** (which is all that remains of St Martin's Church) dates from the 14th century, and from the top you get a good view of the city (daily Apr–Sept 10am–5pm, Mar and Oct until 4pm, Nov–Feb until 3pm).

CHRIST CHURCH COLLEGE

From Carfax, walk south along St Aldate's to the impressive, neo-Jacobite Town Hall on the left. Inside, is the **Museum of Oxford ⓑ** (tel: 01865-252 761; Mon–Sat 10am–5pm; free). The displays highlight the history of the city from prehistoric times to the present day. The most macabre exhibit is the skeleton of Giles Covington, an Oxford Freeman who was convicted of murder and executed in 1791. While the Museum of Oxford is currently closed

Cornmarket shopping.

for major refurbishment, the temporary Micro-Museum will house a small selection of works until the renovation is complete. Afterwards, carry on down St Aldate's to **Christ Church ⓒ**, the grandest of the colleges (www.chch.ox.ac.uk; Mon–Sat 10am–5pm, Sun 2–5pm, last entry at 4.15pm), founded in 1525 by Cardinal Wolsey, Henry VIII's chancellor, on the site of an earlier priory. **Tom Tower**, a bell tower, built by Sir Christopher Wren in 1681, looms over the main entrance (visitors enter through the **War Memorial Gardens**)

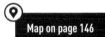
Map on page 146

⊙ Main attractions
Christ Church College
Botanic Garden
Magdalen College chapel
  and cloisters
Bodleian Library
Bridge of Sighs
Pitt-Rivers Museum
Ashmolean Museum
Blenheim Palace

Carfax Tower on Queen Street.

Christ Church chapel is also the city **Cathedral**; the 13th-century spire is one of the earliest in England, and the building contains some exquisite stained glass, including the St Catherine Window and other works by Pre-Raphaelite artist Edward Burne-Jones. Lining the south side of the vast **Tom Quad** is the enormous **Hall**, with a magnificent hammerbeam ceiling. It may already be familiar to some visitors, since it was used for certain scenes in the Harry Potter films. To the north is the neoclassical **Peckwater Quad** and the smaller Canterbury Quad, where the **Picture Gallery** (tel: 01865-276 172; July–Sept Mon–Sat 10.30am–5pm, Sun 2–5pm, Oct–May Mon, Wed–Sat 10.30am–1pm, 2–4.30pm, Sun 2–4.30pm, June Mon, Wed–Sat 10.30am–5pm, Sun 2–5pm) has a fine collection of Renaissance paintings and drawings.

MERTON AND MAGDALEN

South of Christ Church, extending to the confluence of the Thames and Cherwell, is the glorious **Meadow** where cows graze. Along the Thames are the university boathouses, and it's here, in Eights Week in late May, that the college rowing races take place. The Broad Walk runs east–west across the Meadow, and from it a path cuts north to **Merton College D** (www.merton.ox.ac.uk; Mon–Fri 2–5pm, Sat–Sun 10am–5pm), founded in 1264. The **library** in **Mob Quad** (the oldest complete quadrangle in Oxford) was built in the 1370s (guided tours for a maximum of eight people, for details email tours@merton.ox.ac.uk). Much of the medieval structure remains, and the 16th-century bookshelves make it the first of its kind in England, where the books were set upright instead of being kept in presses. The **Max Beerbohm Room** in the Mob Quad's west wing is devoted to drawings by the writer and caricaturist (1872–1956), one of Merton's illustrious alumni.

From Merton make your way to Rose Lane and the **Botanic Garden E** (www. botanic-garden.ox.ac.uk; daily May–Aug 9am–6pm, Mar–Apr and Sept–Oct until 5pm, Nov–Feb until 4pm, last entry 45

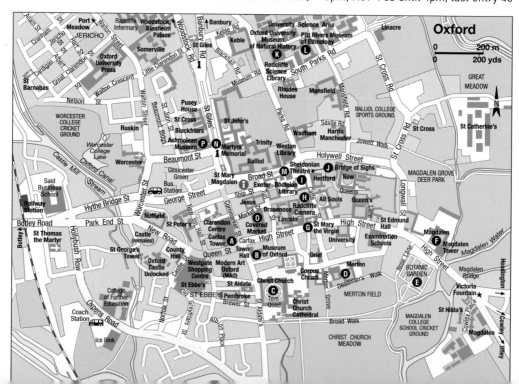

mins before closing). Founded in 1621 by Henry Danvers, Earl of Danby, as a physic garden for the School of Medicine, this is the oldest Botanic Garden in Britain. From the central pond, the view through the arch to Magdalen bell tower is magnificent. A great variety of roses are grown, and there's a wide range of tropical plants in the massive **glasshouses** next to the Cherwell. Leaving the gardens you arrive at the High Street, just opposite **Magdalen College F** – pronounced "maudlin" (www.magd.ox.ac.uk; daily July–Sept 10am–7pm, Oct–June 1pm–6pm), founded in 1458 by William of Waynflete. The chapel is a fine example of Perpendicular architecture, and the cloisters, which are at the heart of the college, are stunning. The **bell tower** (1505) was used as a vantage point by Royalist forces during the Civil War (1642–6) and is famous for the Latin grace sung from the top by choristers on May Morning. Behind the college's New Buildings is the deer park, **Magdalen Grove**, and the lovely **Water Walks**, a maze of stream-side paths.

THE HISTORIC CORE OF THE UNIVERSITY

From Magdalen, follow the High Street to **St Mary the Virgin G**, the original hub of the university, where all ceremonies were held and documents kept. The main entrance is the Baroque **South Porch**: built in 1637, it was directly inspired by the canopy that Bernini had just built over the high altar of St Peter's in Rome. The 15th-century nave is a fine example of the Perpendicular style, with slender columns and large windows. It was here, in 1556, that Archbishop Thomas Cranmer faced his persecutors for the last time. Refusing to denounce the Reformation, and retracting all previous recantations, he was dragged from the church and burned at the stake in Broad Street. The **tower** (Mon–Sat 9.30am–5pm, Sun noon–5pm, July–Aug until 6pm) offers a magnificent view of the city.

On the north side of Radcliffe Square stands the **Radcliffe Camera H** (not open to the public), founded as a library in 1749 and absorbed into the Bodleian

Radcliffe Camera.

The view of Radcliffe Camera over Oxford spires from Sheldonian Theatre.

⊘ FACT FILE

Location At the confluence of the Thames (the Isis) and the Cherwell.

By air Heathrow (40 miles/64km), connected by National Express and The Airline coach services every half-hour, journey time 1 hour 20 minutes; Gatwick (70 miles/112km), same operators run services every hour, journey time 2 hours 20 minutes; Birmingham International (65 miles/104km), trains from Birmingham International run hourly, journey time 1 hour.

By road M40 motorway from London (Junction 8) and the Midlands (Junction 9); journey time about 90 minutes from Central London except during rush hour.

By bus Oxford Tube from near London Victoria about every 15 minutes during the daytime and every 20 minutes for most of the evening up until 3am (tel: 01865-772 250; www.oxfordtube.com).

By train Every half an hour from London Paddington, tel: 0845-748 4950, journey time approximately 1 hour.

Guided tours Walking tours start at Oxford Information Centre, Broad Street; open-top bus tours, tel: 01865-790 522, www.citysightseeingoxford.com.

Bike hire Tel: 01865-316 885; www.summertowncycles.co.uk.

Tourist information Oxford Information Centre, 15–16 Broad Street; tel: 01865-686 430; www.experienceoxfordshire.org.

The Bodleian Library Quadrangle.

Christ Church College was used to represent Hogwarts' dining hall in the Harry Potter film series.

as a reading room in 1860. "Camera" simply means chamber, and John Radcliffe was a physician who, despite his renowned ill temper, made a huge fortune by treating the wealthy – including the monarch, William III. The Radcliffe Camera was built after his death in 1714 to house a library devoted to the sciences. The gracious round form of the Camera was suggested by Nicholas Hawksmoor, but it was another great 18th-century architect, James Gibbs, who produced the detailed designs.

The **Bodleian Library** ● itself dominates the square on the north side; it is one of the world's largest libraries, founded in 1602, and now houses over 12 million printed items, including 50,000 precious manuscripts. The **Old Schools Quadrangle**, in Jacobean-Gothic style, is the centrepiece, and just inside the main entrance on the far side is the old **Divinity School** (tel: 01865-287 400; guided tours of the library buildings, Mon–Sat 10.30 and 11.30am, 1, 2 and 3pm, university ceremonies permitting). Begun in 1426, it is noted for its elaborate, lierne-vaulted ceiling.

NEW COLLEGE LANE AND PARKS ROAD

Nearby, the **Bridge of Sighs** ● marks the beginning of New College Lane and links the two parts of Hertford College. This pretty bridge is an anglicised version of the Venice original. From here you could follow the lane to **New College** (not new at all, it was founded in 1379 and has lovely original cloisters), but our tour goes north, up Parks Road to the **Oxford University Museum of Natural History** ● (www.oum.ox.ac.uk; daily 10am–5pm; free), a splendid neo-Gothic structure begun in 1855, with slender iron columns and wrought-iron vaulting in the glass roof. It is a treasure house of zoological, entomological and geological exhibits, among them the skeleton of an iguanodon dominating the main hall, and a model of a dodo (plus a few remains of the real thing) brought to England in 1638.

Through the doors to the rear is the **Pitt Rivers Museum of Ethnology** ● (www.prm.ox.ac.uk; Mon noon–4.30pm, Tue–Sun 10am–4.30pm; free), an exotic collection of artefacts from all

corners of the world, begun by Lt-General Pitt Rivers (1827–1900) when serving abroad with the Grenadier Guards. A cabinet containing shrunken heads (*tsantas*) from Ecuador, along with shrinking instructions, is one of the more ghoulish exhibits in this temple to Victorian scientific curiosity.

BROAD STREET

Retrace your steps down Parks Road to the **Sheldonian Theatre** (www. sheldon.ox.ac.uk; Fri–Wed 10am–4pm, university ceremonies permitting, check website for specific dates), the first architectural scheme of the young Christopher Wren, which he designed in 1669 at the age of 30 while still a professor of astronomy. The bestowal of honorary degrees takes place here each June, but for most of the year the Sheldonian is used for concerts, talks and lectures. The ceiling is held up by huge wooden trusses in the roof, details of which can be seen on the climb up to the cupola.

Adjacent to the theatre is the **Museum of the History of Science** (www.mhs.ox.ac.uk; Tue–Sun 2–5pm; free), which displays the apparatus used during World War II to prepare penicillin for mass production. Opposite the Sheldonian, on the aptly named **Broad Street**, stands **Trinity College** (tel: 01865-279 900; www.trinity.ox.ac.uk; call to check opening times), founded by monks from Durham Abbey in 1286. Unlike most Oxford colleges, the Front Quad is not closed off from the street, and its lawn almost invites visitors to enter. Apart from the Baroque chapel, with its splendidly carved wooden panelling, stalls, screen and reredos, the principal attraction of Trinity is its fine gardens, entered through a wrought-iron screen from the Garden Quad.

Next to Trinity is **Blackwell's**, one of the world's most famous academic bookshops. Opened in 1879, the original shop was tiny, and even today the initial impression is of an average-sized provincial bookstore. Downstairs, however, is the underground Norrington Room, an enormous space stacked with shelves devoted to every topic under the sun.

⊙ Fact

It was in the pool known as Mercury in the centre of Tom Quad that Anthony Blanche was dunked in Evelyn Waugh's novel *Brideshead Revisited*. The pool is currently strictly out of bounds for undergraduates, with a heavy fine imposed for those who flaunt the rules.

Oxford's Bridge of Sighs.

A detail on Radcliffe Camera.

On the other side of Trinity is **Balliol College** (www.balliol.ox.ac.uk; daily 10am–5pm), renowned for having produced a greater number of politicians and statesmen than any other college in Oxford. They include former prime ministers Harold Macmillan and Edward Heath. Founded in 1263, Balliol vies with University College and Merton for the claim to be the oldest college in Oxford. Little of the original college remains; what we see today is mostly Victorian.

Much of the southern side of Broad Street is distinctive for its colourful facades above shops selling art and music books and artists' materials. Outside Balliol College, a cross in the road marks the point where the Protestant Martyrs, bishops Thomas Cranmer, Hugh Latimer and Nicholas Ridley, were burned at the stake. Around the corner at the southern end of broad St Giles', they are further commemorated by the **Martyrs' Memorial** , which was erected in 1841. Before Latimer and Ridley were consumed by the flames in 1555 (Cranmer followed a year later), Latimer offered these words to his colleague: "Be of good comfort, Master Ridley, and play the man. We shall this day light such a candle, by God's grace, in England, as I trust shall never be put out."

Oxford University Eights Week rowing races.

OXFORD'S SHOPPING DISTRICT

Now head south down the pedestrianised shopping street of Cornmarket and turn left into Market Street for the **Covered Market** . Established by the Paving Commission in 1774 as a permanent home for the stallholders cluttering the streets, this is an Oxford institution that can't be missed. The central range is dominated by the butchers, whose fronts are hung with a variety of carcasses. There are also a high-class delicatessen and a pasta shop; shops selling sausages and meat pies; as well as teashops and cafés – including the traditional "greasy spoon" – all vying for custom alongside smart boutiques and florists.

You can leave by an arcade via the tastefully restored **Golden Cross Yard**. Now equipped with a pizzeria, boutiques

⊘ ANNUAL EVENTS

May Morning the choir of Magdalen College sings a Latin grace from the Magdalen bell tower at 6am – an unforgettable sound. This is followed by bells ringing out over the city for 20 minutes and Morris dancing performances in the centre.

Ascension Day the ancient ceremony of Beating the Bounds starts at St Michael's Church in Northgate, and reconfirms the limits of the parish.

Eights Week held in May, in the fifth week of the Trinity (summer) term, when eight-oared crews from all colleges compete for the distinction of "head of the river". The boat that crosses the finishing line first without being bumped is the winner.

Spring Bank Holiday Monday the Lord Mayor's Parade of splendidly decorated floats and tableaux runs from St Giles to South Park.

Encaenia in the week following the end of the summer term (in June). This is the main honorary degree ceremony, when dignitaries process to the Sheldonian Theatre.

St Giles' Fair the Monday and Tuesday following the first Sunday of September is the date of this colourful and much-loved local fair, which has been taking place since 1624.

and shops selling organic products, this stands on the site of one of Oxford's oldest inns, where Shakespeare's plays are said to have been performed in the cobbled yard. Leaving the yard, you'll find yourself back at Carfax, where the tour began, but if you still have any energy left you could take a right turn onto Pembroke Street to **Modern Art Oxford** (www.modernartoxford.org.uk; Tue–Sat 10am–5pm, Sun noon–5pm; free), which occupies an old brewery warehouse, is devoted to modern and contemporary art, and mounts some interesting changing exhibitions – past artists have included Tracey Emin and Sol LeWitt. The café in the museum is a good place to relax and rest your legs after all your exertions.

THE ASHMOLEAN MUSEUM

Retracing your steps back to the Martyrs' Memorial, you will find, just beyond, the **Ashmolean Museum**  (www.ashmolean.org; Tue–Sun 10am–5pm; free), with its neoclassical facade stretching along the north side of Beaumont Street. Built from 1841 to 1845, the Ashmolean is the oldest museum in the country. Set up by Elias Ashmole in 1683, its first home was in purpose-built premises on Broad Street (now the Museum of the History of Science). The origin of the collection goes back to Lambeth, London. There, in a pub called The Ark, the 17th-century naturalist and royal gardener John Tradescant displayed the extensive collection of rarities and curiosities gathered on his trips to Europe or given to him by sea captains. After his death in 1638, Tradescant's son, also called John, added numerous items from the New World. The collection was bequeathed to Ashmole, who presented it to the university. The museum has been extensively redeveloped, with a new building and 39 new galleries opened by the Queen in 2009. In 2011, in the second phase of development, the galleries of Ancient Eygpt and Nubia opened, enabling the display of previous unseen works. You can still view items from Tradescant's collection in the Ark to Ashmolean gallery (room 8,

The Ashmolean Museum.

⊙ Where

Around 40 miles (70km) northeast of Oxford is a place that was once Britain's best-kept secret. **Bletchley Park** (www.bletchleypark.org.uk; Mar–Oct daily 9.30am–5pm, Nov–Feb daily 9.30am–4pm) was a rambling country estate that became the heart of Britain's codebreaking operations during World War II. It was here that Germany's seemingly impenetrable Enigma code was broken, and where the genius Alan Turing worked to build the Bombe, the machine that helped to break it. If travelling from London, you can reach Bletchley by train from Euston in 40 minutes.

Morris's early production line at Cowley.

level 1), which includes the star attraction, **Powhattan's Mantle**. Powhattan was a Virginian Native American chief and, as any child from the USA will tell you, the father of Pocahontas.

The **Antiquities Department** has a fine Egyptian section, and extensive collections covering Ancient Greece, Rome and the Near East, as well as Dark Age Europe and Anglo-Saxon Britain. The museum's most famous artefact is an Anglo-Saxon item, the **Alfred Jewel**. Found in Somerset in 1693, it is regarded as the finest piece of Saxon art ever discovered. It bears the inscription *Aelfred mec heht gewyrcan* ("[King] Alfred had me made").

The other main attraction is the collection of **Western Art**, which includes drawings by Michelangelo and Raphael, as well as *The Hunt in the Forest*, painted by the Florentine artist Paolo Uccello in 1466. In addition to its world-renowned collections, the museum holds temporary exhibitions of contemporary art; past big-hitters have included Jeff Koons and Georgia O'Keeffe.

PORT MEADOW

At the end of Beaumont Street, stretching north, is Walton Street. Look out for the turning on your left down Walton Well Road, via which you come to a bridge over the railway and canal, leading to the 400-acre (160-hectare) Port Meadow. Used for grazing ever since its first mention in the Domesday Book (1087), the meadow is a rare piece of Old England; it has never been ploughed. Dotted with cattle and horses, it is also rich in birdlife and wild flowers. Annual winter floods bring flocks of wildfowl and waders, and the meadow is a magnet for migrating birds, especially geese.

In summer, you can often make out the outlines of Iron Age farming enclosures and hut circles, delineated by the buttercups that grow taller over buried features such as ditches and foundation trenches. At weekends, students wander along the footpaths to The Trout and Perch pubs, while others ply the river on punts or sailing dinghies.

⊙ CAR CONNECTIONS

In 1901, young William Richard Morris, who had begun his working life in his early teens repairing bicycles, set up his own cycle shop in Oxford High Street.

An ambitious and talented young man, he saw that the future lay with the horseless carriage, and by 1912 had progressed to building the prototype of the "Bullnose" Morris Oxford car in a garage in Longwall Street. Just one year later he established his automobile plant at nearby Cowley, Britain's first mass-production line for affordable cars. He sold 393 cars in his first year and by the end of the 1920s he was producing 100,000 annually. He also built a separate factory for his successful MG Super Sports model.

Knighted in 1928, Morris became Viscount Nuffield a decade later, partly in honour of his generosity to hospitals and other medical projects.

In 1937, he donated the site and funds to build Nuffield College. He had always had a prickly relationship with the university and city authorities, and was anxious that the new college should help build a bridge between the academic and non-academic worlds. He would be proud of the research developments that have taken place there in recent decades.

THE GREAT PALACE OF BLENHEIM

Blenheim Palace, near Woodstock, is a Baroque masterpiece, a place of pilgrimage and a good day out for children.

Some 8 miles (13km) northwest of Oxford is the attractive little Georgian town of **Woodstock,** which originally grew prosperous through glove-making. Pleasant as it is, it is overshadowed by its grand neighbour, **Blenheim Palace** (www.blenheimpalace.com; house and gardens: mid-Feb–mid-Dec daily 10.30am–5.30pm; park: all year 9am–6pm or dusk). In the early 18th century this great palace, designed by Sir John Vanbrugh and his assistant Nicholas Hawksmoor, was given by a grateful nation to John Churchill, 1st Duke of Marlborough, after his victory over the French at the Battle of Blenheim in 1704. Although recognised as a masterpiece of English Baroque, its sheer ostentation made it an object of controversy right from the start.

THE PALACE AND GROUNDS

The gilded **State Rooms** are the most impressive, decorated with tapestries, paintings and sculpture; and the beautiful **Long Library** contains more than 10,000 volumes. Many visitors are most interested in Blenheim as the birthplace and home of Sir Winston Churchill (1874–1965). There is a large collection of his manuscripts, paintings, books and letters, and visitors can also see the room in which the great man was born. The stately home sometimes hosts solo art exhibitions, featuring artworks and installations by the likes of Jenny Holzer, Ai Weiwei and Yves Klein. The last attraction at the palace is The Untold Story, a high-tech, interactive exhibition on lesser-known aspects of the history of the palace.

It is quite possible to spend an enjoyable day at Blenheim without even going into the house. The park in which it stands, covering some 2,100 acres (800 hectares), was landscaped by "Capability" Brown (1715–83). Its centrepiece is the **lake**, spanned by Vanbrugh's Grand Bridge. The shallow side of the lake, called the Queen Pool, is home to a variety of waterfowl, which makes it popular with birdwatchers.

It was in the little Temple of Diana overlooking the lake that Sir Winston proposed to Clementine Hozier in August 1908. The young couple made their home in London, but spent a lot of time at Blenheim.

Another of the park's attractions is the **Marlborough Maze,** the second-largest in the world. It occupies the Walled Garden at the south side of the estate, an area known as the **Pleasure Gardens,** which includes putting greens, giant chessboards and bouncy castles for children, together with a herb garden, butterfly house, tearoom and adventure playground. The area can be reached on a miniature railway which trundles through the grounds, but it's also nice to walk, admiring the ancient oak trees as you go.

The 1st Duke has a large monument in the palace chapel, but Sir Winston and his wife are buried in Bladon parish churchyard, just outside the walls of the park.

The west facade of Blenheim Palace.

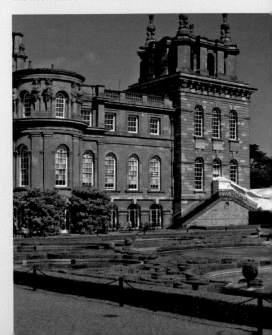

Sheep graze at Chipping Campden.

THE COTSWOLDS

To many people, this area, with its Roman remains and ancient castles, its picturesque villages and leafy lanes, its lush river valleys and riverside pubs, represents the essence of England.

The creamy-white limestone of the Cotswold Hills defines the boundaries of the region and gives it its character, a harmonious landscape of fields bordered by dry-stone walls, churches with majestic towers, opulent townhouses and snug cottages with roofs of limestone tiles. Its historic villages and small towns remain remarkably intact, and the region conforms with many visitors' idea of rural England. These charms have not been lost on the English themselves, and an influx of homebuyers from London has made the area an affluent one.

Many people start a visit to the Cotswolds at **Oxford ❶**, usually combined with a trip to **Blenheim Palace ❷** (see page 145). From Oxford, go west on the A40 and make a short detour off to the right to the romantic ruins of 15th-century manor house **Minster Lovell Hall** with its interesting dovecote (daily during daylight hours, exterior only; free). Then it's back on the road again to **Burford ❸**, which has one of the region's finest high streets, lined with 17th- and 18th-century cottages and descending sharply to a packhorse bridge over the River Windrush. A massive church stands beside the bridge, with a splendid Renaissance monument to Henry VIII's barber and surgeon, Edward Harman.

West of Burford the Windrush flows through a series of unspoilt villages,

but we are heading a short way south on the A361 to **Lechlade**, where Percy Bysshe Shelley (1792–1822) was inspired to write *A Summer Evening Churchyard*. You can follow his footsteps on a path inevitably called Shelley's Walk, to **St John Bridge**, at the highest navigable point on the Thames. Beside the bridge is the **Trout Inn** (very pretty, but often crowded) and a minor road to **Kelmscott Manor ❹** (www.sal.org.uk/kelmscott-manor; currently closed for restoration, set to reopen in spring 2020), a Tudor farmhouse that became

⊙ Main attractions
Chedworth Roman Villa
Westonbirt Arboretum
Painswick Rococo Garden
Berkeley Castle
Gloucester Cathedral
Hidcote Manor Garden
Kiftsgate Court

Map on page 156

Kelmscott Manor.

famous as the summer residence of the poet and craftsman William Morris (1834–96). A typical Cotswold stone-built house, the manor has a roof of split stones of which Morris said: "It gives me the same sort of pleasure in their orderly beauty as a fish's scales or a bird's feathers." There is a comprehensive account of Morris's life and the Arts and Crafts Movement which he co-founded, and works by several members of the movement, including Burne-Jones and Rossetti. The old kitchen is open to the public, with displays of carved panels from the Society of Antiquaries London collection. William Morris and his wife, Jane, are buried beside the rustic and unspoilt village church – the kind he loved most.

FAIRFORD TO CHEDWORTH

Some 5 miles (8km) west in **Fairford** ❺ is the finest of Cotswold churches, St Mary the Virgin, with an extraordinary 15th-century stained-glass window, which depicts the biblical story from the Creation to the Crucifixion. The Last Judgement window, with its fiery red devils with spiked teeth and yellow horns, and grim details of eternal punishment, is a masterpiece.

Continue along the A417 to Ampney Crucis – which also has a fine church – then take a right turn on the B4425 to **Barnsley** ❻, where you skirt Barnsley Park before entering the main street of a village where overhead cables and television aerials were once banned in an attempt to preserve its timeless

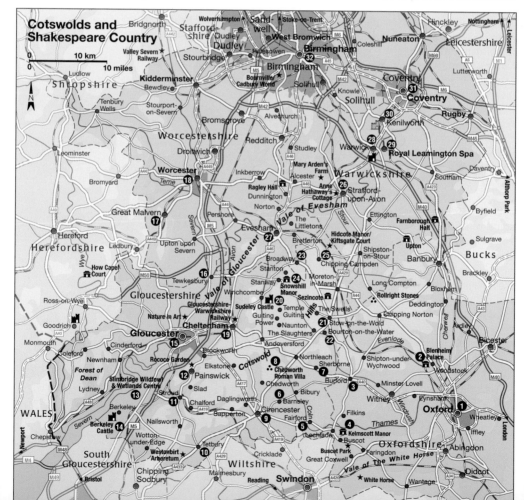

tranquillity. The village is best known for **Barnsley House**, where the splendid 4-acre (1.6-hectare) garden created by Rosemary Verey (1918–2001) became one of the most visited in Britain. The house is now an exclusive hotel, but the garden is open to the public on selected days (for details tel: 01285-740 000; www.barnsleyhouse.com).

The B4425 joins the A40. Turn left here, then look for a right turn signposted to **Sherborne ❼** (estate: daily; free), where 18th-century **water meadows** have been restored to working order by the National Trust. Sherborne was built as a model estate village in the mid-19th century and consists of rows of attractive identical stone cottages. Also here is Lodge Park, a beautiful 17th-century hunting lodge, created in 1634 for high-living gambler John "Crump" Dutton (www.nationaltrust.org.uk/lodge-park-and-sherborne-estate; Mar–Oct Fri–Mon 11am–4pm, Nov–Feb closed Sat).

Turn left when the A429 joins the A40, and just south of Northleach you'll see signs to **Chedworth Roman Villa ❽** (www.nationaltrust.org.

uk/chedworth-roman-villa; daily Apr–Oct 10am–5pm, Mar and early Nov 10am–4pm), in a delightful woodland setting overlooking the Coln Valley. Chedworth is one of the largest Roman villas discovered in Britain, with two bathhouses, a latrine and a water-shrine. Mosaics here include a wonderful depiction of the seasons, with Winter personified as a peasant in a billowing hooded cloak bringing home a hare for the pot. In one corner of the site is a *nymphaeum*, a small sanctuary to the goddess of the spring who supplied the villa with water. The Romans introduced the edible snails that are found around the villa and inhabit the railway cuttings, which are now a nature reserve. They used to be fed on milk to fatten them up. Chedworth village has a handsome Norman church with a fine stone-carved 15th-century pulpit, and a good pub, the Seven Tuns, in which to relax after your sightseeing. It dates back to 1610.

CIRENCESTER

Whether you pronounce it "Cissiter", as purists suggest, or "Ciren", as

Parish Church of St John the Baptist, Cirencester.

The Bath House at Chedworth Roman Villa.

Cycling in Bourton-on-the-Hill.

the locals say, the market town of **Cirencester ⑨** used to be Corinium, the hub of a network of Roman roads, and it retains the rectilinear street plan of a Roman town. Gardeners are used to turning up pieces of mosaic, and there are some spectacular examples in the excellent **Corinium Museum** (www.coriniummuseum.org; Apr–Oct Mon–Sat 10am–5pm, Sun 2–5pm, Nov–Mar Mon–Sat 10am–4pm, Sun 2–4pm). Here, you can come face-to-face with Roman daily life through reconstructions of rooms from a town-house and interactive displays. The Anglo-Saxon Gallery reveals treasures from a cemetery site at Lechlade, and substantial remains of the town walls are still in evidence along with a well-preserved amphitheatre. The museum also hosts film screenings, creative workshops and history lectures.

Cirencester also has the interesting **Parish Church of St John the Baptist**, with a fine 15th-century wine-glass pulpit, one of the few to survive the Reformation. If the magnificent tower is open (tel: 01285-659 317; times vary), climb

to the top for a view of **Cirencester Mansion**, otherwise hidden from view by what is said to be the world's tallest yew hedge. Beyond the mansion the broad tree-lined avenues of **Cirencester Park** are open to the public. An early example of English landscape gardening, it was laid out by the 1st Earl of Bathurst in the 18th century, with some help from his friend the poet Alexander Pope (1688–1744). The walk to the park takes you past handsome houses built by wealthy wool merchants.

TETBURY TO BERKELEY CASTLE

We are going a little way south now, to **Tetbury ⑩** off the A433, which was a quiet backwater until Prince Charles moved to nearby Highgrove. It's an attractive little place, with a 17th-century market hall, numerous antiques shops and a wonderfully theatrical church, a rare example of Georgian Gothic built between 1777 and 1781. The Highgrove Shop on Long Street sells Prince Charles's range of organic foods as well as gifts for homes and gardens.

⊘ FACT FILE

By car The M40 and M4 motorways provide easy access to the Cotswolds from London, as does the M5 from Bristol, the Midlands and the north.

By bus National Express from London Victoria to Oxford, Cheltenham, Cirencester and Gloucester, www.nationalexpress.com.

By train Regular services from London Paddington to Oxford, Cheltenham and Gloucester. National Rail Enquiries, tel: 03457-484 950; www.national-rail.co.uk; to buy tickets online, www.thetrainline.com.

Main festivals The Cheltenham Festival of horseracing (Mar), http://cheltenham.thejockeyclub.co.uk; Cheltenham Festivals of Music (July) and Literature (Oct), www.cheltenhamfestivals.co.uk; Treefest, Westonbirt Arboretum (Aug bank holiday), www.forestryengland.uk/westonbirt-the-national-arboretum.

Outdoor activities Guided walks, The Cotswold AONB Partnership, www.cotswoldsaonb.org.uk; cycle hire, Cotswold Country Cycles, tel: 01386-438 706, www.cotswoldcountrycycles.com; horse riding, Camp Riding Centre, tel: 01285-821 219, www.cotswolds.info/equestrian/riding-schools.

For children Berkeley Castle, tel: 01453-810 303, www.berkeley-castle.com; Slimbridge Wildfowl & Wetlands Centre, 01453-891 900, www.wwt.org.uk/wetland-centres/slimbridge.

Information Oxford, tel: 01865-686 430; Bourton on the Water, tel: 01451-820 211; Cheltenham, tel: 01242-522 878; Gloucester, tel: 01452-396 572.

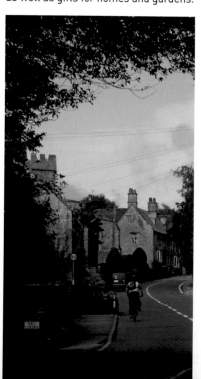

Just south of the town lies the **Weston-birt Arboretum** (tel: 0300-067 4890; daily 9am–4.30pm), a glorious estate covering around 600 acres (240 hectares), its trees interplanted with camellias, azaleas, rhododendrons, cherries and maples which bring thousands of visitors during May and October for the spring and autumn colour. There are around 3,000 species of trees and shrubs, many of them rare or endangered. It's a great place for families too, with plenty of children's activities.

Next we head north for **Stroud ⑪**, on the A46. The steep-sided valleys around the town provided it with fast-running streams, ideal conditions for woollen mills in the 18th century, when Stroud was the capital of this industry. A few of the grand old mills continue to produce high-quality cloth. The popular farmers' market is held every Saturday 9am–2pm.

Some 3 miles (5km) north along A46 is **Painswick ⑫**, known for its elegant stone houses; a churchyard with 99 topiaried yews forming a series of avenues to the church; and some elaborately carved "table top" and "tea caddy" tombs. North

of the town is Painswick Rococo Garden (www.rococogarden.org.uk; mid-Jan–Oct daily 10.30am–5pm, Nov 10.30am–4pm), designed as an 18th-century pleasure ground for the gentry. Dotted with temples and gazebos and surrounded by woodland, the garden is magical throughout the year, and is particularly impressive at snowdrop time (February), when the flowers carpet the ground.

Those interested in wildlife could make a slight detour here (take the A419 which crosses the M5, then turn left on the A38) to the **Slimbridge Wildfowl & Wetlands Centre ⑬** (www.wwt.org.uk; daily Apr–Oct 9.30am–5.30pm, Nov–Mar until 5pm), founded by artist and naturalist Sir Peter Scott (1909–89) in 1946 on a marshy site beside the River Severn. The ponds are home to an array of wildfowl from around the world, and viewing hides are dotted around at strategic points. It's possible to take a canoe safari, watch birds flying freely in the heated tropical house and even visit Crane School, where young cranes are being hand-reared and prepared for life in the wild. Scott House, located on site, is a new museum

Berkeley Castle's Great Hall

Inside Gloucester Cathedral.

Houses in Painswick.

designed to recreate the former home of Sir Peter Scott and his family, filled with personal artefacts, original artworks and conservationist memorabilia, opened in September 2019.

While you're on this side of the motorway, you might wish to visit a splendid castle just south of Slimbridge. At **Berkeley Castle** ⑭ (www.berkeley-castle.com; Apr–Oct Sun–Wed 11am–5pm), with its massive Norman keep, you can see the Great Hall, where the barons met before riding to Runnymede to force King John to sign Magna Carta in 1215; and the cell where Edward II spent his last days before he was murdered in 1327. Despite this regicide, the castle has remained in the hands of the same family from 1153 to the present – Shakespeare apparently wrote *A Midsummer Night's Dream* for a Berkeley family wedding.

GLOUCESTER

Back on the A38, we are now heading north for **Gloucester** ⑮, not one of the most beautiful cities but one of great historical interest and full of unusual and fascinating museums (see box). Founded by the Romans, it became an important Saxon town, and later one of the country's busiest ports. From the renovated docklands area you can take a short cruise through the port and along the canal on the *King Arthur* (tel: 01452-318 200 for details and bookings; times vary, check ahead; departure from the quayside of the Gloucester Waterways Museum). Gloucester's Norman **Cathedral** (www.gloucestercathedral.org.uk; daily 7.30am–6pm; guided tours Mon–Sat 10.30am–4pm, Sun noon–2.30pm; donation requested), small by cathedral standards, has two fine tombs: that of Robert, Duke of Normandy, William the Conqueror's eldest son, and of Edward II, murdered at nearby Berkeley Castle (see page 160). Today it's famous as the setting for many scenes in the Harry Potter films.

You may now decide to go north to Tewkesbury and Great Malvern, or east to Cheltenham. For **Tewkesbury** ⑯ take the A417/B4211. It's a pretty little town on the confluence of the Severn and Avon rivers, and a number of its half-timbered buildings now serve as pubs – the 17th-century Bell Inn, now a hotel, is worth a stop. **Tewkesbury Abbey** is a fine Norman church (open daily; donation) with splendid views of the Malvern Hills from the top of its square tower.

Twelve miles (20km) northwest is **Great Malvern** ⑰, once a spa town and still known for Malvern water which gushes from the spectacular surrounding hills. It's a lively cultural centre, synonymous with the composer Sir Edward Elgar (1857–1934) who lived nearby. The annual Autumn in Malvern Festival (tel: 01684-892 277; www.malvernfestival.co.uk; Sept/Oct) offers a feast of music, literature and fine-arts events.

A few miles further north will take you to the historic city of **Worcester** ⑱. Perched above the River Severn is the fine 12th-century **cathedral** (www.worcestercathedral.co.uk; daily 7.30am–6pm; free), while on New Street there are impressive timbered buildings from the

Tudor period. On the High Street is the Georgian Guildhall with its grand assembly rooms hung with historic portraits.

Worcester also paid an important role in the English Civil War. Visitors can learn more at the **Commandery** (www.museumsworcestershire.org.uk/museums/the-commandery; tel: 01905-361 821; Tue–Sat 10am–5pm, Sun 1.30–5pm), which the Royalists used as their headquarters, and now functions as the city's history museum.

During the Industrial Revolution, canals were introduced and porcelain factories flourished to complement the city's longstanding trade in textiles and gloves. The **Worcester Porcelain Museum** (www.museumofroyalworcester.org; Mon–Sat Mar–Oct 10am–5pm, Nov–Feb 10am–4pm) charts this industrial history and houses the world's largest collection of the fine local porcelain.

For many, though, Worcester will be forever associated with the music of Sir Edward Elgar. The composer was born in 1857, at Broadheath, just 3 miles (5km) from Worcester, and his birthplace is now a **museum** (https://www.

nationaltrust.org.uk/the-firs; daily 10am–5pm, winter until 4pm). In Worcester itself, the Elgar Walk takes enthusiasts on a tour of significant Elgar landmarks, beginning and ending at the junction of College Street and College Precincts, near the cathedral.

ROYAL CONNECTIONS

If you opted for this short diversion you could now return south on the M5 to **Cheltenham** ⑲, the gracious Regency spa town which became popular as a summer resort after George II visited to "take the waters" in 1788. To get the feel of the town, stroll along the broad leafy avenue known as The Prom, where a splendid fountain is dominated by a statue of Neptune. To one end of The Prom lie the Imperial Gardens and elegant Montpellier Walk; to the other, The Wilson, Cheltenham Art Gallery and Museum (www.cheltenhammuseum. org.uk; Tue–Wed, Fri–Sat 9.30am–5.15pm, Thu until 7.45pm, Sun 11am–4pm; free), housed in smart, spacious quarters. Among the treasures in its collection are fine items of furniture

⊙ Kids

Children will love a steam-train ride on the Gloucestershire–Warwickshire Railway (days vary; check tel: 01242-621 405 or www. gwsr.com), which runs for 15 miles (24km) between Cheltenham Racecourse and Broadway.

Gloucester's historic waterfront.

⊙ GLOUCESTER'S BEST MUSEUMS

Gloucester Waterways Museum (www.canalrivertrust.org.uk; check for opening times) is set in Gloucester's historic docks. This excellent, child-friendly museum tells the story of England's waterways.

City Museum and Art Gallery (www.bit.ly/GloucesterCityMuseum; Tue–Sat 10am–4pm, with exceptions) houses a varied collection that includes dinosaur displays and fossils, local flora, 10th-century Saxon sculpture and medieval metalwork.

Soldiers of Gloucester Museum (www.soldiersofglos.com; daily 10am–5pm). The history of local regiments, and a section on women at war.

House of the Tailor of Gloucester (www.tailor-of-gloucester.org.uk; Mon–Sat 10am–4.30pm, Sun noon–4pm; free) reveals the real-life tale behind the Beatrix Potter story of the mayor's magic waistcoat.

Nature in Art (Wallsworth Hall, Twigworth, 2 miles/3km north of the city on A38; www.natureinart.org.uk; Tue–Sun 10am–5pm). A collection inspired by nature, with works by artists from Picasso to David Shepherd.

In the picturesque village of Chipping Campden.

Enjoying a sunny day at Cheltenham's Imperial Gardens.

made by members of the Arts and Crafts Movement. Nearby, in Clarence Road, the **Holst Birthplace Museum** (www.holstmuseum.org.uk; Apr–mid-Dec Tue–Sat 10.30am–4pm) pays homage to composer Gustav Holst (1874–1934), who spent his early years here. The house offers a delightful glimpse into the upstairs-downstairs world of the town's Victorians and Edwardians.

North of Cheltenham on the B4632 is a place with royal connections of a different kind: **Sudeley Castle** ⑳ (www.sudeleycastle.co.uk; daily mid-Mar–Oct 10am–5pm, Nov–mid-Dec 10am–5pm; last admission 1hr before closing) was briefly the home of Katherine Parr (1512–48), the last of Henry VIII's six wives, who survived him. Only six weeks after becoming a widow she married Lord Admiral Seymour, Sudeley's owner, but died a year later and was buried in the chapel. The castle was ruined during the Civil War which erupted in 1642, but restored during the 19th century. Among its glories are some fine furnishings, paintings by Rubens and Van Dyck, and romantic English gardens.

Continue north for a short way on the B4632, then turn right on the B4077 for **Stow-on-the-Wold** ㉑, the Cotswolds' highest town ("Stow-on-the-Wold where the wind blows cold", as the local rhyme has it). Here, royal connections were nothing to boast about: the church was used as a prison for Royalists during the Civil War and suffered considerable damage. The unusual north porch, with two yew trees growing out of the masonry, was added as part of the 1680 restoration. The enormous market square was in use until the 1980s, and the wooden stocks on the green were used to punish those who looked on market days as an opportunity for pilfering. Stow now has a reputation as an antiques centre, and you will find numerous interesting shops and galleries.

MODEL VILLAGES AND MANOR HOUSES

Around Stow are some of the Cotswolds' most attractive villages, among them **Upper** and **Lower Slaughter**, and **Bourton-on-the-Water** ㉒. The latter has far too many gift shops and cafés, but it remains a pretty little place, with elegant 18th-century bridges spanning the Windrush as it flows through the centre. The **Model Village** (www.themodelvillage.com; daily 10am–4pm, summer until 6pm), in the garden of the Old New Inn, is a delightful miniature reconstruction of Bourton; and the **Model Railway** (www.bourtonmodelrailway.co.uk; June–Aug daily 11am–5pm; Sept–May Sat–Sun only) will delight anyone who is nostalgic about train sets.

Close by is **Birdland** (www.birdland.co.uk; daily Apr–Oct 10am–5pm, Nov–Mar 10am–4pm), where most of the 500 or so birds were bred and can wander freely in natural surroundings. The best time to visit is at penguin feeding time, which commences at around 11am and 2.30pm.

Backtrack now to the A424/A44 to visit **Broadway** ㉓, a manicured and

mellow village, crammed with antiques shops, art galleries and teashops. The original parish church, about a mile away, has ancient topiaried yew trees, rustic monuments and a sense of tranquillity. In the village itself, the imposing Lygon Arms Hotel is a 16th-century building restored by members of the Arts and Crafts Movement in the early 20th century.

William Morris, co-founder of the movement, spent holidays at Broadway Tower, in nearby **Broadway Tower Country Park** (www.broadwaytower.co.uk; daily 10am–5pm). On a clear day it is possible to see 13 counties from the 18th-century tower.

Close to Morris's tower (and reached by a turning off the A44 at Broadway Green just before you enter the village) is **Snowshill Manor** ㉔ (www.national trust.org.uk/snowshill-manor-and-garden; mid-Mar–Oct daily, manor: noon–5pm, gardens: 11am–5.30pm), an attractive Tudor manor house, restored by the eccentric Charles Paget Wade from 1919 to 1951. The Arts and Crafts influence is evident in his work. He also assembled an eclectic range of 22,000 objects, ranging from musical instruments to toys to Japanese armour. For some, Snowshill's greatest appeal is the garden, conceived as a series of outdoor rooms around the house.

CHIPPING CAMPDEN

Chipping Campden ㉕ is an idyllic Cotswolds town, kept in a state of perfect preservation by the Campden Trust, which ensures that power cables are hidden and modern shopfronts banished. The sheer variety of buildings here is unusual, from the flamboyant Jacobean gateway of Campden House to the Perpendicular-style church of St James, the 14th-century house of a wealthy merchant, William Grevel, and the Renaissance-style Market Hall, built in 1627. A scattering of eclectic boutique shops, quaint cafés and fire-warmed pubs

makes it one of the most favoured Cotswolds getaways.

Three miles (5km) outside town are two delights for garden-lovers. **Hidcote Manor Garden** (www.nationaltrust.org.uk/hidcote; Mar–Oct daily 10am–5pm, with exceptions), created at the beginning of the 20th century by Lawrence "Johnnie" Johnstone, is a highly architectural garden, known for its rare shrubs and trees and for some outstanding herbaceous borders. Laid out in a series of "rooms", it influenced Vita Sackville-West when she created her garden at Sissinghurst. Even those who prefer a more naturalistic style of gardening are usually won over by Hidcote.

Just down the road is another stunning garden, **Kiftsgate Court** (www.kiftsgate.co.uk; Apr and Sept Sun–Mon, Wed 2–6pm, May–July Sat–Wed noon–6pm, Aug Sat–Wed 2–6pm), an informal terraced garden famous for its roses, especially the *rosa filipes* (Kiftsgate Rose), which grows at will and flowers profusely in June. If you are visiting at this time, it makes a lovely last stop on your tour of the Cotswolds.

The ancient market at Chipping Campden.

Honey-coloured buildings in Chipping Campden.

Anne Hathaway's Cottage in Stratford.

SHAKESPEARE COUNTRY

You may go to Warwickshire to see Stratford, Shakespeare's town, but it has many other treasures – great castles, cathedrals and the art galleries of Birmingham, England's second city.

The novelist Henry James (1843–1916) described his much-loved, adopted county of Warwickshire as "mid-most England, unmitigated England..." and this is the heart of the region covered in this chapter. It is a land of patchwork fields, mellow brick houses and country lanes, with the River Avon running through it. But this area of the West Midlands also contains Birmingham, England's second-largest city, and Coventry, which was once synonymous with the British car industry.

STRATFORD-UPON-AVON

A tour of Shakespeare Country must begin in **Stratford-upon-Avon** ㉖, where the Bard was born on 23 April 1564, St George's Day. Stratford is a pleasant town, set on an attractive stretch of the Avon, where it is joined by the Stratford Canal. Start your tour at the point where the two bridges over the Avon funnel pedestrians and traffic into town, and where there is a large car park and the ever-busy Tourist Information Centre. Beyond the traffic, in **Bancroft Gardens**, overlooking the canal basin, is the **Gower Memorial** Ⓐ, on which Shakespeare sits, surrounded by characters from his plays: Hamlet, Prince Hal, Falstaff and Lady Macbeth.

Follow Bridge Street now to Henley Street, where the informative

Shakespeare Centre (tel: 01789-204 016; www.shakespeare.org.uk) stands next door to **Shakespeare's Birthplace** Ⓑ (daily Apr–late Oct 9am–5pm, late Oct–Mar 10am–4pm). This timber-framed building was the Shakespeare family home and business premises – his father was a glove-maker, wool merchant and moneylender, and became mayor in 1568. The building has been authentically restored and furnished (it served as a pub before it was bought for the nation in 1847).

Main attractions
Shakespeare's Birthplace
Royal Shakespeare
  Theatre
Anne Hathaway's Cottage
Warwick Castle
Royal Leamington Spa
Kenilworth Castle
Birmingham Back to
  Backs

Maps on pages
156, 167

Harvard House in Stratford.

⊙ Tip

Save money and buy a pass that covers entry to all five historic Shakespeare houses – Shakespeare's Birthplace, Anne Hathaway's Cottage, Harvard House, New Place and Hall's Croft. The ticket also includes Mary Arden's Farm (3miles/5km from Stratford at Wilmcote), a fully working Tudor farm. To book tickets tel: 01789-204 016 or online at www.shakespeare.org.uk.

William Shakespeare.

In the nearby High Street is a building not associated with Shakespeare: **Harvard House** (tel: 01789-204 016; daily 10am–5pm, with exceptions), covered with ornate carved heads and friezes. This was the childhood home of Katherine Rogers, who married Robert Harvard and whose son John emigrated to America in the 17th century before becoming principal benefactor of the university that bears his name.

Continue to Chapel Street, where **Nash's House**, former home of Shakespeare's granddaughter Elizabeth, is a Tudor building stocked with 17th-century tapestries and furnishings. It adjoins **New Place** (check opening times), the house where Shakespeare died in 1616. These sites both received a facelift and reopened in July 2016 to commemorate the 400th anniversary of Shakespeare's death. The entrance is now through the original gatehouse and upgraded displays relate to Shakespeare's family life and works he wrote while living here. Beyond lies a Tudor-style knot garden and the Great Garden where two mulberry trees stand, one planted by the actress Peggy Ashcroft; her ashes were scattered there after her death in 1991.

Opposite the site of New Place stands the **Guild Chapel**, mostly 15th-century but originally founded in 1269. Over the chancel arch are the remains of what must have been a spectacular wall painting of the Last Judgement. Continue along Church Street, past the wonderfully intact **Almshouses**, and turn into the street appropriately named Old Town where stands Hall's Croft, home of Shakespeare's daughter, Susanna. At the bottom, go right into Trinity Street to **Holy Trinity Church** (www.stratford-upon-avon.org; Apr–Sept Mon–Sat 9am–5pm, Sun 12.30–5pm, Oct–Mar Mon–Sat 10am–4pm, Sun 12.30–5pm; donation), dating mostly from the 14th century. It is worth a visit for its own sake, but most people come to pay homage at **Shakespeare's grave** beneath a simple stone in the chancel.

The riverside park can be entered through Old Town. Dominating the far

⊙ FACT FILE

By car The area is fringed with motorways: the M5 to the west, and the M1 and M6 to the north and east; the M42 orbits Birmingham from the south; the M40 from London and Oxford gives direct access to Stratford, Warwick and Royal Leamington Spa.

By coach There are National Express services from London Victoria Coach Station, as well as between major towns in the area; www.nationalexpress.com.

By rail Direct services run from London Paddington to Evesham, with other services to Stratford and Leamington; from London Marylebone to Warwick; and from London Euston to Birmingham and Coventry; tel: 0345-748 4950, www.nationalrail.co.uk.

By air From Birmingham Airport there are flights to and from New York, plus internal flights and scheduled and charter flights to more than 40 European cities; www.birminghamairport.co.uk.

Tourist information Birmingham, www.visitbirmingham.com; Coventry and Warwickshire, tel: 024-7622 5616; Evesham, tel: 01386-446 944; Leamington, tel: 01926-742 762; Stratford, www.shakespeare-country.co.uk.

Guided tours Stratford Town Walks, tel: 01789-292 478, daily; City Sightseeing, open-top bus tours to Shakespeare sites, tel: 01789-299 123.

end is the **Royal Shakespeare Theatre** (image), adjacent to the galleried Elizabethan-style **Swan Theatre**. Built in the early 1930s, after the previous building was destroyed by fire, the theatre, which has some marvellous Art Deco interior fittings, is home to the Royal Shakespeare Company (RSC). The entire complex has been revamped, with state-of-the-art facilities, including a thrust-stage (for various tours, tel: 01789-403 493; www.rsc.org.uk).

We are now back at Bancroft Gardens and the nine-arched bridge where we began, but there is one more pilgrimage to make: **Anne Hathaway's Cottage** (image) (daily Apr–late Oct 9am–5pm, late Oct–Mar 10am–4pm) is in **Shottery**, about 1 mile (1.6km) west of town. It's a delightful timber-framed thatched cottage, with an idyllic cottage garden (not the working farmyard it would have been in Anne's day). The house remained in the Hathaway family until 1892, when it was bought by the Birthplace Trust. Beyond the house is the **Shakespeare Tree Garden**, planted with most of the trees mentioned in the plays.

THE VALE OF EVESHAM

Follow the River Avon now for a bit of a detour, crossing into Worcestershire to the Vale of Evesham, with its orchards and market gardens. The river swings in a great bend around the town of **Evesham** (27), once the site of one of the most important abbeys in the Midlands, founded in 701. The abbey's wealth funded the great Perpendicular **Bell Tower**, still the town's most important landmark. Attractive parkland popular with picnickers drops gently towards the river.

At the town museum housed in the **Almonry** (www.almonryevesham.org; Mon–Sat 10am–5pm, Nov–Feb closed Wed) you can learn about the great Battle of Evesham in 1265, which ended the rebellion of Simon de Montfort against Henry III. De Montfort's mutilated remains were buried in the abbey church, but such was the veneration shown them by pilgrims that they were removed to a secret resting place.

Royal Shakespeare Theatre

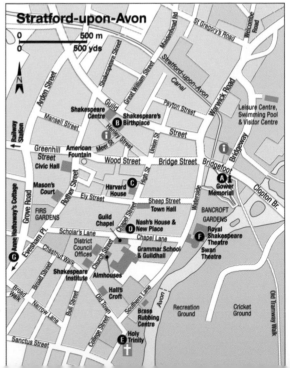

Stratford-upon-Avon

WARWICK AND ROYAL LEAMINGTON SPA

We head north again, past Stratford to **Warwick** ㉘, the county town, built on a rise above the Avon, and dominated by the majestic tower of **St Mary's Church**, which can be climbed for a splendid view over the town and surrounding countryside. The tower and nave were rebuilt after a great fire in 1694, but the 15th-century **Beauchamp Chapel** was spared the flames. The gilded brass effigy of Richard Beauchamp, Earl of Warwick, is splendid.

Warwick is a delightful town, with a wealth of Georgian buildings and a few medieval ones that survived the fire. Chief among these is the timbered and gabled **Lord Leycester Hospital** (www.lordleycester.com; Tue–Sun summer 10am–5pm, winter 10am–4pm). It has been a home for old soldiers ever since Robert Dudley, favourite of Queen Elizabeth I, renovated the old guildhall as almshouses in 1571.

Most people come here, however, to see **Warwick Castle** (www.warwick-castle.co.uk; daily June–Sept 10am–5pm, Nov–May 10am–4pm, with exceptions; tickets are cheaper if bought online in advance), described as "the most perfect piece of castellated antiquity in the kingdom". It has everything you expect of a castle: a wonderful site, great towers and walls, grim dungeons, sumptuous state rooms and glorious grounds, re-landscaped during the 18th century by "Capability" Brown. There are also interactive and walk-through attractions, recreated displays and a rather gruesome Castle Dungeon experience. The castle also hosts classical concerts and events such as medieval banquets.

Royal Leamington Spa ㉙, close by, began as a spa town in the late 18th century, and the focal point is still the **Royal Pump Rooms** by the bridge over the River Leam. These now shelter a museum and gallery, but a sample of the spa water is available to those visitors intrepid enough to ask – it flows from a fountain and cups are available from the museum information desk. To the east are the showpiece Jephson Gardens, named after the 19th-century physician and philanthropist who contributed so much to the town. They are just part of the Grade II-listed sequence of parks that unfolds along the river. Some of the finest buildings are to be found along Newbold Terrace opposite the Pump Room; in The Parade, an elegant thoroughfare running north; and in the superb curve of Lansdowne Crescent.

KENILWORTH AND COVENTRY

Some 4 miles (7km) north is another splendid castle, **Kenilworth** ㉚ (www.english-heritage.org.uk; Apr–Sept daily 10am–6pm, Oct until 5pm, Nov–Mar Sat–Sun until 4pm). Despite years of neglect and deliberate destruction after the Civil War (1642–9), the extensive ruins remain an evocative setting, full of the echoes of history. The 14th-century Great Hall is one

Stratford-upon-Avon celebrates Shakespeare's birthday every year, with streets around the town closed off to allow performances, celebrations and a procession.

of the many additions made by John of Gaunt (1340–99), which turned the grim Norman stronghold into a fine palace. In 1563 Elizabeth I granted the castle to her favourite, Robert Dudley, who added the gatehouse and apartments. When the queen came to visit she was entertained by a "lady of the lake" floating with her nymphs on a torch-lit vessel, firework displays and lavish feasts. A re-created Elizabethan garden has a magnificent fountain and carved arbours. You can now ascend 60ft (18m) up the tower for the first time in 350 years, with new stairs leading to the queen's former bedroom and private gallery, offering glorious views over the grounds and countryside.

Coventry ㉛ is known principally for three things: for the destruction it suffered during World War II and the cathedral which sprang phoenix-like from the ashes; for the story of 11th-century Lady Godiva, a noblewoman, who rode naked through the streets, protected only by her long hair, in protest against her husband's imposition

of taxes; and as the birthplace of the British car industry.

A medieval doorway at Ford's Hospital.

All three are celebrated in the city: the first is the reason many come to Coventry. The second is commemorated more light-heartedly every July at the costumed **Godiva Procession**, and by the **Herbert Art Gallery and Museum** (www.theherbert.org; Mon–Sat 10am–4pm, Sun noon–4pm; free), which aims to spotlight the city's heritage in its History Centre along with the local creative scene through contemporary art exhibitions and cultural events. And the third, which began with Daimler in 1896, can be explored in the **Coventry Transport Museum** (www.transport-museum.com; daily 10am–5pm; free), where the largest collection of British road transport in the world evokes Coventry's special contribution to the industry.

Much of Coventry was, necessarily, redeveloped after the war, but some historic buildings do remain: **St Mary's Guildhall** with its spectacular Arras tapestry is a reminder of Coventry's wool-trading past; and **Ford's**

Warwick Castle.

Where

Althorp Park (July–Aug only noon–5pm; booking advised; tel: 01604-770 107; www.spencerofalthorp.com) lies off the A428 northwest of Northampton. This is the family estate of the Earl of Spencer and the burial place of his sister Diana, Princess of Wales.

Hospital is an outstanding medieval building which has functioned as an almshouse since 1509. For a change from the urban, head for the peaceful canal towpath, where 5.5 miles (9km) of waterside art make up the **Coventry Canal Art Trail**.

BIRMINGHAM

Birmingham 32, at the forefront of the 19th-century Industrial Revolution and still one of the major manufacturing centres, has a history studded with the names of industrial greats – like James Watt, inventor of the steam engine, and Matthew Boulton, who pioneered gas lighting. In the 1960s, the city also became one of the country's most famous examples of revolutionary urban planning. However, by the 1990s, many aspects of its urban design had come to be recognised as short-sighted, and Birmingham was looking decidedly run-down. Efforts have since been made to transform the situation, and the city has become a centre for services, shopping and cultural activities, as exemplified by the dramatic redevelopment of the glass-covered environment of the **Bullring** shopping centre.

Many visitors arrive in Birmingham by rail, at New Street Station. From here, Cannon Street climbs to **St Philip's Cathedral**, an outstanding example of English Baroque, with glorious stained-glass windows designed by Edward Burne-Jones (1833–98). Other members of the Pre-Raphaelite Brotherhood are also represented in the city: in Chamberlain Square the **Museum and Art Gallery** (www.birminghammuseums.org.uk; Mon–Thu, Sat–Sun 10am–5pm, Fri 10.30am–5pm; free) has a matchless collection of their work. In addition to fine art, some of the rarest artefacts in the country are showcased in the museum's 40-plus permanent galleries, and there's a diverse programme of temporary exhibitions too. A pedestrianised area makes a link on one side with **Victoria Square**, where the grandiose 19th-century Town Hall, modelled on the Temple of Castor and Pollux in Rome, and the Council

COVENTRY CATHEDRAL

The ruins of the old cathedral (www.coventrycathedral.org.uk; daily 9am–5pm), which form a poignant introduction to the city, are now a place of contemplation, and a venue for Mystery Plays, performed as a symbol of peace and reconciliation. Located in the ruins is the Blitz Experience Museum, which has five 1940s room reconstructions.

The new cathedral (www.coventrycathedral.org.uk; Mon–Sat 10am–5pm, Sun noon–4pm), Modernist in style, was designed by Sir Basil Spence and built between 1955 and 1962. It stands strikingly juxtaposed with the ruined Gothic shell of the old. The broad steps leading to the entrance on the university side are guarded by a striking bronze figure by Sir Joseph Epstein of St Michael triumphing over the devil, while the vast glazed screen is engraved with saints and angels.

Inside, the eye is led past slender supporting columns to Graham Sutherland's celebrated tapestry showing Christ in Glory surrounded by symbols of the Evangelists. The baptistery is dominated by a window of equal scale and renown, the abstract stained glass the work of John Piper and Patrick Reyntiens, and by a font consisting of a rugged boulder brought from Bethlehem. The small Chapel of Gethsemane is protected by a screen in the form of the crown of thorns, designed by Spence himself. Climb the cathedral tower for the best views over the city.

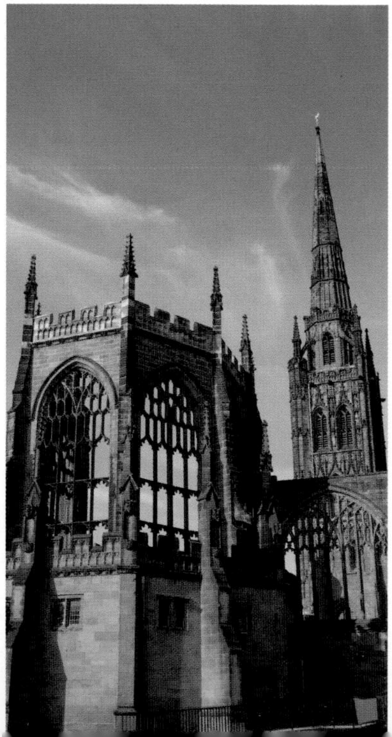

The ruins of Coventry Cathedral.

House contrast with some monumental contemporary sculptures.

On the other side of Victoria Square, a bridge crosses a section of Queensway to the Hall of Memory and **Centenary Square**, the setting for the huge **International Convention Centre**. Its Symphony Hall has been acclaimed as one of the world's finest auditoriums. Towering above the square, the 10-storey Library of Birmingham (Mon, Tue 11am–7pm, Wed–Sat until 5pm) – one of the largest in Europe – is housed in an eye-catching building, with great views of the city from its lofty outdoor terraces and crowning gold dome. The pedestrianised area leads on to **Gas Street Basin**, once the hub of a transport network on Birmingham's canals – the aggregate length of which is greater than the canals of Venice. This part of Birmingham has now been revamped as a district of bars and restaurants known as **Brindleyplace**. The site is home to the **National Sea Life Centre** (www.visitsealife.com/birmingham; Mon–Fri 10am–4pm (with exceptions), Sat 9.30am 6pm Sun 10am–5pm), which has a completely transparent underwater tunnel. On a more intimate scale, the **Ikon Gallery** (www.ikon-gallery.org; Tue–Sun 11am–5pm; free), housed in a Victorian building, is a laid-back venue for contemporary art with a good café.

Stroll south along the water's edge to come to the **Mailbox**, an exclusive complex of designer shops and eateries, and the home of BBC Birmingham.

FURTHER SOUTH

On the fringes of Chinatown, the National Trust's **Back to Backs** (www.nationaltrust.org.uk/birmingham-back-to-backs; pre-booked tours only, call 0121-666 7671) is Birmingham's last surviving courtyard of working people's houses which were built literally back to back, a common feature in the industrial towns of 19th-century Britain.

Visitors are taken through four of the dwellings, restored and decorated to reflect the lives of chosen inhabitants from the 1840s, 1870s, 1930s and 1970s. The retro, fully operational sweet shop hugging the end of the row is a great touch. Three more houses can be rented as holiday accommodation. A short walk west takes you to the independent shopping centre Custard Factory in Digbeth, an emerging cultural quarter splashed with street art by artists from around the world. There's a rich indie scene, from artisanal coffee shops and music venues to ruin bars and pop-up street food haunts.

A short bus or train journey from the city centre is the University of Birmingham at Edgbaston, home of the **Barber Institute of Fine Arts** (www.barber.org.uk; Mon–Fri 10am–5pm, Sat–Sun 11am–5pm; free), an Art Deco building housing an unmissable collection of paintings, from the Renaissance artists to the Impressionists. The museum also houses one of the finest collections of Byzantine coins anywhere in Europe.

Birmingham's Bullring shopping centre.

Punting on the River Cam.

CAMBRIDGE

Like Oxford, Cambridge isn't car-friendly. But, with most of its architectural glories concentrated along a short stretch of the River Cam, it is an easy place to find your way around on foot.

In 1209, when riots in Oxford resulted in the hanging of three students, a group of scholars settled in the market town of **Cambridge**, already a thriving community, and the seeds of England's second university were sown, although the first college was not founded until 1284. Feuds between townspeople and students ("town and gown") soon erupted, and these continued to flare up on and off over the following six centuries. The university's dominant role was established in the 1440s by the demolition of a large tract of the medieval centre to make way for the construction of King's College. Today there are 31 colleges in Cambridge; most of them are open to the public – though restrictions apply during the examinations period (May–mid-June). Some of the more famous ones – King's, Queens', St John's, Trinity – charge an admission fee, although Clare only charges in the summer

KING'S AND CLARE

Start your walk at **King's College**  (www.kings.cam.ac.uk; term time Mon–Fri 9.30am–3.30pm, Sat 9.30am–3.15pm, Sun 1.15–2.30pm, out of term daily 9.30am–4.30pm), which was founded in 1441 by Henry VI – although the pinnacled gatehouse was added nearly 400 years later by Gothic Revivalist William Wilkins, and the neoclassical Fellows'

Building on the west side is an 18th-century structure. To the right soars the beautiful Perpendicular **King's College Chapel** with the largest fan-vaulted stone ceiling in the world, its only apparent support the slender columns of the nave. There are also some exquisite stained-glass windows, the work of 16th-century Flemish and English craftsmen. The intricately carved rood screen, donated by Henry VIII, is a magnificent example of Early Renaissance woodwork. The chapel also contains a stunning painting: Rubens'

Main attractions
King's College Chapel
Trinity College
Museum of Zoology
Fitzwilliam Museum
Christ's College Garden
Pepys Library, Magdalene
Kettle's Yard

Map on page 176

Queen's College.

King's College.

Adoration of the Magi. The renowned **King's College Choir**, whose carol performance is broadcast live across the world on Christmas Eve, sings here daily during term time and visitors are welcome to attend services.

Leave King's by the north gate to find the entrance to **Clare College** (founded in 1326) **on Trinity Lane.** The college's Old Court backs onto the River Cam, and Clare Bridge – the oldest of the college bridges – offers picture-postcard views of punts drifting past weeping willows and banks of daffodils in spring. Back on Trinity Lane, head north past Trinity Hall, one of the smaller, more intimate colleges, and turn right down Senate House Passage. On your left you'll pass the domed Gate of Honour of Gonville and Caius College, one of the earliest Renaissance stone structures in the city, while on the right is the Senate House, used nowadays mainly for degree ceremonies. As you emerge from the passage, you see the **Church of Great St Mary** Ⓑ in front of you. It was here that the great 16th-century Protestant martyrs – Hugh Latimer

and Archbishop Thomas Cranmer – preached. From the tower (123 steps) there is a wonderful view of the town (charge). This church is regarded as the very centre of Cambridge, the point from which all distances are measured.

FROM TRINITY COLLEGE TO THE BACKS

From here, head north on Trinity Street. Immediately on your right is the **Cambridge University Press Bookshop** Ⓒ, the oldest bookshop site in Britain: books have been sold here since 1581. Further up Trinity Street on your left is the Great Gate of **Trinity College** Ⓓ (www.trin.cam.ac.uk), the largest and richest college, founded by Henry VIII just before his death in 1546. Trinity has produced 33 Nobel Prize-winners, six prime ministers and numerous poets, philosophers and scientists – Francis Bacon, Lord Byron, Isaac Newton, Ernest Rutherford, Lord Tennyson and Vladimir Nabokov among them. You can visit the **Wren Library** (term time Mon–Fri noon–2pm, Sat 10.30am–12.30pm),

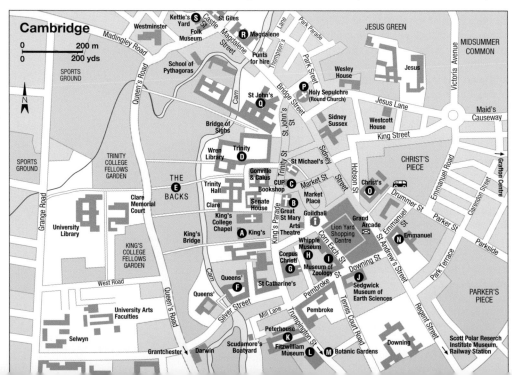

one of the finest classical buildings in the country, designed by Sir Christopher Wren as a gift to the college. The 16th-century Great Court is the site of the Great Court Run, in which students must try to run round the perimeter (400 yards/metres) within the time it takes the clock to strike 12 (43 seconds), a scene memorably captured in the 1981 film *Chariots of Fire*. The Olympic runner Lord Burghley was the first successful contestant (in 1927). You can view the Great Court from beneath Queen's Gate on Trinity Lane (daily 10am–4.30pm, free).

Leaving the college at the rear, cross **Trinity Bridge** to visit **The Backs ⑤**, the picturesque lawns, meadows and gardens that border the Cam and offer classic views of the architectural variety of Cambridge's colleges. Walking south, past Clare and King's, you soon reach Queens' Green and Silver Street just beyond. From here, head east to the porters' lodge of **Queens' College ⑥** (www.queens.cam.ac.uk; summer daily 10am–4.30pm, varies at other times of the year). The Cam divides the college in two and is spanned by the **Mathematical Bridge**, an early 20th-century copy of the one designed in 1749 by William Etheridge (and not Isaac Newton, as the myth runs). On the east side of the river is the Old Court, a fine example of a medieval quadrangle, and Cloister Court, flanked by the President's Lodge, a half-timbered building.

UNIVERSITY MUSEUMS

At the end of Silver Street, turn left onto King's Parade to find **Corpus Christi ⑥**, the only college founded by trade guilds. Its Old Court has resisted 18th-century refurbishment and looks much as it would have done in the 14th century. At the back of Corpus, on Free School Lane (accessed from Pembroke Street), lies the **Whipple Museum of the History of Science ⑩** (www.hps.cam.ac.uk/whipple; Mon–Fri 12.30–4.30pm; free),

housing a selection of scientific and navigational instruments dating from the 14th century. Just round the corner on Downing Street is the **Museum of Zoology ⓵** (www.museum.zoo.cam.ac.uk; Tue–Sat 10am–4.30pm, Sun noon–4.30pm), which was reopened in 2018 by Sir David Attenborough after a £4m redevelopment. The project included renovating the displays, adding new exhibits and moving the famous fin whale skeleton to hang from the ceiling of the glass-fronted foyer – best viewed from the museum's new café (which has a live bee hive). Among its exhibits are specimens discovered by Charles Darwin (1809–82) on his 1831 voyage on the *Beagle*: most famous of these are some of the Galapagos finches.

On the other side of Downing Street is the **Sedgwick Museum of Earth Sciences ⓶** (www.sedgwickmuseum.org; Mon–Fri 10am–1pm, 2–5pm, Sat 10am–4pm; free), which houses Britain's oldest intact geological collection. Exhibits include the skeleton of one of the smallest known dinosaurs, the compsognathus. The adjacent

Paintings at the Fitzwilliam Museum.

Museum of Archaeology and Anthropology (www.maa.cam.ac.uk; Tue–Sat 10.30am–4.30pm, Sun noon–4.30pm; free) is devoted to prehistory.

SOUTH ALONG TRUMPINGTON STREET

Now heading south on Trumpington Street, very soon on your left is **Pembroke College**. It is best known for its chapel, the first chapel to be completed (1663–5) by Sir Christopher Wren. Further down, on the right, is **Peterhouse College Ⓚ**, the oldest and most traditional of the colleges, founded in 1284 by the Bishop of Ely. The Gothic chapel on the east side is its most outstanding building. Sir Frank Whittle, inventor of the jet engine, was a student here, as was Charles Babbage, whose work led to the modern computer.

Just beyond Peterhouse, to the south, is the **Fitzwilliam Museum Ⓛ** (www.fitzmuseum.cam.ac.uk; Tue–Sat 10am–5pm, Sun noon–5pm; free). The museum contains a priceless collection of paintings, books and manuscripts belonging to the museum's founder, Viscount Fitzwilliam; antiquities, sculpture, sarcophagi, ceramics and jewellery from Egypt, Asia, Greece and Rome; and masterpieces by Italian Renaissance artists, Flemish masters, and French Impressionists. The fan gallery has displays of European and oriental fans. In addition, the museum has an ongoing programme of temporary exhibitions, courses, family activities and musical events, including regular lunchtime concerts.

Further south still, Trumpington Street becomes Trumpington Road, and before long on your left you come to the **Botanic Gardens Ⓜ** (www.botanic.cam.ac.uk; daily Apr–Sept 10am–6pm, Feb–Mar and Oct 10am–5pm, Nov–Jan 10am–4pm). A huge variety of plants provides all-year colour; there are also glasshouses full of tropical plants, a Woodland Garden, a Winter Garden and a Genetics Garden, which illustrates how genetic variation plays on the appearance of plants, plus a summer plants festival and various tours. It's a reminder that the garden was established by Professor Henslow, the tutor who inspired Charles Darwin.

EMMANUEL, CHRIST'S AND SIDNEY SUSSEX

On the east side of the city centre, opposite the top end of Downing Street, is **Emmanuel College Ⓝ**, the first Protestant college, founded in 1584. The chapel was designed by Christopher Wren and the garden known as The Paddock has a large pool where Dominican monks used to fish, before Henry VIII dissolved their friary.

On the other side of St Andrew's Street is the Grand Arcade, a smart shopping centre, and further north, on the right, is **Christ's College Ⓞ**. The Fellows' Building is attributed to Inigo Jones; some have their doubts, but it is a splendid piece of 17th-century Classicism. **Fellows' Garden** (Mon–Fri usually 9am–4pm) is a magical oasis in the city centre. Milton's Mulberry Tree (said

⊙ PUNTING

One of the most enduring images of Cambridge is of languid summers spent punting along on the river. The calm and shallow waters of the River Cam are ideally suited to the flat-bottomed punts, which are propelled by someone standing at the back of the boat and pushing a pole (usually about 10ft/3 metres long) against the riverbed. Pleasure punts were introduced in Edwardian times; before that they were used by fishermen and reed cutters in the Fens. In Cambridge, the tradition is for the punter to stand on the boat's short deck (the 'counter' or 'till'), whereas in Oxford, you stand at the other end, with the till at the front.

Punts can be hired at the bottom of Mill Lane (tel: 01223-359 750; www.scudamores.com) or from outside the nearby Granta pub on Silver Street (tel: 01223-354 164; www.punting-in-cambridge.co.uk). Most visitors choose to glide along The Backs and under the bridges behind Trinity, King's and several other colleges – though this stretch of river does become congested in summer. Those in the know prefer to punt instead along the lower reaches of the river through the meadows to Grantchester, where you can stop for a picnic.

to have shaded the poet John Milton as he worked) was one of several planted by James I in 1608 to stimulate the silk industry. The most famous alumnus is Charles Darwin, and a garden dedicated to his name marks his achievements.

Further north, St Andrew's Street merges into Sidney Street and before long you come to Sidney Sussex College on your right. One of the smaller colleges, it is notable as the last resting place of the head of Oliver Cromwell, leader of the Roundheads in the English Civil War. He had briefly been a student here, until his father's death obliged him to return home and take on family responsibilities. In 1643 he returned as military leader, looted the colleges – which supported King Charles I – and requisitioned their courts as barracks.

ST JOHN'S AND MAGDALENE

Sidney Street eventually becomes Bridge Street, and soon afterwards on your right is the 12th-century **Church of the Holy Sepulchre** ❷ (Mon–Sat 10am–5pm, Sun 1.30–5pm), one of only four surviving Norman round churches in England. Just opposite is the turning for St John's Street, which is dominated by the ornate 16th-century gate tower of **St John's College** ❶ (www.joh.cam. ac.uk; daily Mar–Oct 10am–4pm, Nov–Feb 10am–3.30pm). The neo-Gothic chapel, inspired by Sainte-Chapelle in Paris and designed by George Gilbert Scott, is well worth a visit. To the rear of the college, the delicate **Bridge of Sighs**, modelled on its Venetian namesake, was built in the 19th century to form a link with newer buildings on the other side of the river.

From St John's, continue up Bridge Street to **Magdalene College** ❶ on your right. The showpiece here is the **Pepys Library** (late Apr–Sept Mon–Fri 2–4pm, Sat 11.30am–12.30pm, 1.30–2.30pm, mid-Jan–mid-Mar, Oct–mid-Dec Mon–Sat 2–4pm; free). Samuel Pepys bequeathed his 3,000-volume

collection to the college in 1703. The library's greatest treasure is the original manuscript of the great man's diary, recording daily life in the 1660s.

Continue up Magdalene Street and you come to the **Folk Museum** (www.folkmuseum.org.uk; Mon–Sat 10.30am–5pm, Sun 11.30am–4.30pm), filled with the evidence of local life since 1700. Almost next door is **Kettle's Yard** ❺ (www.kettlesyard.co.uk; Tue–Sun 11am–5pm), an unusual museum in four cottages, which Tate Gallery curator Jim Ede restored and made into his home in the 1950s. With Kettle's Yard, Ede founded a haven of peace and welcome, filled with works by Ben Nicholson, Henry Moore, Barbara Hepworth and many other artists and sculptors; and one where music, light and natural objects, such as pebbles, would also greet the senses. The house-gallery was extended again in 2018, where an understated design by award-winning architect Jamie Fobert (of Tate St Ives and National Portrait Gallery fame) has made space for temporary exhibition galleries and an education wing, along with a café and shop.

> **✪ Fact**
>
> Due east of Sidney Street via Jesus Lane is Jesus College, noted for its Cloister Court and medieval chapel. The latter dates from 1200 but was restored in the Gothic style by the Victorian Augustus Pugin, with new ceilings designed by William Morris's firm. Behind the college lies Jesus Green, and on the other side of Victoria Avenue is Midsummer Common, scene of an annual summer fair.

The Bridge of Sighs at St John's College.

Sailing boat on the Norfolk Broads.

EAST ANGLIA

The main attractions here include boating on the Norfolk Broads, exploring the Fenlands, discovering medieval churches and timber-framed houses, and following in the footsteps of John Constable.

London

It's hard to believe now, when driving through the empty landscapes and sleepy villages of Suffolk and Norfolk, that East Anglia had formerly – in medieval times – been one of the most densely populated and commercialised regions of England. The broad acres of chalk and grassland provided ideal grazing for sheep, and huge quantities of wool were exported, boosted by the arrival of expert Flemish weavers in the mid-14th century. The main legacy of this era of wealth and prosperity is the region's medieval churches – more than 1,000 of them – from Saxon and Norman to Gothic Perpendicular. The great timber-framed houses you will see were also built on the proceeds of wool.

Our tour begins in **Cambridge ❶** (see page 175) and first goes some 15 miles (24km) south on the A1301 to **Saffron Walden ❷**, which gets its name from the orange crocus dye that made the town wealthy. Today it's a delightfully unspoilt market town with a number of timber-framed buildings, several of them decorated with ornamental plasterwork called pargetting. The huge church that dominates the town is a fine example of Perpendicular style.

About 1 mile (1.6km) west is **Audley End House** (tel: 01799-522 842; www.english-heritage.org.uk; house: Apr–Sept daily noon–5pm, Oct daily noon–4pm; grounds: Apr–Sept daily 10am–6pm,

Oct daily 10am–5pm; some further openings at school holiday times). The biggest house in England at the time, it takes its name from Sir Thomas Audley, Henry VIII's Lord Chancellor, who adapted the buildings of Walden Abbey. This mansion was enlarged in grandiose Jacobean style in 1614 for his grandson Thomas Howard, the Lord Treasurer to James I who described it as "too large for a king, but it might do for a Lord Treasurer". Substantial changes were made in the 18th century when Robert Adam (1728–92)

Main attractions
Ely Cathedral
Sandringham House
Norwich
The Broads
Southwold
Flatford Mill
Lavenham

Map on page 183

A hops farm near Wells-next-the-Sea.

⊙ Fact

Each winter, two large drainage channels in the Fens flood over onto grazing land and create what are known as the Ouse Washes. These marshy areas to the northwest of Ely attract over 100,000 wildfowl, including all three types of swan. The RSPB (www.rspb.org.uk) and the Wildfowl & Wetlands Trust (www.wwt.org.uk) manage the Washes as nature reserves. In cold weather, visitors can watch the birds being fed from the comfort of the hides provided.

remodelled the Great Drawing Room and many other parts, although the Great Hall retains its hammerbeam ceiling and Jacobean oak screen. Lancelot "Capability" Brown landscaped the grounds at the same time. The Service Wing gives a fascinating insight into life "below stairs" in Victorian times. Just across the road is a miniature railway (tel: 01799-542 134; www.audley-end-railway.co.uk).

THE FENS

On the other side of Cambridge is the flat Fenland of north Cambridgeshire, which was marshland until it was drained in the 17th century. About 16 miles (25km) north of Cambridge on the A10 is the city of **Ely** ❸. Rising ship-like above the city and surrounding fenlands is **Ely Cathedral** (www.elycathedral.org; summer daily 7am–6.30pm, winter Mon–Sat 7am–6.30pm, Sun 7am–5.30pm). The cathedral, sometimes referred to as the "Ship of the Fens", stands on a knoll that used to be known as the Isle of Eels, after the staple diet of the villagers. St Etheldreda selected the

Ely Cathedral.

site for a monastery site in AD 673, and the present cathedral was built in the 11th century. It was around this time that Hereward the Wake famously used Ely as a refuge when being pursued by William the Conqueror. Hereward seemed unreachable on Ely (then an island), but eventually the monks tired of the siege and showed the conqueror's men the secret pathway through the marshes, giving Hereward away.

The splendour of Ely Cathedral lies in its unusual situation and in its unique lantern. In the evening, the lantern – an octagonal tower of wood and glass built high on the back of the nave in an extraordinary feat of engineering – reflects the rays of the dying sun. By night its glass gleams with the light within. The **Lady Chapel** is the largest of its kind in the country. A museum in the south triforium traces the history of stained glass.

Follow the A10, and the River Ouse, to the north, and branch off on the A1101 towards **Wisbech** ❹, a market town that styles itself the capital of the Fens. The two impressive Georgian streets – South

⊙ FACT FILE

Location The counties of Essex, Suffolk, Cambridgeshire and Norfolk between the Thames Estuary and The Wash.

By car From London, Colchester is about 60 miles (100km) on the A12 and Norwich is 115 miles (185km) on the A12/A140; journey time from Norwich to Cambridge about 80 minutes; Norwich to King's Lynn 1 hour.

By bus National Express from London Victoria to Norwich, about 3 hours 15 minutes; tel: 0871-781 8181; www.nationalexpress.com.

By rail 50 minutes by train from London Liverpool Street to Colchester; 1 hour 50 minutes to Norwich; London King's Cross to King's Lynn 1 hour 40 minutes; tel: 03457-484 950, www.nationalrail.co.uk.

Nearest airport Stansted; four train services per hour to London Liverpool Street; hourly train service to Cambridge.

Nearest port Harwich (to Hook of Holland and Hamburg).

Major towns Bury St Edmunds, Colchester, Ipswich, King's Lynn, Norwich.

Attractions The Broads; medieval churches; wool towns; coastal birdlife.

For children Pleasurewood Hills, Lowestoft, tel: 01502-586 000; www.pleasurewoodhills.com, one of the largest theme parks in England.

Tourist information Bury St Edmunds, tel: 01284-764 667; Colchester, tel: 01206-282 920; Ipswich, tel: 01473-258 070; King's Lynn, tel: 01553-763 044; Norwich, tel: 01603-213 999.

Brink and North Brink – illustrate the prosperity that marsh drainage brought. The eccentric **Wisbech and Fenland Museum** (www.wisbechmuseum.org.uk; Tue–Sat 10am–4pm; free) has the complete furnishings of a Victorian post office. **Peckover House** (www.nationaltrust.org.uk/peckover; mid-Mar–end Oct Mon–Wed, Sat–Sun noon–4pm; garden: Mon–Wed, Sat–Sun 11am–5pm), built in 1722, is an interesting town house on North Brink renowned for its Rococo decoration. It also has an outstanding Victorian garden, with a summerhouse, orangery and croquet lawn. Opposite stands the **Octavia Hill Birthplace Museum** (www.octaviahill.org; mid-Mar–Oct Mon–Wed, Sat–Sun 1–4.30pm). Hill (1838–1912) was a Victorian reformer and a co-founder of the National Trust.

Take the A47 for about 12 miles (20km) to the next stop, **King's Lynn** ⑤, a port and market town on the Great Ouse, south of the Wash. Its port is still active, and the heart of the town has retained its character with some fine Georgian houses and medieval monuments. Worth seeing are the elegant Custom House, St Margaret's Church on the Market Place, and the 15th-century Trinity Guildhall, Old Gaol House and Town Hall which make up the complex that houses the interactive Stories of Lynn exhibition (daily 10am–4.30pm).

Leaving King's Lynn by the A149, before long you will see a turn to the right for **Sandringham** ⑥ (tel: 01553-612 908; www.sandringhamestate.co.uk; daily Easter–mid-Oct 11am–5pm, Oct until 4pm; last admission 30mins before closing closed for flower show during late July, check online as date varies). This great house was built in 1870 by the Prince of Wales, who later reigned as Edward VII. Largely 18th-century in style, it has many Edwardian embellishments, and is now the Queen's country retreat and the place where she usually spends Christmas. There are extensive grounds, with lakes and nature trails, and an eclectic museum of royal gifts, personal memorabilia and motor cars.

HUNSTANTON TO CROMER

Continue on the A149, now a coast road, past **Hunstanton**, an old-fashioned

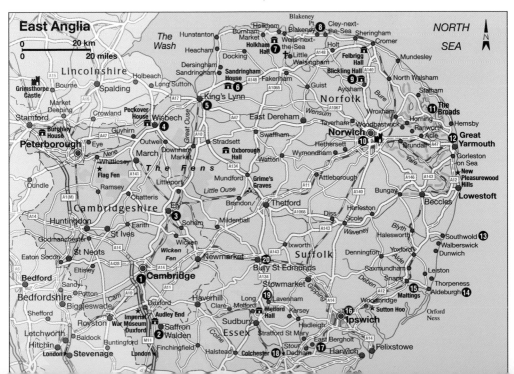

A beach hut in Wells-next-the-Sea.

resort with broad sandy beaches and 60ft (18-metre) cliffs with distinctive strips of carrstone and red-and-white chalk. It's the only East Anglian resort facing west, and you get some glorious sunsets over The Wash. The A149 follows the coast east through a series of small villages, seven of which have "Burnham" in their names – including Burnham Thorpe, the birthplace of Lord Nelson. At Holkham is one of Norfolk's finest stately homes, **Holkham Hall** ❼ (www.holkham.co.uk; house and garden Apr–Oct Sun–Mon, Thu noon–4pm; grounds daily 9am–5pm; free but car park charge). Set in magnificent parkland, the sombre Palladian facade hides a grand hall and state rooms with paintings by Van Dyck, Rubens and Gainsborough. The stunning sandy beach at Holkham famously featured in the closing scenes of the film *Shakespeare in Love.* Access is via Lady Anne's Drive on the A149. The Coasthopper bus service, which runs from Hunstanton to Cromer, is the perfect way to access the villages and take excellent walks along the north Norfolk coast.

East of Holkham is **Wells-next-the-Sea**, a genuine working port with coasters along the quay and fishing boats bringing in crabs and shrimps – served day-fresh in local seafood restaurants. It's also a popular holiday spot, with amusements and fish-and-chip shops along the quay and brightly coloured beach huts strung along its sands. Between April and October, a miniature steam railway (www.wwlr.co.uk) will take you inland from Wells to **Little Walsingham**, still a place of pilgrimage for Catholics, with a well-preserved medieval high street.

A little further on from Wells, **Blakeney** ❽ is a pretty coastal village of flint-knapped cottages, known for its sand-and-shingle spit. **Blakeney Point** at its tip is the summer home for a dozen species of seabirds, including terns, oystercatchers, plovers and redshanks. Common and grey seals bask on the sands when the tide is low, and in summer they can be spotted on a ferry trip from Morston Quay (some allow you to land on Blakeney Point for up to an hour). The next town along is Cley next the Sea a lovely little village with a white-sailed windmill, small deli, award-wining bakery and local pottery and book shops. From here the Georgian town of Holt is located just inland, and is worth a detour for its antiques stores, art galleries, gift shops and food hall.

The last coastal stop for the moment is at **Cromer**, a pleasant Victorian resort with a long sand-and-shingle beach and a town centre dominated by the soaring church tower. There's a Victorian pier, too, on which stands the Pavilion Theatre, still putting on shows. Fishing boats bring in the famous Cromer crabs (don't miss the Crab and Lobster Festival in May), which you can buy throughout Norfolk in the summer months.

INLAND TO NORWICH

Head inland now on the A140 to Aylsham and **Blickling Hall** ❾ (www.

Norwich's Royal Arcade.

nationaltrust.org.uk/blickling; Mar–Oct daily noon–5pm; park: all year), one of England's greatest Jacobean houses. Covered with turrets and gables, bordered by lawns and huge yew hedges, it is also known for its spectacular Long Gallery, fine furniture and tapestries. The gardens are colourful year-round and the park offers splendid walks.

Continue south on the A140 to **Norwich** ⑩. Before the Industrial Revolution this was one of the most prosperous cities in England. Set amid rich agricultural land, it rose to prominence in the Middle Ages as a market and trading centre. This prosperity is evident in the 31 medieval churches and a host of historic houses. There's also a large and colourful **market**, and a pleasantly relaxed atmosphere. The 12th-century **Castle** (Mon–Sat 10am–4.30pm, Sun 1–4.30pm, July–Sept until 5pm) has a museum in its keep, with collections of archaeology and natural history, as well as galleries displaying works by the Norwich School of landscape painters and a wide range of temporary art exhibitions. It also has the world's largest collection of ceramic teapots.

Down in the town, close to the lively market, is an elegant Art Nouveau thoroughfare, the **Royal Arcade**, where you'll find independent art galleries, boutique stores, jewellery shops and a chocolatier.

The magnificent **Cathedral** (www.cathedral.org.uk; daily 7.30am–6pm; donation) was founded in 1096 by Bishop Losinga. There are over 1,000 carved and painted bosses throughout the building, and the cloisters are the largest in England. Within the outer flint walls is a modern version of a Norman refectory, designed by Sir Michael Hopkins. Nearby is Elm Hill, a quaint cobbled street lined with interesting little shops and buildings. You can admire the cathedral spire from **Pull's Ferry**, a medieval flint-and-stone water gate on the River Wensum.

Sir Michael also designed the **Forum**, a horseshoe-shaped building encompassing the regional library and tourist office. At the University of East Anglia don't overlook the **Sainsbury Centre for Visual Arts** (www.scva.org.uk; Tue–Fri 10am–6pm, Sat–Sun until 5pm; free), which houses a wonderful collection featuring Picasso, Henry Moore and Giacometti, juxtaposed with ethnographic pieces. Highlights include Moore's *Mother and Child,* and an Inca llama effigy, which would probably have been buried with a human sacrifice. A growing sculpture park, set across 320 acres of parkland fringing the campus grounds, sees new works by acclaimed artist Antony Gormley sitting alongside existing pieces by the likes of Moore, Lynn Chadwick and John Hoskin.

FROM THE BROADS TO THE MALTINGS

You can take the A1151 northeast, or the A47 or B1140 east from Norwich to reach **the Broads** ⑪, a national park containing a network of navigable

Seals at Blakeney Point.

rivers and lakes in Norfolk and Suffolk, formed by the flooding of medieval peat diggings. Catering for every type of craft, and uninterrupted by locks, these 200 miles (320km) of quiet waterways are a haven for boating enthusiasts. Many people spend their holidays on the water in a narrow boat, but you can also hire a sailing boat or motor cruiser, by the hour or by the day (see www.broads-authority.gov.uk for information). There are also trips to see the wildlife of the area. The floating **Broads Wildlife Centre** (tel: 01603-270 479; visitor centre Apr–Oct daily 10am–5pm; reserve dawn to dusk all year; free) at Ranworth offers a wealth of information and a boardwalk trail.

If you're doing your navigating through the Broads by road, the A47 will take you to **Great Yarmouth** , where Charles Dickens (1812–70) set part of *David Copperfield*. The town once flourished on its herring catch, but over-fishing killed the industry and now, as the most popular resort on the Norfolk coast, it relies mainly on tourism. Golden sands are hidden from

Old Moot Hall in Aldeburgh.

view behind helter-skelters and roller-coasters. The nicest area of town is the historical part around **South Quay**, where the **Old Merchant's House** (tel: 01493-857 900; Apr–Sept Sat–Sun 11am–4pm), with its Jacobean plaster ceilings, is worth a visit, as is the historic **Hippodrome Circus** (www.hippodromecircus.co.uk; tel: 01493-844-172;), Britain's only surviving total circus building, which has seen the likes of Charlie Chaplin, Houdini and Lillie Langtry perform.

Some 10 miles (16km) south is **Lowestoft**, England's most easterly town, which still retains a small fishing fleet. About 15 miles (24km) down the coast lies **Southwold** ⓭, a remarkably unspoilt and rather old-fashioned little place that is renowned for its brewery, Adnams. Set on a cliff top, it is distinguished by its open greens, created after a fire destroyed much of the town in the 17th century. Victorian seafront terraces, Georgian houses and fishermen's cottages blend smoothly together, and colourful beach huts face the sea across a sand-and-shingle

⊙ DISAPPEARING DUNWICH

Dunwich was once the capital of medieval East Anglia, a prosperous town with eight churches, two monasteries, two hospitals, major shipyards and a population one-sixth the size of London's. But coastal erosion changed all that. It was kept at bay for two centuries, but a terrible storm in 1328 deposited vast amounts of sand and shingle in the harbour and ended its role as a port. Constant erosion over the centuries has reduced the village to a handful of cottages, a pub, one church, and a beach with a café and a few fishing boats. All that remains of medieval Dunwich are the ruins of Greyfriars monastery and those of the Leper Chapel by the church. A solitary tombstone is sole testimony to All Saints', the last of the medieval churches, which collapsed into the sea in 1921. Locals say that when a storm is threatening, the sound of the bells tolling can be heard from beneath the waves.

Dunwich Museum (daily Apr–Sept 11.30am–4.30pm, Mar Sat–Sun 2–4pm; tel: 01728-648 796 for winter hours; free) charts the potted history of the town from Roman times to the present day, showing all the buildings lost to the sea. At the present rate of erosion, with recent storms scooping up more of the steeply shelving beach, the museum has about 70 years to go.

beach. Its charms have lured many artists over the years, from Turner to Damien Hirst. The **Southwold Museum** (www.southwoldmuseum.org; Easter–Oct daily 2–4pm; free) is largely devoted to the Battle of Sole Bay, fought against the Dutch in 1672. The church of **St Edmund** is said to be the finest medieval seaside church in England.

You have to go around the estuary of the **River Blyth** to pick up the B1125 to **Aldeburgh ⑭**, the birthplace of the international music festival which now takes place at Snape. But Aldeburgh – an unspoilt and architecturally-interesting town which has been a port since Roman times – is still very much a festival centre, and its hotels and restaurants cater well for visitors to the concert hall nearby at Snape. Aldeburgh's High Street, lined with galleries and bookshops as well as food shops, runs parallel to a steeply shelving shingle beach where fresh fish is sold straight from the boats. The brick and timber-framed **Moot Hall**, which houses a small museum, stands near the promenade, but used to be some way inland, until erosion ate away the land.

Take the A1094 inland, then turn left (on the B1069) to reach the **Snape Maltings ⑮** on the River Alde. These 19th-century red-brick granaries and malt houses were converted by composer Benjamin Britten (1913–76) into a concert hall in 1967. Born in Lowestoft, Britten moved to Snape in 1937, and his most famous opera, *Peter Grimes*, was performed here eight years later. The main events of the **Aldeburgh Festival** take place here in June (www.aldeburgh.co.uk; box office tel: 01728-687 110) – though other events are held throughout the summer, and the riverside galleries and craft, furniture and antiques shops are open all year.

CONSTABLE AND CAMULODUNUM

Get on the A12 now for **Ipswich ⑯**, the county town of Suffolk. The centre is mostly modern, but there's an atmospheric Victorian dockland on the River Orwell, and a local museum and gallery in the **Christchurch Mansion** (www.

Ⓞ Tip

Left-hand turns off the B1125 between Southwold and Aldeburgh take you to Dunwich (see page 186), to the Sizewell Nuclear Power Station, and to Thorpeness, with its "House in the Clouds" and pleasant boating lake. Thorpeness was developed as a private "fantasy" holiday village by Scottish barrister Glencairn Stuart Ogilvie, who acquired the land in 1910. He invited his friends and colleagues for summer holidays, providing a country club with tennis courts and swimming pool, a golf course and many holiday homes built in Tudor and Jacobean revival style.

See a classic Punch and Judy show on Southwold's pier.

⊙ Tip

A circular route through Constable Country starts at the car park near Flatford Mill and takes in East Bergholt and Dedham. Guided walks (provided a guide is available) visit the scenes of paintings (National Trust Information Centre at Bridge Cottage, tel: 01206-298 260). There are also longer guided rambles of Dedham Vale and circular self-guided walks available.

cimuseums.org.uk; Mar–Oct Tue–Sun 10am–5pm, Sun 11am–5pm, Nov–Feb Tue–Sun 10am–4pm, Sun 11am–4pm; free), which has a splendid collection of Constable's paintings as well as works by Gainsborough in its Wolsey Art Gallery (as well as great temporary exhibitions featuring the likes of Rodin and Picasso). There's also 15th-century St Margaret's Church, with a wonderful hammerbeam roof and a Tudor gateway.

The pretty village of **East Bergholt** ⑰, birthplace of John Constable, lies to the left of the A12 between Ipswich and Colchester. A plaque on railings just before the church marks the painter's birthplace, and the graves of his parents lie in **St Mary's Churchyard**, where a large wooden cage houses the heaviest ring of five bells in England – unique as they are still rung by hand. From the church, follow the signs for **Flatford**, which take you to a car park from where a path leads down to the River Stour, to **Flatford Mill**, and **Willy Lott's Cottage**, both recognisable as subjects of *The Hay Wain*. The B1029

will bring you to the attractive village of **Dedham,** where you'll see the soaring tower of the **Church of St Mary**, which dates back to the early 16th century and features in several of Constable's paintings. Dedham is also home to the **Munnings Art Museum** (mid-Mar–Oct Wed–Sun 2–5pm), displaying the works of Sir Alfred Munnings, who is particularly recognised for his fine paintings of horses.

Now we're back on the road for **Colchester** ⑱. Set on the River Colne, this was Camulodunum, the first capital of Roman Britain, and a long section of Roman wall and a large gateway still stand. In 1076 William the Conqueror began his castle on the ruins of a Roman temple to Claudius. The great **Norman Keep** is all that remains: it houses the **Castle Museum** (www.cimu seums.org.uk; Mon–Sat 10am–5pm, Sun 11am–5pm), which features many interactive displays on Roman, Norman and medieval history, the siege of Colchester during the Civil War, as well as a medieval prison.

From Colchester our route goes northwest on the A134 towards **Sudbury**, just north of which the village of **Long Melford** makes an interesting diversion, to see the mellow Tudor mansion **Melford Hall** (www.national trust.org.uk/melford-hall; May–Sept Wed–Sun noon–5pm, Sat–Sun in Apr and Oct), where Elizabeth I once stayed; and the village church, which is one of the best examples of Perpendicular architecture in Suffolk.

LAVENHAM

Lavenham ⑲ (reached via the B1071) is one of the finest of East Anglia's wealthy wool towns, with a large number of medieval buildings, many half-timbered and tilting at alarming angles. Best known is the lovely ochre-coloured **Little Hall** (www.little hall.org.uk; Easter–Oct Mon 10am–1pm, Tue–Sun 1–4pm) in the market place. It dates back to the 14th century. The

Timber-framed houses, Lavenham.

Perpendicular-style church has a magnificent tower, bearing the coats of arms of local cloth merchants; and the early 16th-century **Guildhall** (www.nationaltrust.org.uk/lavenham; Mar–Oct daily 11am–5pm, Feb, Nov, Dec Fri–Sun 11am–4pm), meeting place of the Guild of Corpus Christi, now houses a museum on the wool trade and a walled garden which contains dye plants used since the Middle Ages. Telegraph poles have been removed and the wires buried underground to preserve the village's Tudor appearance.

BURY ST EDMUNDS

North of Lavenham is the last stop on our route, the ancient market town of **Bury St Edmunds ⓴**, aptly named to honour Edmund, the last Saxon king of East Anglia, who was canonised and buried here.

In *The Pickwick Papers*, Charles Dickens, who stayed here at the Angel Hotel, called Bury "a handsome little town of thriving and cleanly appearance". Nearby is The Nutshell, reputedly Britain's smallest pub. The town is now a mixture of architectural styles, but retains much of its original layout.

There are 980 listed buildings, including the 12th-century **Moyse Hall** (Mon–Sat 10am–5pm, Sun noon–4pm; last admission 1hr before closing), the oldest merchant's house in East Anglia, which is now a local museum. Inside are Bronze Age and Saxon artefacts found in the area.

The **Cathedral of St James** stands guard over the ruins of **St Edmunds Abbey** (daily Mar–May, Oct 7.30am–6pm, Sun 9am–6pm, June–Sept 7.30am–7.30pm, Sun 9am–7.30pm, Nov–Feb 7.30am–4.30pm, Sun 9am–4.30pm), one of the richest Benedictine foundations in England. It was here in 1214 that a group of barons swore to take up arms against King John if he did not sign Magna Carta. The **Gate Tower**, the best-preserved feature, gives an idea of the abbey's former splendour. Originally founded in the 7th century, it was an important place of pilgrimage after the body of Edmund, last king of the East Angles who was killed by the Danes, was placed here in about 900.

Flatford Mill.

Canterbury Cathedral at night,
through Christchurch Gate.

CANTERBURY AND THE SOUTHEAST

The county of Kent is known as the Garden of England, thanks to its orchards. It is also the cradle of Christianity in Britain, a land of castles, moated manors and delightful villages.

Hops, apples and cherries are the traditional crops from the country's most southeastern county of Kent, known as "the Garden of England". Market forces and agricultural policies have driven all but the fair women to the wall, but the agriculture of the past has shaped the countryside, giving it its distinctive hop kilns, while an abundance of wood has led to white weatherboard buildings. The High Weald is a lovely, rolling landscape, and at Dover the chalk Downs spill dramatically into the sea, giving England its ancient name, Albion, from the Latin *alba* (meaning white).

This is the nearest England gets to the Continent, and it was here that the invaders landed: Julius Caesar in 55 BC, Angles, Saxons and Jutes in the Dark Ages, William of Normandy in 1066. Christianity also arrived here with Augustine in 597, establishing the Church at Canterbury. And it was in the skies over Kent that the ferocious dogfights of the Battle of Britain took place in 1940. Today England is linked to the Continent through the Channel Tunnel.

CHARLES DICKENS COUNTRY

The south side of the Thames Estuary in Kent is Charles Dickens country. He drew inspiration from the bleak marshes, and the people who lived by the tidal river. Some marshlands remain, still bleak, but ideal for waders and seabirds. Dickens lived at Gad's Hill in **Rochester 1**. You can still see sites that inspired Dickens around the town – notably Restoration House, Crow Lane, which was Satis House in *Great Expectations*. For free walking tours of Rochester (Apr–Sept; charge for groups) tel: 01634-721 886. This ancient town on the River Medway has always been of strategic importance: Watling Street, the Roman road from Canterbury to London, passes through it, and the Normans built a fine **castle** (www.english-heritage.org.uk; daily Apr–Sept 10am–6pm, Oct–Mar 10am–4pm)

Main attractions
Canterbury Cathedral
Leeds Castle
Sissinghurst Castle
Hever Castle
Knole
Battle Abbey

Map on page 194

Hastings old town.

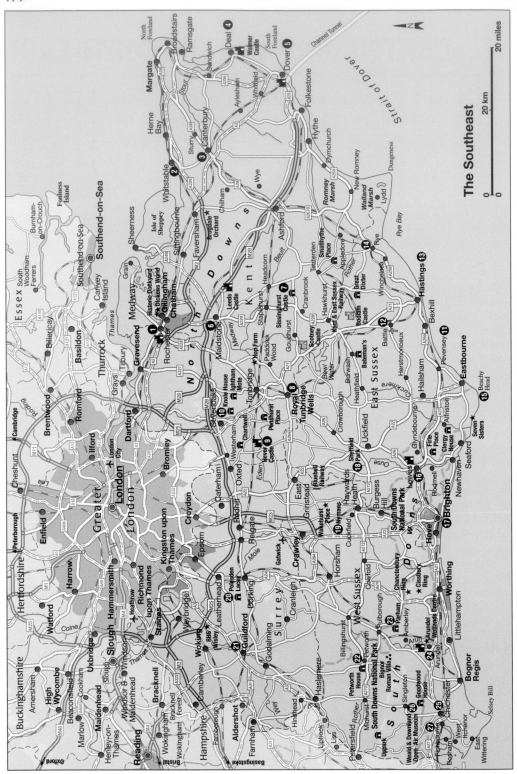

The Southeast

0   20 km

0   20 miles

with the tallest keep in England (113ft/32 metres). The Normans also built an exemplary **cathedral** (www.rochestercathe dral.org; Mon–Fri 7.30am–6pm, Sun until 5pm, Sat 8.30am–5pm; free) here, on the site of an earlier Saxon cathedral which had been founded in AD 604. It is sturdy, simple and reminiscent of the Norman churches of France. The cathedral is an important place of pilgrimage and has been so since the 13th century.

Chatham is a neighbour in this seamless clutter of Medway towns. Its famous Royal Navy dockyards, established by Henry VIII, were closed by the Admiralty in 1984 with a loss of 8,000 jobs, but found a new lease of life as a museum. The **Historic Dockyard** (https://thedock yard.co.uk; daily Apr–Oct 10am–6pm, early Feb 10am–3pm, mid-Feb–Mar, Nov 10am–4pm) covers 80 acres (32 hectares) and has the largest concentration of listed buildings in Britain. Visitors can see the shipbuilding sheds, the sail lofts, and the impressive 1,140ft (350-metre) Ropery, built in 1792. Ships on display include the submarine HMS *Ocelot* and the last Victorian sloop, HMS *Gannet*.

More of a backwater is **Faversham**, a pretty town on the River Swale, and also on Watling Street. Among its ancient quays is a pervading smell from the local brewery, Shepherd Neame. Apples trees are prolific at nearby **Brogdale Orchard** (www.brogdalecollections.org; Mar–Oct daily 10am–4pm), which holds the national fruit collection. There are almost 2,000 varieties of apple alone, including the earliest known in England and the variety that is said to have fallen on Newton's head, prompting him to muse on gravity. Back on the coast, another attractive town is **Whitstable ❷**, known since Roman times for its oysters. Buy them in the old harbour or try them at the seafront Whitstable Oyster Fishery Company restaurant, or at the Pearson's Arms, the pub and restaurant opposite. In 1830 George Stephenson built one of the first passenger railway lines, which ran the half dozen miles from here to Canterbury.

CANTERBURY

Canterbury ❸ is the cradle of English Christianity. Its main attraction is, of

Charles Dickens, tireless writer and social campaigner.

Rochester Cathedral.

⏲ FACT FILE

Main town Canterbury.

By car M2 and A2 from London, 50 miles (80km).

By train From London Charing Cross.

By sea Dover is the principal ferry port to France; the Channel Tunnel is outside nearby Folkestone (from Dover on the M20, London is 75 miles/120km, Canterbury 20 miles/32km on the A2).

By air Gatwick Airport (www.gatwickairport.com) is in West Sussex, 28 miles (45km) south of London. Fast trains link the airport with Victoria Station approximately every 15 minutes. Journey time 30 minutes.

Big attraction Canterbury Cathedral.

Best garden Sissinghurst Castle.

Best train ride Romney, Hythe and Dymchurch Railway.

What to eat and drink English wines from Lamberhurst and Tenterden; hundreds of types of fruit at Brogdale Orchard; lamb from Romney Marsh.

Annual events Summer concerts at Leeds Castle; opera and theatre companies tour historic buildings in summer, particularly National Trust properties.

Tourist information Canterbury, Beaney House, 18 High Street, tel: 01227-862 162; Royal Tunbridge Wells, The Pantiles; tel: 01892-515 675.

CANTERBURY CATHEDRAL

The Church of England's spiritual home is a delightful hotchpotch of styles.

Canterbury, the birthplace of Christianity in England, is the mother church of the Anglican Communion, its archbishop the Primate of England. In AD 597 Pope Gregory the Great sent Augustine to England to convert the English, whose religion had lapsed after the Romans had departed. He converted King Ethelbert of Kent, who gave him land on which he founded a monastery (outside the city walls) and the cathedral (within).

MURDER OF THOMAS BECKET

In 1170 four knights, thinking they were doing King Henry II a favour, murdered the "turbulent priest", Archbishop Thomas Becket, in the northwest transept. Becket was promptly canonised and in 1174

Stained glass window depicting Thomas Becket at Trinity Chapel, Canterbury Cathedral.

Henry performed a penance at his tomb. From then until the Reformkation, the cathedral was a place of pilgrimage, not just in England, but throughout Europe. The 14th-century poet Geoffrey Chaucer gives a vivid account of the characters who joined the pilgrimages in the prologue to *The Canterbury Tales*. In 1220 Becket's bones were transferred to a shrine in the Trinity Chapel and in 1935, T.S. Eliot's play about Becket, *Murder in the Cathedral*, was first performed in the Chapter House leading off the Great Cloister.

THE CATHEDRAL'S ARCHITECTURE

The cathedral (www.canterbury-cathedral.org; summer Mon–Sat 9am–5.30pm, Sun 9am–4.30pm, winter Mon–Sat 9am–5pm, Sun 10am–4.30pm, last entry 30 mins before closing) has spectacular features. The oldest part is the well-lit crypt, from the 11th century, and there are traces of earlier work; some of its fine carved capitals are unfinished. Four years after Becket's death a fire resulted in the building of the Trinity Chapel to contain his tomb and remodelling by William of Sens of the choir, which was used by the monks of the adjoining monastery for singing daily psalms.

The glorious, soaring, Perpendicular nave, rebuilt in the late 14th century, is the longest medieval nave in Europe; above the central crossing rises the main Bell Harry Tower (249ft/90 metres), added a century later. Among the many noble tombs, perhaps the finest is that of the Black Prince in the Trinity Chapel, a copper effigy encumbered in full armour.

The cathedral's stunning stained glass dates from the 12th and 13th centuries and rivals the best in France. The windows in the Trinity Chapel portray the life of Jesus; a noted window of Adam, formerly part of a series showing the ancestors of Jesus in the choir and Trinity Chapel, is now in the west end of the cathedral.

During World War II, Canterbury was badly damaged by a series of bombing raids, known as the "Baedeker Blitzkrieg". The raids occurred after the Battle of Britain, when the Luftwaffe's capacity to cause widespread damage was severely limited, and specifically targeted rural and coastal communities. Miraculously, the cathedral remained completely unscathed.

course, the **cathedral** (see opposite), which is steeped in the history of its glorious and infamous past. As a place of pilgrimage for Christians from all over Europe, it provided the setting for one of the first great works of English literature, Geoffrey Chaucer's *The Canterbury Tales* (1387). In St Margaret's Street the **Canterbury Tales** (www.canterburytales. org.uk; Apr–Aug daily 10am–5pm, Sept–Oct until 4pm, Nov–Mar Wed–Sun 10am–4pm) promises a "medieval adventure" with the sights, sounds and even the smells of the journey made by five of Chaucer's characters.

Despite German aerial bomb attacks in 1942, much of Canterbury's medieval character remains. The town's delights include parts of the original Roman wall which once enclosed it. Also worth visiting are the excavated ruins of **St Augustine's Abbey** (www.english-heritage.org. uk; Apr–Sept daily 10am–6pm, Oct until 5pm, Nov–Mar Sat–Sun 10am–4pm). Further east along Longport is **St Martin's Church** (Tue, Thu, Fri 11am–3pm, Sat until 4pm, Sun 9.45–10.30am; free), where continuous Christian worship

has taken place since AD 597. It was Augustine's first base in Canterbury. The cathedral, the abbey and the church are all part of a Unesco World Heritage Site. In the 4th century this area was selected by rich Romans for their villas, and remains can still be seen. The Canterbury Roman Museum (www.can terburymuseums.co.uk; daily 10am–5pm) is a family-friendly spot built around the remains of an original Roman townhouse, while the Beaney House of Art & Knowledge (Tue–Sat 10am–5pm, Sun 11am–4pm) contains a small museum, art gallery, library and café.

But Canterbury doesn't just offer a window to the past – the university town's narrow streets are lined with pubs, restaurants, independent shops and the modern Marlowe Theatre (www.mar lowetheatre.com). Located in The Friars, the theatre is named after Christopher Marlowe (1564–1593), who was born and attended school in the city. It is hailed as one of the landmark theatres in the country, and the main auditorium, with seating for 1,200, hosts touring productions and a programme featuring plays,

Canterbury pilgrims, as described by Chaucer.

Sunset over Whitstable's beach huts.

An oast house in the Kent countryside.

musicals, comedy, dance and much more. The Marlowe Studio supports local projects and the youth theatre.

Further east is **North Foreland**, the tip of the duck's tail of Kent, marked with a famous lighthouse – the last to be manned in the UK, going automated only in 1998. The lighthouse keepers' cottages now provide accommodation for holidaymakers (visit www.ruralretreats. co.uk for details). Just around the coast above North Foreland is the town of Margate, a holiday resort that suffered decades of decline since its Victorian heyday, but which is now attracting investment and tourism again. Leading the regeneration is the **Turner Contemporary Art Gallery** (www.turnercontemporary.org; Tue–Sun 10am–5pm; free), named after the great landscape painter J.M.W. Turner, who went to school in the town and continued to visit long afterwards. Exhibitions range across the high points of modern and contemporary art – past commissions include Grayson Perry and Tracey Emin (who now has a studio in the town). The cobbled streets of the old town are filled with boutique shops and antique stores, and a crop of smart hotels and restaurants are also springing up. There is also Dreamland (www.dreamland.co.uk), the UK's original pleasure park.

ALONG THE KENT COAST

On the other side of North Foreland, just to the south, is **Broadstairs**, a pretty, old-fashioned seaside town with a sandy bay and landscaped cliffs, which Dickens described as being "left high and dry by the tide of years". When he knew it, the cliff-top **Bleak House** was called Fort House. He spent many long summer holidays there in the 1850s and 1860s. It was here that he wrote much of his novel *David Copperfield*.

Sandwich lies along the River Stour, 2 miles (3km) from the sea. In the 9th century it was an important port, but by the 17th century, progressive silting of the estuary left it high and dry, and it is now surrounded by a 500-acre (200-hectare) coastal bird sanctuary. In the 11th century, Sandwich became one of the original Cinque Ports (pronounced "sink"), a string of harbours from here

⊙ THE HOP GARDENS OF KENT

A distinctive feature of the landscape of Kent are the white-painted, angled wooden cowls of the round (and later square) hop-drying kilns known as oast houses. These once turned with the wind to act as chimneys above the slatted wooden floors over which hop flowers were scattered above some form of heating. After the hops were dried they were cooled and stored, and packed into bags before being dispatched to the breweries. There are only a handful of hop farms left in Kent and most kilns have been converted for residential use, though hop bines – the long plants that spiral clockwise around taut twine attached to wires supported by hop poles – which have a pleasant smell, often decorate pubs. There was a time, however, when hops, a principal ingredient of English ale, were a mainstay of the local agriculture. They were also an integral part of the lives of the working-class families from the East End of London, who every September would come down to Kent in their thousands, living in special hopper huts and harvesting the bines.

Much of it was neck-aching, overhead work, and after the shout of "pull no more bines" the evening's rewards were singsongs and gatherings on the farms or in the local pubs. However, by the mid-20th century, mechanised harvesting methods had finally consigned these working holidays to history.

to Hastings with special trading privileges granted in return for maintaining vessels to defend the English Channel from the French. **Walmer Castle** (www.english-heritage.org.uk; Apr–Sept daily 10am–6pm, Oct 10am–5pm, Nov–Mar Sat–Sun 10am–4pm) in **Deal** ❹ is still the official residence of the Lord Warden of the Cinque Ports, a post held by the late Queen Mother for 24 years. Here, too, is the simple camp bed where the great Duke of Wellington, who vanquished Napoleon at Waterloo, chose to die like a simple soldier. It was on the beach of this small resort that Julius Caesar landed in 55 BC.

Sandwich, Deal and **Dover** ❺ are now billed as "White Cliffs Country", and at Dover, Britain's busiest passenger port, the chalk massif of the South Downs dramatically drops into the sea. The Romans built a lighthouse on these cliffs and the Normans a **castle** (www.english-heritage.org.uk; Apr–Sept daily 10am–6pm, Oct 10am–5pm, Nov–Mar Sat–Sun 10am–4pm), where you can experience a medieval siege and visit tunnels used by the military in World War II. The Roman Painted House (www.theromanpaintedhouse.org.uk; early Apr–mid-Sept Tue–Sun 10am–5pm, except mid-Apr–May: Tue and Sat only) in New Street, which was excavated in the 1970s, is also worth a visit. Built around AD 200, it was probably an official hotel for those crossing the channel. The neighbouring channel port of **Folkestone** is also built beside steep cliffs. The town has a large market by the sea on Sunday where you can buy, among many things, dried dogfish called "Folkestone beef". The nearby **Channel Tunnel** provides fast train and car-shuttle services between England and France. **Ashford**, along with Ebbsfleet, on the high-speed rail link from France to London, is a handy jumping-off point for the rest of Kent.

CASTLES AND GARDENS

Maidstone ❻ is the county town of Kent, built alongside the River Medway. Places to visit are just out of town: the **Museum of Kent Life** (www.kentlife.org.uk; daily 10am–4.30pm, mid-July–Aug until 6pm, Dec until 3pm, with exceptions), in Sandling on the north side of the town,

Dover Castle.

The Roman pharos, or lighthouse, at Dover Castle.

The view over Sissinghurst Castle's gardens from the Elizabethan Tower.

has Britain's last working oast house and hop-pickers' huts, and tells the story of how Kent was once filled with seasonal workers from the East End of London. Southwest at Yalding, near Paddock Wood, is the **Hop Farm Family Park** (www.thehopfarm.co.uk; daily 10am–5pm), based around a large collection of oast houses. A highlight at the park are the shire horses, which once pulled the brewers' drays, and special shire horse "experience" days are run. There are music festivals, glamping huts and various attractions for children, including funfair rides.

Six miles (10km) to the south of Maidstone, **Leeds Castle** (www.leeds-castle. com; daily Apr–Sept 10.30am–5.30pm, Oct–Mar until 4pm) dates back to the 12th century and later passed into royal hands, becoming the residence of the widowed queens of medieval England. Henry VIII visited frequently with his wife Catherine of Aragon. This fairy-tale place, built on islands in a lake amidst 500 acres (200 hectares) of parkland, is one of England's finest castles. As well as visiting the grand interior of the castle

itself, visitors can see the quirky museum of dog collars – some of which date back 500 years – and wander through the elaborate yew maze. Apart from formal gardens, the extensive grounds feature a bird of prey centre and children's playgrounds. Black swans swim on the large lake. Grand open-air concerts, classic motor shows, food and flower festivals, and *son et lumière* shows are put on in the grounds in summer.

Sissinghurst Castle ❼ (www.national trust.org.uk/sissinghurst-castle; mid-Mar– Oct daily 11am–5.30pm) is not a castle at all, but the ruins of a 16th-century manor house and a perfect backdrop for one of the most popular gardens in England. During the Seven Years War it served as a prison for captured French soldiers. It was bought by Vita Sackville-West (1892–1962), poet, novelist and gardener, and her politician husband Harold Nicolson, both key members of the Bloomsbury set, in 1930. The beautiful gardens arranged as "outdoor rooms" are delightful, though belated revelations about Vita's love life – which included an affair with the writer Virginia Woolf – no

doubt have helped to bring the curious. The White Garden has a stunning array of white foliage and blooms and is particularly appealing. There is a vegetable garden that supplies the licensed restaurant with fresh fruit and vegetables. Visitors can also see the room where Vita sat and wrote.

WEAVERS AND THE WEALD

The surrounding white weatherboarded High Weald towns of **Tenterden**, **Cranbrook** and **Goudhurst** are peaceful country places. In 1747 the villagers of Goudhurst locked themselves in the church while a gang of smugglers from nearby **Hawkhurst** fought the local militia in the churchyard. From this half-timbered village there are wonderful views south over hop and fruit country. These Wealden towns grew rich on wool and weaving. Large, half-timbered hall houses remain. Among the most interesting are **Smallhythe Place**, near Tenterden (www.nationaltrust.org.uk/small-hythe-place; Mar–Oct Wed–Sun 11am–5pm), a charming 16th-century house where the actress Ellen Terry lived,

and **Great Dixter** (www.greatdixter.co.uk; Apr–Oct Tue–Sun, house: 1–5pm, gardens: 11am–5pm) in Northiam, a rival of Sissinghurst, which was home to the horticulturalist Christopher Lloyd, who set major trends in gardening in recent years. Nearby is **Bodiam Castle** (www.nationaltrust.org.uk/bodiam-castle; Mar–Oct daily 11am–5pm, Nov–Dec until 4pm, Jan–Feb Sat–Sun only), a classic medieval fort, dating from 1385 and set in a generous moat; while **Scotney Castle** (www.nationaltrust.org.uk/scotney-castle; daily 10am–5pm or dusk if earlier, winter until 4pm), 5 miles (8km) southwest, is a thoroughly romantic spot with a ruined 14th-century moated castle, and gardens landscaped in the 18th-century pictorial tradition.

TAKING THE WATERS IN TUNBRIDGE WELLS

To the west, halfway down the A21 between London and Hastings, lies **Royal Tunbridge Wells** ❽, a place with a reputation for retired colonels who write letters of complaint to the *Daily Telegraph* and sign themselves "Disgusted of

⊙ Tip

The Kent and East Sussex Railway (tel: 01580-765 155; www.kesr.org.uk) starts its journey to Bodiam from Tenterden. Full-sized steam trains normally run daily in July and August (check the website for the rest of the year). Try a cream tea in the restaurant car. Wending its way for just over 10 miles (16km), through idyllic countryside, it's a perfect family outing.

Leeds Castle.

Tunbridge Wells". The town first rose to fame and fortune in 1606, when Dudley, Lord North, a hypochondriac, discovered the health-giving properties of a spring on the common. Court and fashion followed, and the waters, rich in iron salts, were, and still are, taken at the Pantiles. This terraced walk, with shops and cafés behind a colonnade, is named after the tile work laid in 1638, some of which is still there. The Forum (https://www.twforum.co.uk/; daily 7.30–11pm) is a grass-roots music venue with a 250-person capacity in a unique setting: a former public toilet on Tunbridge Wells Common. Despite being tiny, it's managed to attract an impressive line-up – Adele and Oasis played here as emerging artists. More recently, the likes of Coldplay and Mumford & Sons have graced its stage.

Penshurst Place (www.penshurstplace.com; Apr–Oct daily, house: noon–4pm, grounds: 10.30am–6pm), just to the northwest of Tunbridge Wells, is one of Kent's finest mansions, dating from 1340. Home of the Viscount de L'Isle, it was for two centuries the seat of the Sidney family, notably Sir Philip Sidney,

The Mermaid Inn in Rye.

the Elizabethan soldier and poet. A few miles to the west lies **Hever Castle ⑨** (www.hevercastle.co.uk; Apr–Oct, Dec daily, castle: noon–6pm, gardens: 10.30am–6pm, Mar, Nov Wed–Sun until 4.30pm). Henry VIII, who first met Anne Boleyn in this, her father's house, seized Hever after her execution and murdered her brother, George. William Waldorf, 1st Viscount Astor (1848–1919), applied his American millions to make massive and sympathetic improvements to the moated castle, the 35-acre (15-hectare) lake and gardens where flowerbeds are laid out exactly as they were in Tudor times 400 years ago.

CHARTWELL

Some 10 miles (16km) to the north on the B2026 is **Westerham**, where General James Wolfe, who decisively beat the French in the battle for control of Canada in 1759, was born. His birthplace, **Quebec House** (www.nationaltrust.org.uk/quebec-house; Mar–Oct Wed–Sun noon–5pm, Nov Sat–Sun 1–4pm), displays Wolfe memorabilia.

South of the village is **Chartwell** (www.nationaltrust.org.uk/chartwell; Mar–Oct Mon–Fri 11.30am–5pm, Sat–Sun 11am–5pm), where Sir Winston Churchill lived from 1924 until his death in 1965. There is often quite a queue to see his home and studio, where many of his paintings are on display. The grounds contain the famous brick wall that he built, and a fine kitchen garden – as well as the views of the Kentish Weald that inspired him.

Sevenoaks is 5 miles (8km) to the east on the far side of the A21, and on its outskirts is **Knole ⑩** (www.nationaltrust.org.uk/knole; mid-Mar–Oct Tue–Sun 11–5pm), one of the largest private houses in the country and the birthplace of Vita Sackville-West. It was the Archbishop of Canterbury's residence until confiscated by Henry VIII. It has 365 rooms, 52 stairways and seven courtyards. There are exceptionally fine portraits of the Sackville family by

Gainsborough and Van Dyck (though protective low lighting makes some hard to see), as well as some rare furniture. There is a 1,000-acre (400-hectare) deer park and a visitor centre too.

Southeast of Knole is **Ightham Mote** (www.nationaltrust.org.uk/ightham-mote; mid-Mar–Oct daily 11am–5pm), a stunning 14th-century timber and stone, secluded, moated manor house. Ightham Mote has many special features including a Great Hall, a Tudor Chapel with hand-painted ceiling, and a Grade I-listed dog kennel in the courtyard, built for a St Bernard.

WILLIAM THE CONQUEROR'S COUNTRY

In the Levels to the east, the village of **Pevensey** ⓫ features a castle (www.english-heritage.org.uk; Apr–Sept daily 10am–6pm, Oct 10am–5pm, Nov–Mar Sat–Sun 10am–4pm) that was the landing place in 1066 of William, Duke of Normandy, the last man successfully to invade Britain. The Norman conqueror did not meet up with Harold of England until some 10 miles (16km) inland; Senlac Field, the spot where Harold fell, his eye pierced by an arrow, was marked by William, who built upon it the high altar of the abbey church at **Battle** ⓬ as a thanksgiving. An imposing 14th-century gatehouse leads to the grounds and ruins of the **abbey** (www.english-heritage.org.uk; daily Apr–Sept 10am–6pm, Oct until 5pm, Nov–Feb Sat–Sun only 10am–4pm, Mar Wed–Sun 10am–4pm), where there is a Visitor Centre and the 1066 Battlefield attraction.

The place where William prepared for battle is just 6 miles (9km) southeast of Battle. The hilltop Norman castle at **Hastings** ⓭ stands above a warren of caves where Smugglers' Adventure (www.smugglersadventure.co.uk; Mar–Oct daily 10am–5pm), a family attraction, can be visited. The castle is now a ruin, but a siege tent inside tells the battle story on which the town has thrived. On the Stade, the stretch of shingle beach, tall,

black weatherboarded sheds, known as the Net Shops and used by fishermen for hundreds of years for storing nets, are architectural curiosities.

To the east is the ancient town of **Rye** ⓮, which has suffered from floods and the French, but now lies high and dry. Edward III (1327–77) gave Rye its walls and gates. The **Landgate** and **Ypres Tower** (www.ryemuseum.co.uk; Apr–Oct 10.30am–5pm, Nov–Mar until 3.30pm) survive, as well as much half-timbering.

Rye has long been a home to writers: Lamb House (www.nationaltrust.org.uk/lamb-house; mid-Mar–Oct Fri–Tue 11–5pm) in Mermaid Street was the home of Henry James from 1898 to 1916, and later, E.F. Benson, whose *Mapp and Lucia* books were inspired by life in the town. Today, it is a popular seaside getaway for Londoners, with its cobbled streets, seafood restaurants, cosy pubs and boutique hotels.

From Rye the land lies flat across the great expanse of **Romney Marsh**, a strange, haunting area of water weeds, rare-breed sheep and wading birds, including the Kentish plover.

Sheds for drying fishing nets, on the shore at Hastings.

The Pantiles in Royal Tunbridge Wells.

Seaford Head cliffs, Sussex.

BRIGHTON AND THE DOWNS

The resorts of the south coast have a raffish air. Around about, and to the north, are the bracing hills of the Downs with hill forts, horseracing and welcoming pubs.

The Downs, a parallel chalk range that stripes the south of England, gives the region a distinctive outdoor flavour. Here are the famous horseracing tracks of Epsom, Goodwood, Fontwell and Brighton; the fine golf course at Wentworth; the parklands of Petworth, Glyndebourne and Sheffield Park; tennis at Eastbourne; as well as many fine flowering gardens. Close to the capital, the whole area is well explored and much of the northern "home county" of Surrey is suburban. Many people commute to the city from as far away as the Sussex coast, which has long been a favourite place for a day's outing, particularly Brighton, one of the world's first bathing resorts.

THE SOUTH DOWNS COAST PATH

The **South Downs** were a highway into Britain for early settlers who started clearing land for farming here 6,000 years ago, leaving it crew-cut by sheep and striated by ploughshares. Today in the high spots where Iron Age forts and flint mines flourished, the wind whispers through copses, windmill sails and woodland clumps that rise over voluptuous gullies and coombs, remnants of the last Ice Age that scooped out devils' dykes and punch-bowls. Along the crest runs the white streamer of the South Downs Way,

A Brighton seagull.

Britain's first designated long-distance bridleway, and a popular path for walkers of all abilities. The beauty of the area led to a large chunk of it being designated a National Park in 2009.

The South Downs make their final majestic bow at **Beachy Head** ⑮, where chalk cliffs reach 530ft (160 metres) and crumble yearly into the sea. The lighthouse has been moved further inland, and the steps down the cliff at Birling Gap are only temporary. From the cliff top there is a view down on Eastbourne, a pristine resort which in sunshine can

⊙ **Main attractions**
Beachy Head
Lewes
The Royal Pavilion, Brighton
Sheffield Park
Wisley Gardens
Parham House
Chichester
Weald and Downland Open Air Museum

Maps on pages
194, 208

LITERARY FRIENDS IN THE SOUTH

The Bloomsbury Set, which started in London, ended up in the country, where its cultural traces can still be seen.

In his 1903 *Principia Ethica* the philosopher G.E. Moore stated, "By far the most valuable things are the pleasures of human intercourse and the enjoyment of beautiful objects. It is they that form the rational ultimate end of social progress." This served as a springboard from old, stern Victorian values, into a new spirit of freedom. It was a spirit that infused a group of friends who began to meet two years later at 46 Gordon Square in Bloomsbury, near the British Museum. Among them were the writers Virginia Woolf and Vanessa Bell (then the

Vanessa Bell's self-portrait at Charleston.

Stephen sisters), Lytton Strachey and E.M. Forster, the economist John Maynard Keynes, and the artists Duncan Grant and Roger Fry.

HOMES IN SUSSEX

Little evidence of their creative spirit remains in London, but a visit to a number of sites in the south gives a clue of this intimate and influential group. Virginia and Leonard Woolf bought Monk's House in Rodmell in 1919, seven years after they married. Virginia's sister, Vanessa Bell, took over Charleston near Firle, a delightful small house and garden, now fully restored with their hand-painted cupboards and doors.

Woolf also found a good friend in Vita Sackville-West, who was born at Knole in Kent and, with her husband Harold Nicolson, bought Sissinghurst Castle. Woolf's 1928 novel *Orlando* is based on their friendship; a copy of the manuscript is displayed at Knole.

VIRGINIA WOOLF AND FRIENDS

Part of the interest in these literary figures was their private lives, and the sexual ambiguity and freedom that they relished. Duncan Grant, though homosexual, was Vanessa Bell's lover and father of her daughter Angelica; Angelica later married David "Bunny" Garnett, who had been Duncan's lover; Vita Sackville-West, and her husband, Harold Nicolson, both pursued same-sex affairs whilst remaining happily married: as well as the famous fling with Virginia Woolf, Sackville-West also had a long relationship with Violet Treyfusis, daughter of the mistress of Edward VII.

World War II ended the good times. Virginia Woolf, who had suffered from mental illness for most of her life, found her sensitivity tried by the incessant drone of fighters and bombers overhead. Finally one day she walked across the meadows from her house to the River Ouse, filled her pockets with stones, walked into the water and drowned. The 12th-century church of St Michael and All Angels at nearby Berwick suffered bomb damage, and after the war Angelica and Quentin Bell painted it in the bright country colours they had grown up with at Charleston.

gleam like a slice of the French Riviera. The town was well planned from the start, around the middle of the 19th century, by the 7th Duke of Devonshire: shops are banned from the seafront and there are 200 acres (80 hectares) of public parks. Each year visitors flock to see the pier, the early 19th-century fortress and other attractions, including lawn tennis courts in Devonshire Park where women's championships are held prior to Wimbledon each year. Alongside The Beacon, a new shopping complex that replaced the Arndale Centre in 2018, is a scattering of second-hand books and antiques shops, record stores and galleries in the Little Chelsea area (around Grove Road and South Street). A 10-minute walk south, the Towner Art Gallery (Tue–Sun 10am–5pm) houses fine paintings by Eric Ravilious (1903-1942) – who focused on the South Downs landscape in his work – along with temporary exhibitions and a top-floor café that opens onto a wide balcony with views of the Downs.

West of Eastbourne, Beachy Head is the highest of seven undulating waves of chalk hills known as the **Seven Sisters**. The fire-warmed Beachy Head Pub, on the headland, is a great spot for lunch. Behind them the **Seven Sisters Country Park** leads into the **Cuckmere Valley**, a good place for walks, especially starting around the pleasant village of **Alfriston** where the **Clergy House** (www.national trust.org.uk/alfriston-clergy-house; Sat–Wed mid-Mar–Oct 10.30am–5pm, Nov–mid-Dec Sat–Sun 11am–4pm), a 14th-century thatched hall by the village green, was the first property to be acquired by the National Trust, in 1896.

HISTORIC SUSSEX HOUSES

Between the two world wars, this corner of England between Eastbourne and Brighton was a favourite spot of London's literary Bloomsbury set (see page 206). At **Charleston** (www.charles ton.org.uk; Mar–Oct Wed–Sat guided tours only 11.30am–5pm, Sun noon–5pm), an 18th-century farmhouse, Vanessa Bell and Duncan Grant drew the literary crowd, and their enthusiastic painting and decoration gives the house great charm. The family's

Bateman's, the 17th-century Jacobean house at Burwash.

Audience members picnicking on the Glyndebourne lawns.

⊘ FACT FILE

County towns Lewes (East Sussex), Chichester (West Sussex), Guildford (Surrey).

By car Brighton is 50 miles (80km) from London, and the journey takes about 75 minutes, depending on traffic.

By train Trains go from London Victoria to Chichester, Worthing, Brighton and Eastbourne.

By air Gatwick, London's second airport, is halfway between Brighton and London: trains from Gatwick to Brighton and Worthing take about 30 minutes.

By sea Ferries and Seacats from Newhaven to Dieppe.

Best family day out Weald and Downland Open Air Museum.

Local words Twitten (passages between streets), catcreeps (steps between streets on different levels).

The cultural year Brighton Festival (major multifarious events, three weeks in May); Brighton Fringe Festival (largest annual arts festival in England, four weeks in summer); Glyndebourne opera (summer).

Sports Eastbourne Women's Lawn Tennis Championship (June); Glorious Goodwood horseracing (July); Goodwood Festival of Speed (June/July).

Tourist information Brighton tel: 01273-290 337; www.visitbrighton.com; Chichester tel: 01243-775 888; Guildford tel: 01483 444 333.

handiwork can also be seen at the nearby church at **Berwick**. In 1919 Vanessa Bell's sister, the writer Virginia Woolf, and her husband Leonard bought **Monk's House** (www.nationaltrust. org.uk/monks-house; Apr–Oct Wed–Sun 1–5pm), a weatherboarded building among thatched houses in **Rodmell**. The village lies in the meadowlands around the River Ouse, where Virginia Woolf drowned in 1941.

Nearby **Firle Place** (www.firle.com; June–Sept Tue–Thu, Sun 2–4.30pm) in West Firle was refashioned in the 18th-century Georgian style from the Tudor original. Firle has been in the Gage family for more than 500 years; Sir Thomas Gage was Commander-in-Chief of the British forces in America during the skirmish of Lexington that began the American War of Independence in 1775. In the Great Hall are paintings by Reynolds, Gainsborough and Van Dyck, and a 17th-century map of New York shows Wall Street running behind the city wall.

On the other side of the A27 is **Glynde Place** (www.glynde.co.uk; May–June

Wed–Thu, Sun guide tours only 2pm and 3.30pm; tearoom 1–5pm), an Elizabethan manor belonging to Viscount Hampden with portraits of a family that has owned this land for 800 years. A mile to the north is **Glyndebourne** (www. glyndebourne.com), where John Christie and his wife, the opera singer Audrey Mildmay, built an opera house in their Elizabethan home in the 1930s. Operagoers have picnic dinners on the extensive lawns.

LEWES

Lewes 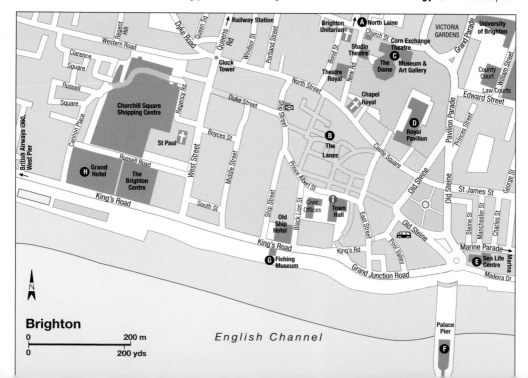, the county town of East Sussex (at the junction of the A26 and A27), has been the scene of battles since Saxon times and today it is best known for its explosive Guy Fawkes celebrations on 5 November. Lewes is also an antiques and antiquarian book centre. Thomas Paine, author of *The Rights of Man*, which helped to fuel American Independence, lived at Bull House in the High Street from 1768–74. The Barbican in the High Street is the entrance to the Norman **castle** and **Museum of Sussex Archaeology** (www.sussexpast.

Brighton

0 200 m
0 200 yds

English Channel

co.uk; Tue–Sat 10am–5.30pm, Mon, Sun 11am–5.30pm, Nov–Feb until 3.45pm), the high point of the town, built by William de Warrene in the wake of the Norman Conquest. From here there are views over Harry Hill, where in 1264 Simon de Montfort and England's barons defeated Henry III, forcing him to sign the Mise of Lewes, which brought about parliamentary government to England.

From 1890 the Anglophile New England art collector Edward Perry Warren lived with a "male brotherhood" in Lewes House, now occupied by the local council. He commissioned from the French sculptor Auguste Rodin a version of *The Kiss*, with instructions that the man's genitals should be "seen in their entirety". The result horrified the town council and it was only briefly displayed; today it is in the Tate Britain gallery in London. The High Street drops steeply to the River Ouse, and over the bridge is Harvey's, brewers of one of the best Sussex beers, and **Anne of Cleves's House** (www.sussexpast. co.uk; Feb, Nov Tue–Sat 10am–4pm, Sun–Mon 11am–4pm, Mar–Oct until 5pm), a 16th-century timber-framed hall house given to Anne of Cleves in her divorce settlement with Henry VIII. Beyond it are the outline foundations of **Lewes Priory**, once one of the greatest Cluniac priories in Europe.

BRIGHTON

London's favourite resort is an hour's train journey from the capital and a short drive west along the A27 from Lewes. The story of **Brighton** ⑰ begins with a local doctor, Richard Russell, who in a tract in 1750 extolled the efficacy of sea water, both to drink and to bathe in. The practice became so sociably desirable that when Russell opened an establishment with attendants called "bathers" (for men) and "dippers" (for women), he could count on the patronage of the Prince Regent (later George IV). It became the favourite haunt of "Prinny", and in 1784 he drove a coach from London on a new, direct road in 4 hours 30 minutes. Today the journey is accomplished in a quarter of that time. On summer weekends, day-trippers

North Laine in Brighton.

The Seven Sisters.

⊙ Eat

The Brighton Foodies Festival (www.foodiesfestival. com/brighton-food-festival) is a popular year-round event combining top chefs, food and drink stalls, live music, workshops and masterclasses, held in May each year. This provides a wonderful opportunity to showcase the food of the city and the Sussex countryside, with local producers, growers, chefs, restaurants and bars coming together to champion the region. The Big Sussex market features some 90 stalls and was attended by around 57,000 people on Good Friday and Easter Saturday in 2012. There is also a Children's Food Festival giving kids the opportunity to attend food workshops and partake in food-related activities.

Brighton Pier.

arrive at **Brighton Station**. From there it's a short walk down Queen's Road and West Street to the promenade, the stony beach and sparkling sea.

The town has a raffish air, attracting artists, street performers and alternative lifestylers, who are catered for in a variety of restaurants and bars. Much of the enjoyment in the town is simply in walking the streets. From the station, heading into the old town, the first encounter is with an area called **North Laine** Ⓐ. Here there remains a spirit of the 1960s, with candle and craft shops, vegan specialists and tattoo parlours. A more recent influx of independent boutiques and artisanal coffee shops caters for the town's increasingly wealthy population. The town also has a reputation for antiques. The more respectable shops are in **The Lanes** Ⓑ, a warren of alleys between North Laine and the sea. The Lanes have various etymologies, but they follow an agricultural pattern, possibly from former fields where hemp was grown to make fishermen's nets. They are one of the best

places to head to when it's time for something to eat.

North Laine and The Lanes are divided by Church Street, where the Pavilion Gardens provide the entrance to the excellent **Brighton Museum and Art Gallery** Ⓒ (www.brightonmuseums.org. uk; Tue–Sun 10am–5pm), which fills an ornate Victorian building. Its galleries exhibit everything from fine Victorian paintings and an extensive collection of Art Deco furniture, to contemporary clothing and a scientific facial reconstruction of a Saxon man, made from a skull discovered locally. The museum is part of an interesting assortment of buildings, which includes the **Dome Theatre** in the old Royal Stables, the **Corn Exchange** in the old riding house, and **The Studio Theatre**.

These galleries and theatres all lie on the north side of the town's great attraction, the **Royal Pavilion** Ⓓ (www. brightonmuseums.org.uk; daily Apr–Sept 9.30am–5.45pm, Oct–Mar 10am– 5.15pm). In 1785 the Prince Regent rented a small farm on the Old Steine, and on this site Henry Holland and

John Nash, inspired by the architecture of Mughal India, built his lavish Pavilion. The brilliant oriental interiors, designed by Frederick Grace and Robert Jones, are decorated with golden dragons, chinoiserie, burnished palms and coloured glass. The opulent Banqueting Room is laid ready for a feast from the ballroom-sized Great Kitchen, which has 500 copper pieces in its *batterie de cuisine*. Concerts are sometimes held in the lovely Music Room. On the first floor Queen Victoria's bed is furnished with six mattresses, made of straw, hair and feathers.

Across the Old Steine down by the seafront is the **Sea Life Centre** Ⓔ (www2.visitsealife.com; daily 10am–5pm, mid-Sept–Oct, Nov–Dec until 4pm, with exceptions), which has a modern walk-through aquarium, and the **Brighton Pier (Palace Pier)** Ⓕ. Brighton's other pier, at the west end of the seafront, is now a mere skeleton after ferocious storms and a fire all but destroyed it. The futuristic British Airways i360 tower now marks the spot. Take the vertical cable car 162m

(531ft) up to the glass observation pod for amazing views.

On the east side of the Palace Pier is Madeira Drive, where the London to Brighton Veteran Car Run ends every November. The Volks Railway (www.volkselectricrailway.co.uk) goes more than a mile (2km) from here along the seafront. Built in 1883, this is said to be the oldest electric railway in the world.

The road above, Marine Parade, leads to **Brighton Marina**, a man-made harbour lined with bars, restaurants, shopping arcades, supermarkets and cinemas.

Most of the seafront action takes place on the other side of the pier, along the lower promenade, where restaurants tucked beneath the arches serve fresh seafood, live bands play in the summer and impromptu dancing can break out at any time. By the small **Brighton Fishing Museum** Ⓖ (www.brightonfishingmuseum.org.uk, daily 10am–4pm; free), barely bigger than the clinker-built fishing "punt" inside it, stalls sell cockles and whelks and other delights of the deep. Behind it is

The Royal Pavilion, Brighton.

WE DO LIKE TO BE BESIDE THE SEASIDE

England's coastal resorts have long attracted a holiday crowd in search of bracing air and a little fun.

The Brighton Parish register of 12 November 1641 records the burial of a woman who "came for cure". This is thought to be the earliest record in England of anyone using the sea for its curative properties. Within a century bathing in the sea had become a pastime for visitors to this fishing village and elsewhere. A 1735 print from Scarborough, on the Yorkshire coast, shows bathing machines on the beach. These wooden huts on wheels, used as changing rooms, were drawn by horses into the sea. At Margate "modesty hoods" were fitted over the steps of these machines, designed by a local Quaker. Male bathers did not always wear costumes at first and,

Victorian bathers.

though there are instances of female bathers also swimming naked in Brighton and Scarborough, they generally wore long flannel gowns.

THE BURGEONING RESORTS

The fashionable arrived, and the populace followed just as soon as there were railways to take them there. Wakes Week in Lancashire took cotton workers to Blackpool in their thousands, and it became the first resort to reach borough status, in 1876. Brighton burgeoned and became, in effect, London-on-Sea (a soubriquet still used today), though Southend and Margate on the Thames Estuary became just as accessible. On bank holidays, introduced in 1871, special trains ran, entertainments were laid on and songs about the seaside were played by promenade bands.

A hero of the hour was Captain Webb. In 1875 this dashing former captain of the Cunard line, covered in porpoise oil and wearing a scarlet costume, swam the English Channel in 21 hours 41 minutes. It was the world's first marathon aquatic event.

THE RESORTS TODAY

Today, England's seaside resorts retain a Victorian air: seafront promenades with deckchairs and bandstands; rusting piers in need of repair, and racks of seaside rock in every imaginable flavour. An aroma of vinegar may mingle with the ozone: fish and chips are the traditional seaside fast food. There are even nudist enclaves (Brighton's was the first, in 1981) with a certain bracing innocence.

Some resorts – Hove, Eastbourne – have their smart addresses. But even their airs and graces cannot hide the breezy cheeriness that earlier generations of holidaymakers brought to the English seaside. In recent years, the seaside resort has also enjoyed something of a renaissance: celebrities have settled in Brighton, Whitstable has attracted some trendy "second homers" who want a beach retreat, and some fashionable bars and restaurants have opened all along the coast. Moreover, at the first sign of unseasonably sunny weather during a weekend or bank holiday, Londoners still flock to the coast and the beaches are as packed as ever.

the historic Old Ship Hotel, from where Charles II escaped to France.

The best-known hotel is the **Grand Hotel ⓗ**, the ritzy joint on the seafront that became synonymous with naughty weekends. Following the devastating IRA bomb attack on the building during the 1984 Conservative Party Conference, which left two dead and more than 30 injured, the hotel was defiantly restored to its former glory.

ROTTINGDEAN, WORTHING AND BOGNOR

Four miles (6.5km) east of Brighton is **Rottingdean**, a pleasant village by the sea, though rather cut off from it by the A259 coastal road. From 1897 to 1902 Rudyard Kipling, the great literary figure of Britain's Empire days, lived at The Elms, where he wrote *Kim*, *Just So Stories* and *Stalky & Co*. His 18th-century house cannot be visited, but its walled garden on The Green is open to be enjoyed. He was related to the Pre-Raphaelite painter Edward Burne-Jones (1833–98), who lived in North End House on the west side of The Green.

To the west of Brighton, ribbon development connects the Sussex resorts of **Worthing**, **Littlehampton** (there is a good sandy beach at **Climping**, on the west side of Littlehampton) and **Bognor Regis**. Straddling the River Arun, Littlehampton is a pleasant seaside town with a clutch of good food and drink spots, including 47 Mussel Row for seafood; the Thomas Heatherwick-designed East Beach Cafe, with its coastal design and sea views; and sister West Beach Cafe by architect Asif Khan. A ferry also traverses the river from Littlehampton up to Arundel – great for children. However, Worthing is perhaps the most amiable of these resorts. Shaking off its image as a place for retirees, it has become a popular centre for hi-tech industries. Oscar Wilde took its name for his main character, John Worthing, in his 1895 play *The Importance of Being Earnest*, which he wrote while staying here.

Just inland from Worthing is the fine church at **Sompting**, visible from the main A27. Dating from AD 960, it is the only Saxon church in the country with a Rhenish helm spire. Faithful parishioners have embroidered views of the Downs on the hassocks.

IRON AGE FORTS

Behind Worthing are **Chanctonbury** and **Cissbury Ring**s, sites of Iron Age hill forts. There is little actually to see, but they are atmospheric places and make excellent walks. Cissbury was named after the Saxon leader Cissa, but the hill fort was built long before him, in 240 BC. It covers 650 acres (260 hectares), making it the second-largest in the country after Maiden Castle in Dorset. For the ramparts a wooden wall was constructed to contain 60,000 tons of chalk excavated from the ditch. The site had already been occupied for around 4,000 years when some

The main gate to Lewes Castle.

300 flint mine shafts were dug, to a depth of up to 75ft (23 metres), using deer's antlers as digging tools. The thick grass is springy underfoot; it has never been ploughed, and the rich and ancient flora includes eight kinds of orchids and fleawort, used in bedding to fend off fleas.

Chanctonbury, just to the north, is privately owned by the Goring family. In 1760 Charles Goring planted a beech copse around the hill fort, and it maintains mythical properties: run round it seven times on a moonless night to summon the Devil. Chanctonbury can be reached from **Steyning** (pronounced Stenning), a pleasing small town of 61 listed buildings. Its church of St Andrews has the most impressive Norman nave in Sussex and gives an idea of the importance that this town, formerly on a navigable river and with its own mint, once had.

THE NORTH DOWNS

Surrey and Sussex are now home to a few good vineyards.

Departing now from the coast and following the northern borders of Sussex, from east to west, there are a number of outstanding gardens, all in the hands of the National Trust. **Bateman's** (www.nationaltrust.org.uk/batemans; daily mid-Mar–Oct 11am–5pm, Nov–Dec 11am–4pm) in Burwash, East Sussex, was home of the writer and Nobel laureate Rudyard Kipling from 1902 to 1936. This lovely Jacobean building is full of mementoes of the Empire Kipling so powerfully evoked, and there is a romantic garden where you can take a boat out on the pond. North of the Downs, between East Grinstead and Lewes beside the A275, is **Sheffield Park** ⑱ (www.nationaltrust.org.uk/sheffield-park-and-garden; mid-Feb–mid-Sept 10am–5pm, mid-Sept–Oct 9.30am–5pm, Nov–Dec 10am–4pm or dusk if earlier), laid out in the 18th century by "Capability" Brown with lakes, waterfalls and cascades. There is a generous show of bluebells in spring, and the Bluebell Railway steam train (www.bluebell-railway.co.uk) runs from here to Kingscote, 9 miles (14km) away. Further west, beside the A23, is **Nymans Garden** ⑲ near Hayward's Heath

⊘ ENGLISH WINES

The popularity of wine-drinking in Britain has increased dramatically in the last 20 years or so. In the unenlightened days, many pubs served only Liebfraumilch and perhaps Lambrusco, but nowadays you can expect a more grown-up selection, and New World wines are at least as widely offered by pubs as European wines. The growing popularity of wine in Britain, coupled with a changing climate, has encouraged the production of English varieties to soar and the UK is becoming a major player in wine production. Sparking white wine is a particular forte, with recommended producers including Camel Valley, Ridgeview and Nyetimber.

If you are interested in visiting a vineyard, Chapel Down Winery (tel: 01580-763 033; www.chapeldown.com) near Tenterden in Kent runs guided tours daily between April and November, while in Sussex, off the A23 between Crawley and Brighton, Bolney Wine Estate (tel: 01444-881 894; www.bolneywineestate.com) offers tours and tastings year-round. In Surrey, on the outskirts of Dorking, Denbies' Wine Estate (tel: 01306-876 616; www.denbies.co.uk) has two fine restaurants, a range of tours, and the opportunity to purchase their award-winning Chalk Ridge Rosé, which is widely hailed as one of the best rosé wines in the world. In East Anglia, the Wyken Vineyards (tel: 01359-250 287; www.wykenvineyards.co.uk) are situated idyllically on the edge of a country estate near Bury St Edmunds.

(www.nationaltrust.org.uk/nymans; house: Mar–Oct daily 11am–4pm; gardens: daily Mar–Oct 10am–5pm, Nov–Feb 10am–4pm). This fine Wealden garden boasts a historic collection of flora. Northeast of Nymans is **Wakehurst Place** (www.kew.org/visit-wakehurst; daily Mar–Oct 10am–6pm, Nov–Feb 10am–4.30pm), an outstanding botanical garden and home of the Millennium Seed Bank, the world's largest seed-conservation project.

To the northwest, in Surrey (and just outside the M25 near Great Bookham), the best of the North Downs flora can be seen at **Polesden Lacey ⑳** (www.nationaltrust.org.uk/polesden-lacey; house: Apr–Oct 11am–5pm; gardens: daily Apr–Oct 10am–5pm, Nov–Mar until 4pm). This large Regency villa is where George VI and Queen Elizabeth spent their honeymoon in 1923.

A little further west, just north of **Guildford ㉑** on the A3, is the Royal Horticultural Society's showpiece, **Wisley Gardens** (www.rhs.org.uk; Mon–Fri 10am–6pm, Sat–Sun 9am–6pm; last admission 1 hour before closing).

Guildford itself, Surrey's county town, has a castle with Norman walls and a modern cathedral. There are a number of attractive small towns nearby, including **Farnham**, **Godalming**, **Haslemere** and **Shere**.

BACK ON THE SOUTH DOWNS

A trio of stately homes lies to the south of Guildford. Near Petersfield (on the A3) is the magnificently restored 17th-century house of **Uppark** (www.nationaltrust.org.uk/uppark-house-and-garden; house: daily mid-Mar–Oct 12.30–4pm; gardens: 10am–5pm), with a fine art collection and a grand view from its high point 350ft (106 metres) on the top of the South Downs. Just to the east, **Petworth ㉒** is a town of myriad antiques shops overshadowed by the great wall of **Petworth House** (www.nationaltrust.org.uk/petworth-house-and-park; mid-Mar–Oct daily 11am–5pm). This has been home to the Percy family since 1150 and it contains the National Trust's largest painting collection, with works by

Sheffield Park.

⊙ **Fact**

The remains of Boxgrove Man, found at Boxgrove Priory near Chichester in 1993, date from 500,000 BC and are thought to belong to England's oldest inhabitant. The site, now owned by English Heritage, has yielded a tibia bone and two incisors, enough to date this as the earliest hominid so far found in England.

Van Dyck, Gainsborough, Reynolds, Blake and Turner, who had a studio here and executed many paintings of the house and extensive deer park, landscaped by "Capability" Brown. Finally, **Parham House** ㉓ (www.parhaminsussex.co.uk; house: mid-Apr–mid-Oct, Wed–Fri, Sun 2–5pm, gardens open from noon), situated between Petworth and Arundel, is one of the finest Elizabethan buildings in England, and its gardens include a 4-acre (1.6-hectare) walled garden, orchard, maze and heronry.

Due west of Parham, on a high point of the Downs by Bury Hill, is **Bignor Roman Villa** (www.bignorromanvilla.co.uk; Mar–Oct daily 10am–5pm). The site dates from the first century and covers more than 4 acres (1.8 hectares) where, beneath thatched buildings, there are mosaics depicting cherub gladiators, the goddess Venus and snake-haired Medusa. Nearby is the delightful village of Amberley, with mellow, robust thatched, flint-stone houses. The castle ruins are all that remains

Bateman's was once the home of author Rudyard Kipling.

of the palace of the bishops of Chichester.

To the south of Amberley the River Arun cuts through the South Downs to reach **Arundel** ㉔, home of the Dukes of Norfolk. This under-the-radar town is emerging as a coveted weekend getaway for Londoners, with its beautiful castle, independent shopping scene, rambling riverside walks and traditional pubs. The narrow streets are brimming with cool boutiques; try Gallery 57 for handmade ceramics and Zimmer Stewart Gallery for contemporary art. There are also vintage stores – don't miss Antiquities or Spencer Swaffer – and quaint tearooms (Belinda's is one of the best – and the oldest). The South Downs Pig hotel is set to open here in 2020, marking it as one to watch.

Its fairy-tale **castle** (www.arundelcastle.org; Apr–Oct Tue–Sun 10am–5pm) dates from 1070, but had a Victorian make-over, and has provided the backdrop for films such as *The Young Victoria* and *The Madness of King George*. The Norfolks are the premier Catholic family in England: the parish church is intriguingly divided between Anglican church and Catholic chapel, the two separated by a glass wall.

The castle is surrounded by 2 sq miles (5 sq km) of landscaped parklands, which contain a lake and a **Wildfowl and Wetlands Centre** (www.wwt.org.uk; daily Apr–mid-Oct 9.30am–5.30pm, mid-Oct–Mar until 4.30pm).

CHICHESTER AND AROUND

Chichester ㉕ is a small market town centred on a traditional Market Cross with many Georgian buildings. The modern Festival Theatre, a theatre-in-the-round, has a reputation for excellence. It lies in Priory Park by the old Norman motte and bailey and the remains of the city wall. The **Cathedral** (daily subject to services; free) is light and graceful and full of interest. Construction was begun in 1091, and

its mixture of Gothic and Norman is enhanced by works of modern art from Marc Chagall, Graham Sutherland, Patrick Procktor and, most notably, John Piper, who created the altar tapestry in 1966. Pallant House in West Pallant has further works collected by Walter Hussey, Dean of the Cathedral from 1955–77. Together with Bishop Bell, he was instrumental in giving modern art a place in the cathedral.

North of Chichester, on the top of the Downs, is **Goodwood**, the country estate of the Earl of March, where there is a racecourse in a wonderful Downland setting. "Glorious Goodwood" is the most important horseracing meeting here, held annually at the end of July. For those who prefer motorised racing, elsewhere on the estate there is a circuit for the Goodwood Festival of Speed, which is held annually at the end of June. The four-day event features historic racing cars and motorbikes, appearances (and demonstration drives) from famous champions of the recent past and a hill-climb competition.

Just beyond it is the **Weald and Downland Open Air Museum ㉖** (www.wealddown.co.uk; daily summer 10.30am–6pm, winter until 4pm, with exceptions). Around 50 historic buildings, ranging in age from 13th-century to 19th-century, have been brought to this 40-acre (17-hectare) site. They include houses and shops, mills and barns as well as a farmhouse uprooted in the building of the Channel Tunnel.

Chichester grew up as a port, and the sea is not far away. In 1960 the largest Roman domestic building north of the Alps was found at **Fishbourne ㉗** (www.sussexpast.co.uk; daily Feb–Oct 10am–5pm, Nov–mid-Dec until 4pm, mid-Dec–Jan Sat–Sun only 10am–4pm). Begun in AD 75, it had a quayside and 100 rooms, with impressive mosaic floors, but it was burnt down some 200 years later.

Among **Chichester Harbour**'s tidal estuaries, **Bosham** stands out as the most timeless, attractive backwater. Its Saxon church claims to be the oldest site of Christian worship in Sussex.

⊙ Tip

Chichester Harbour is a safe place to learn to sail and has many sailing clubs to choose from. If you just want a 90-minute trip round the harbour, boats leave from Itchenor; Easter to October, weather permitting. A two-hour birdwatching trip is also available in the winter months to see the migrant waders and huge flocks of Brent geese. For more information on all trips contact Chichester Harbour Water Tours, tel: 01243 670504; www.chichesterharbourwatertours.co.uk.

Arundel Castle.

THE ENGLISH GARDEN

England's temperate climate encourages a great diversity of gardens, which blend the grand and the homely in a cosmopolitan range of styles.

The formal gardens of great houses have both followed fashion and set the style for the nation's favourite hobby. In medieval times, fruit trees, roses and herbs were grown in walled enclosures. In the 16th century, aromatic plants were incorporated in "knots" (carpet-like patterns). Tudor Gardens (like those at Hatfield House in Hertfordshire) were enclosed squares of flowers in geometric patterns bordered by low hedges and gravel paths.

A taste for small flowerbeds persisted through the 17th and 18th centuries, when fountains and canals began to be introduced.

THE ART OF THE LANDSCAPE

In the 1740s a rich banker, Henry Hoare, inspired by Continental art during his Grand Tour, employed William Kent (1685–1748) to turn his gardens at Stourhead in Wiltshire into a series of lakes dotted with buildings in the classical style. This was the birth of the landscape garden, known as le jardin anglais.

"Capability" Brown rejected formal plantings in favour of natural parkland and restricted flowers to small kitchen gardens. But Humphry Repton (1752–1815) reintroduced the formal pleasure garden. The Victorians put the emphasis on plants, and Gertrude Jekyll (1843–1932) promoted the idea of planting cycles to ensure that colour lasted through the year.

This Wiltshire garden at Stourhead, birthplace of England's landscape movement, is dotted with lakes and temples and has many rare trees and shrubs. The artful vistas were created in the 1740s, and their magnificence contrasts with the severe restraint of the Palladian house (1721–4).

Hidcote Manor, a 17th-century Cotswold house at Mickleton in Gloucestershire, has one of the most beautiful English gardens, mixing different types of plot within various species of hedges. Although covering 10 acres (4 hectares), it's like a series of cottage gardens on a grand scale, prompting Vita Sackville-West to describe it as "haphazard luxuriance".

Classical statues graced many gardens in the 17th century. This one is at Belvoir Castle, Leicestershire. Until the late 18th century many statues were made of lead.

Lancelot "Capability" Brown.

The great gardeners

Lancelot Brown (1715–83) was nicknamed "Capability" Brown when he rode from one aristocratic client to the next pointing out "capabilities to improvement". His forte was presenting gardens in the "natural" state, and his lasting influence lay in his talent for combining quite simple elements to create harmonious effects.

Brown liked to create elegant lakes for his parks, as at Blenheim Palace in Oxfordshire. He was also involved with the gardens at Stowe in Buckinghamshire, which the National Trust today describes as "Britain's largest work of art", and with the gardens at Kew, Britain's main botanical establishment, just outside London.

One of the 20th century's most influential gardeners was Vita Sackville-West (1892–1962), who developed her gardens at Sissinghurst Castle in Kent. She revived the 16th-century idea of dividing a garden into separate sections, combining a formal overall style with an informal choice of flowers.

The 4th Duke of Marlborough employed "Capability" Brown (see right) in 1764 to impose his back-to-nature philosophy on Blenheim Palace. Brown's most dramatic change was to create a large lake by damming the River Glyme.

Thanks to the influence of the Gulf Stream, sub-tropical flora can flourish at England's south-western tip. Tresco Abbey Gardens, on the Isles of Scilly, were laid out on the site of a Benedictine priory and contain many rare plants.

This example at Henry VIII's Hampton Court Palace outside London shows the Tudor liking for knots – small beds of dwarf plants or sand and gravel laid out in patterns resembling embroidery. Topiary, statues and mazes provided a counterpoint to the mathematical order.

HAMPSHIRE, WILTSHIRE AND DORSET

The area's highlights include the splendid cathedrals of Salisbury and Winchester, the ancient stone circle of Stonehenge, Stourhead's stunning gardens and some of the best beaches in England.

This region of England offers plenty of variety – from the ports of Portsmouth and Southampton, to the Isle of Wight, to the cathedral city of Winchester, and the megalithic remains of Stonehenge and Avebury. The landscape ranges from the pretty scrubland of the New Forest in the south to the grassy sprawl of Salisbury Plain further north, while in the west are the country lanes, patchwork fields and rolling hills of Dorset. The tour described below is roughly circular, running anticlockwise from Portsmouth all the way round to finish at Bournemouth.

THE SOUTH COAST PORTS

Portsmouth ❶ is a good place to start: it's a large and confusing city, owing to post-war reconstruction, but the main sites are clearly signed. "Historic Ships" signs lead you to the *Mary Rose*, HMS *Victory* and HMS *Warrior*. An inclusive ticket allows you to visit all three and to explore a number of museums and sites dotted around the **Historic Dockyard** (www.historicdockyard.co.uk; daily Apr–Oct 10am–5.30pm, Nov–Mar until 5pm). The **Mary Rose Exhibition** details the history of Henry VIII's flagship, sunk in 1545, and the **Mary Rose Ship Hall** displays the recovered ship itself. The tour of **HMS *Victory***, on which Lord

Nelson died at the Battle of Trafalgar in 1805, gives a good idea of life for an 18th-century sailor. On **HMS *Warrior***, the first iron-clad warship, you can take a tour or explore independently. The city's most striking attraction is the contemporary Emirates **Spinnaker Tower** (www.spinnakertower.co.uk; daily 10am–5.30pm), which soars high above the harbour; it's even taller than the London Eye. The tower has three viewing platforms: the first has a glass floor and multimedia displays about the

Map on page 222

The beach at Studland Bay.

harbour's history, the second has a café, and the third is open to the elements. Further south, the D-Day Story museum (www.theddaystory. com; Apr–Sept 10am–5.30pm, Oct–Mar until 5pm) commemorates the Normandy landings; it reopened in 2018 with three new exhibition galleries, a café and shop, following a £5m revamp. New items on display include "the pencil that started the invasion", used by Lt Cdr John Harmer to sign the order for Force G naval forces to depart for Gold Beach, along with newly conserved landing craft and beach armoured recovery vehicles (BARV).

The M27 motorway will take you the short distance to **Southampton ❷**, the port from which the *Mayflower* sailed to America in 1620, and the *Titanic* set out on its ill-fated voyage in 1912. It is still a busy port, and, like Portsmouth, it suffered badly in World War II. Post-war planning left much to be desired, but it makes the most of what heritage is left. The 13th-century **Medieval Merchant's House** on French Street (www.english-heritage.org.uk; Apr–Sept Sat–Sun 11am–4pm) has been furnished to reflect how it would have appeared in the 14th century. Walking north up Castle Way and Portland terrace, you soon come to Southampton City Art Gallery (www.southamptoncityart gallery.com; Mon–Fri 10am–3pm, Sat 10am–5pm; free), which is particularly noted for its series of Perseus paintings by Burne-Jones. Just nearby is the SeaCity Museum (www. seacitymuseum.co.uk; daily 10am–5pm), a magnificent complex that contains a wealth of exhibits ranging from archaeological finds to memorabilia associated with the Titanic.

THE ISLE OF WIGHT

From Southampton you can take a ferry or hydrofoil to the **Isle of Wight ❸**. It's England's largest island, with pretty towns, lovely beaches and an old-fashioned feel. It's been a popular holiday destination since Victorian times, and the poets Swinburne and Tennyson had

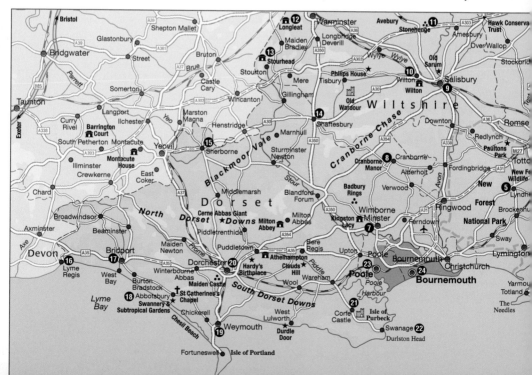

houses here, while Dickens stayed here while working on his magnum opus David Copperfield. Probably its most famous resident, though, was Queen Victoria herself, who spent much of her time at **Osborne House** (www.english-heritage.org.uk; daily Apr–Sept 10am–6pm, Mar and Oct 10am–4pm, with exceptions) at **East Cowes**. It was designed by Prince Albert in 1845 in an Italianate style, and the richly furnished interior remains much as it was when Victoria died here in 1901.

Just outside **Newport**, in the centre of the island, is **Carisbrooke Castle** (www.english-heritage.org.uk; Apr–Sept daily 10am–6pm, Oct until 5pm, Nov–Mar Sat–Sun 10am–4pm). A 12th-century keep survives, but most of the rest is 16th-century. Charles I was imprisoned here in 1647 before being taken to London for trial and execution. The star attraction is the 18th-century treadmill, still operated by donkey-power.

Nearby, the town of Cowes itself is the base for Britain's most famous

sailing event – Cowes Week (www.aamcowesweek.co.uk), held at the beginning of August each year. Nearly 1,000 yachts and some 8,000 competitors participate in the dozens of races that take place each day on the Solent (the channel between the south coast and the Isle of Wight). Many people enjoy the associated onshore festivities as much as the sailing. Live music and innumerable cocktail parties are on offer every day in Cowes itself, and on the final Friday a spectacular fireworks display is launched from barges out on the Solent.

WINCHESTER

Back in Southampton, it's a brief journey on the M3 to **Winchester ④**, which once shared with London the honour of being joint capital of England. Start your tour at the **Cathedral** (www.winchester-cathedral.org.uk; Mon–Sat 9.30am–5pm, Sun 12.30–3pm). All architectural styles are represented, from the 11th-century Romanesque north transept to

The Medieval Merchant's House in Southampton.

Beaulieu stately home.

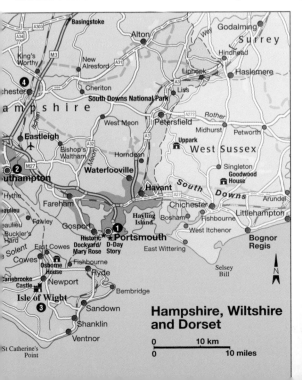

Hampshire, Wiltshire and Dorset

At the Beaulieu Motor Museum.

the glorious Perpendicular-style nave. Look out for the oldest choir stalls in England (c.1305); the grave of Jane Austen (1775–1817) in the north aisle; the Edward Burne-Jones windows in the Epiphany Chapel; and contemporary sculptor Antony Gormley's bronze in the crypt. The precious 12th-century Winchester Bible is displayed in the library.

There's much else to be seen in the town: the **Great Hall** (www.hants.

HMS Victory at Portsmouth Dockyard.

gov.uk/thingstodo/greathall; daily 10am–4.30pm; donation), which houses the **Round Table**, improbably linked with King Arthur and his knights, is all that remains of William the Conqueror's castle. **Winchester College** (tel: 01962-621 209; guided tours only) has a chapel rich enough to rival the cathedral; and the ruined **Wolvesey Castle** (www.english-heritage.org.uk; Apr–Sept daily 10am–5pm; free) was the former home of the Bishops of Winchester.

THE NEW FOREST

Now head southwest on the M3/M27 motorways to **Lyndhurst** ⑤, which is capital of the **New Forest** national park. You can learn about the area at the excellent **New Forest Centre** (www.newforestcentre.org.uk; daily 10am–5pm; free, charge for museum), which contains a museum, visitor centre and tourist information. There's information in the museum on Alice Liddell, the girl for whom Lewis Carroll (1832–98) wrote *Alice in Wonderland*. She became Mrs

Reginald Hargreaves, and it is under this name that you'll find her tomb in **Lyndhurst Church**, an exuberant building full of stained glass by William Morris and Edward Burne-Jones, with life-sized angels supporting the timber roof.

Many people come to the New Forest especially to visit **Beaulieu** (www.beaulieu.co.uk; daily mid-May–mid-Sept 10am–6pm, mid-Sept–mid-May until 5pm), one of the first stately homes to open its doors to the public. The magnificent **Cistercian Abbey** (now a ruin) was built in the 13th century. The cloister – the best-preserved part – is now planted with herbs, and the monks' refectory has been converted into a parish church. The abbey was confiscated and sold by Henry VIII during the 1530s Dissolution, and in the 19th century the abbey gatehouse was turned into the baronial-style **Palace House**; beautifully vaulted ceilings survive, and the walls are hung with portraits.

From here you can walk through attractive gardens to the ugly

building that houses the **National Motor Museum**; hop on an open-topped veteran bus for a tour of the grounds; or queue for a ride on the monorail that encircles them, and gives a fine aerial view. The museum possesses a huge collection covering more than a century of motoring, concentrating more on the social history of the car than the mechanical aspects. There are also displays of cars that have broken the land-speed record; and trams, buses and fire engines for children to clamber on. Beaulieu also houses an exhibition on Britain's Secret Army, the World War II Special Operations Executive (SOE), who completed their training there.

WEST TO WIMBORNE

Leave the forest on the A31 for **Wimborne Minster** , where the imposing twin towers of the church rise above Georgian houses. The original minster was built in 705, but then destroyed by the Danes; the present one is Norman. Opposite stands the **Priest's House Museum**

Inside Winchester Cathedral.

Burne-Jones's stained-glass window in Winchester Cathedral.

⊘ FACT FILE

By car The region is easily accessible from most parts of England, although the A3, A4/A36, M3 and M27 are very busy with commuter traffic during rush hours.

By coach National Express services to Dorchester, Portsmouth, Salisbury, Bournemouth and other main towns; www.nationalexpress.com.

By rail Salisbury, Dorchester, Bournemouth, Southampton, Portsmouth and Winchester are on main lines to London; from Southampton there are local trains to the heart of the New Forest; tel: 03457-484 950, www.nationalrail.co.uk.

By ferry Daily car and passenger ferries operate from Poole and Portsmouth to Bilbao, Caen, Cherbourg, Le Havre and St Malo; contact Brittany Ferries, tel: 0330-159 7000, www.brittany-ferries.co.uk or P&O Ferries, tel: 0800-130 0030, www.poferries.com; Red Funnel Ferries, tel: 0844-844 9988, www.redfunnel.co.uk, operate services to the Isle of Wight.

New Forest Animals Tel: 023-8028 2052 (Mon–Fri) or 0300-067 4600 (24 hours), to report animals injured or in distress).

Tourist information Portsmouth, tel: 023-9282 6722; Dorchester, tel: 01305-267 992; Lyme Regis, tel: 01297-442 138; Southampton, www.discoversouthampton.co.uk; Salisbury, tel: 01722-342 860; New Forest, www.thenewforest.co.uk.

A wild New Forest pony.

(www.priest-house.co.uk; the museum is closed for refurbishment until spring 2020), an interesting little place whose attractions include a Victorian kitchen and stationer's shop, an archaeology gallery, a fine garden and a teashop (the teashop will remain open during the works).

West of town is **Kingston Lacy** (www.nationaltrust.org.uk/kingston-lacy; daily mid-Mar–Oct 11am–5pm, Nov until 4pm, with exceptions), a 17th-century mansion containing works by Rubens, Titian and Van Dyck, and set in grounds farmed by traditional organic methods. North now on the B3078 to **Cranborne Manor** ⑧ (www.cranborne.co.uk; Mar–Sept Wed 9.30am–4pm) where, set around the Jacobean house (not open to the public), is one of England's most appealing gardens, originally planted with roses, clematis and topiary hedges by John Tradescant in the 17th century. The village is pretty, too.

SALISBURY TO STONEHENGE

The best place to begin a visit to **Salisbury** ⑨ is on a windswept hill just outside it, **Old Sarum**, where extensive ruins of the earlier town are set within the ramparts of an Iron Age hill fort. Salisbury itself is dominated by the creamy-white limestone **Cathedral** (www.salisburycathedral.org.uk; Mon–Sat 9am–5pm, Sun noon–4pm), with its wonderful spire (the tallest in Britain), timber roof and cloisters. It was built in the 13th century and is a stunning example of the Gothic style. In the Chapter House is displayed one of the four original copies of Magna Carta (1215). The cathedral is not the only attraction; stroll around the town enjoying the gracious Queen Anne buildings, or stop for tea or a light lunch at one of them, **Mompesson House** (www.nationaltrust.org.uk/mompesson-house; mid-Mar–Oct daily 11am–5pm).

Only 3 miles (5km) west of Salisbury is **Wilton** ⑩, dominated by **Wilton House** (www.wiltonhouse.com; May–Aug Sun–Thu 11.30am–5pm), the estate of the Earl of Pembroke. The 17th-century house was designed by Inigo Jones, and the

⏱ A FOREST TRAIL

An exploration of the forest could begin at Lyndhurst, going south to Brockenhurst, where one of England's oldest trees, a magnificent 1,000-year-old yew, stands in the churchyard. Stock up with picnic provisions in the village then follow Rhinefield signs to three beauty spots. The first, Ober Water, is a forest stream alive with minnows, where boggy margins support such flowers as the bog asphodel and insect-eating sundew plant. Information boards at the car park indicate a choice of walks.

About 1 mile (1.6km) on, you come to Rhinefield Drive, an arboretum planted with rhododendrons, azaleas and giant conifers. Again, there is a choice of marked walks. A right turn off the A35 will take you to Bolderwood Drive, another 19th-century arboretum where you can follow marked walks, keeping an eye out for red, fallow and roe deer.

Heading towards Ashurst you'll find the New Forest Wildlife Park (www.newforestwildlifepark.co.uk; daily summer 10am–5.30pm, winter until 4.30pm), where an array of small mammals, including three species of otter and several species of owl, live in old farm buildings and forest enclosures that approximate their natural habitat. Most people go there to please the children and then find themselves fascinated by the place.

grounds have an excellent adventure playground.

Between Wilton and Salisbury, the A360 leads about 11 miles (16km) north to **Stonehenge** ⓫ (www.english-heritage.org.uk; daily June–Aug 9am–8pm, mid-Mar–May and Sept–mid-Oct 9.30am–7pm, mid-Oct–mid-Mar 9.30am–5pm; timed tickets only, book in advance), which stands on **Salisbury Plain**. England's most famous ancient monument, it has been declared a Unesco World Heritage Site. It spans the period 3000–1600 BC (the central ring of stones dates from *c.*2000 BC) and was built in phases. Part of it is constructed of large bluestones, which appear to have come from the Preseli Mountains in Pembrokeshire, 200 miles (320km) away – perhaps transported at least part of the way here by glaciers in the last Ice Age. There are also enormous sarsen stones that outcrop locally.

The purpose of Stonehenge has battled archaeologists and other experts for centuries and engendered many myths. Inigo Jones, one of the first to investigate the monument formally, at the behest of James I in the 17th century, concluded it was a Roman temple to Uranus. Though the alignment of the major axis with the midsummer sunrise suggests a religious significance, no firm evidence has been found, and theories about it range from the practical – that it was some kind of calendar – to the extraterrestrial. Whatever its purpose, its builders must have had some knowledge of mathematics and astrology. It is popularly associated with the Druids, but in fact pre-dated them by about 1,000 years. Regardless of this, present-day Druids and many other people regard it as a place of ritual and worship on Midsummer Eve, and the police regard it as a priority to stop them trespassing.

Stonehenge stands within the ancient Kingdom of Wessex, a region that was later mythologised further in the novels of Thomas Hardy. The name referred to "West Saxons"; it is particularly rich in ancient remains.

Shaftesbury's Gold Hill.

The great circle of Stonehenge.

From Stonehenge, visitors can make a detour north on the A360/361 to the village of **Avebury**, the site of one of the most important megalithic monuments in Europe, as well as Bronze Age burial mounds. Northwest of Stonehenge, on the A303/A36, you reach **Warminster** and **Longleat** ⑫ (tel: 01985-845 420; www.longleat.co.uk; daily Mar–Oct 10am–5pm, until 6pm or 7pm in summer months, closed Mar Tue–Thu, with exceptions). The property of the Marquess of Bath, this was the first stately home to be opened to the public (in 1948). The house, Elizabethan in origin and with an eclectic mixture of styles spanning the past four centuries, is splendid, but it is the safari park, where animals roam freely in grounds originally landscaped by "Capability" Brown, which is now the greatest draw.

After your safari, return to the A303, then take a right turn at Mere to visit **Stourhead** ⑬ (www.nationaltrust.org.uk/stourhead; house: Mar–Oct daily 11am–4.30pm, early–mid-Nov until 3.30pm; garden: all year daily 9am–5pm). The Palladian-style house, built for banker Henry Hoare in the 18th century, is surrounded by one of the loveliest landscaped gardens in England. Classical temples dedicated to Flora and Apollo stand beside the dark waters of the lake. In spring the walks are vivid with azaleas and rhododendrons.

Returning to the A303, retrace your route a short way and take the A350 to **Shaftesbury** ⑭, one of southern England's few hill towns. Climbing cobbled **Gold Hill**, lined with 18th-century cottages and the remaining wall of a demolished abbey, is like stepping back into a picturesque version of the past. Thomas Hardy (1840–1928) used Shaftesbury, renamed Shaston, as the setting for his 1896 novel *Jude the Obscure*.

Heading west on the A30, our next destination is **Sherborne** ⑮, the burial place of two Saxon kings. There is a wealth of medieval buildings here, including the Abbey Church and Almshouse. **Sherborne Castle** (www.sherbornecastle.com; Apr–Oct Tue–Thu, Sat–Sun 11am–5pm) is an interestingly eccentric pile, built for Sir Walter Raleigh (1552–1618).

At **Yeovil**, 5 miles (8km) west, is the Elizabethan **Montacute House** (www.nationaltrust.org.uk/montacute-house; Mar–Oct daily 11am–4.30pm), built in golden stone with ornamental gazebos for the lawyer who prosecuted Guy Fawkes, one of the conspirators who tried to blow up the Houses of Parliament in 1605. In the church at **East Coker**, 3 miles (5km) south, are the ashes of T.S. Eliot (1888–1965), whose ancestors emigrated to the USA. "In my beginning is my end," he wrote in the poem named after the village.

THE DORSET COAST

Continue west on the A30 and drop down to the coast at **Lyme Regis** ⑯, just east of the Devon border. This old

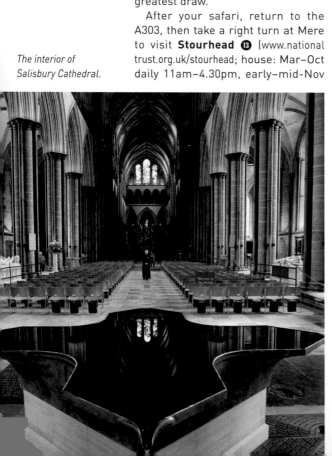

The interior of Salisbury Cathedral.

fishing town was once as fashionable as Bath. Regency bow windows and trellised verandas on Victorian villas line The Parade on the way to the tiny harbour and the projecting arm called **The Cobb**. It was here that the Duke of Monmouth landed in 1685, aspiring to the crown, and here on the steps called Granny's Teeth that Jane Austen's Louisa Musgrave tumbled in *Persuasion*. **Bay Cottage** at the harbour's end, now **Jane's Cafe**, is thought by some to be where Austen (1775–1817) lived while writing much of the novel: the Jane Austen garden marks the location of a cottage where she certainly stayed. The sea-lashed walls also formed a backdrop for Meryl Streep in the 1981 film of John Fowles's novel *The French Lieutenant's Woman*. The town retains its popularity with artistic types to this day, and lining its narrow lanes there are numerous galleries selling the creations of painters, sculptors, potters and photographers.

The road east takes you to **Bridport** ⑰. It is 2 miles (3km) from the sea, yet there is no denying its marine character. **West Bay** is Bridport's improbable harbour, a narrow channel dug in the shingle bank and flanked by two high piers only feet apart. In the old days, coasters had to be hauled in with ropes.

The next town is **Burton Bradstock**, a pretty spot with thatched cottages, smoky stone and bright window boxes, and a stream that used to drive the flax mills until the last one closed in 1931. Here the **Chesil Bank** begins, curving away eastwards until it becomes the slender link that means the Isle of Portland is not really an island at all, but a peninsula. Chesil Bank has no mercy: to bring a boat in here spells almost certain disaster. Stretching eastwards to Exmouth and westwards to Studland Bay, these 95 miles (153km) of coastline have been named the "Jurassic Coast" and designated a World Heritage Site for their geological importance. Charmouth is the prime location for finding fossils, such as ammonites, on the beach. Before you start searching, take a Fossil Hunting

⊙ **Fact**

Thomas Hardy, who used Dorset locations for most of his novels, renamed Bridport, Port Bredy. It is featured in his short story Fellow Townsmen, in which Hardy describes how hemmed-in Port Bredy is by the hills; and it has changed very little since those days.

A view of The Cobb, Lyme Regis.

⊙ Tip

If time is at a premium, an alternative, more direct route from Dorchester to Corfe Castle is on the A352, but this cuts out several of the Hardy sites, as well as Athelhampton House.

Walk. There's a charge, but they last two hours and are extremely informative. To book, contact the Charmouth Heritage Coast Centre (tel: 01297-560 772; www.charmouth.org).

Portland is a place apart: Hardy called it "the Gibraltar of Wessex" and claimed the people had customs of their own. Everything is made of Portland stone, the material used for many of London's best-known buildings. The lighthouse on the southern tip overlooks the water of the treacherous Portland Race. Portland's harbour was the location for the sailing events in the 2012 London Olympics.

St Catherine's Chapel on a green hill above the bank at **Abbotsbury** ⑱ is a vital mark for sailors and fishermen, as well as a place of prayer. On the land side it overlooks a surprising subtropical garden, which contains the ruins of a substantial 15th-century monastic barn, built as a wheat store and a swan sanctuary.

George III put **Weymouth** ⑲ on the map when he went there to convalesce in 1789, and much of the character

The statue of Thomas Hardy in his hometown of Dorchester.

of an 18th-century watering place remains. The king's statue stands at the end of the Esplanade, which is lined on one side with stuccoed terraces, on the other by an expanse of golden sands. **Brewers Quay** is a re-developed Victorian brewery in Weymouth's old harbour that houses an antiques emporium and the **Weymouth Museum**.

Turn inland now and take the A354 some 8 miles (13km) towards Dorchester. Just outside the town you will come to **Maiden Castle**, a massive Iron Age hill fort: excavations show that the hilltop was occupied some 6,000 years ago. The name derives from "mai dun", meaning great hill; the fort is believed to be the world's largest earthworks.

DORCHESTER

Dorchester ⑳ is the county town of Dorset and a place well aware of its past. It was the setting for Thomas Hardy's *Mayor of Casterbridge*, and there is a collection devoted to him, including the original manuscript of the 1886 novel, in the **Dorset County Museum** (www.dorsetcountymuseum.org;

⊙ THOMAS HARDY

Thomas Hardy (1840–1928) was born at Higher Bockhampton, near Dorchester, the son of a stonemason, and although he spent considerable periods of time in London and travelled in Europe, all his major novels are set in the region. He trained as an architect, but after the success of *Far From the Madding Crowd* in 1874 he was able to concentrate on writing.

A recurrent theme in Hardy's work is the indifference of fate and the arbitrary nature of the suffering it inflicts on mankind. In his own time he was widely criticised for his pessimism, and it must be said that many of his novels, particularly the later ones such as *Jude the Obscure*, are extremely gloomy. In his later years Hardy turned to poetry, which he considered a superior art form, but it is for his novels that he is remembered.

Hardy sites that can be visited, as well as the Dorset County Museum and the Hardy Cottage, mentioned above, are Max Gate, in Alington Avenue, Dorchester (www.nationaltrust.org.uk/max-gate; mid-Mar–Oct daily 11am–5pm), which he designed himself and inhabited from 1885 until his death; and the churchyard at Stinsford, just east of town, where his heart was buried alongside his family, although his body was interred at Westminster Abbey.

closed for renovation until summer 2020, when it will open with new galleries, a learning centre and library). **Hardy's Cottage** (www.nationaltrust.org.uk/hardys-cottage; mid-Mar–Oct daily 11am–5pm), the writer's birthplace, is 3 miles (5km) northeast of the town in the village of Higher Bockhampton.

But Dorchester isn't all Hardy: it's a pleasant town in its own right, where the pace of life is a little slower than elsewhere. It has another claim to fame (or infamy) in the **Shire Hall**, the courtroom where six farm workers, who became known as the **Tolpuddle Martyrs**, were sentenced to transportation in 1834 for the crime of forming a branch of the Labourers' Union. Such was the public outcry that the men were returned to England after serving two years in Australia, rather than the seven their sentence demanded. The village of Tolpuddle lies just off the A35 to the east of Dorchester, and there is a monument to the men, who became heroes of the later union movement.

To the north of town, on the A352, is the village of **Cerne Abbas**, which has a magnificent tithe barn but is best known for the **Cerne Abbas Giant**, the 180ft (55-metre) tall priapic club-wielding fertility figure carved into the chalk downs nearby. Some believe he dates from the time of the Roman occupation, but there are no written records of him until the 17th century.

Also worth a stop as you head east from Dorchester on the A35 is **Athelhampton House** (www.athelhampton.co.uk; Mar–Sept Sun–Thu 10am–5pm, Nov–Feb Sun only 10.30am–4.30pm), a fine medieval hall surrounded by impressive Victorian gardens adorned with fountains, statuary and topiaried pyramids. Continuing a few miles further east, and then south along the B3390, you come to Clouds Hill (www.nationaltrust.org.uk/clouds-hill; mid-Mar–Oct daily 11am–5pm), a tiny cottage that was once home to T.E. Lawrence – or Lawrence of Arabia, as he is popularly known.

CORFE CASTLE AND THE ISLE OF PURBECK

Turn off the A35 on to the A351 for **Corfe Castle ㉑** (www.nationaltrust.org.

The chain ferry connects Sandbanks and Studland.

Weymouth Harbour.

uk/corfe-castle; daily Apr–Sept 10am–6pm, Oct, Mar 10am–5pm, winter until 4pm) at Wareham. Sitting on a rocky pinnacle, this is one of England's most impressive ruins. It was an important stronghold from the time of the Norman Conquest, but its finest hour was during the Civil War, when the owner, Lady Bankes, defended it against a six-week siege by parliamentary troops, who later demolished it to prevent any repetition. Corfe Common nearby is rich in wildlife, and there are splendid views from the folly of Crech Grange Arch.

Head for the coast now (staying on the A351) to **Swanage** ㉒, between Durlston and Swanage bays, "lying snugly between two headlands as between a finger and a thumb", as Hardy put it when he fictionalised the village as Knollsea. Look out for a stone globe 10ft (3 metres) in diameter, flanked by panels giving sobering information on the nature of the universe; and for the ornate 17th-century Town Hall facade, made from the famous local marble.

This region is the **Isle of Purbeck** (although it is not an island at all) and is famous both for its marble and for its wonderful white sandy beaches. A whole swath of the coast is National Trust land, designated the **Studland Bay and Nature Reserve**. As well as one of the best beaches in England, the area supports a variety of rare birds and plants, butterfly habitats and other wildlife. There are a number of public paths and nature trails, plus car parks and the usual National Trust facilities. There is also a cliff-top walk westwards to lovely **Lulworth Cove** and the strangely eroded rock formation of **Durdle Door**.

At **Studland Heath**, the eastern tip of the area, a car ferry goes from Shell Bay to Sandbanks, a small peninsula that has been dubbed "Britain's Palm Beach" on account of its wealthy residential areas. From here, it's a short drive up to Poole (though it's also possible to drive all the way round the bay on the A351/A350 via Wareham). **Poole** ㉓ is a thriving port sitting on a huge harbour and has a delightful quayside.

Durdle Door at Lulworth Cove.

Curving steps meet under the portico of the **Customs House** with its coat of arms representing an authority the Dorset smugglers never acknowledged. The galleries of the **Poole Museum** (www.poolemuseum.co.uk; summer daily 10am–5pm, winter Mon–Sat noon–4pm; free) tell the story of this maritime town. A small display is devoted to the Boy Scout movement, which was founded by Sir Robert Baden-Powell in 1908 after running the first Scout camp on nearby Brownsea Island.

From the quay, ferries (www.brownseaislandferries.com; mid-Mar–Oct 10am–4.30pm), run regularly to **Brownsea Island** which is now National Trust-owned – although part of it is leased to the Dorset Wildlife Trust as a nature reserve. A lovely area of heath and woodland, the island is a haven for the now rare red squirrel, and has a waterfowl sanctuary. The island is also accessible by ferry from Sandbanks.

BOURNEMOUTH

Sedate and elegant **Bournemouth** ㉔ was established as a resort at the end of the 19th century and has remained popular ever since, largely due to a great sweep of sandy beach and the attractive parks and gardens that cover its surrounding cliffs. It has all the accoutrements of a modern seaside resort: amusement arcades, and clubs and bars. It's also a favourite spot for surfers. If you are there during the summer months, it's worth getting tickets for a performance by the Bournemouth Symphony Orchestra.

Bournemouth's best museum is the **Russell-Cotes Art Gallery** (www.russellcotes.com; Tue–Sun 10am–5pm), which has good oriental exhibits. East of town, next to a ruined Norman castle, stands **Christchurch Priory**, which has an impressive Norman nave, but most of the remainder dates from the 13th–16th century. If you've seen enough churches and castles for a while, you might just like to climb nearby **Hengistbury Head** for splendid views over the Channel, or go a little further to **Mudeford**, where bright beach huts line the shore.

Corfe Castle.

BATH

Visitors no longer come to Bath to take the curative waters, but most go away feeling a lot better after even a short stay in this lively and beautiful city.

Cradle in the folds of the Mendip Hills and dissected by the River Avon, **Bath** has a long history. The Romans built the baths that give it its name – they are among the most impressive Roman remains in the country – and after years as a popular spa it was transformed, early in the 18th century, into one of the most beautiful cities in Europe. In 1988 Bath was designated a Unesco World Heritage Site. The transformation of the city was largely thanks to three men: Richard "Beau" Nash, a dandy, a gambler, and the town's master of ceremonies; Ralph Allen, a far-sighted businessman; and John Wood the Elder, an innovative architect. Their influence will be seen everywhere on this tour.

Our visit to Bath begins at the **Pump Room** Ⓐ, which was built in the 1790s. Here the therapeutic waters could be sampled in comfort – but it was also a social arena, complete with musical entertainment, a place to see and be seen. Admire the room from one of the elegant tables, entertained by the Pump Room Trio or the regular pianist, with a Bath bun and coffee to hand. At the far end of the room, a statue of Beau Nash presides over the scene, and in an alcove on the south side, overlooking the King's Bath, spa water is dispensed from a lovely late

In the Pump Room.

19th-century drinking fountain graced by four stone trout.

The city's greatest attraction is the **Roman Baths** Ⓑ (www.romanbaths.co.uk; daily Mar–mid-June, Sept–Oct 9am–5pm, mid-June–Aug until 9pm, Nov–Feb 9.30am–5pm); try to visit early or late to avoid the queues, even during the week, as there are lots of school groups. The Great Bath, seen from above on entering, was discovered in the 1880s during investigations into a leak in the King's Bath that was causing hot-water floods

Main attractions

Pump Room
Roman Baths
Bath Abbey
Bath Spa
Royal Crescent
Pulteney Bridge

Map on page 236

Sally Lunn's famous traditional bun.

in local cellars. The Victorians were excited by archaeology, and the discovery was greeted with great interest throughout Britain.

From here the route leads down to the heart of the baths, the **Temple Precinct**, excavated in the early 1980s. The temple was built around AD 60, on the site of the native Sanctuary of Sulis, a Celtic goddess whom the Romans conflated with their own Minerva, whose attributes included medicine. Finds from the period include coins, votive offerings and petitions to the goddess. There are also curses inscribed on pewter or lead sheets, some written backwards. Other highlights include a gilded bronze head of Minerva; the Gorgon's head that originally adorned the main temple's pediment; the corner blocks of a sacrificial altar; and a sea beast mosaic.

The museum emerges next to the **Great Bath**, from where free guided tours leave (subject to availability), taking in the East and West baths, and the medieval King's Bath. The Great Bath is the best place to see the water at close quarters, bubbling up at a temperature of 115°F (45°C) and replete with 43 minerals, including iron that stains the stone red. The water's green colour is caused by light reacting with algae; when the baths were roofed over in Roman times, the water would have been clear. The **King's Bath**, overlooked by the Pump Room, is named after King Bladud, mythical founder of Bath, who, when he was a prince, suffered from leprosy and roamed the countryside as a swineherd. According to legend he was miraculously cured when he stumbled upon some hot springs. Duly rehabilitated, he went on to found the city on the site of the curative hot springs.

BATH ABBEY

From the Baths it is a short hop across Abbey Churchyard to **Bath Abbey** (www.bathabbey.org; Mon 9.30am–5.30pm, Tue–Fri 9am–5.30pm, Sat until 6pm, Sun 1–2.30pm, 4.30–6pm; donations welcome), the heart of medieval Bath. In 675 a Convent of Holy Virgins was founded here, and although

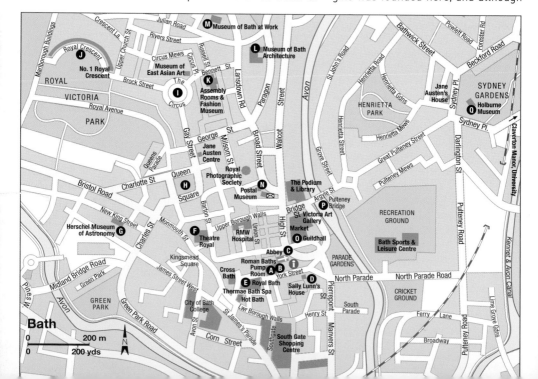

Bath

there is no further record of the convent, there is evidence that a Saxon abbey existed by 757. Edgar, the first king of all England, was crowned in the abbey church in 973. He introduced the Benedictine monks who were to control the abbey and the town for the next 500 years.

In 1107, in the wake of the Norman Conquest, the Bishop of Somerset moved the seat of the bishopric from Wells to Bath and built a Norman church on the site of the Saxon one. This lasted until 1499, when Bishop Oliver King rebuilt the church in the Perpendicular style characterised by flying buttresses, wide windows and fan vaulting. The Dissolution of the Monasteries by Henry VIII in 1539 brought the work to a halt, leaving the nave without a roof for many years.

The entrance to the abbey is through the **West Front**, with its Jacob's Ladder ("the angels of God ascending and descending on it": Genesis 28: 12–17). Inside, the vast windows fill the abbey with light. The east window depicts 56 scenes from the life of Christ in brilliant stained glass. Overhead stretches the exquisite fan vaulting. Among the other delights of the abbey are the memorials to famous residents and guests who died in Bath for want of the desired cure. Don't miss the one dedicated to Beau Nash ("Ricardi Nash, Elegantiae Arbiter"), who died at the age of 86, impoverished and enfeebled. Tower tours are available throughout the year (Mon–Sat); climb the 212 steps to the top for spectacular views over the city.

Not far from the abbey, along North Parade Passage, you may want to visit **Sally Lunn's House** ⓓ, a restaurant-cum-café occupying the oldest house in Bath (15th century, with a prettified 17th-century facade). It is famous for a highly versatile bun, made on the premises since the 1680s, and served with sweet or savoury toppings.

West of the Pump Room, along colonnaded Bath Street, the state-of-the-art luxury **Thermae Bath Spa** ⓔ (www.thermaebathspa.com; daily 9am– 9.30pm) has been created from a cluster of historic baths harnessing

In Bath's pedestrianised shopping centre.

The Assembly Rooms, once the centre of Bath's social scene.

Inside the American Museum at Claverton Manor.

the waters of two of Bath's three hot springs. They include the **Cross Bath**, built by Thomas Baldwin in 1791, the neighbouring **Hot Bath**, and the **New Royal Bath**. During the 17th century the Cross Bath had a reputation for curing sterility, and Mary of Modena, the wife of James II, conceived a much-needed heir after bathing here. The modern complex includes a rooftop pool with views over the historic centre; while the vistas are scenic, be prepared to share this small pool with crowds of other tourists, especially in the warmer months. There's the larger indoor Minerva Bath too, plus steam rooms, sauna, ice chamber and treatment rooms.

GEORGIAN ARCHITECTURE

Head now to Sawclose and one of the oldest and loveliest theatres in England, the **Theatre Royal ⑤**. This grand theatre attracted some of the best-known actors of the late 18th century – including David Garrick and Sarah Siddons. The Royal presents a year-round programme of plays, opera,

dance and concerts (tel: 01225-448 844; www.theatreroyal.org.uk).

From the theatre, go up Monmouth Street and turn left for the **Herschel Museum of Astronomy ⑥** (www.bath-preservation-trust.org.uk; Mon–Fri 1–5pm, Sat–Sun 10am–5pm), the home and observatory of William Herschel, who came to Bath from Hanover in 1761 as an organist, and became musical director of the Assembly Rooms. From this garden, with the aid of a home-made telescope, he discovered Uranus in 1781. A replica of the telescope is in the museum. He was subsequently appointed Director of the Royal Astronomical Society.

Queen Square ⑪ is our next stop. It was built in the 1730s by John Wood the Elder, the architect credited with introducing the Palladian style to Bath. The north side, with Roman portico, is particularly striking. Now walk up Gay Street to **The Circus ①**, again designed by John Wood, although completed after his death by his son. This was England's first circular street and there is a wealth

⊘ THE AMERICAN MUSEUM

Visiting an American Museum in a city with a Roman and Georgian heritage may seem odd, but this one is rather special. It is housed in Claverton Manor, set in grounds based on George Washington's garden at Mount Vernon, overlooking a beautiful wooded valley, yet barely 3 miles (5km) from the city.

A series of rooms have been furnished in different styles: there's the 18th-century Deer Park Parlor from Maryland; the Greek Revival Room, based on a mid-19th-century New York dining room; and the New Orleans Bedroom that, with blood-red wallpaper and an ornate Louis XV-style bed, evokes the antebellum world of Scarlett O'Hara.

There are also galleries devoted to the history of Native Americans, to westward expansion, whaling and American crafts such as quilting and Shaker furniture. The Library holds over 11,000 books and periodicals, and is free to use by appointment. There is also a superb collection of maps, most dating back to the 16th century. A programme of special events features re-enactments of Civil War camp life and Independence Day displays. You can reach the museum (www.american museum.org; mid-Mar–Oct Tue–Sun 11am–5pm) by bus to the university, then a 15-minute walk, or take the shuttle from Bath city centre; or by car via the A36 towards Bradford-on-Avon.

of architectural detail, with all three types of column on the facades: Doric at the bottom, Ionic in the middle and Corinthian at the top.

John Wood the Younger designed another architectural first: the **Royal Crescent ❶**, built from 1767–74, a short walk west of The Circus. This is Bath's star turn, set in a dramatic position above Royal Victoria Park, and comprising 30 separate properties. **No. 1 Royal Crescent** has become a delightful museum (www. bath-preservation-trust.org.uk; daily 10am–5pm), restored and furnished by the Bath Preservation Trust as it would have been in the 18th century. The crescent had its share of famous residents: Isaac Pitman, inventor of shorthand, lived at No. 17; and Elizabeth Linley, who was painted by Gainsborough and who eloped with playwright Richard Sheridan, lived at No. 11.

Retrace your steps now past The Circus to the **Museum of East Asian Art** www.meaa.org.uk; Tue–Sat 10am–5pm, Sun noon–5pm), with an impressive collection of Chinese art. Opposite are the **Assembly Rooms and the Fashion Museum ❻** (www.national trust.org.uk/bath-assembly-rooms; www. fashionmuseum.co.uk; daily 10.30am–4pm, Mar–Oct until 5pm; rooms free). The **Assembly Rooms'** magnificent ballroom is lit by cut-glass chandeliers, and there are separate rooms once used for gambling and taking tea. The Fashion Museum is dedicated to the fickleness of fashion over the past four centuries, with the exhibits on the Georgian period being the most fascinating. The collection was started by Doris Langley Moore, who gave her collection to Bath in 1963.

OTHER MUSEUMS AND ATTRACTIONS

Go north from here, up Paragon, to the **Museum of Bath Architecture ❶** (www. museumofbatharchitecture.org.uk; mid-Feb–Nov Mon–Fri 1–5pm, Sat–Sun 10am–5pm), which offers an illuminating account of the talents and techniques that created the facades of the city. The particular crafts involved in

Rooftop pool at Thermae Bath Spa.

The spa water fountain at the Pump Room.

Georgian interior design are explained in sections including furniture-making, painting, wallpaper, soft furnishings and upholstery.

The next stop, in nearby Julian Road, is the **Museum of Bath at Work** Ⓜ (www.bath-at-work.org.uk; Apr–Oct daily 10.30am–5pm, Nov–Mar Sat–Sun only). The museum relates the story of a 19th-century family firm that operated for 100 years without, it seems, ever throwing anything away. You can wander through the workshop, storeroom, office and factory and imagine yourself back in a less fashionable part of Bath.

Retrace your steps down Paragon to Broad Street and the **Bath Postal Museum** Ⓝ (www.bathpostalmuseum.co.uk; Mon–Tue 11am–5pm, Wed–Sun 2–5pm, until 4.30pm in winter), from where the world's first postage stamp, the Penny Black, was sent in May 1840. Exhibits track the history of the postal service and touch on some delightful peripheral topics, such as a collection of Cupid-covered Victorian Valentine cards.

It's not far now to the **Guildhall** Ⓞ (Mon–Fri 9am–5pm, except when there are private functions; free), designed in the Adam style in the 1770s by the young Thomas Baldwin, who went on to become the city architect. The **Banqueting Hall** is splendid, lined with portraits of city notables and lit by the finest chandeliers in the city.

Next door is a covered market, a lively cut-through to **Grand Parade**, and then the **Victoria Art Gallery** (entrance on Bridge Street; www.victoriagal.org.uk; daily 10.30am–5pm; free). Several Sickerts and a Whistler are on display along with Gainsborough portraits and J.M.W. Turner's *West Front of Bath Abbey*.

Bridge Street leads to **Pulteney Bridge** Ⓟ, designed by Robert Adam from 1770 to 1774 and lined, like the Ponte Vecchio in Florence, with tiny shops on either side. On the right side of the bridge steps lead down to the Avon, from where river cruises depart every hour or so, and there are riverside walks to North Parade

Victoria Gardens and the Royal Crescent.

Bridge. There's a little café below the bridge with views over the weir.

At the east end of imposing **Great Pulteney Street** (another Thomas Baldwin design) is the **Holburne Museum** Q (www.holburne.org; Mon–Sat 10am–5pm, Sun 11am–5pm; free), housed in an elegant 18th-century mansion that was originally the Sydney Hotel, and which, in 2007, featured prominently in the film *The Duchess*, starring Keira Knightley. Visitors today can see paintings by Turner, Stubbs, Reynolds and Gainsborough. The last made his name in Bath, portraying the rich and famous. There are excellent temporary exhibitions here, too.

The museum stands on the edge of **Sydney Gardens**, which are frequently mentioned in the letters of Jane Austen, who lived nearby at 4 Sydney Place from 1801 to 1804, as the scene of public galas and fireworks displays. In the 19th century they were the site of daring balloon ascents. The gardens are dissected by Brunel's Great Western Railway

(1840–41) and the Kennet & Avon Canal (1810), elegantly incorporated by means of landscaped cuttings and pretty stone and cast-iron bridges. And if you want to do something different, you can cycle along the Kennet & Avon Canal for a scenic ride.

Artefacts on display at the Museum of Bath at Work.

At the Jane Austen Centre.

⦿ JANE AUSTEN'S BATH

Jane Austen (1775–1817) is the star of Bath's literary firmament, but she was far from its biggest fan. In her novels, she often portrays Bath as a petty city that is only good for gossip, parties and balls. Having departed for good, she wrote: "It will be two years tomorrow since we left Bath, with happy feelings of escape!" In *Northanger Abbey*, one of her characters reflects Austen's views: "I get so immoderately sick of Bath… though it is vastly well to be here for a few weeks, we would not live here for millions."

Large parts of *Persuasion* and *Northanger Abbey* are set in the city, giving an insight into the life Jane Austen led in Bath from 1799 to 1806. She stayed in four houses, living at 4 Sydney Place, 13 Queen Square, 27 Green Park Buildings and 25 Gay Street. The writer's association with the city is celebrated at the Jane Austen Centre (40 Gay Street; www.janeausten.co.uk; Apr–June, Sept–Oct daily 9.45am–5.30pm, July–Aug 9.30am–6pm, Nov–Mar Sun–Fri 10am–4pm, Sat 9.45am–5.30pm). The permanent exhibition recalls her story in an interesting and illuminating way.

THE WEST COUNTRY

A tour around England's southwestern corner offers a wide variety of scenery, architecture and activities, and the best climate in the country in which to enjoy them.

The West Country is many things to many people. For some it's the bleak moorlands of Bodmin, Dartmoor and Exmoor; for others it is quaint fishing villages and artists' colonies, or the gardens for which Cornwall is famous. It is an area steeped in legend – the land of King Arthur, Camelot and the Holy Grail; history here takes on a romantic quality, with facts obscured by time, and fictions embellished with tales of piracy, smuggling and shipwrecks. Yet its rugged coastline – and bright summer weather – has also made it Britain's most popular holiday destination.

The tour starts at **Bath ❶** (see page 235), then goes 8 miles (13km) east to the former mill town of **Bradford-on-Avon ❷**, which is focused around its picturesque main bridge, and has one of the best Saxon churches in the country – St Laurence's, founded in 700.

BRISTOL TO EXETER

After this, go northwest of Bath on the A4 to **Bristol ❸**, a major port since the time of the Phoenicians and in the 18th and 19th centuries an important gateway to the British Empire. Bristol became wealthy on the back of this colonial trade – though it's important to remember that a significant component of the import-export business model at that time was the slave trade between West Africa and the Americas.

Bristol's trading port moved several miles downstream from the city (to Avonmouth Docks and Royal Portbury Dock) during the 20th century. The old docks have now been redeveloped, and attractions and museums have moved in. **We The Curious** (www.wethecurious. org; Mon–Fri 10am–5pm, Sat–Sun and daily in school holidays 10am–6pm) is an interactive science museum geared to children. Nearby, the **Watershed** is an arts venue with cinemas, events space and a bar on the Floating Harbour. Further round the dock you can visit the

⊘ **Main attractions**
Bristol
Wells Cathedral
Dartmoor
Bodmin
Eden Project
St Michael's Mount
St Ives
Tintagel Castle

Maps on pages
244, 247

The north coast of Exmoor National Park.

The West Country

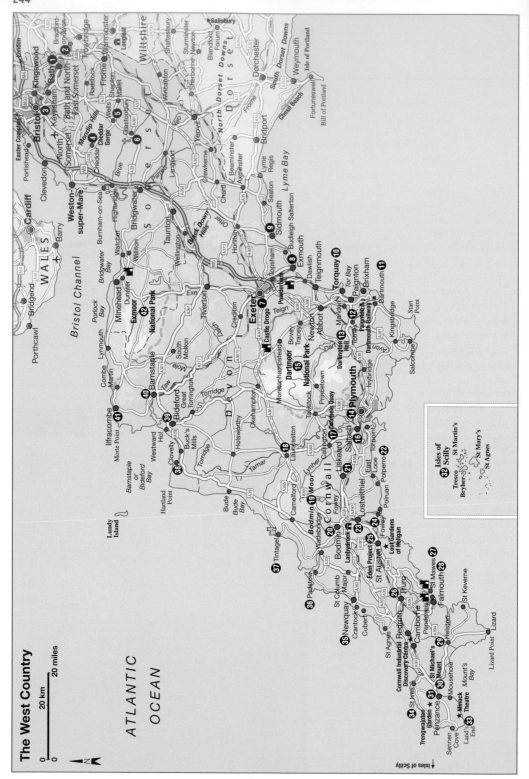

SS *Great Britain* (www.ssgreatbritain.org; daily 10am–6pm, winter until 4.30pm). Designed by Isambard Kingdom Brunel (1806–59), the ship represents Bristol's heyday as a shipbuilding centre, a theme explored further in the associated **Dockyard Museum** (same hours as ship). Your ticket also grants access to Being Brunel, a new museum that traces the life and legacy of the engineering mastermind, opened in 2018. Brunel is generally credited as Britain's greatest civil engineer, and was also responsible for the Great Western Railway, a series of steamships, and numerous bridges and tunnels.

Bristol is famed for its street art, with home-grown artist **Banksy** the most famous (anonymous) face on the scene. Although a walking tour is the best way to discover the city's graffiti-splashed walls (see www.visitbristol.co.uk for local operators), art-lovers can walk around the docks to Hanover Place to stumble across Banksy's The Girl with the Pierced Eardrum – a parody of Vermeer's famous Girl with a Pearl Earring. Another of the mysterious street artist's works – the Grim Reaper – can be found nearby at the waterside **MShed** city museum (www.bristolmuseums.org.uk/m-shed; Tue–Sun 10am–5pm; free).

In the city centre, uphill from the waterfront, is the **Cathedral**, founded in 1140 (www.bristol-cathedral.co.uk; Mon–Fri 8am–5pm, Sat–Sun until 3.15pm; donations welcome). From here, Park Street rises to Bristol University, passing independent shops, cafés and restaurants, to the Bristol Museum and Art Gallery (tel: 0117-922 3571; Tue–Sun 10am–5pm; free), and Clifton Village, where Brunel's **Suspension Bridge** spans the Avon Gorge. This corner of Bristol is a charming huddle of boutique shops, pubs and restaurants, with pretty squares hidden away behind the main street. North of the city centre, in Easter Compton, will be Bristol's massive new surfing attraction: **The Wave** (www.thewave.com; tel: 0117-915 3402), due to open in autumn 2019. This man-made surfing lake will use cutting-edge technology to produce up to 1,000 artificial waves an hour, with different zones for

Clifton Suspension Bridge.

There are over 230 panes of glass in the windows of Mol's Coffee House.

Steep cliffs at Porthcurno.

different abilities (ranging from 50cm-high waves up to almost 2m).

From Bristol take the A38 towards **Cheddar Gorge** , at 3 miles (5km) long the biggest gorge in England, carved out of karst limestone by the River Yeo. **Gough's Caves** (www.cheddargorge.co.uk; daily 10am–5pm, with exceptions) were discovered by local resident Richard Gough in 1890, and 13 years later the skeleton of the 9,000-year-old Cheddar Man was found here. A walkway leads through a series of stalactite-encrusted chambers. The **Cheddar Gorge Cheese Company** (www.cheddaronline.co.uk; daily from 10am, closing times vary), in the lower gorge, has a viewing gallery where you can watch England's most popular cheese being made.

The A371 leads southeast from Cheddar to **Wells** ❺, a market town centred on the stunning **Cathedral** (www.wellscathedral.org.uk; daily Apr–Sept 7am–7pm, Oct–Mar until 6pm; donation). Among the highlights of this early English Gothic building are the intricately carved West Front, the Choir, with England's oldest Jesse Window,

and the 14th-century scissor arches. Look out for the stunning clock, which dates back to 1390. The face shows the universe as imagined before Copernicus – with the earth at the centre. On the quarter-hour, jousting knights appear and race around the clock.

Also well worth a visit is the **Bishop's Palace** (www.bishopspalace.org.uk; daily Apr–Oct 10am–6pm, Nov–Mar until 4pm), approached over a drawbridge spanning the moat. The ruins of the 13th-century Great Hall stand in tranquil grounds, where you can see the springs that gave the town its name. South of Wells lies the ancient market town of **Glastonbury** ❻ (see page 249).

Now it's time to get on the M5 motorway and go straight to the university town of **Exeter** ❼. The Roman city wall was completed in AD 200; much of it still stands, and most main sites are within its circumference. The focal point of Exeter is the **Cathedral** Ⓐ (www.exeter-cathedral.org.uk; Mon–Sat 9.30am–5pm), which is largely 14th-century but has two Norman towers. The most significant feature is the fan vaulting of the

⊙ FACT FILE

The gateways to the West Country are Bath, Bristol, Exeter, Plymouth and Newquay.

By rail Trains leave from London Paddington for all the above destinations. Journey times: about 2 hours to Bath and Bristol; 2 hours 30 minutes to Exeter; 3 hours 30 minutes to Plymouth. For all rail information, tel: 03457-484 950.

By coach National Express coaches from London Victoria are slower, but cheaper. For information, www.nationalexpress.co.uk.

By car Bath and Bristol are easily accessible from London via the M4, Exeter via the M5, fed from London by the M4, from the north by the M6, Plymouth via the M5/A38.

By air Flybe operates flights to Newquay from London Gatwick and Manchester among other places; www.flybe.com.

Best museum Tate Gallery, St Ives, www.tate.org.uk/visit/tate-st-ives.

Walking trails Information on guided walks around Dartmoor, www.dartmoor.gov.uk or www.moorlandguides.co.uk.

Tourist Information Exeter, tel: 01392-665 700; Plymouth, tel: 01752-306 330; Penzance, tel: 01736-335 530; Torquay, tel: 01803-211 211.

world's longest Gothic vault. The building contains hundreds of carved images of "green men", pagan symbols of fertility. In the elegant Cathedral Close the most eye-catching building is 16th-century **Mol's Coffee House** Ⓑ (sadly a coffee house no longer), where Sir Francis Drake (1540–96) is supposed to have met his sea captains.

Beneath the pavements of the nearby pedestrianised High Street are the **Underground Passages** Ⓒ (tel: 01392-665 887; June–Sept and school holidays Mon, Sat 9.30am–5.30pm, Tue–Fri 10.30am–4.30pm Sun 10.30–4pm, Oct–May Tue–Fri 10.30am–4.30pm, Sat 9.30am–5.30pm, Sun 11.30am–4pm, subject to change, call to check), 14th-century subterranean aqueducts through which you can take an entertaining guided tour. At the top end of Gandy Street (enlivened with murals) is the **Exeter Phoenix Arts Centre** (www.exeterphoenix.org.uk) Ⓓ, which has a popular café and a lively schedule of events; straight ahead stands the **Royal Albert Memorial Museum** Ⓔ (www.rammuseum.org.uk; Tue–Sun 10am–5pm;

free). Descending to the River Exe and the cobbled **Quayside** Ⓕ you'll find shops and cafés, plus bikes and canoes for hire. Visit the **Custom House Visitor Centre** (tel: 01392-271 611; Apr–Oct daily 10am–5pm, Nov–Mar Thu–Sun 11am–4pm; free) for an audiovisual presentation on local history.

EXMOUTH AND SIDMOUTH

South of the city, where the estuary meets the sea, is **Exmouth** Ⓖ (take the

Babbacombe Model Village.

Glastonbury Tor at sunrise.

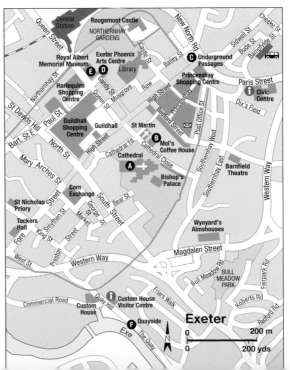

Exeter

⊘ Tip

Dartmouth Riverboat Company, tel: 01803-555 872, www.dartmouthrailriver. co.uk, has daily sailings from Dartmouth to Totnes (Apr–Oct). The relaxing cruise twists and turns along the river past pretty villages, and the home of the late Dame Agatha Christie, to a humorous commentary from the Skipper. They also offer various other cruises.

A376). Its 2 miles (3km) of golden sand are the finest in East Devon, and made it the county's first beach resort, in the 18th century.

To the east (A3052) is **Sidmouth** ❾, which is considered to be the most attractive and best preserved of East Devon's resorts. Narrow lanes back onto a grand seafront dominated by Regency houses, and the shingle beach is bordered with cliffs. Just east of the town is the **Donkey Sanctuary** (www.thedonkey-sanctuary.org.uk; daily 9am–dusk; donations welcome), a home for abused and abandoned donkeys, which has cared for over 9,000 animals over the years.

Head west after this short diversion, via the A379, down the west side of the estuary, to **Powderham Castle** (www.powderham.co.uk; Apr–Oct Sun–Fri 11am–4.30pm). This impressive medieval fortress is set in a deer park and has a lakeside picnic area and a Children's Secret Garden.

THE ENGLISH RIVIERA

The road continues via **Teignmouth** to the great sweep of Torbay, a conurbation of Torquay, Paignton and Brixham. **Torquay** ❿ is a town that likes to emphasise its Mediterranean influences. At night, with the illuminations on, palm trees rustling and people promenading, it could almost be part of the French Riviera. The **Pavilion** (currently closed to the public) on the seafront is a wonderful example of Edwardian wedding-cake architecture.

On the north side of town, reached by the **Babbacombe Cliff Railway** (Feb–Dec), is the **Babbacombe Model Village** (www.model-village.co.uk; daily 10am–4pm, with exceptions), a microcosm of contemporary England that is particularly charming when the lights go on at dusk. A couple of miles east is **Kent's Cavern** (www.kents-cavern.co.uk; daily 10.30am–4pm, with exceptions), a network of caves with a massive bear fossilised in a chamber roof. The guided tour is good, but many of the best remains are in the **Torquay Museum** (www.torquaymuseum.org; Mon–Sat 10am–4pm) at the foot of Babbacombe Road. The museum also has a gallery devoted to the crime writer Agatha Christie, who spent much of her life in the town, and a reconstruction of a 19th-century farmhouse.

Torquay blends seamlessly into Paignton, which has little of the former's elegance, but does have two of the region's best stretches of sand – one off the promenade, the other at **Goodrington**, reached by the **Paignton and Dartmouth Steam Railway** (www.dartmouthrailriver.co.uk; Mar–Nov), which chugs through attractive scenery. Behind Goodrington is **Paignton Zoo** (www.paigntonzoo.org.uk; daily 10am–4.30pm, with exceptions in summer), where there are several recreated habitats providing a home for a variety of animals.

Brixham is the third town in Torbay, a pretty resort where tourism and fishing harmoniously coexist (don't miss the BrixFest and FishStock festivals for food and music, and Funfish trips for the likes of mackerel fishing

Dartmouth's Boat Fleet.

experiences and "sea-fari" cruises). The harbour area, with its active fish market, has real character, and there's a full-size reconstruction here of the *Golden Hind*, the ship that took Sir Francis Drake around the world.

DARTMOUTH AND PLYMOUTH

Take the A379 south now to Kingswear, clinging to the steep banks of the Dart Estuary, from where it is a short ferry ride to **Dartmouth** ⑪, where the waters are thick with boats in one of England's best anchorages. Dartmouth has a long maritime history and a strong naval presence, with the Britannia Royal Naval College on the hill. The town focuses on the **Boat Fleet** (an inner harbour) and the streets running off it, crowded with historic buildings with fine frontages.

Just outside town, clamped to a shoulder of rock, is the formidable, well-preserved **Dartmouth Castle** (www.english-heritage.org.uk; Apr–Sept daily 10am–6pm, Oct until 5pm, Nov–Mar Sat–Sun 10am–4pm). It comprises the original 14th-century castle, a

Victorian fort and 17th-century St Petrock's Church.

From Dartmouth head inland to **Totnes** ⑫, an elegant town often described as Elizabethan even though its history goes back much further than that. Its face has not changed for centuries, the castle concealed from view by a tumble of houses and the arch of the East Gate spanning the main street.

The **Guildhall** is a fine building with a pillared portico, and 15th-century St Mary's Church has a delicate Saxon rood screen. In the granite-pillared Butterwalk, an Elizabethan market is held on Tuesdays (May–Sept), with traders in period dress. Turn right, and **Totnes Castle** (www.english-heritage.org.uk; Apr–Sept daily 10am–6pm, Oct until 5pm, Nov–Mar Sat–Sun 10am–4pm) soon comes into view, a perfectly preserved Norman motte-and-bailey structure.

Just off the A384, 2 miles (3km) north of Totnes, is the 14th-century **Dartington Hall** ⑬, the nerve-centre of the Dartington Estate, run by philanthropists Leonard and Dorothy

Sir Francis Drake looks out to sea at Plymouth Hoe.

Exeter Cathedral.

⊘ GLASTONBURY

Glastonbury is best known these days as the site of a hugely popular music festival held over the summer solstice, its profits donated to charity. But Glastonbury is also the site of the oldest Christian foundation in Britain. The ruined abbey is built on the site of an earlier church, founded in the 1st century when Joseph of Arimathea, the man who gave his tomb to Christ, is believed to have brought here either the Holy Grail or the Blood of the Cross. The winter-flowering hawthorns in the abbey grounds are said to have sprung up when Joseph dug his staff into the ground and it rooted – an omen that he should settle here. Three early kings – Edmund I (died 946), Edgar (died 975) and Edmund Ironside (died 1016) – are buried here.

The existing buildings date from 1184–1303, when Glastonbury was the richest abbey in England, after Westminster. They fell into ruin after the Dissolution of the Monasteries in the 1530s. The remains of a warrior and his female companion interred deep beneath the Lady Chapel are identified by local legend as those of King Arthur and Queen Guinevere.

Glastonbury Tor, high above the little town, offers views as far as the Bristol Channel. On this spot the last abbot and his treasurer were executed in 1539 for opposing Henry VIII.

Elmhirst. The hall has a cobbled quad and magnificent hammer-beamed Great Hall; outside, sculptures and a 14th-century barn cinema are set in mature woodland. The glorious gardens are open to the public (www.dartington.org; dawn to dusk; free), with lots to see, plus craft shops, places to eat and a Visitor Centre.

Follow the road to the A38, where you will find **Buckfast Abbey** (www.buckfast.org.uk; Mon–Sat 9am–6pm, Sun noon–6pm, subject to services; free), an 11th-century foundation bought in 1882 by a group of French Benedictines who dedicated their lives to its restoration. Today the monks keep bees, and make and sell tonic wine.

Now take the A38 straight to **Plymouth** ⑭, the largest conurbation in Devon. Being a naval base, it was badly bombed during World War II. Subsequent building leaves much to be desired. The **Hoe** survived – a broad grassy shoulder between town and sea, where Francis Drake was playing bowls when the Spanish Armada was sighted (1588). **Smeaton's Tower** (a former Eddystone lighthouse) stands on the Hoe, not far from the formidable walls of the **Royal Citadel** (www.english-heritage.org.uk; guided tours only May–Sept Tue, Thu, Sun 2.30pm). Further along the seafront is the Barbican, where the huge **National Marine Aquarium** (www.national-aquarium.co.uk; daily 10am–5pm) has impressive displays that recreate the different levels of aquatic habitat, from high moorland to deepest ocean. Among the species on show are sharks, turtles and several species of seahorse, which have been successfully bred at the centre.

DARTMOOR NATIONAL PARK

Dartmoor National Park ⑮ covers some 368 sq miles (954 sq km). Reaching 2,000ft (600 metres), the moor is the highest land in southern England. Around half of it is open moorland, the rest steep wooded valleys with secluded villages. Many visitors enter the park from **Tavistock** on the B3357, which leads to the **National Park Visitor Centre** – with varied displays and information on guided walks – and **Princetown**,

the highest, bleakest settlement, with Dartmoor Prison looming nearby. The road continues to **Widecombe-in-the-Moor**, a captivating little place with two claims to fame: the well-known song that advertises its annual fair in September and its church, known as the cathedral of the moor, because of the height of its tower. Narrow lanes south lead to two pretty villages, **Buckland-in-the-Moor**, with some of the most photographed thatched cottages in Devon; and **Holne**, birthplace in 1819 of writer Charles Kingsley – author of *The Water Babies* – where you'll find the 14th-century Church House Inn.

Back on the B3357 you will soon reach **Hay Tor** (1,490ft/450 metres), with far-reaching views, and **Becky Falls** (www.beckyfalls.com; mid-Feb–Oct daily 10am–5pm), where there are nature trails through pleasant woodland, plus a restaurant, gift shop, family activities and picnic area surrounding the waterfalls. Nearby, the little granite-built town of **Bovey Tracey** is worth a stop for the **Devon Guild of Craftsmen** (www.crafts.org.uk;

daily 10am–5.30pm), housed in a historic riverside mill. You will find a high-quality selection of ceramics, glass and textiles on display and for sale.

Take the A382 towards Okehampton, where a right turn leads to Drewsteignton and **Castle Drogo** (www.national trust.org.uk/castle-drogo; mid-Mar–Oct daily 11am–5pm), the last castle to be built in England, begun in 1910, and designed by Sir Edwin Lutyens. The formal terraced gardens are open all year (Sat–Sun only in winter) with access to various walks through the beautiful River Teign Gorge.

Now join the A30 to visit the market town of **Okehampton**, where the **Museum of Dartmoor Life** (www. museumofdartmoorlife.org.uk; Apr–Oct Mon–Fri 10am–4.15pm, Sat 10am–1pm, Nov Mon–Sat 11am–1pm) offers insights into life on the moor. **Okehampton Castle** (www.english-heritage. org.uk; Apr–Oct daily 10am–5pm) has been a ruin since it was seized by Henry VIII in 1538, but its hilltop setting, with a riverside picnic area below, is delightful. Our tour follows the road

Brunel's bridge at Saltash.

Rock formations on Bodmin Moor.

Launceston Steam Railway.

Buckland Abbey.

south past picturesque **Lydford Gorge** back to Plymouth and into Cornwall.

ACROSS THE TAMAR

It is said that nothing has done more to keep Cornwall Cornish than the River Tamar. To get a sense of how different from Devon it is, cross via Brunel's **Royal Albert Bridge** at **Saltash** ⑯. 18th-century houses cluster on the quayside, and visitors can go inside the home of Drake's first wife – **Mary Newman's Cottage** (tel: 01579-384 381; Apr–Sept Wed–Thu and Sat–Sun noon–4pm; free). Outside the town (off the A38) stands the imposing Norman church at **St Germans**, and there are several stately homes in the vicinity: **Trematon Castle** (also Norman) can only be glimpsed from the road, but visitors can look around **Antony House** (www.nationaltrust.org.uk/antony; Apr–Oct Tue–Thu 12.30–4.30pm, June–Aug also Sun) and **Mount Edgcumbe House** (www.mountedgcumbe.gov.uk; Apr–Sept Sun–Thu 11am–4.30pm).

The route now takes you north, leaving the main road to visit **Cotehele Quay** ⑰ (www.nationaltrust.org.uk/cotehele; mid-Mar–Oct daily 11am–4pm), perched above the wooded riverbanks. Here, there's a medieval house, remarkably unchanged, and a collection of wharf buildings, including a watermill, forge and cider press.

Rejoin the main road (A388) to **Launceston** ⑱, Cornwall's only walled town, founded in the 11th century. **Launceston Castle** (www.english-heritage.org.uk; Apr–Sept daily 10am–6pm, Oct until 5pm) sits in immaculate grounds, with views across Bodmin and Dartmoor. The castle was once a prison, where George Fox, the founder of the Quakers, was held in 1656. The 16th-century parish church, **St Mary Magdalene**, covered with decorative motifs, is the town's other important building. The **Launceston Steam Railway** (www.launcestonsr.co.uk; see website for opening times), with a museum, workshop and buffet, will take you on a trip down memory lane.

BROODY BODMIN

Pick up the A30 here and follow it through the brooding but magnificent **Bodmin**

⊘ WEST DEVON HIGHLIGHTS

Saltram House (www.nationaltrust.org.uk/saltram; mid-Mar–Oct daily noon–4.30pm) is set in 470 acres (190 hectares) of grounds in Plymouth's eastern suburbs. Virtually all the furnishings are original, which is rare. This National Trust property contains several portraits by Sir Joshua Reynolds (who was born in Plympton) and a magnificent salon, reworked by Robert Adam in the 1770s.

Buckland Abbey (www.nationaltrust.org.uk/buckland-abbey; mid-Mar–Oct daily 11am–5pm, Nov–Dec until 4pm, late Feb–early Mar Sat–Sun 11am–3pm) was a 13th-century Cistercian monastery, and the vast barn and abbey church are original. Sir Francis Drake (1540–96), the first Englishman to navigate the globe, and the man who brought potatoes and tobacco from Virginia to England, bought it in 1580, and the rooms house an exhibition devoted to his life. Look out for Drake's Drum – it is said that it beats when England is in danger and needs his help: the last time it was heard was at Dunkirk.

Morwellham Quay (www.morwellham-quay.co.uk; daily Mar–Oct 10am–5pm, Nov–Feb 10am–4pm, with exceptions), set in a Designated Area of Natural Beauty at the highest navigable point on the Tamar, is a superbly presented reconstruction of industry and transport in Victorian times. A small railway takes visitors into the disused copper mine.

Moor ⑲. The road enters the moorland at Altarnun, where you can visit the **Wesley Cottage** (www.wesleycottage.org. uk; May–Oct Tue–Sat 10am–4pm), where John Wesley (1703–91), founder of Methodism, stayed when preaching in Cornwall. At Bolventor you cannot miss the **Jamaica Inn**. The attached Smugglers' Museum (www.jamaicainn.co.uk; daily 8am–9pm) gives a theatrical presentation of Daphne du Maurier's story and has a collection of smuggling relics.

A minor road follows the River Fowey, passing **Dozmary Pool** in the wildest part of the moor. Fed by underground springs, it is the stuff of legend: according to Alfred Lord Tennyson, it was here that King Arthur's sword was consigned to the waters after his death. A little further south is **St Cleer's Holy Well**; its waters were reputed to cure madness.

You are close to Liskeard (pronounced "Liskard") here, and roads to the coast, but an exploration of the moor is best rounded off by a visit to **Bodmin** ⑳, the western gateway, an old trade route from Ireland that attracted early saints. St Petroc, Cornwall's senior saint, founded a priory here in the 6th century (only fragments remain) and the 15th-century **Church of St Petroc** (daily 9am–5pm) houses a cask containing his remains. This is the county's largest church.

Bodmin Museum (tel: 01208-77067; Easter–Sept Mon–Fri 10.30am–4.30pm, Sat until 2.30pm, Oct Mon–Sat 10.30am–2.30pm; free) has good exhibitions on local life through the ages, and there's a nostalgic taste of sulphur on the **Bodmin and Wenford Steam Railway** (www.bodminandwenford railway.co.uk; May–Sept daily). Bodmin's bypass skirts the grounds of **Lanhydrock House** (www.nationaltrust.org. uk/lanhydrock; Mar–Sept daily 11am–5.30pm, Oct until 5pm), an enormous country house with 50 rooms to explore and a pleasing lived-in atmosphere. Highlights are the long gallery with a splendid plasterwork ceiling, the servants' quarters and extensive grounds planted with rare shrubs.

Double back now to **Liskeard** ㉑ on the A38. Its tin-mining heyday is long

St Mary Magdalene Church at Launceston.

St Michael's Mount.

gone, but there remains a wealth of Georgian buildings, a Regency Market Hall and the **Stuart House**, where Charles I spent several nights during the Civil War (1642–6).

CORNWALL'S FISHING VILLAGES

Head down to the coast now to **Looe Bay**, where East and West Looe are linked by a bridge. The former is the larger and more prosperous, dependent on tourism and the revived fishing industry. The **Old Guildhall Museum** (Apr–mid-Nov Mon–Fri 11am–4pm, Sat until 1.30pm, Sun until 4pm) is devoted to fishing and smuggling.

Go west a few miles to **Polperro** ㉒ which lives up to its reputation as one of Cornwall's most picturesque fishing villages. Clinging to the steep hillside, colour-washed cottages bedecked with flowers crowd the narrow alleys. The paths winding up the hill offer splendid views over the harbour.

Inland now to **Lostwithiel** ㉓, Cornwall's former capital is a serene, rather French-looking place beside the Fowey. There are many attractive Georgian buildings in the town, and the 14th-century **Duchy Palace** stands in Quay Street. **Lostwithiel Museum** (www.lostwithielmuseum.org; mid-Apr–Sept Mon–Fri 10.30am–4.30pm; free) has an excellent collection of local photographs, and domestic and agricultural implements.

Fowey ㉔ (pronounced Foy), at the mouth of the river of the same name, is a pretty place, its houses huddled daintily above a deep-water harbour, one of the south coast's best sailing areas (see www.fowey.co.uk for details of boating opportunities). Henry VII built a fort above **Readymoney Cove**; **St Catherine's Castle** contains the mausoleum of the locally powerful Rashleigh family – their townhouse is now the Ship Inn. For many years Fowey was the home of Daphne du Maurier, and there is a festival in her honour each May. The **Fowey Museum** (www.museumsincornwall.org.uk; Easter–Sept Mon–Fri 10.30am–4.30pm), housed in part of the Town Hall, commemorates the town's maritime past.

Polperro's cove.

FROM TRURO TO LAND'S END

Leaving Fowey, take the A3082, which joins the A390 to **St Austell** and the **Eden Project** ❷ (www.edenproject.com; daily 9.30am–6pm, mid-July–Aug until 6.30pm). This vast global garden is accommodated within huge domed conservatories called biomes; it has become one of Cornwall's major attractions. Built on the site of a huge disused china clay pit, the biomes recreate rainforest and Mediterranean habitats. The lush Rainforest biome is filled with all sorts of exotic plants, including chocolate, bananas, cola and sugar. The Mediterranean biome contains plants such as olive trees, vines, citruses and cork trees. There's also plenty of information on the impact that people have on plants and habitats around the world. There are also extensive gardens outside. On from here to **Truro** ❷: every inch a city – although the ring road has separated its heart from its maritime heritage. The triple towers of the neo-Gothic **Cathedral** (www.trurocathedral.org.uk; Mon–Fri 7.30am–6pm, Sat until 4.30pm, Sun until 5pm; donation) soar above the

rooftops of 18th-century houses. **Lemon Street** is one of the most homogeneous Georgian streets in England. The past is well documented in the **Royal Cornwall Museum** (www.royalcornwallmuseum.org. uk; daily 10am–4.45pm), which has galleries for archaeological finds, including an Egyptian room with an unwrapped mummy, as well as collections relating to local and natural history, ceramics and costume.

Turn off the A39 onto the B3289 to reach **St Mawes** ❷, on the Roseland Peninsula. Ferries bustle in and out of the harbour, and yacht owners fill the Victory Inn. Thatched cottages line the seafront road to the three huge circular bastions of **St Mawes Castle** (www. english-heritage.org.uk; Apr–Sept daily 10am–6pm, Oct 10am–5pm, Nov–Mar Sat–Sun 10am–4pm), built by Henry VIII in 1543 as a defence against a French attack from the sea. The garden of **Lamorran House** (www.lamor rangarden.co.uk; Apr–Sept Wed and Fri 10am–5pm; charge) in Upper Castle Road has a Mediterranean feel, with sub-tropical plants flourishing on the

Jamaica Inn, on the borders of Bodmin Moor.

The walled garden at the Lost Gardens of Heligan.

⊘ CORNISH GARDENS

Cornwall's mild climate has produced some beautiful gardens. Among the best are:

Glendurgan, which is set in a wooded valley near Falmouth. Rare and exotic subtropical plants flourish here, and there is an unusual 19th-century laurel maze; tel: 01326-252 020.

Trebah, Falmouth. Hydrangeas, rhododendrons and azaleas, plus a water garden and cascades, produce wonderful colour year-round; tel: 01326-252 200.

Lost Gardens of Heligan, Pentewan, St Austell. These "lost" Victorian gardens have been superbly restored. The Italian garden, kitchen garden, walled garden and "jungle" area have been returned to their former glory; tel: 01726-845 100. This is a must on your itinerary.

Trelissick, near Truro. This is a plantsman's garden, famous for its tender exotic plants and shrubs, as well as its setting. Enjoy delightful woodland and riverside walks, with wonderful views down to Falmouth; tel: 01872-862 090.

Trewithen, Truro, is internationally known for its camellias, rhododendrons, magnolias, plus many rare trees and shrubs; tel: 01726-883 794.

Caerhays Castle, Gorran, St Austell. An informal woodland garden overlooking the sea, where camellias, magnolias and rhododendrons thrive; tel: 01872-501 310.

hillside. Level with the top of the tower below, the lych-gate of the church at **St Just-in-Roseland** frames what may be the most perfect view in Cornwall. The 13th-century church itself, reflected in St Just Pool, is almost as pleasing.

On the other side of the estuary lies **Falmouth** ㉘ (there are ferries; otherwise return to Truro and continue on the A39). This town developed after Sir Walter Raleigh (1552–1618) decided it would make a good harbour. Henry VIII built **Pendennis Castle** (www.english-heritage.org.uk; Apr–Sept daily 10am–6pm, Oct daily 10am–5pm, Nov–Mar Sat–Sun 10am–4pm) at the same time as the one at St Mawes, but the expected French attack never came. The town received a charter in 1661 and the church of King Charles the Martyr was built the following year.

On the redeveloped Discovery Quay, the **National Maritime Museum** (www.nmmc.co.uk; daily 10am–5pm) occupies a splendid building. Lots of interactive exhibits make it popular with children as well as marine enthusiasts; highlights include the underground gallery, with large windows framing fish swimming in the harbour, and the 30m-high lookout tower. The **Falmouth Art Gallery** (www.falmouthartgallery.com; Mon–Sat 10am–5pm; free) in the central square, The Moor, puts on exhibitions of paintings, sculpture, photographs and textiles. The town centre is crammed with artisanal coffee shops (music-lovers should visit Jam Records to browse vinyl post-caffeine hit) and local craft shops – try Old Brewery Yard, also home to a gallery and craft beer bar/shop. Visit in October for the Falmouth Oyster Festival, a four-day event hosting some of the top names in cooking and a celebration of all things seafood and wine.

Helston ㉙ is the next port of call. It really comes alive on 8 May, the celebration of Flora Day, a pagan ritual to welcome spring. The **Helston Museum** (www.helstonmuseum.co.uk; Mon–Sat 10am–4pm; free) has interesting displays on life in the region in days gone by. Just outside Helston is the **Flambards Experience** (www.flambards.co.uk; Easter–Oct daily 10am–5pm, with

The geodesic domes of the Eden Project.

exceptions), a theme park with various rides, as well as exhibitions that include a re-creation of a Victorian village.

The A394 takes you west past the rocky island of **St Michael's Mount** ❸⓿ (www.stmichaelsmount.co.uk; Easter–Oct Sun–Fri 10.30am–5pm, with exceptions). A Benedictine monastery was founded here in the 12th century (the Priory Church crowns the summit). It was then fortified by Henry VIII after the Dissolution to form part of his string of coastal defences. To reach the island, you must walk across the causeway at low tide or board a boat.

Across **Mount's Bay** lies **Penzance** ❸❶, the star of Cornish resorts and the warmest place in the British Isles, with subtropical plants flourishing in **Morrab Gardens**, off Morrab Road. At the other end of the road, in Penlee Park, the **Penlee House Gallery and Museum** (www.penleehouse.org.uk; Mon–Sat Apr–Oct 10am–5pm, Nov–Mar until 4.30pm) displays paintings from the Newlyn School.

The ship-eating **Isles of Scilly** ❸❷ (pronounced "silly"), 28 miles (45 km) west of Land's End, can be reached by ferry from Penzance or plane from Land's End, Newquay and Exeter. Highlights are the **Tresco Abbey Gardens** (www.tresco.co.uk; daily 10am–4pm), which contain the Valhalla collection of figureheads; and the **Isles of Scilly Museum** on St Mary's (www.iosmuseum. org; Easter–Sept Mon–Fri 10am–4.30pm, Sat 10am–noon, Oct–Easter Mon–Sat 10am–noon). In season there are races of six-oar gigs off St Mary's.

Travelling south from Penzance on the B3315, two picturesque villages sit on the south shore of Penwith. Newlyn has the **Newlyn Gallery** (Mon–Sat 10am–5pm, closed Mon in winter), featuring work by regional artists, while **Mousehole** (pronounced *mowzel*) is as tiny as the name suggests; a cluster of granite cottages and half-timbered pubs. The village is named after an old smugglers' cave called the Mouse Hole. Further west, Porthcurno is home to a delightful beach cove as well as the open-air **Minack Theatre** (tel: 01736-810 181; www.minack.com; daily 10am–5pm, with exceptions, closed to visitors during performances), which is

Tintagel Castle.

In the Tate St Ives.

○ Tip

The Tarka Trail stretches from Ilfracombe to Meeth, via Barnstaple. Named after Henry Williamson's Tarka the Otter – the story was based on many locations along the Trail – the route follows a disused railway through beautiful countryside. For more information on hiring bikes for this traffic-free cycle route, tel: 01271-324202.

spectacularly set carved into the cliffs overlooking the sea. During the summer season productions include everything from Shakespeare to musicals and children's shows.

Return to the B3315 and travel on to **Land's End ❸**, the most westerly point in England. No longer the romantic, isolated spot it once was, it is now developed. The **Land's End Centre** (www.landsend-landmark.co.uk; Mar–Nov daily 10am–4pm last admission) has the iconic signpost, a discovery trail, five family attractions and lots of shops and restaurants.

ST IVES AND NEWQUAY

On the road to St Ives (the B3306 that hugs the coast) you'll pass **St Just**, where Cornish miracle plays are performed in a grassy amphitheatre called the Playing Place; and **Botallack**, which has the most picturesque of the ruined mine buildings. The **Levant Mine** (www.nationaltrust.org.uk/levant-mine; mid-Mar–Oct daily 10.30am–5pm) has the oldest working beam engine in Cornwall. Along the cliff is the **Geevor Tin Mine Museum** (www.geevor.com; Sun–Fri Apr–Oct 9am–5pm, Nov–Mar until 4pm). A little further up the coast is **Zennor**, a place of magic and legends; where a legendary mermaid lured a chorister beneath the waves after he'd fallen in love with her voice

But the goal for many visitors is **St Ives ❹**, the most interesting of the resorts, and in recent years the most fashionable and upmarket. It is distinguished by its "island", which divides the Atlantic surfing beach of Porthmeor from the harbour and beach of Porthminster, with the little granite chapel of St Nicholas on its topmost point. St Ives grew prosperous on pilchards and tin mining, and the houses of the pilchard fishermen still crowd the tangled streets of Downalong, while the tin miners lived in Upalong. Both industries collapsed, but the town was saved by its scenic beauty and the quality of its light, which attracted artists here.

The **Tate St Ives** (www.tate.org.uk; daily 10am–5.20pm) has a small permanent exhibition of works by artists connected with the region, complemented

Pendennis Castle.

by temporary exhibitions of modern art. The top-floor café has an outdoor terrace and spectacular views across St Ives and the ocean.

Nearby on Barnoon Hill is the **Barbara Hepworth Museum** (tel: 01736-796 226; daily 10am–5.20pm), where her work is displayed in her studio and garden. For more paintings, go to the excellent **St Ives Society of Artists Gallery**, in Norway Square (www.stisa.co.uk; Mon–Sat 10.30am–5.30pm, Apr–Oct also Sun 2–5pm; free), and the **Penwith Gallery** (www.penwithgallery.com; Mon–Sat 10am–5pm; free).

Continue up the north coast, which is beautiful despite the plethora of seaside bungalows and caravan sites, to **Newquay** ㉟, the largest, brashest resort on the coast, with beautiful sandy beaches popular with surfers. Nearby Watergate Bay is a real surfer's Mecca, offering excellent conditions for beginners and professionals, as well as surfing schools and surfer-friendly hotels. Just inland, at Kestle Mill, is **Trerice** (www.nationaltrust.org.uk/trerice; Mar–Oct daily 11am–5pm, Nov–Dec

Sat–Sun 11am–4pm), an exquisitely decorated and furnished Elizabethan manor house.

PADSTOW AND TINTAGEL

Our route continues inland (A392/A39) to reach **Padstow** ㊱ on the River Camel Estuary. It's a picturesque little place with a small harbour and cobbled streets. If you're here on 1 May you'll see the famous **Padstow 'Obby 'Oss** (Hobby Horse) and his colourful entourage in a procession celebrating the coming of summer. **Prideaux Place** (www.prideauxplace.co.uk; Easter–mid-Apr and mid-May–Sept Sun–Thu 1.30–4pm, grounds 10.30am–5pm), which overlooks the town and deer park, is one of the stops on the procession's route, and one of the nicest of Cornwall's stately homes. Padstow is also noted for its seafood restaurants, including several owned by famous chef Rick Stein. Although they are pricey, they come recommended nevertheless.

Pick up the A39 at Wadebridge and turn left at Camelford for **Tintagel** ㊲, where the **Old Post Office** (www.

Surfers paddle out into the water at Newquay.

nationaltrust.org.uk/tintagel-old-post-office; daily Apr–Sept 10.30am–5.30pm, Mar, Oct 11am–4pm), a 14th-century yeoman's farmhouse, has been restored. It's amazing that so much remains of **Tintagel Castle** (www.english-heritage.org.uk; Apr–Sept daily 10am–6pm, Oct 11am–4pm, Nov–Mar Sat–Sun only 10am–4pm), on a headland of black craggy cliffs, accessible only by footbridge. Once a Celtic stronghold, then home to the earls of Cornwall, it's best known as the legendary birthplace of King Arthur, and home to Merlin the magician. Carry on north to **Bude**, where surfers flock to the golden sands and strong waves.

WESTWARD HO!

Here you cross back into Devon to visit **Clovelly** ❸ (www.clovelly.co.uk), a perfectly preserved fishing village, where steep cobbled streets lined with brightly-painted houses lead up from the harbour. It was made famous by Charles Kingsley (1819–75) in *Westward Ho!* The resort of the same name, a 19th-century development, lies nearby.

The Great Hangman cliffs at Exmoor National Park.

Follow the road round Barnstaple Bay to the pleasant town of **Bideford** ❸, also closely associated with Kingsley. There's an impressive medieval bridge, and the quay is the mainline station for **Lundy Island**, a peaceful sliver of land 11 miles (18km) offshore, home to puffins and a wealth of other bird- and marine life.

Nearby **Barnstaple** ❹, on the Taw Estuary, is best known for its glass-roofed 19th-century Pannier Market, the finest in Devon, where fresh produce is on sale.

The major resort on Devon's north coast is **Ilfracombe** ❹, although its beach is not remarkable. (For the finest beach in Devon, turn off on the B3343 instead and wind down to the sands and dunes of **Woolacombe**.) All the same, Ilfracombe has a port full of character, and a highly eccentric **Museum** (www.ilfracombemuseum.co.uk; Apr–Oct Mon–Fri 10am–5pm, Nov–Mar Tue–Fri 10am–1pm), which concentrates on maritime history, but incorporates plenty else besides (including a shrunken head and pickled bats).

⊘ EXMOOR NATIONAL PARK

Exmoor ❹ contains a great variety of landscape and wildlife; whilst parts are open heather-covered moor, it also includes some of Britain's most dramatic and beautiful coastline. It is not as high as Dartmoor and is more extensively farmed, with habitation more widely spread; many of its hills are topped with Iron Age forts. Among the many highlights (starting from Combe Martin on the moor's western edge) are:

The Great Hangman, the highest sea cliff in England.

The Cliff Railway (www.cliffrailwaylynton.co.uk; mid-Feb–Oct daily 10am–5pm, with exceptions), linking Lynton and the seaside town of Lynmouth.

Valley of the Rocks, a dramatic, dry land formation running parallel to the coast.

Doone Valley, a magical place made famous by R.D. Blackmore's novel *Lorna Doone*.

Selworthy, a pretty village full of preserved thatched cottages.

Dunster, with its striking castle and circular Yarn Market.

Dunkery Beacon, the highest spot (1,704ft/519 metres) on Exmoor.

Landacre Bridge a medieval structure crossing the River Barle.

Tarr Steps, a clapper bridge near Withypool.

For information and details on various walks, contact the Exmoor Visitors' Centre, 7/9 Fore Street, Dulverton, TA22 9EX; tel: 01398-323 841.

WEST COUNTRY WRITERS

Whether crafting poetry or thrillers, family sagas or anthropomorphic tales, writers from all over can't help but find the West Country inspirational.

The West Country is a region that has produced and inspired numerous writers, some of whose works have even been immortalised in place names. R.D. Blackmore's *Lorna Doone* (1869) was set in the 17th century and gave its name to the Upper East Lyn, which became the Doone Valley. Much of mid-Devon has been christened Tarka Country, after *Tarka the Otter* (1927), written by Henry Williamson (1895–1977).

Charles Kingsley (1819–75), whose father was vicar of Clovelly, wrote *Westward Ho!* (1855) while living in nearby Bideford, and the name was borrowed for the resort.

MORE DEVON WRITERS

Other writers associated with Devon are Sir Arthur Conan Doyle (1859–1930), who used Dartmoor as the location for *The Hound of the Baskervilles* in 1902, and John Galsworthy (1867–1933), who wrote *The Forsyte Saga* series while living in Manaton on the east side of the moor. Two centuries earlier, John Gay (1685–1732), author of *The Beggars' Opera* (1728), was born and educated in Barnstaple.

Perhaps the most famous of Devon's writers is Agatha Christie (1890–1976), Britain's most prolific author, whose thrillers still sell about 4 million copies a year. She was born in Torquay and wrote two of her books while staying at the Art Deco hotel on Burgh Island (www.burghisland.com), which today is accessed by sea tractor. Greenway, Christie's family home, overlooking the River Dart, is now managed by the National Trust, and is open to the public (www.nationaltrust.org.uk/greenway; daily mid-Feb–Oct 10.30am–5pm). Parking must be pre-booked (tel: 01803-842 382).

CORNWALL WRITERS

Cornwall also has its share of literary figures. D.H. Lawrence (1885–1930) wrote *Women in Love* at Zennor, where he sat out World War I. Virginia Woolf (1882–1941) used early memories of Godrevy Lighthouse in her 1927 novel *To The Lighthouse*. Sir John Betjeman (1906–84) also spent childhood holidays in Cornwall, in Trebetherick at the mouth of the Camel Estuary. His verse autobiography, *Summoned by Bells*, recalls bicycle trips to churches, and he later described travelling by rail to Padstow as "the best train journey I know".

More recently, Winston Graham, in his immensely popular Poldark novels, has drawn on the 19th-century mining industry around Perranporth.

Most inextricably associated with Cornwall, however, is Daphne du Maurier (1907–89); she wrote several of her early works at Bodinnick, near Fowey, and later ones at Menabilly. She used Jamaica Inn on Bodmin Moor as the setting for the eponymous novel, and gave evocative Cornish settings to *Frenchman's Creek* and *Rebecca*, the latter published in 1938 and later memorably filmed by Alfred Hitchcock.

Agatha Christie.

Ludlow Castle and town,
Shropshire.

Ross-on-Wye.

HEREFORD AND THE WELSH BORDERS

The border counties play host to literary and arts festivals, produce world-famous pottery, and lay claim to some splendid castles and cathedrals as well as the world's first iron bridge.

The great border castles of Herefordshire are a legacy of the time when this green and pleasant region was a fiercely disputed frontier between England and Wales, where the Norman lords established the Marches. This chapter explores the castles and valleys, the pretty towns of the Wye Valley and takes in the world's first iron bridge at Coalbrookdale, as well as the pottery town of Stoke-on-Trent.

The tour starts with a visit to **Ross-on-Wye ❶**, which stands on a red sandstone cliff above a bend in the River Wye. The slender spire of **St Mary's Church**, which tops the cliff, can be seen for miles around. The church is known for its hedgehogs: stone ones, wooden ones, painted and embroidered ones. The area of parkland that surrounds the church is called The Prospect, and it does indeed offer a wonderful prospect across the river. Ross is a busy market town centred on a 17th-century arcaded **Market Hall**, which is set in a square where markets are still held.

The 136-mile (218km) **Wye Valley Walk** passes through Ross, a stunning and diverse trail waymarked by a distinctive leaping salmon logo. It follows the banks of the Wye from Chepstow to the source of the river on the slopes of Plynlimon in Powys, Wales.

AROUND THE FOREST OF DEAN

From Ross, make a diversion some 8 miles (13km) southwest to **Symonds Yat ❷**, a rocky outcrop with stunning views over the Wye. The ferry that links Symonds Yat East and West across the river runs on an overhead chain and is operated by hand. The **Amazing Hedge Puzzle** (www.mazes.co.uk; daily 11am–5pm, Oct and Mar until 4pm, Nov–Feb until 3pm), along with the Jubilee Maze and the adjoining Museum of Mazes, explain some of the mysteries of maze-making.

⊘ Main attractions
Hereford Cathedral
Hay-on-Wye
Ludlow Castle
Ironbridge Gorge Museum
Wedgwood Museum

Map on page 266

Royal Albert tea set.

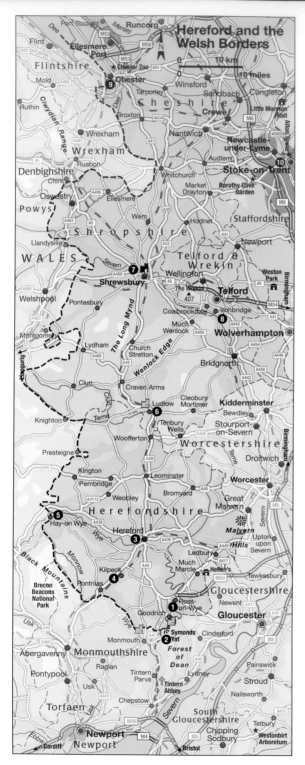

Symonds Yat is a springboard for walks in the **Forest of Dean**, a former royal hunting ground, over the border in Gloucestershire. The forest's ancient mining industry can be explored at **Clearwell Caves** (www.clearwellcaves.com; mid-Feb–Mar, Sep–Oct 10am–4pm, Apr–Aug until 5pm) near Coleford.

On your way back to Ross, take a look at **Goodrich Castle** (www.english-heritage.org.uk; tel: 01600-890 538; Apr–Sept daily 10am–6pm, Oct daily 10am–5pm, Nov–Mar Sat–Sun 10am–4pm), the best-preserved and most intact of the border fortresses.

From Ross, take the A449/B4224 towards Hereford. There are opportunities for riverside and woodland walks. To the right of the road, at **Much Marcle**, is **Hellens** (www.hellensmanor.com; Easter–Sept Wed, Sun by guided tour at 1pm, 2pm and 3pm, or you can just visit the gardens 12.30–5pm), a Tudor house set in extensive grounds with fish ponds and coppices. There's also a ridge-top picnic spot near Much Marcle.

Continuing north the road brings you to the pleasant market town of **Ledbury**, with some fine examples of black-and-white timber-framed houses, such as the 17th-century Market House. The town offers some good independent shopping and an excellent choice of restaurants.

HEREFORD

Ignoring all other tempting diversions, make your way now to **Hereford** ❸, the pleasant cathedral city that is the capital of the Wye Valley. Its greatest treasure is the 12th-century **Cathedral** (www.herefordcathedral.org; daily 9.15am–5.30pm, Sun until 3.30pm), with a lovely early English Lady Chapel and the restored Shrine of St Thomas of Hereford. The **Mappa Mundi Centre** (Mon–Sat Mar–Sept 10am–5pm, Oct–Feb 10am–4pm) displays the largest and finest medieval map of the world, as well as the famous **Chained Library**. Here is an amazing collection of books and manuscripts dating from the 8th–18th century. Every three years the cathedral plays host to the world's oldest music festival, the **Three Choirs Festival** (www.3choirs.org; next July 2021). On other years the festival is held in Worcester or Gloucester.

The **Hereford Museum and Art Gallery** (tel: 01432-260 692; Wed–Sat 11am–4pm; free) opposite the cathedral offers a good introduction to the city and area, as well as changing art exhibitions. In Edgar Street on the ring road, the **Courtyard Centre for the Arts** (www.courtyard.org.uk) is a light and modern venue for theatre, music and dance; it also has an art gallery, cinema and restaurant. You may just want to wander along pedestrianised Church Street, linking the cathedral to **High Town**, where you can visit the **Old House** (tel: 01432-260 694; Tue–Sat 10am–4pm, Sun 11.30am–2.30pm), a handsome half-timbered Jacobean house. In the other direction, south of the cathedral, is the Old Bridge, from where you can walk along the Wye.

The village of **Kilpeck** ④, about 8 miles (13km) south on the Abergavenny road, has the most wonderfully ornate, red sandstone Norman church in England. **St Mary and St David** was built around 1134–45 and is well preserved, with unusual carvings on the south door, chancel arch and the semi-circular apse.

SECOND-HAND BOOK CENTRE

Backtracking a little on the A465, take a left turn on to the B4348 for the trip to the border town of **Hay-on-Wye** ⑤ (most of the town is in Wales). Hay became a major literary centre in the 1970s when an eccentric businessman, Richard Booth, seeing how many shops and cinemas were losing business to the bigger towns, began converting the empty premises into bookshops. Financial difficulties foiled his plan to

rule the town unchallenged, and other booksellers moved in. Today, Hay is a book enthusiast's paradise, and in late May/early June the **Hay Festival of Literature** (www.hayfestival.com) attracts thousands of readers and high-profile writers to the little town.

INTO SHROPSHIRE

The A438/A4112 leads via Leominster to **Ludlow** ⑥, a charming town where lie the ashes of A.E. Housman (1859–1936), the poet who immortalised the dreamy slopes of this part of rural England in *A Shropshire Lad*. It's an architecturally interesting place, with 13th-century taverns and Tudor market buildings. **Ludlow Castle** was the seat of the presidents of the council of the Marcher lords, and it was here that John Milton's play *Comus* was first performed in 1634.

Modern-day Ludlow has spearheaded an English gastronomic revival based on the region's high-quality agricultural produce and the "slow food" movement. Ludlow's restaurants have won numerous Michelin stars, and

☉ Tip

To the left and right of the A4112 lie what are known as the black and white villages – clusters of black and white cottages, shops and inns, clustered around village churches. Weobley, dating from the 7th century, Eardisland, which stands on the River Arrow, and Pembridge, also on the river and with over 90 listed buildings, are among the most picturesque.

☉ HEREFORD CIDER

Herefordshire is the place to go for cider. If you are there in spring you will see orchards of trees loaded with pale pink apple blossom, in late summer with rosy cider apples. Perry (made from pears) is also produced. Numerous cider breweries open their doors to visitors, providing demonstrations of cider-making, tastings and opportunities to buy. Among the most interesting are Ross On Rye Cider & Perry Company, which offers orchard tours and hosts annual cider and music festivals (tel: 01989-562 815; www.rosscider. com), perry specialists Gregg's Pit Cider & Perry (tel: 01531-660 687; www. greggs-pit.co.uk) and Dunkerton Cider Mill (tel: 01544-388 653; www.dunkerton scider.co.uk) which has a well-stocked cider shop. Then there's award-winning Once Upon a Tree (tel: 01531-637 119; www.onceuponatree.co.uk), which produces fine ciders and apple juices. Call in advance for tours. If you want to explore the history of the industry in more detail, visit the Cider Museum and King Offa Distillery (tel: 01432-354 207; www.cidermuseum.co.uk; Mon–Sat 10.30am–4.30pm) in Ryelands Street, Hereford (the museum is signposted on the ring road), which has a well-stocked shop and café. All these distilleries suggest that you check availability in advance if you would like a tour.

If you fancy exploring Hereford's cider producers by bike or staying on a cider-producing farm, check out the website www.ciderroute.co.uk. It also details any upcoming festivals or special events to do with cider.

the town hosts its own food festival in September each year (www.foodfestival.co.uk). West of Ludlow (and just over the Welsh border) is Knighton, a good centre for exploring **Offa's Dyke**. This 8th-century earthwork, built by the Saxon King Offa to protect England from the marauding Welsh, runs the length of the England–Wales border and was the first official boundary between England and Wales. Its exact purpose – military or administrative – is uncertain. Compared to Hadrian's Wall, built to keep the Scots at bay, it can hardly be regarded as a serious line of defence. This 1,200-year-old barrier has vanished along some of its route, but walkers can trace its course on the long-distance Offa's Dyke Path (www.nationaltrail.co.uk/offas-dyke-path). Hay-on-Wye, Monmouth and Knighton, 17 miles (28km) west of Ludlow, are good access points.

North on the A49 lies **Shrewsbury** ❼, beautifully situated on a meander in the River Severn, crossed by the English bridge and the Welsh bridge. It has 15th-century houses, some quaint half-timbered shopfronts, and some fine parks and gardens. The pink sandstone castle near the station was converted into a museum by Thomas Telford and now incorporates the **Shropshire Regimental Museum** (www.shropshireregimentalmuseum.co.uk; mid-May–mid-Sept Fri–Wed 10.30am–5pm, Sun until 4pm, mid-Sept–mid-Dec and mid-Feb–mid-May Fri–Sat, Mon–Wed 10.30am–4pm). The solid and unassuming **Cathedral** (www.shrewsburycathedral.org; Easter–Oct Mon–Fri 1–4pm, Sat 10am–4pm, rest of the year Sat only 10am–4pm and services; free) is built of the same reddish stone as the castle.

Shrewsbury is the birthplace of scientist Charles Darwin (1809–82), whose *On the Origin of Species* articulated the theory of evolution. The World War I poet Wilfred Owen (1893–1918) was also born here.

IRONBRIDGE TO CHESTER

East of Shrewsbury on the A5/M54 is **Telford**, a new town named after the 18th-century engineer Thomas Telford.

Ironbridge.

Initiated in the 1960s, the ambitious project takes in **Coalbrookdale** and **Ironbridge**  on the River Severn, where the world's first iron bridge was built in 1779 by Abraham Darby III, of the well-known Darby family of iron-masters from Coalbrookdale. It was here, a region rich in natural resources that had been a mining centre since the time of Henry VIII, that Bristol brass-maker Abraham Darby pioneered the use of coke to smelt iron, thus making the process much cheaper while retaining high quality, and turning the area into the busiest industrial centre in the world.

Ten different museums, which include original furnaces, foundries, brickworks, the Coalport china works and a recreated Victorian town (Blists Hill), are incorporated in the splendid **Ironbridge Gorge Museum** (www.iron bridge.org.uk; daily 10am–5pm, with exceptions; a passport ticket allows repeated entry to all museums for one year).

Our next destination (north on the A442/A41) is **Chester** ❾, the most northerly and the most exciting of the timbered Tudor towns of the Welsh Marches. Its particular architectural character can be seen in the so-called **Rows** of double-tiered and covered walkways as you walk down Eastgate, Westgate or Bridge Street. The oldest of the Rows dates from 1486, though most of them are 16th century.

In Roman times Chester was an important stronghold called Deva; part of an amphitheatre can be seen just outside the city walls, by St John's Street. The **Grosvenor Museum** (www. westcheshiremuseums.co.uk; Mon–Sat 10.30am–5pm, Sun 1–4pm; free) records the Roman legacy with models of the ancient fortress city. Under the Normans, Chester became a near-independent state governed by a succession of earls. The tidal estuary of the River Dee allowed the city to flourish as a port until the 15th century, when the estuary began to silt up. After that, shipping was transferred to the natural port of Liverpool.

The 2-mile (3km) walk around the city walls will help you to get

Chester Cathedral's south transept.

The Hay-on-Wye Festival.

⦿ FACT FILE

Location The area follows the Welsh border from south to north, taking in parts of Herefordshire, Shropshire and Cheshire.

By car Via the M4/M5/M50 from London to Ross-on-Wye; M5 from Birmingham; M56 from Manchester to Chester.

By coach Tel: 0871-781 8181, www.nationalexpress.co.uk.

By rail London Paddington to Hereford, journey time approximately 2 hours 45 minutes; tel: 03457-484 950.

Main events Hay Festival, literature and the arts (www.hayfestival.com), Food Festival (www.foodfestival.co.uk), Hereford Three Choirs Festival (www.3choirs.org).

For children Alton Towers Theme Park, tel: 0871-222 3330; Gladstone Working Pottery Museum. Come along and make a souvenir to take home (tel: 01782-237 777).

Most famous sons Industrial pioneer Abraham Darby (1678–1717); naturalist Charles Darwin (1809–82); poet Wilfred Owen (1893–1918).

Tourist information Chester, tel: 0845-647 7868, www.visitchester.com; Hay-on-Wye, tel: 01497-820 144, www.hay-on-wye.co.uk/tourism; Hereford, tel: 01432-268 430, www.visitherefordshire.co.uk; Ludlow, tel: 01584-875 053, www.ludlow.org.uk; Shrewsbury, tel: 01743-258 888, www.visitshrews bury.co.uk; Stoke-on-Trent, tel: 01782-236 000, www.visitstoke.co.uk.

*Screams galore at
Alton Towers.*

*Painting Moorcroft
pottery in Stoke.*

orientated. This is one of the few British cities with its medieval walls still intact, with those on the north and east sides following the original Roman plan. The **Cathedral** (www. chestercathedral.com; Mon–Sat 9am–5pm, Sun 1–4pm; donation) was a Benedictine abbey until the Dissolution of the Monasteries under Henry VIII. An unusually square building, it has a massive south transept with a grand Victorian stained-glass window.

Meanwhile, at Upton, 2 miles (4km) north of the city, is **Chester Zoo** (www. chesterzoo.org; daily 10am–5pm, with exceptions). It's the country's largest zoo outside London, with over 20,000 animals in a setting of 125 acres (51 hectares) of grounds.

Well worth an eastward trip via the A54/34 is **Little Moreton Hall** (www. nationaltrust.org.uk/little-moreton-hall; mid-Feb–Oct Wed–Sun 11am–5pm, daily late July–Aug), an ornately decorated, half-timbered and moated manor house, built in the late 15th century.

THE POTTERIES

Stoke-on-Trent ⑩ was made famous by Arnold Bennett (1867–1931) in his novels of the "Five Towns", in which he described provincial life with a discernment and attention to detail that has rarely been matched.

Thousands of people come here simply to pick up a bargain at the factory shops, selling everything from dinner services to ceramic jewellery, and with "seconds" on sale at reduced prices. But Stoke is also a progressive town with a lively centre and **Cultural Quarter,** where the Victoria Hall stages classical and rock music, comedy and children's shows, and the Regent Theatre hosts touring productions of opera, ballet and musicals.

All the big names in pottery were once represented here, but many have sadly closed down in recent years. **Wedgwood**, however, has a visitor centre (www.world ofwedgwood.com; daily 10am–5pm), which – in an imaginative and entertaining way – allows you to explore the history and craft of ceramics, to have a go at throwing or painting a pot and, of course, to

visit their working factory. Next to the visitor centre is the excellent Wedgwood Museum (www.wedgwoodmuseum.org.uk; hours as above; combined tickets available with visitor centre), which tells the story of 250 years of ceramic history. The collection includes a vase thrown by Josiah Wedgwood himself.

When you've had enough of pottery, there are a number of places to visit in the vicinity. About 7 miles (12km) north of Stoke-on-Trent is **Biddulph Grange Garden** (www.nationaltrust. org.uk; Apr–Sept daily 9am–5.30pm, Oct 10am–5.30pm, Nov–Dec 10am–3.30pm, mid-Feb–Mar daily 11am–3.30pm), an unusual Victorian garden in which visitors are taken on a miniature tour, from an Egyptian Court to a mini-Great Wall of China, as well as to a pinetum and a fernery. Alternatively there's the **Dorothy Clive Garden** (www. dorothyclivegarden.co.uk; mid-Mar–Sept daily 10am–5.30pm, Oct–mid-Mar Fri–Sun 10am–4pm) near Market Drayton, which is glorious in early summer when the rhododendrons are in full bloom, and has pleasant woodlands year-round. Another option is the **Shugborough Estate** (www.nationaltrust.org.uk; mid-Mar–Oct daily 11am–4.30pm), the magnificent ancestral seat of the Earls of Lichfield. It is a rare example of a complete working estate. The stable block houses the original 18th-century kitchens, there is a walled garden and, of course, the mansion itself. The grounds contain eight nationally important monuments, including the Shepherd's Monument, which many believe has links to the Holy Grail.

When the children have tired of all this, cart them off on the short trip to **Alton Towers** (www.altontowers.com; Apr–mid-July, Sept Mon–Fri 10am–4pm, Sat–Sun until 5pm, Mid-July–mid-Sept Aug daily 10am–6pm, Oct 10am–9pm, with exceptions), the country's leading theme park, which is constantly updating its thrills. The rides range from adrenalin-filled Nemesis to gentle ones that are suitable for small children. There's also Galactica, a virtual reality rollercoaster ride, a pirate-themed aquarium, a water park – and even two hotels (one with a spa) and a log cabin development.

Biddulph Grange garden.

Ferris wheel, Nottingham.

DERBY TO THE EAST COAST

The Pilgrim Fathers, Robin Hood and D.H. Lawrence all have links with this region, which spans the Midlands, incorporating blooming bulb fields and excellent family-friendly beaches.

Often referred to collectively as the East Midlands, the counties of Derbyshire, Nottinghamshire, Leicestershire and Lincolnshire offer many attractions to the visitor – from stately homes to Stilton cheese, and from medieval cathedrals to the National Space Centre. Away from the big cities, the region contains some of the least spoilt parts of the country. To the east is the extensive and sparsely- populated farming county of Lincolnshire, while to the north, like a vast rockery garden, is the Peak District National Park, which offers opportunities for walkers, rock-climbers and pot-holers.

DERBY

Settled snugly in the centre of England, **Derby ❶** is a useful jumping-off point for the Peak District (see page 283), but it's also a lively city in its own right, with plenty to see and do, and with good public transport. In Irongate, the oldest (and most upmarket) part of town, there's the **Cathedral** (www.derbycathedral.org; daily 8.30am–5.30pm; donation) with a fine wrought-iron screen. Just to the south is the vibrant Cathedral Quarter with independent shops, restaurants, cafés and bars. Nearby, on the Strand, is the **Derby Museum and Art Gallery** (tel: 01332-641 901; www.derbymuseums.org;

Derby Cathedral.

Tue–Sat 10am–5pm, Sun noon–4pm; free), home to the world's largest public collection of works by 18th-century local artist Joseph Wright. On Friar Gate is **Pickford's House Museum** (Tue–Sat 10am–5pm), a fine Georgian house with interiors that recapture the house's heyday. On the top floor is a servant's bedroom with a straw mattress. The house also contains a large costume collection.

Kedleston Hall (www.nationaltrust. org.uk/kedleston-hall; house: Mar–Oct Sat–Thu, 11am–5pm, park: daily

⊙ Main attractions
Derby Museum
Nottingham Castle
Lincoln Cathedral
Burghley House

Map on page 274

10am–6pm, until 4pm in winter), 5 miles (8km) from the city centre, is a splendid 18th-century Palladian mansion complete with Robert Adams interiors, a huge collection of paintings, and an **Eastern Museum**, housing objects collected by Lord Curzon, the owner, when he was Viceroy of India (1899–1905). The property, which has extensive grounds, was used as a location in the film *The Duchess* starring Keira Knightley.

To the south of Derby is Calke Abbey (www.nationaltrust.org.uk/calke-abbey; Mar–Oct daily 11am–5pm), another grand house – but with a very different atmosphere. The interiors have been left untouched, retaining a feel of aesthetic decay and faded gentility.

NOTTINGHAM

Return to Derby (or skirt it to the south) and take the A52 to **Nottingham ❷**, the cultural and nightlife hub of the East Midlands, with two popular universities. It's an attractive city centred on a broad market square, with two large shopping centres, a major arts complex and numerous bars and restaurants. In popular imagination, the city is still associated with Sherwood Forest, Robin Hood and the evil sheriff. **Nottingham Castle** today bears little resemblance to its medieval predecessor (it's mostly a Victorian construction), but it does provide a splendid home for the **Castle Museum and Art Gallery** (tel: 0115-876 1400; www.nottinghamcastle. org.uk; the museum and gallery is currently closed for refurbishment, due to reopen in 2020), with collections of silver, glass, armour and paintings. There are also tours of the castle caves (days as museum noon, 1pm, 2pm and 3pm), but be warned, they are quite strenuous.

Nottingham is also famous as the birthplace of the writer D.H. Lawrence (see page 277), and for its lace making. To discover more about the history of life in the city, visit the Museum of Nottingham Life (tel: 0115-876 1400; Sat–Sun noon–4pm) in Brewhouse Yard at the base of the castle rock. Set in five 17th-century cottages, it covers

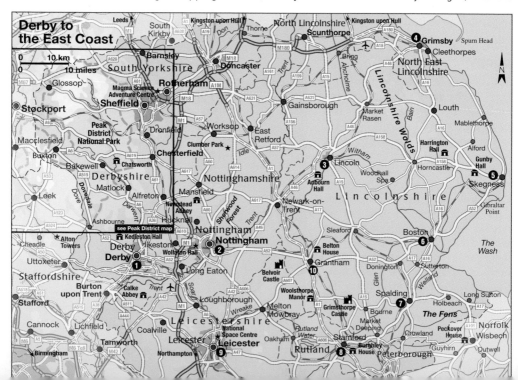

300 years of social history and contains a reconstructed Victorian schoolroom. North of here, Nottingham Playhouse is a modern venue for top-notch theatre as well as comedy, dance and music performances.

Until the 20th century, Nottingham was world-renowned for its lace-making industry. The historic Lace Market district in the city centre has been revamped in recent years, with shops, restaurants and now also **Nottingham Contemporary** (tel: 0115-948 9750; www.nottinghamcontemporary.org; Tue–Sat 10am–6pm, Sun 11am–5pm), a stylishly designed art gallery.

On the west side of the city is **Wollaton Hall** (tel: 0115-876 3100; daily 11am–4pm; free, charge for car park), a fine Elizabethan mansion that is also home to the city's Natural History Museum and Industrial Museum. Visitors can also see the Tudor kitchens (on guided tour only), as well as the Regency Dining Room and Salon.

Go to Ravenshead on the northern outskirts of Nottingham to visit **Newstead Abbey** (www.newsteadabbey.org.uk;

house: Sat–Sun noon–4pm, gardens: daily 9am–dusk). The ancestral home of Lord Byron, the house is surrounded by lakes, terraces and Japanese and Spanish gardens. A little further north is **Clumber Park** (www.nationaltrust.org.uk/clumber-park; daily 7am–7pm, until 4pm Nov–Mar), one of Nottingham's famous "Dukeries" or large hunting estates, consisting of park, farm and woodland, a serpentine lake, and a walled garden enclosing a Victorian apiary, fig house and vineries.

LINCOLN

Now take the A57 towards **Lincoln ❸**, which towers impressively over its flat Fenland setting. It's a city with Roman, Norman, medieval and Georgian influences, with a well-preserved historic area at the top of the hill, and the modern town below. You can get a good look at the city by taking a canal trip on the *Brayford Belle* (tel: 01522-881 200; Easter–mid-Oct daily 11am, 12.15pm, 1.30pm, 2.45pm and 3.45pm).

The three towers of its magnificent **Cathedral** (www.lincolncathedral.com;

○ **Tip**
Lincolnshire is well known for its markets, which are held throughout the county. If you enjoy the bustle of a market and the chance to buy fresh produce, contact the local tourist offices for times and venues. One market not to miss is Lincoln's Christmas Market, which runs for four days in early December. The medieval square and surrounding cobbles make the perfect setting for over 250 stalls that turn out for this truly festive occasion.

Statue of Robin Hood in front of Nottingham Castle.

○ FACT FILE

Location Lying just to the south of the Peak District (for which Derby and Nottingham are good jumping-off points) and covering a swath of middle England between The Wash and the mouth of the River Humber.

By car The M1 to Derby or Nottingham (Exit 25) takes about 2 hours from north London (allow at least 3 hours from Central London).

By coach National Express coach service from London Victoria, about 3 hours, tel: 0871-781 8181, www.nationalexpress.co.uk.

By train About 1 hour 40 minutes to both Derby and Nottingham from London St Pancras, tel: 03457-484 950.

For children The beaches of Skegness, Cleethorpes and Mablethorpe; Skegness Natureland Seal Sanctuary, www.skegness natureland.co.uk.

Best theatres Nottingham Playhouse.

Famous locals Alfred, Lord Tennyson; D.H. Lawrence; Sir Isaac Newton; Margaret Thatcher.

Tourist information Derby, tel: 01332-643 411, www.visitderby.com; Leicester, tel: 0116-299 4444, www.goleicestershire.com; Lincoln, tel: 01522-545 458, www.visitlincolnshire.com; Nottingham, tel: 08444-775 678.

Lincoln Cathedral.

Enjoy a traditional donkey ride on Skegness Beach.

Mon–Sat 7.15am–6pm, Sun until 5pm, with exceptions) dominate the skyline from afar. The building, which featured as a location in the film the *Da Vinci Code*, is an attractive blend of Norman and Gothic, and has some extraordinary misericords in the choir stalls. Concerts, recitals and exhibitions are often staged here.

Lincoln Castle (tel: 01522-782 040; www.lincolncastle.com; daily Apr–Sept 10am–5pm, Oct–Mar 10am–4pm) is also Norman in origin, although there have been many later additions. For 900 years it served as the town prison. It contains a copy of Magna Carta, one of only four left in the country, signed and sealed by King John at Runnymede in 1215. A walk along the top of the outer walls was opened in 2015.

Among the city's many fine Norman and medieval buildings is the **Jew's House**, now a restaurant, which dates back from the 1170s and is a reminder of when a large Jewish community flourished here. It is believed to be the oldest surviving example of domestic architecture in the country.

If you have time for only one museum or gallery, make it the **Usher Gallery** (www.thecollectionmuseum.com; daily 10am–4pm; free) in Lindum Road. It has works by Peter de Wint, J.M.W. Turner, L.S. Lowry and Henry Moore, as well as memorabilia relating to the Lincolnshire-born Poet Laureate Lord Alfred Tennyson (1809–92), whose statue stands in the cathedral grounds. The gallery has joined forces with the adjacent archaeological museum to form The Collection, which includes a wealth of artefacts from the Iron Age and the Roman, Saxon, Viking and medieval eras.

THE LINCOLNSHIRE COAST

Grimsby ❹ (about 50 minutes' drive northeast of Lincoln on the A46) is situated on the east coast at the mouth of the River Humber, with access to miles of safe and sandy beaches. Sadly, the fishing industry that brought prosperity to the town in the 19th century has dwindled to almost nothing in recent years, but the ethos and atmosphere remain.

At the **National Fishing Heritage Centre** (tel: 01472-323 345; Tue–Sun 10am–5pm, closes 4pm Nov–Mar), interactive displays take you on a trip through old Grimsby and its port, and allow you to roam around a restored 1950s trawler. Afterwards, you can buy good smoked fish from **Alfred Enderby Traditional Fish Smokers** in Fish Dock Road (www.alfredenderby.co.uk).

Popular family resorts on this coast include Cleethorpes (closest to Grimsby), Mablethorpe and, best known of all, **Skegness** , with 6 miles (10km) of safe and sandy beaches. Here, accommodated in one of the many small hotels or bed-and-breakfast establishments, children can build sandcastles and enjoy donkey rides, and parents can take advantage of gardens and bowling greens as they did in the days before the Costa Brava beckoned. It was here in 1936 that Billy Butlin opened the first Butlin's Holiday Camp.

Fantasy Island (www.fantasyisland. co.uk; mid-Mar–Sept daily 11am, closing times vary) offers rides and fun for all the family when the beach palls or the weather is bad; and the **Skegness Natureland Seal Sanctuary** (www.skegnessnatureland.co.uk; daily 10am–5.30pm) in North Parade aims to combine education and conservation with entertainment. Many unusual animals have been guests at the sanctuary, including dolphins, whales, oiled seabirds and injured birds of prey. You can also meet the permanent residents – penguins, meerkats, alpacas and butterflies; visit at 11am or 3pm to coincide your visit with feeding time for the seals and penguins.

BOSTON

From Skegness the A52 parallels the coast and then turns inland a short way to **Boston** on the banks of the River Witham. It's an attractive little town, and has one of the finest produce markets in Lincolnshire, held each Wednesday and Saturday. On Wednesdays, produce is auctioned in Bargate Green; it's an entertaining event even if you don't intend to buy. Boston also has one of the tallest working

The entrance gate at Lincoln Castle.

England's oldest pub, Ye Olde Trip to Jerusalem, on Drewhouse Yard, Castle Road, Nottingham.

⊘ D. H. LAWRENCE

The first thing that most people associate with D.H. Lawrence is *Lady Chatterley's Lover*, first published in 1928, but later banned because of its sexual content. It was not published unexpurgated until 1963 after an unsuccessful prosecution for obscenity. This was his last but one novel, finished when he was already slowly dying of tuberculosis, and was the culmination of a prolific writing career that included collections of short stories and poems as well as novels.

Born in Nottingham in 1885, Lawrence was the son of a miner, and a product of the Victorian concern to make education available to the poor. But while far more working-class children were reading books, few were writing them. His mother, an ex-teacher, was determined he should not follow his father down the pit, and encouraged him to study – he eventually won a scholarship to Nottingham University College. The bond between mother and son was recreated in the autobiographical *Sons and Lovers* (1913). In 1912 he met his future wife, Frieda (already married to one of his professors); their life together was turbulent and peripatetic, as they travelled in Australia, the USA and Mexico. His last years, when in failing health, were spent in Italy and the south of France. He died in France in 1930. Visit his Birthplace Museum (Tue–Sat 10am–4pm) in the village of Eastwood.

windmills in England, the Maud Foster Windmill, and a church tower, known as the Boston Stump, which soars to 272ft (83 metres).

Modern artists are much in evidence here: murals are created all over town to disguise empty or neglected properties; the Memorial Gardens Archway is a modern piece in forged steel; and gracefully poised welded steel sculptures of human figures by artist Rick Kirby are displayed in Friary Court.

Most of all, Boston is known for its American connections. It was here that the Pilgrim Fathers were tried and imprisoned for trying to leave the country. The **Guildhall** (www.bostonguild hall.co.uk; Wed–Sat 10.30am–3.30pm; free) contains the cells where the Pilgrim Fathers were confined in 1607, and the **Pilgrim Fathers' Memorial** stands on the riverbank near the sea, on the spot where they were arrested.

SPALDING TO STAMFORD

From Boston take the A16 southwest to **Spalding ❼**, which is at the heart of the Lincolnshire bulb industry. In spring there are acres of tulips, hyacinths and daffodils here, and all summer long visitors can learn more at the **Bulb Museum** (tel: 01775-680 490; Apr–Oct Mon–Sat 9am–5pm, Sun 10am–4pm; free), which depicts the industry from 1880 to the present. Learn more about the history of Spalding at the medieval **Ayscoughfee Hall Museum** (tel: 01775-764 555; Wed–Sun 10.30am–4pm, closes 3.30pm in winter; free)

Keep to the A16 to reach **Stamford ❽**, a mellow stone-built town with five medieval churches, and some streets and squares where all the buildings pre-date the Victorian era. Just to the south of the town is **Burghley House** (www.burghley.co.uk; mid-Mar–Oct Sat–Thu 11am–5pm), one of the most glorious Elizabethan mansions in the country. Built in the late 16th century for William Cecil, the 1st Lord Burghley and treasurer to Elizabeth I, this has been a family home ever since, which gives it a special atmosphere lacking in many stately homes.

The state rooms hold a wonderful collection of paintings, furniture,

Foxton Locks on the Grand Union Canal.

porcelain and tapestries; and the deer park, landscaped by "Capability" Brown, is delightful. Of special interest are the Sculpture Garden and the fascinating Garden of Surprises, open on the same days as the house.

LEICESTER AND GRANTHAM

Leicester ❾ lies due west on the A47, a busy modern city with ancient origins. **Castle Park** is the historic heart: the castle gardens and riverside are tranquil spots for walking, and the city's Saxon, Roman and medieval forebears are all represented. Visit the **New Walk Museum** (tel: 0116-225 4900; Mon–Sat 10am–5pm, Sun 11am–5pm) for a wonderfully eclectic display, ranging from Ancient Egyptian artefacts to dinosaurs. The museum's art collection contains works by Bacon, Dürer, Turner and Lowry, as well as examples of German Expressionism.

Leicester's markets are also worth seeing: the great food hall in the **Market Centre** (Mon–Sat 9am–5pm) and the outdoor **Retail Market** (Mon–Sat 7am–6pm) both offer a vast array of fresh food and other goods such as books, clothes and flowers. Since the 1960s, Leicester's textile industry has attracted large numbers of immigrants from the Indian Subcontinent, who have made the city one of the most vibrant and cosmopolitan in the region. Among the by-products of this influx is the profusion of ethnic cuisines served at the city's restaurants. Melton Road and Belgrave Road have particular concentrations of ethnic eateries.

A couple of miles north of Leicester city centre (just off the A6) is the **National Space Centre** (www.spacecentre.co.uk; Mon–Fri 10am–4pm, Sat–Sun 10am–5pm). Perennially popular with children, this museum has spacecraft, a chance to "walk on the moon" and a planetarium.

From here you can return to Nottingham or head south to London on the M1, but if you have time, pay

a visit to **Grantham** ❿, a pleasant old town of red-brick and half-timbered houses with a parish church complete with steeple. It used to be famous for its connections with Sir Isaac Newton (1642–1727), who propounded the theory of gravitation, and who was born at nearby Woolsthorpe Manor. These days, however, it is better known as the birthplace of Margaret Thatcher, the Conservative prime minister who dominated British politics in the 1980s; she was brought up here above her father's grocer shop. Friendly little **Grantham Museum** (www.granthammuseum.org.uk; Thu–Sat 10am–4pm; free) on St Peter's Hill explores the town's links with both of them, and much more.

Just north of the town on the A607 is the elegant 17th-century **Belton House** (www.nationaltrust.org.uk/belton-house; mid-Mar–Oct Wed–Sun 12.30–5pm), with a formal topiary walk and an Orangery. For those too young to be interested in such things as houses and gardens, there's an adventure playground and a discovery centre.

Fruit and veg for sale in Leicester's historic heart.

Splendid Burghley House.

HOWZAT!

England's special gift to the world is cricket. Most countries don't want it, and the ones that do have often proved to be rather better at it.

A Frenchman reporting on the state of cricket in England in 1728 wrote: "Everyone plays it, the common people and also men of rank. They go into a large open field and knock a ball about with a piece of wood. I will not attempt to describe this game." Apart from a lack of sensitivity to the music of leather balls on willow bats, this foreigner was sensible in not attempting a description of a game that involves two teams of 11 players, two wickets, two umpires, tea and sandwiches and which, in county and international Test Matches, takes five days to play. It has been said that the English, not being spiritual people, invented the game to give themselves some conception of eternity.

BATTING FOR A BETTER WORLD

Many see cricket as a civilising influence. Writing on the French Revolution, the historian G.M. Trevelyan reflected, "If the French noblesse had been capable of playing cricket with their peasants, their châteaux would not have been burnt." In this idealised pursuit the village blacksmith had the opportunity to hurl balls down at the Lord of the Manor. It was a very English sporting spirit, in which one did one's best, never cheated, and played with a "straight bat".

One delight of the game is seeing in what bizarre circumstances it might be played. The players pictured here in the Solent on the south coast meet for a 90-minute match once a year, the only time when the Brambles Bank sandbar is revealed by an abnormal tide.

Lord's cricket ground in London is home to the Marylebone Cricket Club (MCC), the game's governing body whose members are identified by red-and-gold ties, known as "egg and bacon" (right). Lord's hosts international matches known as Tests.

An MCC member looking out over Lord's during an Ashes match, the celebrated test series between fierce rivals England and Australia.

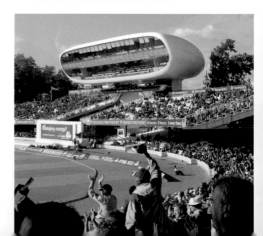

W. G. Grace.

W.G. Grace, Hero at the Wicket

The colossus of cricket was William Gilbert "W.G." Grace, depicted here in *Vanity Fair* magazine in 1877. He was a giant on the field, knocking up runs with consummate ease. Born in Bristol, he played for a Gloucester team of Gentleman v Players at the age of 16. He twice captained England and toured the US and Canada. At home, crowds flocked to see him wherever he appeared. He had a doctor's practice, and remained a gentleman player, though this amateur status did not prevent him making money from the game where he could. His reputation for fairness and a straight bat excused the odd occasion when he would replace bails claiming that the wind had blown them off. He went on playing until he was 66, and Sir Arthur Conan Doyle watched him in old age, recording, "At the end of a century he had not turned a hair."

Howzat! If a batsman is thought to be out, a cry goes up for the umpires to adjudicate. The headgear shows that it can be a dangerous game.

Cricket's popularity in England is long-standing; the game's known history dates to the 16th century.

Cricket is still played on village greens. Games last all afternoon, with a break for tea, and there's beer when stumps are pulled.

The view from Mam Tor.

THE PEAK DISTRICT

Bleak and challenging in parts, but threaded with pure rivers and dotted with idyllic villages and some splendid stately homes, the Peaks are a walker's paradise.

The Peak District is a region of outstanding beauty lying at the southern end of the Pennines, which form the "backbone" of England. Over the years, as a centre of lead mining, then of silk and cotton production, it has been greatly changed by man, but even so, it retains some wonderfully wild walking country. It was Britain's first National Park, founded in 1950, and is highly accessible and much visited. Surrounded by the conurbations of the North and the Midlands, it has over 100 roads running through it, and the north–south artery of the M1 motorway passes just to the east.

This tour begins in Matlock, in the southern Peaks. The largest town and the administrative centre of the district, modern **Matlock ❶** was created by John Smedley, a 19th-century industrialist who watched over its development from **Riber Castle**, which overlooks the town from its commanding hilltop to the south. From here, take the A6, crossing the bridge over the River Derwent and passing into the Derwent Gorge, where high limestone crags crowd in on the left. Soon, the biggest of the lot, the 300ft (90-metre) **High Tor** appears, almost overhanging the road, with rock-climbers clinging to the rock face like flies on a wall. Just beyond

Matlock sits on the banks of the Derwent.

High Tor the swinging gondolas of the **Heights of Abraham Cable Cars** (www.heightsofabraham.com; mid-Mar–Oct daily 10am–4.30pm, until later at peak times) can be seen. The Heights of Abraham, named after General Wolfe's 1759 victory in Quebec, are reached by turning left as you enter Matlock Bath. They encompass the **Rutland and Great Masson Caverns** (times as above), former lead mines that now provide exciting underground tours, picnic sites and nature trails up to the **Victoria Prospect Tower**, built

⊘ Main attractions
Arkwright's Cromford Mill
Dovedale
Chatsworth House
Bakewell
Buxton

Maps on pages 284, 290

⊘ Fact

English inventor and industrialist Richard Arkwright (1732–92) invented a horse-driven spinning frame before the water-powered one at Cromford. Arkwright's achievements were widely recognised and in 1786 he was knighted, and became High Sheriff of Derbyshire the following year.

in 1844. There are also stupendous views across the gorge.

CROMFORD AND THE CRADLE OF THE INDUSTRIAL REVOLUTION

Matlock Bath ❷ became popular as a holiday spot in Victorian times when the railways arrived. Today, it is well known as a weekend destination for motorbikes and for its illuminations over the Lovers' Walks along the Derwent from early September to early October. Among its modern attractions is the **Peak District Mining Museum** (www.peakdistrictleadminingmuseum.co.uk; daily Apr–Oct 10am–5pm, Nov–Mar Wed–Sun 11am–3pm) in the Pavilion – a fascinating introduction to the world of the lead miner, with tunnels through which children can crawl. **Gulliver's Theme Park** (www.gulliversfun.co.uk; June–Aug daily 10.30am–4.30pm; times vary at other periods of the year) is set high on a hillside above Matlock Bath and has river rides and a mine train.

Follow the A6 through Matlock Bath to **Cromford ❸**. Richard Arkwright, one of the architects of the Industrial Revolution, came here in 1771 to build the world's first water-powered cotton mill and create an industrial village that was a wonder of the age. It was poor communications that stopped the Derwent Valley becoming one of the principal

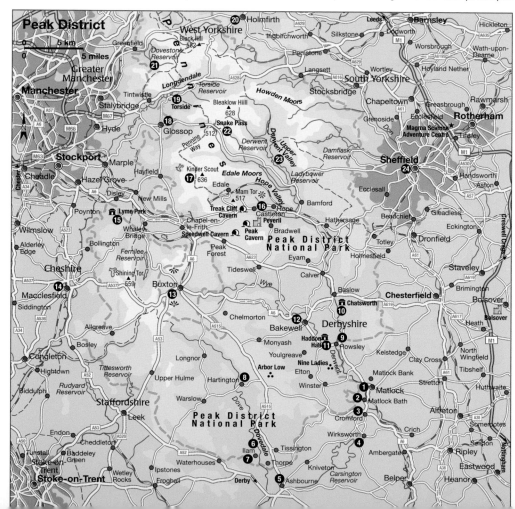

centres of that world-changing revolution. **Arkwright's Cromford Mill** (www.cromfordmills.org.uk; daily 9am–5pm; free to site, charge for car park and tours), a World Heritage Site, is clearly signposted. Tours around the village are arranged from the Arkwright Mill. Workers' cottages in North Street off the Wirksworth road, completed in 1776, show how Arkwright wanted his workers to live.

A little further on is Cromford Wharf and the **High Peak Junction Visitor Centre** (tel: 01629-533 105; Apr–Oct daily 10am–5pm, Nov–Mar Sat–Sun 10.30am–4pm) of the **Cromford Canal**, which runs for 5 miles (8km) to Ambergate. Turn right at Scarthin Nick crossroads and left up a steep hill, passing the outstanding viewpoint of the **Black Rocks of Cromford**. Here there's a picnic site and access to the **High Peak Trail**, a route that follows the line of the former Cromford and High Peak Railway, completed in 1831 as an extension of the Cromford Canal. As the road enters quarry-scarred

Wirksworth ④, signs indicate the **National Stone Centre** (www.nationalstonecentre.org.uk; daily Apr–Sept 10am–5pm, Oct–Mar until 4pm; free), which offers treasure trails, audiovisual shows and exhibitions (charge), set in a former limestone quarry by the High Peak Trail.

Roam the narrow streets to appreciate the atmosphere of Wirksworth, which has been a lead-mining centre for centuries. The Wirksworth Heritage Centre (www.wirksworthheritage.co.uk; daily 9am–5pm) reopened in 2019, now in new premises on St John's Street in the heart of the town. The museum's permanent collection celebrates local heritage, with interactive displays ranging from piecing together the history of T'Owd Man to discovering the town's connection with George Eliot. It also hosts talks, workshops, walks and events, while the new café opens onto an outdoor courtyard. Nearby, the sloping **Market Place** has many fine 18th and 19th-century buildings, including the Moot Hall (not open to the public). The

Cable cars to the Heights of Abraham.

St Oswald's church spire dominates the skyline in Ashbourne.

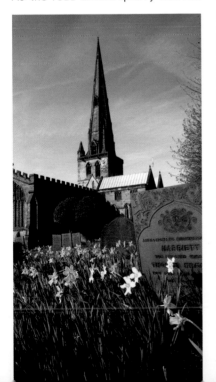

⊘ FACT FILE

By car About 2.5 hours on the M1 motorway from North London; leave at Exit 28 (Matlock) for the southern dales, Exit 29 (Chesterfield) for the central and northern areas.

By coach National Express daily coach services from London and Manchester. A good coach service also links the main Peak District towns, tel: 0871-781 8181.

By train About 2 hours from London St Pancras to Derby, Nottingham, Chesterfield and Sheffield. Local services link with the main Peak District towns, tel: 03457-484 950.

Main towns Matlock, Buxton, Bakewell.

Special events Buxton International Festival of Music and the Arts (2 weeks in July); well-dressing ceremonies throughout the summer.

For children Chatsworth Farm and Children's Adventure Playground; Gulliver's Kingdom Theme Park, Matlock Bath; the Ranger Service runs children's fun days and activities throughout the summer, www.peakdistrict.gov.uk.

Local specialities Bakewell puddings; Stilton cheese.

Tourist information Bakewell, tel: 01629-816 558; Buxton, tel: 01298-25106; Chesterfield, tel: 01246-345 777; Matlock, tel: 01629-583 388.

Honey for sale in Hartington.

Parish Church of St Mary is mainly 13th-century, and contains a wonderful 7th-century carved coffin lid.

DOVEDALE

Continue along the B5035 to **Ashbourne** ❺, "the gateway to Dovedale". The **Parish Church of St Oswald** is one of the finest in the Peak District, and its soaring 14th-century spire is an elegant landmark. Nearby, in Church Street, is the beautiful gabled and mullion-windowed Elizabethan Old Grammar School (private). On the way to the cobbled Market Place, you will come to the restored timber-framed **Gingerbread Shop**, which still makes the local delicacy on the premises. The **Tourist Information Centre** (tel: 01335-343 666) is in the Market Place.

Take the A515 Buxton road up a steep hill to the north, then turn left on a minor road signposted to Thorpe and Dovedale. Thorpe is an unpretentious limestone village standing at the foot of **Thorpe Cloud** (942ft/287 metres), one of the

The River Dove running through Dovedale.

sentinels of **Dovedale** ❻, probably the most famous of the White Peak dales. Over a million people visit it every year, and the National Park and footpath authorities run a continuous programme of repairs to the 7-mile (11km) path that runs north through the dale to Hartington. Go beyond the famous **Stepping Stones** beneath Thorpe Cloud and Bunster Hill (many people don't) to the famous series of rock pinnacles and caves such as Tissington Spires, Ilam Rock, Pickering Tor and Reynard's Cave, with its natural archway.

Just beyond the Dovedale turn is the quaint estate village of **Ilam** ❼, largely rebuilt by 19th-century shipping magnate Jesse Watts Russell in neo-Gothic style. Russell lived at mock-Gothic **Ilam Hall** (tel: 01335-350 503; grounds and park: daily during daylight hours; hall private). In the grounds stands the beautiful **Church of the Holy Cross**, a mixture of Saxon, Norman and Early English.

Make your way back to the A515 and head north to **Hartington** ❽.

You'll cross the line of the **Tissington Trail** at a railway-signal box, formerly used as a National Park Visitor Centre. Hartington has a wonderful youth hostel in a Jacobean hall, and is also the home of the **Hartington Creamery**, based at the Old Cheese Shop, which produces high-quality cheeses, including Stilton. It was launched in 2014 after the closure of the former cheese factory in 2009. Afterwards, return to the main road and take the A5012 back towards Matlock.

Some 10 miles (16km) up the A6 from Matlock is **Rowsley ⑨**, with the splendid 17th-century Peacock Hotel. Opposite it, a road leads to **Caudwell's Mill** (www.caudwellsmill.co.uk; Mon–Sat 10am–4pm, Sun 11am–3pm). This 19th-century mill on the Wye, a rare working water-powered roller mill, was lovingly restored by a group of enthusiasts and the machinery is in complete working order and tours can be taken. A large range of flour is available in the shop, a small craft centre and a restaurant.

CHATSWORTH TO HADDON HALL

From here, the B6012 takes you to **Chatsworth House ⑩** (www.chatsworth.org; daily mid-Mar–mid-Nov, house 11am–5pm, park until 5.30pm, mid-May–Aug house 10.30am–5pm, park until 6pm). Home of the Dukes of Devonshire for some 400 years, and known as "the Palace of the Peaks", this is one of the finest houses in England, and contains one of the most important private art collections in the country.

Highlights of the house include the magnificent **Painted Hall** by Louis Laguerre, which shows scenes from the life of Julius Caesar, and is the setting for the annual Chatsworth Children's Christmas Party. The **State Rooms** are stunning in their opulence. Look out for the superb 17th-century English tapestries in the Drawing Room, the wonderful painted ceiling, again by Laguerre, in the State Bedroom, and Jan Vandervaart's famous *trompe l'oeil* violin "hanging" behind a door. The **Great**

Grand Chatsworth House.

Dining Room is where the young Princess Victoria had her first dinner with the grown-ups in 1832; it is notable for its gold-encrusted barrel ceiling and fine collection of paintings. On a different scale, but also impressive, is the series of small rooms known as the **Queen of Scots Rooms**, where the unfortunate monarch lodged during several stays between 1570 and 1581.

The house as we see it today is largely the creation of the 4th Earl and the Dutch architect William Talman, and it was built in the Palladian style between 1678 and 1707. The only part of the original 16th-century Tudor house that remains is the **Hunting Tower** (private), up through the trees of Stand Wood behind the house. Also in Stand Wood is the **Chatsworth Farm and Children's Adventure Playground**.

Were you to head east now along the A619, you would soon reach Chesterfield, famed for the crooked 14th-century spire of the parish church. It has a spiral design and a distinct tilt. The design was deliberate, but the crookedness came from a lack of skilled workmen, due to the Black Death, and the use of green timber in construction.

Further east and into Nottinghamshire is the archaeological site of **Creswell Crags** in Welbeck, near Worksop (www.creswell-crags.org.uk; Mar–Sept daily 10am–5.30pm, Oct, Feb until 4.30pm, Nov–Jan Sat–Sun only 10am–4.30pm; free, charge for car park). This limestone gorge contains caves that have the only known examples of Ice Age rock art in Britain. There is a museum and visitor centre, and you can take a guided tour to see the cave paintings (book first, tel: 01909-720 378).

Back in the Peak District and about a mile up the A6 from Rowsley is another famous stately home – **Haddon Hall** ⑪ (www.haddonhall.co.uk; mid-Apr–Oct daily 10.30am–5pm, Dec until 4.30pm). The home of the Duke of Rutland, it is known as "the most romantic medieval manor house in England", a description that

Eyam.

⊘ THE PLAGUE IN EYAM

The village of Eyam (pronounced "eem") is perhaps the most evocative place in the Peak District. In September 1665 a piece of cloth for the tailor arrived from London. It was infested with rat fleas, the carriers of the bubonic plague. By May 1666, 73 villagers had died. So the villagers held a public meeting and agreed to place themselves under quarantine – cutting them off from the world to prevent the disease spreading further afield. Food and medicine was donated from nearby Chatsworth House and left at designated points. The villagers, now unable to flee, suffered terribly and, by the time the plague had run its course, 260 people were dead. Plaques mark plague houses and there are plague graves all over the village, including the churchyard.

is hard to dispute. Haddon has undergone very little restoration: most of what you see from the sloping **Lower Courtyard** dates from the 14th and 15th centuries. The time-worn steps and oak-panelled rooms breathe history. Among the highlights are the wonderful **Banqueting Hall**, the very essence of a medieval manor house, complete with minstrels' gallery and massive 13th-century oak refectory table; the **Long Gallery**, with elaborate oak panelling featuring the boar's head and the peacock of the founding families; and the **Kitchen**, stone-flagged and stone-walled, with massive oak tables, chopping blocks and mixing bowls almost worn through with centuries of use.

The **Chapel of St Nicholas**, one of the oldest parts of the house, originally served the now disappeared village of Nether Haddon. It contains some of the finest 14th- and 15th-century wall paintings in Britain. The tour ends with the famous terraced gardens. a riot of roses, clematis and other blossoms in summer.

BAKEWELL

Beyond Haddon Hall you come to Bakewell ⑫, the history of which goes back to the Saxons, as a visit to the parish church of **All Saints** will reveal. Although heavily restored in Victorian times, this cruciform church still has fragments of Saxon and Norman work, and two of the finest Saxon preaching crosses in the Peak District are situated in the churchyard.

Just behind the church is the **Old House Museum** (www.oldhousemuseum. org.uk; mid-Mar–Oct daily 11am–4pm), one of the finest local museums in the country. It is housed in a 1534 Tudor building, which was used in the 19th century by Richard Arkwright as accommodation for workers employed at his mill on the Wye. There are collections of memorabilia, costumes, lace, samplers and toys, and the Victorian kitchen has been retained, while the craftsmen's workshops have been recreated.

Back in the centre of town, visit the **Bakewell Visitor Centre** (tel:

Try the original Bakewell puddings.

The Long Gallery, Haddon Hall.

01629-816 558; daily Apr–Oct 9.30am–5.30pm, Nov–Mar 10.30am–4.30pm; free) in Bridge Street. The arcaded building dates from the 17th century, and was for many years used as a market hall. Displays tell the story of the town and the Peak District. There is a well-stocked shop where maps and guides are on sale.

Outside the Tourist Information Centre is the **Old Original Bakewell Pudding Shop**, one of three in the town that claim to hold the original recipe to this much-loved almond and pastry confection. The story is that it was created when a flustered cook at the 17th-century Rutland Arms Hotel in nearby Rutland Square poured her pastry mix over the jam instead of the other way around. Whether this is true or not, the pudding (or tart, as it is known outside the region) has become synonymous with Bakewell.

BUXTON

Leaving Bakewell, follow the A6 through the pretty Wye Valley to Buxton ⑬. Start by admiring the elegant Corinthian-styled buildings of The **Crescent** Ⓐ, at the centre of the Buxton Crescent and Thermal Spa Project, which is destined to become a luxury thermal spa and five-star hotel. The £46 million project to restore Buxton's crescent has been many years to come to fruition, with considerable delays in funding. The project was expected to be finished in 2019, but at the time of writing was still ongoing. Designed by York architect John Carr in the 1780s, it was part of the master plan of the 5th Duke of Devonshire to make Buxton a fashionable spa town. The **Assembly Rooms**, once used for church services, will also be central to the project, as will the **Pump Room** Ⓑ, which is located opposite the Crescent and was built in 1894 in the classic style and is due to incorporate an interactive visitor centre, tea room and exhibition area. Outside is the drinking fountain outside, known locally as **St Ann's Well**, which is the scene during July of one of the town's

Paradise Mill.

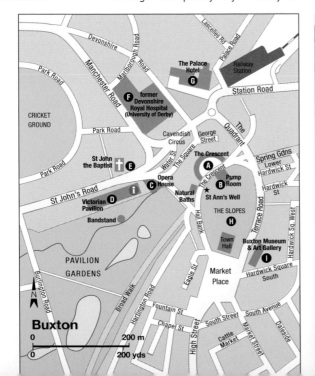

well-dressing ceremonies. There are often queues of people waiting to fill containers with the warm, blue, slightly effervescent water.

Just to the north are the original **Thermal Baths** which now house the Cavendish Shopping Arcade, but have retained an original plunge pool, complete with bosun's chair-type seat, showing how some patients were encouraged to "take the waters".

Walk past the Natural Baths and up to the corner of The Square, where massive gritstone "cloisters" face the attractive Pavilion Gardens. Turn right at the corner and you'll see the ornate, twin-domed frontage of the **Opera House** Ⓒ, designed and built in the grand Edwardian style by the eminent theatre architect Frank Matcham in 1905 and sensitively restored in 1979 (after serving for many years as a cinema). It seats 1,000 people in a magnificently-decorated auditorium lit by a massive gas-fired crystal chandelier. The theatre stages a varied programme

of comedy, drama, ballet and concerts, as well as opera, and is the home of the widely acclaimed **Buxton International Festival of Music and the Arts** (www.buxtonfestival.co.uk), held annually, for two weeks in July.

Beside the theatre is the splendid **Victorian Pavilion** Ⓓ (1871), well supplied with restaurants and bars and now home to Buxton Tourist Information. Its **Conservatory** houses a variety of tropical and native plants and also features a fish pond. In the centre of the Pavilion is the superb **Octagon**, or Concert Hall, which soars above the Pavilion Gardens. Just beyond the Octagon is a large modern swimming pool, filled with warm spa water.

The **Pavilion Gardens**, which reflect the Victorian splendour of Buxton as a hugely popular spa town, provide 23 acres (9 hectares) of landscaped space by the banks of the River Wye. Although the gardens continue beyond Burlington Road, turn right into St John's Road to the parish church of **St John the Baptist** Ⓔ,

A well dressing tableau at Buxton.

⊘ WELL DRESSING

Nothing to do with fashion, well dressing is a Peak District custom that takes place in many villages – about 20 in all – throughout the summer months. Pagan in origin – it was probably an act of thanksgiving for the spring well-water on the high, dry limestone plateau – the ceremony was gradually taken over by the Christian religion, which absorbed what it could not suppress, and is now usually linked to the day that honours the patron saint of the local church, at the beginning of what is sometimes known as Wakes Week.

Designs, usually on biblical themes, are etched into malleable clay on a wooden background and then brought to life, like a natural mosaic, with leaves, berries, bark, grass and flower petals. It is a skilful art involving the whole village, and can take up to 10 days to complete. The tableau is carried in a procession and placed over the local well, where it is blessed by the village priest in a ceremony that generally coincides with the local summer fête.

Well dressing can be seen in Wirksworth and Ashford in May; Rowsley, Bakewell and the Hope Valley at the end of June; in Bamford and Buxton in July; in Fyam in August; and in numerous other villages. Consult the local tourist office or the informative *Parklife* (available free from tourist offices) for details of dates and places.

Working on a Jacquard handloom at Paradise Mill.

Walking the Peaks is a popular weekend activity.

a beautiful example of Italianate Georgian architecture standing in an oasis of green. Designed by Sir Jeffrey Wyatville, who worked closely with the 6th Duke of Devonshire at Chatsworth, it is built in a Tuscan style and contains some fine mosaics and stained glass behind a massive portico under an elegant tower that rises to a copper dome.

Beyond the parish church is the great dome of the **former Devonshire Royal Hospital** (now a campus building for the University of Derby). It was originally the Great Stables, built in 1790 to house the horses of spa visitors. The building was begun in 1880, when, with the widest unsupported iron-framed dome in the world, spanning 152ft (46 metres), it was considered an architectural wonder. Across Devonshire Road stands the imposing facade of the **Palace Hotel**, Buxton's largest and most prestigious, built at the height of the resort's popularity in 1868. It stands close to the **London and North Western Railway Station**, of which, unfortunately,

only the facade remains, with its great semicircular fan window.

From the station, walk down The Quadrant back to The Crescent and the steep paths that wind up **The Slopes**, designed to provide graded paths for exercise. At the top of The Slopes, which offer fine views across the town, is the **Town Hall**, designed by William Pollard and opened in 1889. Hall Bank leads steeply up from The Slopes to the Market Place and the area known as Higher Buxton, where the weekly street market is held. Turn left down Terrace Road and halfway down on the right is the **Buxton Museum and Art Gallery** (tel: 01629-533 540; Tue–Sat 10am–5pm Apr–Sept also Sun noon–4pm; free).

This is an excellent little museum, highlighting the archaeological, geological and sociological history of the Peak district, together with displays of fine and decorative art works. "The Wonders of the Peak" takes you back in a time-tunnel, complete with sounds and smells.

⊘ WALKING THE PEAKS

If you are a seasoned and adventurous walker you will have a fair idea of where you want to go and what kind of terrain to expect in the Peak District, but for those who would like to ramble but are a bit hesitant there is an extensive scheme of Park Ranger-led walks. Some 250 walks cater for differing interests (some specialise in archaeology or botany, for example) and different levels of experience. There are gentle walks that are suitable for children and that are accessible to wheelchairs and tougher hikes for experienced hill walkers.

You can do a rugged 12-mile (20km) moorland walk to Kinder Downfall waterfall, learn about wildlife in the Goyt Valley, walk the hills above Dove Valley, or gently discover the Upper Derwent. The starting point of most walks can be reached by public transport – use it whenever you can, to help cut down on traffic.

All guided walks are free, but for some you need to book in advance. For more information, ring the Peak District National Park, tel: 01629-816 200; check out www.peakdistrict.gov.uk, or ask a local tourist office for the (free) *Parklife*, which gives full details; there is also an online edition. A selection of maps and trail guides are available from visitor centres and tourist offices. Don't forget you need sturdy shoes, waterproofs and a packed lunch for the longer walks.

MACCLESFIELD AND LYME PARK

Macclesfield ⑭ was granted a charter by Edward I to establish a free borough in 1261, but the town's modern prosperity rests on the silk industry that began in 1742. Two excellent museums tell the story of the town's rise to fame as a silk producer, and the best place to start is the **Silk Museum** (www.macclesfieldmuseums.co.uk; Mon–Sat 10am–4pm) in Park Lane – the only museum in the country dedicated to the silk industry. It also has a collection of arts and crafts and archaeology artefacts, which was previously found in the Old Sunday School on Roe Street (now a culture hub with a cinema, film society, creative space and concert hall). The last handloom weaver in Macclesfield retired in 1981, but you can see 25 working Jacquard handlooms at **Paradise Mill** (tel: 01625-612 045; guided tours only Mon–Sat 11.45am, 1pm and 2.15pm, Nov–Mar noon only), just next door. The town has one other museum, the **West Park Museum**

(open by appointment only in term time, call for holiday opening times; free), which houses some ancient Egyptian artefacts (temporarily on display in the Silk Museum) and works by wildlife artist Charles Tunnicliffe.

From Macclesfield take the B5470 to **Lyme Park** ⑮ (www.nationaltrust.org.uk/lyme-park; house: Mar–Aug Thu–Tue 11am–5pm, Sept–Oct also closed Thu; park: daily Apr–Oct 8am–8pm, Nov–Mar 8.30am–6pm). Lyme is one of the Peak District's most impressive stately homes. Originally Tudor, the present Palladian mansion was designed by Leone Leoni in 1720, and its three-storey Ionic portico on the south front is reflected in a peaceful lake. The interior is famous for its intricate carvings by Grinling Gibbons, its clock collection and its beautiful orangery. The extensive 1,320-acre (534-hectare) park is famous for its red deer, maintained here since medieval times, and it backs onto the moorland of Park Moor, where the hunting tower known as the Cage is a prominent landmark.

The Garland King at the Castleton Garland Ceremony.

Buxton's Opera House.

Ⓕ Fact

The six great Victorian reservoirs that fill Longdendale Valley, known as the Longendale Chain, supply Manchester with 24 million gallons (110 million litres) of water a day. Completed in 1877, they were the largest artificial expanse of water in the world at the time.

CASTLETON

From Lyme Park, get on the A6 as far as **Whaley Bridge**, a pleasant little town where colourful canal boats are moored in the canal basin. From here you can follow a minor and at times extremely steep road to the **Goyt Valley**, where there is good rock-climbing for the intrepid and, for the rest, fine views over the Fernilee and Errwood reservoirs, and a forest trail to what is left of Errwood Hall, demolished when the valley was flooded to provide water for Stockport.

After this detour, take the A6 again for about 5 miles (8km) and then turn right towards **Castleton** ⑯, the "capital" of the **Hope Valley**. Prominent in the village is the parish church of **St Edmund** with its 17th-century box pews. It plays an important part in Castleton's **Garland Ceremony** on Oak Apple Day (29 May), when the Garland King and Queen, on white horses, lead a procession, the King encased from head to waist in the "garland", a wooden cage covered in flowers. The procession stops at all the village pubs, where a special tune is played and children dance, and then ends up at the church, where the garland is strung from the top of the tower and left to wither. The custom is thought to have its origins in a pagan ceremony to welcome the return of spring.

Castleton owes its fortune to its strategic importance and its geography. Ever since the Celtic Brigantes tribe built their massive hill fort on the windswept 1,698ft (517-metre) summit of **Mam Tor** (National Trust), this has been a military and administrative centre, although the modern village only came into existence when William Peveril, William the Conqueror's illegitimate son, built **Peveril Castle** (tel: 01433-620 613; www.english-heritage.org.uk; Apr–Sept daily 10am–6pm, Oct until 5pm, Nov–Mar Sat–Sun 10am–4pm). Situated on a limestone spur between the precipitous slopes of Cave Dale and the huge chasm of Peak Cavern, the castle is as impregnable as a castle could be.

Along the Pennine Way.

Not much remains of Peveril's early structure, but the views from the ramparts are impressive.

CAVERNS AND CAVES

But most people come to Castleton to visit the famous caves, which display the unique semi-precious mineral known as Blue John. The oldest of the caves is **Peak Cavern** (www. peakcavern. co.uk; Apr–Oct daily 10am–5pm, Nov–Mar weekends only). Its entrance is said to be the largest in Europe, at 40ft (12 metres) high and 100ft (30 metres) wide, beneath a cliff of limestone over which towers Peveril Castle. Inside, the spacious entrance area was once home to a community of rope-makers, whose equipment still survives. The roof is still blackened with the soot from their sunless homes. Performances by the Orchestra Gallery are held throughout the year in the Great Cave, where the acoustics are incredible.

In the **Speedwell Cavern** (www. peakcavern.co.uk; Apr–Oct daily 10am–5pm, Nov–Mar until 4pm) at the foot of the **Winnats Pass**, you are transported to the Bottomless Pit by a boat that is legged along a flooded lead mine drainage level like a barge in a canal tunnel. The Winnats Pass is a spectacular limestone gorge formed after the last Ice Age. The scene of the tragic murder of a pair of lovers in the 18th century, it is now the only road out of the Hope Valley to the west, since constant landslips from the crumbling slopes of Mam Tor led to the closure of the former A625 turnpike road in the early 1970s.

Treak Cliff Cavern (www.bluejohnstone.com; Mar–Oct daily 10am–5pm, Nov–Feb until 4pm; guided tours only) probably has the most spectacular formations, and it is one of the few sources of the semi-precious banded fluorspar known as Blue John. Ornaments made from this brilliant brittle mineral are sold here and in the village.

The fourth of Castleton's caves, the **Blue John Cavern** (www.bluejohncavern.co.uk; daily 9.30am–4.30pm, or dusk if earlier, guided tours), is the deepest of all and reached by turning right and right again at the top of the Winnats Pass. This cavern was discovered 300 years ago when miners in search of Blue John broke into the previously unknown range of caves.

THE PENNINE WAY

From Winnats Pass you can take the steep, narrow road between Mam Tor and Rushup Edge, which drops steeply down into the Vale of Edale, with magnificent views of **Kinder Scout** , the district's reigning summit (2,088ft/636 metres). At **Edale** is a **National Park Visitor Centre** (tel: 01433-670 207; Apr–Sept daily 9.30am–5pm, reduced hours in winter; free), for this is the southern point of the great long-distance path, the 268-mile (429km) **Pennine Way**, which marches along Britain's backbone between the Peaks and the Scottish border. This is serious walking country, and weather forecasts

Snake Pass winds through the valley.

Castleton's Peveril Castle.

Sid's Cafe in Holmfirth, featured in the long-running sitcom Last of the Summer Wine.

Sheffield Winter Garden, home to more than 2,000 plants.

are available at the centre, which doubles as a mountain rescue point.

Serious walkers might also want to head up to the northern moors: high, wild country of desolate moorland and long valleys, where the trans-Pennine roads are often closed by snow in winter. To reach the northern moors get back on the A6, then the A624 to **Glossop** ⑱, a small industrial town with a surprisingly elegant main square. Glossop's wealth was founded on textiles: there were nearly 60 cotton mills here in the 19th century. **Old Glossop** still has a pleasing pre-industrial air and a range of 17th-century gritstone houses. Glossop is a good stop-off point for some interesting independent shops, chic restaurants and welcoming pubs.

From Glossop head for the A628. Passing through the hamlet of Tintwistle (pronounced "Tinsel") you enter the dramatic cross-Pennine valley of **Longdendale**, an important packhorse route for centuries. The Woodhead Railway ran through the valley in 1847; it included the Woodhead Tunnel, then the longest in the world,

and was built at the cost of many lives. The line is closed now and re-designated the **Longdendale Trail**, a cycle route, and part of the **Trans-Pennine Trail** that links the Irish and North seas. There is a car park at **Torside** ⑲, where there is also direct access to the trail. There are also walks here around the Torside Reservoir.

At nearby **Crowden**, you again cross the line of the Pennine Way, which drops from the peaty heights of **Bleaklow** (2,077ft/628 metres) to the south to climb the boggy wastes of **Black Hill** (1,908ft/582 metres) to the north, on one of the toughest sections of the Pennine path.

THE NORTH OF THE PEAK DISTRICT

From Crowden, take the A6024 to **Holmfirth** ⑳, a pretty town where some of the earliest silent films were produced. The long-running BBC television comedy series *Last of the Summer Wine* was set here, and there is a small exhibition devoted to the series (www.summerwine-holmfirth.co.uk; Mon, Thu–Fri

---

⊘ THINGS TO DO IN SHEFFIELD

Sheffield is easy to get around: the Supertram, a glossy modern tramcar, is a pleasure to ride. A popular university also ensures a lively atmosphere, a hotbed for creativity and plenty of bars and cheapish eateries. Try visiting:

Abbeydale Industrial Hamlet (www.simt.co.uk; Mon–Thu, Sat 10am–4pm, Sun 11am–4.45pm), a museum of the industrial past. Craftsmen demonstrate their skills in this restored steelworks by the River Sheaf.

Bishops' House (www.bishopshouse.org.uk; Sat–Sun 10am–4pm; free), dating from 1500, is the best-preserved timber-framed house in Sheffield.

Krynkl (www.krynkl.co.uk), a growing cultural hub set in a series of Kelham Island shipping containers, is a hotbed of creativity with creative start-ups, a rooftop bar and Jöro, an award-winning New Nordic restaurant. Also check out the 99 Mary Street gallery, Bloc Projects and exhibition space B&B.

The Millennium Gallery (www.museums-sheffield.org.uk; Mon–Sat 10am–5pm, Sun 11am–4pm; free) at Arundel Gate displays arts, crafts and contemporary design. It also includes the Ruskin Gallery, the collection of the Guild of St George, the movement started by the Pre-Raphaelite John Ruskin (1819–1900). Adjacent is the city's **Winter Garden**, a spectacular new glasshouse.

The Weston Park Museum (www.museums-sheffield.org.uk; Mon–Sat 10am–5pm, Sun 11am–4pm; free), which showcases the city's collections of archaeology, natural history, art and social history.

10.30am–4pm, Sat–Sun 10am–3pm, Nov–Mar weekends only, check website for times). Last of the Summer Wine bus tours leave from outside the church most days (tel: 01484-687 231; Sat and Sun only in winter).

Head back now across **Wessenden Head Moor**, recrossing the line of the Pennine Way again, then take a sharp turn just before Greenfield to beautiful **Dovestone Reservoir** ㉑, with good surrounding walks and a thriving sailing club. Head back to Glossop through Stalybridge (in the eastern suburbs of Greater Manchester), then get on the A57, which will take you across the Snake Pass to Sheffield. Best not to try it in winter: the **Snake Pass** ㉒ is one of the highest and most exposed roads in Britain – it reaches 1,680ft (512 metres) at the summit – and is always one of the first to be closed in winter, and the last to reopen.

The road runs above Holden Clough, passing the peat banks of **Featherbed Moss**. It levels out at the summit where the unmistakable line of the Pennine Way is crossed. From the summit, the road swings down in a series of sharp bends to **Lady Clough** then to the isolated **Snake Pass Inn**, a welcome landmark, and sometimes a life-saving one, for walkers or stranded motorists.

As the A57 continues towards Sheffield you pass, on the right, the western arm of the **Ladybower Reservoir** (the largest in the Upper Derwent) and on the left, the **Upper Derwent Valley** ㉓, a man-made landscape, from its reservoirs and dams to the surrounding conifer woods, which has proved so popular that minibus- and cycle-hire services are provided at weekends to keep traffic from choking the entrance road. Bikes can be hired from the Upper Derwent Visitor Centre, at Fairholmes near Bamford.

The main road continues over the Ashopton Viaduct to the western suburbs of **Sheffield** ㉔ (see page 296). Once the steel capital of Britain, the city is only slowly recovering from the industry's decline, and while many see it merely as a convenient base for visiting the Peaks, it does have its own attractions.

Ladybower Reservoir

Canning Dock in Liverpool.

The Titanic memorial and Liver Building in Liverpool.

THE NORTHWEST

Liverpool, home of the Beatles, also has a great waterfront and excellent galleries, while Manchester has emerged as a thriving metropolis, and Blackpool remains a seaside institution.

The northwest is not a prime national or international holiday destination, but it does, all the same, have plenty to offer. There are two vibrant and exciting cities – Liverpool and Manchester – as well as the smaller historical city of Lancaster, the seaside resort of Blackpool and the beautiful Ribble Valley.

LIVERPOOL

It is possible to visit **Liverpool ❶** and avoid references to The Beatles, but it's not easy – the group are still the main reason many people come here, and there are numerous "Beatlemania" attractions to visit (see page 304). Yet there is much more to see and do as well. Liverpool was the European Capital of Culture for 2008, which led to a flurry of regeneration, and large parts of the city – including the renovated **Albert Dock**, a busy development with a variety of shops, bars, restaurants, museums and galleries – were put on the Unesco World Heritage List in July 2004. In 2019 plans were put in motion to develop a 10-year strategy for updating the maritime quarter, with the long-term goal to improve National Museum Liverpool's buildings while making the most of the historic location and public spaces. The **Merseyside Maritime Museum** (www.liverpoolmuseums.org.uk; daily 10am–5pm; free) documents the 800-year-old history of the port.

In Liverpool's Metropolitan Cathedral.

It features a Cunard Trail, following objects of the famous shipbuilding company synonymous with Liverpool, which celebrated its 150th year in 2015. Free tours of the old docks are also available. The museum also incorporates the **International Slavery Museum**, which offers a poignant and thought-provoking view of the slave trade and its legacies. Nearby is the award-winning **Museum of Liverpool** (www.liverpoolmuseums.org.uk; daily 10am–5pm; free), designed by architects 3XN in a futuristic style. The displays chart the social

Main attractions
Albert Dock
Walker Art Gallery
The Beatles Story
Lowry Centre
Old Trafford
Blackpool Pleasure Beach
Morecambe Bay

Map on page 302

and economic history of the city through archaeological material, photographs, costume and decorative art and historical memorabilia. There is plenty that will appeal to children here, including a special gallery, Little Liverpool, for the under-sixes. The film *Kicking and Screaming* charts two young fans from the rival Liverpool and Everton football teams. It creates a poignant reminder of the good and bad times during the clubs' histories, and their effect on the population of the city as a whole. Back from the old docks, on William Brown Street in the city centre, is the **World Museum** (www.liverpoolmuseums.org.uk; daily 10am–5pm; free), with collections of archaeology and ethnology as well as an aquarium.

Among the city's fine art galleries are **Tate Liverpool** (www.tate.org.uk; daily 10am–5.50pm; charge for special exhibitions, permanent collection free), which has the largest collection of modern and contemporary art outside London and hosts some great temporary exhibitions; and, away from the waterfront, the neoclassical **Walker**

Beetham Tower is the tallest building in Manchester.

Art Gallery (www.liverpoolmuseums.org.uk; daily 10am–5pm; free), sometimes known as "the National Gallery of the North", which has an outstanding collection that ranges from the 14th century to the present, and includes works by Rembrandt and the Pre-Raphaelites.

Liverpool's architecture is on a grand scale. Down by the docks it includes the three buildings known as "The Three Graces": the imposing **Royal Liver Building**, with the mythical liver birds sitting atop the two clock towers; the Cunard Building; and the Port of Liverpool Building. All three were built in the early 20th century, when the city and the port were at the height of their prosperity. Near here is the Liverpool Cruise Terminal, highlighting the city's continuing importance as a port and featuring the 1,150ft long (350 metres) floating structure moored on the River Mersey enabling large cruise ships to berth without entering the enclosed dock area. Some 85,000 passengers come to Liverpool a year, which is a great boost to the city's economy. You can take a trip on a Mersey Ferry (www.

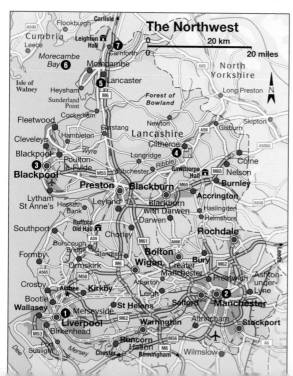

merseyferries.co.uk), used daily by commuters and tourists alike. There have been ferries operating across the river for centuries and it is an excellent way to get a great view of the city skyline.

Behind the docks, in the city centre, you will find the massive shopping, residential and leisure complex of Liverpool One, featuring one of the largest open-air shopping centres in UK. In addition to around 160 stores, there is a cinema with 14 screens, numerous eateries and a jungle-themed indoor golf centre.

Liverpool also has two modern churches, of which the **Roman Catholic Metropolitan Cathedral** (www.liverpoolmetrocathedral.org.uk; daily 7.30am–6pm; free), designed by Sir Frederick W. Gibberd and consecrated in 1967, is the most striking: a circular structure topped with a spire that represents the Crown of Thorns. The crypt, begun in 1930, was the work of Sir Edwin Lutyens, and was the only part of his original design to be carried out before lack of cash halted work.

The **Anglican** Cathedral (www.liverpoolcathedral.org.uk; daily 8am–6pm; free),

Britain's largest, by Giles Gilbert Scott, was begun in 1904 and completed in 1978 after two world wars delayed its construction, but its neo-Gothic style gives it the appearance of a much older building.

There is a good Pre-Raphaelite art collection, along with some Turners and Constables, at **the Lady Lever Art Gallery** (www.liverpoolmuseums.org.uk; daily 10am–5pm; free), built by William Hesketh Lever, later Lord Leverhulme (1851–1928), to house the collection he had assembled to "enrich the lives of his workforce". A major redevelopment of the South End galleries was completed in March 2016 and includes displays of more than 1,500 of Lady Lever's finest objects; highlights include the Wedgwood jasperware collection and stunning Chinese ceramics. The gallery sits in formal gardens in the delightful model village of Port Sunlight (www.port-sunlightvillage.com), across the Mersey in Wirral. Leverhulme, a paternalistic philanthropist and enlightened employer, funded the village for employees of his soap empire (which would later grow into the multinational Unilever). The

Tip

Manchester's most famous attraction is Old Trafford, the home of Manchester United Football Club. The ground was built in 1909 for the sum of £60,000. Today it has changed beyond recognition and has undoubtedly evolved into what is one of the great and most famous sporting arenas in world. The club museum is open Mon–Sat 9.30am–5pm, Sun 10am–4pm, and stadium tours are available daily 9.40am–4.30pm; www.manutd.co.uk.

Some of Antony Gormley's installations on Crosby Beach.

☉ CROSBY

Seven miles (11km) north of Liverpool, via the A565 (or 20 minutes by train from Liverpool Central station) is Crosby, where the wide sands are peopled with 100 cast-iron naked figures all looking out to sea; each of the 6ft (2-metre) figures was moulded by the artist Antony Gormley from his own body. Entitled "Another Place", this haunting installation was originally intended as a temporary one, but after a certain amount of controversy (including from some who complained that the statues were "pornographic"), it has now been given a permanent home here. The figures are dotted about over a 2-mile (3km) area, and as the tides come in and recede again, the figures are submerged and revealed by the sea.

LIVERPOOL AND THE BEATLES

Formed in Liverpool in 1960, The Beatles or "Fab Four" – John Lennon, Paul McCartney, George Harrison and Ringo Starr – became arguably the most successful pop group the world has ever seen.

The Beatles are the best-selling band in history, the album *Sgt Pepper's Lonely Hearts Club Band* is widely regarded as a Pop Art masterpiece, and their enormous popularity (or "Beatlemania") is seen as integral to the social history of Britain in the 1960s

Liverpool's pride in its four famous sons is much in evidence. The National Trust has bought Mendips, the house where John Lennon grew up, as well as Paul McCartney's childhood home, 20 Forthlin Road. Both can also be visited by guided tour (tel: 0151-427 7231; www.nationaltrust.org.uk; book visit online).

The Beatles played many of their early gigs at the Cavern Club on Liverpool's Mathew Street. The

The Fab Four.

original Cavern Club closed in 1973, but was reconstructed in 1984 and is now going strong again as a venue for local bands (tel: 0151-236 9091; www.cavernclub.org). It also stages International Beatleweek (www.internationalbeatleweek.com) in the last week of August, a celebration featuring around 70 bands and attracting a huge number of fans from around the world. Going far beyond live gigs, there are exhibitions, guest speakers, sightseeing tours, sales of memorabilia, tributes and an annual Beatles' convention.

For the rest of the year, Beatles groupies can get their fix by buying memorabilia at the Hard Day's Night shop at 1 Matthew Street, with changing exhibitions in the gallery upstairs, or at the Fab4Store in the Beatles Story (see below) on Albert Dock.

THE BEATLES LEGACY

On Liverpool's dockside, the Britannia Pavilion houses The Beatles Story (tel: 0151-709 1963; www.beatlesstory.com; daily 9am–7pm, 10am–6pm winter), an "experience" of the city's illustrious sons, which is naturally open "eight days a week" and features an underwater trip on the Yellow Submarine and a Fab4D, a mega cinematic experience for all the family (at the Pier Head theatre). Buses for the Magical Mystery Tour (tel: 0151-703 9100; www.cavernclub.org) leave from the ticket office at Albert Dock's Anchor Courtyard daily, and take in all the important landmarks, including Strawberry Field, Penny Lane, Eleanor Rigby's grave and the Cavern Club. Most tours last two hours, though dedicated fans can also join a full-day tour, which includes visits to Mendips and 20 Forthlin Road.

The Beatles finally broke up in 1970 and thereafter pursued individual music careers. Lennon (died 1980) and McCartney each chalked up several more hits of long-lasting appeal, and the late George Harrison brought out a successful triple album, *All Things Must Pass*. Ringo Starr achieved some success as a solo artist in the 1970s, but his post-Beatles career is now chiefly remembered for his narration of the *Thomas the Tank Engine* children's television series.

village is a fascinating place, tranquil and seemingly detached from 21st-century life. It is a Conservation Area, and each of the 900 Grade II-listed buildings is different from its neighbour. To reach **Port Sunlight**, take Queens Way across the Mersey if you are driving, and follow the signs, or use the Merseyrail Wirral Link to Port Sunlight or Bebington stations.

Six miles (10km) to the north of Liverpool, is the world-famous racecourse at **Aintree**, home to the annual Grand National, the most prestigious National Hunt races in the horse-racing calendar. Held each April, it attracts over 70,000 punters, while a further 600 million people across the globe watch the race on television.

THE CHANGING FACE OF MANCHESTER

Manchester ❷ is changing so fast it's hard to keep up with it. The city came to prominence during the 19th century, when it was at the forefront of the Industrial Revolution. Its "dark satanic mills" sprang up when cotton production was revolutionised by Richard Arkwright's steam-powered spinning machines in the late 18th century. When a railway line linked the city with Liverpool in 1830, and the Manchester Ship Canal was completed in 1894, Manchester's prosperity was sealed, and the huge Victorian civic buildings we can see today are evidence of a city that believed in its own destiny. The tenements in which the mill workers lived were razed by slum-clearance projects in the 1950s.

But Manchester's docks went the way of many others, and for years the local economy suffered from post-industrial decline, and the city centre became drab, under-used and under-populated. Eventually, however, a huge revitalisation process began, and today the centre throbs with life once again. There's some of the best shopping in the northwest; a colourful Chinatown; a Gay Village, spanning out from a canalside promenade; and three universities. Manchester's regeneration is as much cultural as physical. The city has been at the cutting edge of pop music since post-punk band Joy Division formed in Salford in the mid-1970s. Other luminaries of the rock and pop scene that came to be known as "Madchester" include Morrissey and The Smiths, the Stone Roses, the Happy Mondays, James, and The Fall. Today, the city remains a hotspot for live music, clubbing and nightlife generally.

For sightseers, Manchester has a treasure trove of first-class museums and galleries. One of the best is the **Museum of Science and Industry** (www.msimanchester.org.uk; daily 10am–5pm; free), an award-winning museum with full working machinery and some splendid examples of transport memorabilia, ranging from steam locomotives to aeroplanes. There are plenty of hands-on and interactive displays to get involved with too. On Mosley Street, the **Manchester Art Gallery** (www.manchesterartgallery.org; Mon 11am–5pm, Tue–Sun 10am–5pm; free) has a fine permanent collection that

Manchester's Lowry Centre.

The City of Manchester, or Etihad, Stadium.

includes works by Ford Maddox Brown and Millais, plus a separate Gallery of Costume at Rusholme.

Part of the University of Manchester since 1889, the **Whitworth Art Gallery** (www.whitworth.manchester.ac.uk; daily 10am–5pm, Thu until 9pm; free) in Whitworth Park, just off Oxford Road, has been the subject of a £15 million redevelopment to showcase its collection of some 55,000 artworks. There is an impressive collection of modern art, including works by Henry Moore, Francis Bacon, Picasso and Jacob Epstein. Another arts development is HOME (www.homemcr.org; main gallery: Tue–Sat noon–8pm, Sun until 6pm; Granada Foundation Gallery: daily 11am–8pm), a popular centre for contemporary theatre, film, art and music, which opened in 2015 and holds regular cultural festivals. On the left bank of the River Irwell is the **People's History Museum** (www.phm.org.uk; daily 10am–5pm; free), a national museum of democracy that showcases the gritty nature of Manchester's character. The collection illustrates the history of working people in Britain, spanning their lives and work over the past 200 years. Further north, on Cheetham Hill, the Manchester Jewish Museum (www.manchesterjewishmuseum.com, Sun–Thu 10am–4pm, Fri until 1pm) is set to reopen in summer 2020 after a major development. The extension will house new galleries, making more space for the museum's 30,000 objects – from personal letters and photographs, to Torah scrolls hidden from the Nazis during World War I.

Try to book for a performance by the resident Hallé Orchestra at the splendid **Bridgewater Hall** (tel: 0161-907 9000; www.bridgewater-hall.co.uk), or make tracks for the **City of Manchester Stadium**, perhaps better known as the **Etihad Stadium** (www.etihadstadium.co.uk), the home of Manchester City Football Club, who have successfully reinvented themselves as the great premiership rival of the legendary Manchester United, thanks to some considerable investment from their Abu Dhabi-based owners.

To the west of the city, Salford Quays, on the banks of the Manchester Ship

Liverpool's Albert Dock.

⊘ FACT FILE

By car Connections to Merseyside via the M6, M56, M58 and M62, about 4 hours from London; to Manchester via the M6, M62, M56, about 3 hours 30 minutes.

By train InterCity services from London Euston to Liverpool, about 2 hours 50 minutes; about 3 hours to Manchester from London Euston; tel: 03457-484 950.

By coach National Express services from London, Birmingham and many other cities to Liverpool, Manchester, Lancaster and Blackpool; tel: 0871-781 8181.

By air Manchester Airport, 10 miles (16km) south of the city centre, tel: 08712-710 711; Liverpool John Lennon Airport, 9 miles (15km) southeast of the city, tel: 0871-521 8484.

City Centre Cruises Tel: 0161-902 0222 for trips around Manchester's canals and waterways.

Manchester United Museum and Tour Tel: 0161-868 8000.

Manchester City Stadium Tel: 0870-062 1894.

Liverpool Football Club Museum and Tour Tel: 0151-260 6677.

Tourist Information Centres Liverpool, tel: 0151-233 2008; Manchester, tel: 0871-222 8223; Blackpool, tel: 01253-478 222; Lancaster, tel: 01524-582 394; Morecambe, tel: 01524-582 808.

Canal, has become a potent symbol of regeneration. This previously run-down area has been the subject of massive inward investment in recent years. MediaCityUK, a huge commercial development, attracted the BBC, which moved much of its television production here, and numerous other companies followed suit. The Quays have become synonymous with culture, sport, art and drama, as well as a mecca for shoppers. One vibrant example is the multimedia **Lowry Centre** (www.thelowry.com; daily 11am–5pm, Sat from 10am; free), which has the world's largest collection of paintings by local artist L.S. Lowry (1887–1976), who is popularly referred to as "the man who painted matchstick men and matchstick cats and dogs". Opposite the centre, on the other side of the canal, a stunning modern building designed by American architect Daniel Libeskind houses the **Imperial War Museum North** (www.iwm.org.uk; daily 10am–5pm; free). The main exhibition hall is devoted to the history of conflicts Britain and the Commonwealth have been engaged in since the onset of the World War I.

BLACKPOOL

On the coast to the northwest of Manchester (up the M61, then M55) is **Blackpool ❸**, which became a popular seaside resort when the arrival of the railways in the mid-19th century enabled Lancashire cotton workers to enjoy a day beside the sea. Even though the grandeur has now somewhat faded, a surge in recent years has seen numbers grow to a record 10 million in 2014.

Fast-food stalls, restaurants, bingo halls and amusement arcades line the **Golden Mile**, which skirts wide stretches of sand, where sand-surfers and kite-flyers have the time of their lives. Trams trundle along the prom, three piers offer traditional summer entertainments, and every kind of fairground ride is available at Blackpool

Pleasure Beach (www.blackpoolpleasure beach.com; Apr–Oct daily 10am–5pm, mid-July–Aug until 8pm, mid-Feb–Mar and early-Nov weekends only, with exceptions; tickets are cheaper if booked online in advance). Above it all looms the famous 518ft (158-metre) Eiffel-style **Blackpool Tower**: in September and October it is outlined in coloured lights as the centrepiece of the spectacular **Blackpool Illumination**s. On Church Street, set back slightly from and perpendicular to the seafront, are the Winter Gardens (www.wintergar densblackpool.co.uk; daily 10.30am–4pm, with exceptions; free), a grand Victorian entertainment complex housing an opera house, a ballroom and several theatres. Events held here range from boxing matches to magic shows to pop concerts. In the past, it has also often been used by Britain's main political parties for their annual conferences.

On the eastern side of the town, next to Stanley Park, is **Blackpool Zoo** (if driving, follow the "brown elephant" signs; www.blackpoolzoo.org.uk; daily 10am–5.45pm, with exceptions). As

Blackpool Tower.

⊘ Tip

You should not attempt to cross the sands of Morecambe Bay without a guide. The tide sweeps across the bay and performs a pincer movement around the sandbars, then spreads over the flats, and in no time at all a peaceful expanse of sand becomes a choppy sea. To book a Cross Bay Walk (approximately 9 miles/14km), tel: 01524-582 808.

well as giraffes, elephants, zebras and lions, the zoo also has a "Dinosaur Safari" and a children's farm.

PRESTON TO THE BOWLAND FELLS

Back along the M55 to the east of Blackpool is Preston, where attractions on the Market Square include the **Harris Museum and Art Gallery** (www.harrismuseum.org.uk; Mon–Sat 10am–5pm, opens 11am Mon; free), with a notable collection of fine and decorative art, as well as textiles and photography. Further east is the former mill town of Blackburn, once a celebrated textiles centre but hard hit by post-industrial decline. Further east still on the Manchester Road is Accrington, home to the **Haworth Art Gallery** (www.hyndburnbc.gov.uk/hag; Tue–Fri noon–4.45pm, Sat–Sun noon–4.15pm; free), which houses the largest public collection of Tiffany Art Nouveau glass in Europe, attractively set within a fine historic Edwardian mansion.

South of Accrington is Helmshore, featuring the **Helmshore Mills Textile Museum** (tel: 01706-226 459; Apr–Oct

The Ribble Valley.

Fri–Sun noon–4pm), which documents Lancashire's textile heritage – in particular wool and cotton production – against the backdrop of two original mills.

Heading northwest from Accrington is the **Ribble Valley**; a good base from which to explore the area is the small, pleasant town of **Clitheroe** ❹. From the remains of its ancient castle, perched on a limestone crag, there are splendid views of the valley. Nearby stand the ruins of the 13th-century Cistercian **Whalley Abbey**, and a parish church with Saxon crosses outside. To the west, **Ribchester**, a pretty village with a 17th-century bridge over the river, has the relics of a huge Roman fort, part of which has been excavated to reveal the foundations of two granaries.

Another attraction partly set within the Ribble Valley is the Forest of Bowland (www.forestofbowland.com), also known as the Bowland Fells. This Area of Outstanding Natural Beauty covers 321 sq miles (808 sq km) of rural Lancashire and North Yorkshire and offers activities including walking, cycling, horse riding and fishing.

⊘ LANCASHIRE'S FINEST

Two of Lancashire's finest stately homes are not far off our route and easily accessible either by car or by public transport:

Gawthorpe Hall (www.nationaltrust.org.uk/gawthorpe-hall; mid-Apr–Oct Wed–Sun noon–5pm, garden: all year daily 8am–7pm) is an Elizabethan masterpiece in Padiham, near Burnley, which was restored in the 19th century by Sir Charles Barry, who created many of the magnificent interiors. The collection of paintings includes some on loan from the National Portrait Gallery in London, and there is a rare collection of needlework, displaying exhibits of samplers and lace work. There is a rose garden and a tearoom, and special children's interactive sessions during term time (tel: 01282-771 004 for details).

Rufford Old Hall (www.nationaltrust.org.uk/rufford-old-hall; house: mid-Feb–Oct Sat–Wed 11am–5pm, Nov–Dec Sat–Sun 11am–4pm; garden: Sat–Wed 11am–5pm, also Nov–late Dec Sat–Sun noon–4pm) is one of Lancashire's finest 16th-century buildings, especially well known for the Great Hall with a hammerbeam roof and carved wooden screen. It is said that Shakespeare performed here for the owner, Sir Thomas Hesketh, whose family owned the house for 400 years. The Carolean Wing has collections of 17th-century furniture and tapestries. The Old Kitchen Restaurant serves light lunches and teas. There are Victorian-style gardens and a wild-flower meadow.

LANCASTER

Head north now up the M6 to **Lancaster ⑤**, the county town of Lancashire, founded by the Romans. In 1322 Robert Bruce razed the castle and much of the town to the ground, but it was rebuilt by John of Gaunt, and his **Gateway Tower** is a fine construction. During the so-called Wars of the Roses of the 15th century, the House of Lancaster was symbolised by the red rose, the House of York by the white. The **castle** (www.lancastercastle.com; daily 9.30am–5pm) and the Shire Hall can be visited – although some parts of the castle are not accessible when the Crown Court is in session. There's also a priory church, **St Mary's**, with a fine Saxon doorway and beautiful choir stalls. Housed within a Georgian building on the Market Square is the **Lancaster City Museum** (tel: 01524-64637; Tue–Sun 10am–5pm; free). Here, visitors can learn about the history of the city from the Romans to the present day. The collection also incorporates the King's Own Royal Regiment Museum.

On the eastern side of the town is the 54-acre (22-hectare) Williamson Park (daily Apr–Sept 10am–5pm, Oct–Mar until 4pm; free). The park's focal point is the imposing Ashton Memorial, a domed folly that has a gallery on the first floor, which offers stunning views out towards Morecambe Bay in the west and the Lake District to the north. The park also has an Edwardian Palm House (charge), which serves as a tropical butterfly house.

MORECAMBE BAY

A short drive west of Lancaster brings you to **Morecambe Bay ⑥**, renowned for its shrimps and its sands – even more so after the five-mile beach starred in the 2019 ITV drama *The Bay*. The shrimps are small, brown and tasty and are gathered in nets dragged across the sand by horse and cart. The sands, a vast spread of tidal flats that are home to thousands of seabirds, can be very dangerous, and you should only walk across in the company of the guides who will lead you, when the tide is right, all the way round the bay. The best way to see the sands and their bird population is by train on a track that trundles over viaducts from Ulverston to Arnside. **Morecambe** is a pleasant holiday resort on the bay, which claims to have originated the idea of autumn illuminations in order to lengthen the summer season. The seaside town will attract even more attention if the team behind Cornwall's Eden Project open an outpost on the Lancashire Coast in 2022, as they promised in 2019.

Carnforth ⑦, a small town just north of Morecambe, is the last stop on our route. Its main claims to fame are the rejuvenated **Carnforth Station and Visitor Centre** (www.carnforthstation. co.uk; daily 10am–4pm; free), including the refreshment room made famous in the film *Brief Encounter*; and **Leighton Hall** (www.leightonhall.co.uk; May–Sept Tue–Fri 2–5pm, also Sun in Aug), home of the Gillow furniture family. In the extensive grounds there are plenty of paths to explore, as well as a walled garden and ornamental vegetable plot.

Morecambe Bay shrimps.

Overlooking the lakes from Morecambe.

THE LAKE DISTRICT

The landscape that inspired the Lakeland poets continues to exert its spell on visitors, who come to walk the fells, to sail the waters, or simply to enjoy the breathtaking scenery.

The **Lake District**, in northwest England, is a small area, but extremely beautiful, with the varied delights of soft hills and woodland; panoramas of the great lakes; unexpected discoveries of smaller waters or tarns; bare contours of the fells and high ground, and the awe-inspiring power of the more remote mountains and mountain passes. The poet William Wordsworth, who was born here at Cockermouth in 1770 and spent most of his life here, rightly remarked: "I do not know any tract of country in which, within so narrow a compass, may be found an equal variety in the influences of light and shadow upon the sublime or beautiful features of landscape."

The Lake District is more frequently visited, both by day-trippers and holidaymakers, than any other region of exceptional natural beauty in the British Isles. On the whole it copes remarkably well with the vast numbers of visitors, but traffic congestion can be a big problem in summer.

The two routes that were popularised by the first tourists in the 1760s and 1770s still carry the greatest share of summer traffic. One is from Penrith to Ambleside by the west shore of Ullswater (scene of Wordsworth's poem *I Wandered Lonely as a Cloud*, popularly known as "Daffodils") and over the Kirkstone Pass, now the A592; the other is from Keswick to

Windermere by the side of Thirlmere, Grasmere, Rydal Water and Windermere, now the A591.

Away from these routes you can find quiet areas of great beauty – particularly if you avoid the high summer – and experience the sense of solitude and oneness with nature that was valued so highly by the 19th-century Romantic poets. The central area of mountains was never much affected by industry or quarrying, and the 19th-century shipbuilding, iron manufacturing and coal mining that once flourished by the coast

⊘ Main attractions

Furness Abbey
Beatrix Potter's Hill Top
Old Man of Coniston
Dove Cottage
Derwentwater
Aira Force
Windermere

Map on page 312

View over Glenridding.

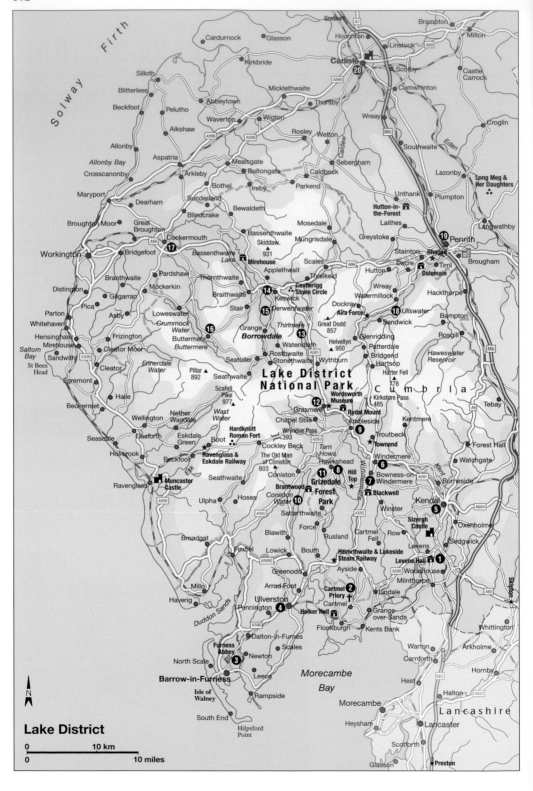

Solway Firth

Solway

Cardurnock
Glasson
Grethe
Houghton
Brampton
Milton

Silloth
Kirkbride
Carlisle
Scoby
Castle
Carrock

Blitterlees
Micklethwaite
Cumwhinton

Beckfoot
Pe}utho
Abbeytown
Thursby
Wreay
Southwaite
Croglin

Allonby
Waverton
Wigton
Welton
Rosley
Caldew

Allonby Bay
Aspatria
Arkleby
Mealsgate
Boltongate
Ireby
Parkend
Unthank
Plumpton
Langwathby

Crosscanonby
Bothel

Maryport
Dearham
Sunderland
Bewaldeth
Mosedale
Laithes
Greystoke

Broughton Moor
Great
Broughton
Blindcrake
Bassenthwaite
Mungrisdale
Wreay

Workington
Cockermouth
Bridgefoot
Thornthwaite
Applethwaite
Skiddaw
931
Mirehouse
Scales
Hutton
Watermillock

Distington
Branthwaite
Pardshaw
Braithwaite
Castlerigg
Stone Circle
Dockray
Aira Force
Ullswater

Lake District

Lake District

0   10 km
0   10 miles

N

have now almost entirely disappeared. Sheep farming was the traditional way of life of the hill folk, and it continues today throughout the area covered by the Lake District National Park, often on farms owned and leased by the National Trust.

THE SOUTH OF THE LAKE DISTRICT

Approaching from the south along the M6, turn off at Junction 36 to Levens. **Levens Hall ❶** (www.levenshall.co.uk; Apr–early Oct Sun–Thu, house: noon–4pm, garden: 10am–5pm) is an Elizabethan house furnished in Jacobean style, and built around a 13th-century pele tower (impregnable tower at the core of a building). The famous topiary garden is little changed since its trees were first shaped in the 17th century.

The A590 south from Levens leads to **Cartmel Priory ❷** (www.cartmelpriory.org. uk; daily except during services, summer 9am–5.30pm, Sunday until 4.30pm, winter daily 9am–3.30pm; donation), near the resort of Grange-over-Sands. It was founded around 1189 by the Baron of Cartmel and was saved from destruction

at the time of Henry VIII's Dissolution of the Monasteries by the quick-wittedness of local people who claimed that it was their parish church. Only the gatehouse and the church remain. Inside the latter there is good medieval carving and old glass; the lovely east window dates from the 15th century, as does the tower. A mother and son who drowned while crossing Morecambe Bay sands are buried next to the font; in the days before the railway linked Cartmel and Lancaster, the treacherous old low-tide route was risked by many. Nearby, the splendid home of the powerful Cavendish family, **Holker Hall** (www.holker.co.uk; mid-Mar–early Nov Wed–Sun 11am–4pm, gardens, café, food hall and shop 10.30am–5pm), is set in attractive gardens. Look out for the Holker Great Lime; planted in the early 17th century, it is one of the largest lime trees in the country.

Furness Peninsula, the southern tip of Lakeland, was in medieval times the heart of a great Cistercian estate farmed by the monks of **Furness Abbey ❸** (tel. 01229-823 420; www.english-heritage. org.uk; Apr–Sept daily 10am–6pm, Oct

A Cumbrian sheep farmer.

The Abbot Hall Museum.

⊙ Fact

The area in which Furness Abbey stands is known as the Vale of Deadly Nightshade because these sinister plants once grew here in such profusion. A story tells of how in 1351 the abbot of Furness Abbey was murdered by three jealous monks. They concocted a lethal poison using deadly nightshade and laced the unsuspecting abbot's food and drink; in the throes of horrendous agony the poor abbot suffered a terrible death.

daily until 4pm, Nov–Mar Sat–Sun 10am–4pm). The abbey, which lies in a lovely setting, was the second-richest Cistercian establishment in England at the time of its suppression in 1537. Its red sandstone buildings, standing out against green lawns, date from the 12th and 15th centuries. The abbey lies to the north of **Barrow-in-Furness**, the peninsula's main town, and once a major shipbuilding centre. **The Dock Museum** (www.dockmuseum.org.uk; Wed–Sun 11am–4pm; free) charts the town's social and industrial history.

Head north now on the A590 to the historic town of **Ulverston** ④ on an old ship canal, where you can visit the **Laurel and Hardy Museum** (www.laurel-and-hardy.co.uk; Easter–Oct daily 10am–5pm, closed Mon and Wed rest of year, with exceptions). It sounds incongruous, but Stan Laurel was born here in 1890, and in addition to telling the story of the silent movie comedy duo's lives, the museum has regular showings of their films. Back on the A591 near Levens, where we began, you will come to **Sizergh Castle** (www.

Levens Hall topiary garden.

nationaltrust.org.uk/sizergh; daily Apr–Oct house: noon–4pm, garden all year: 10am–5pm, winter until 4pm), whose medieval defensive appearance is softened by attractive gardens. About 3 miles (5km) on you reach **Kendal** ⑤, which is a good centre for exploring the Lakes. It is still a working town, not just a holiday centre, carrying on its daily life in the midst of fine 17th- and 18th-century buildings. The church is a Perpendicular structure, and the lively Brewery Arts Centre is worth a look. Beside the church stand **Abbot Hall Art Gallery** and the **Museum of Lakeland Life & Industry** (www.abbothall.org.uk; www.lakelandmuseum.org.uk; Mon–Sat 10.30am–5pm, until 4pm in winter), housed in an 18th-century mansion and its stable block. The former has paintings by John Ruskin and J.M.W. Turner and by local artist George Romney; the latter concentrates on local trades and crafts, and has a room devoted to *Swallows and Amazons* author Arthur Ransome (1884–1967), some of whose books are set on Coniston Water.

⊙ FACT FILE

Location 250 miles (400km) from London, 75 miles (120km) north of Manchester; the Lake District covers 40 miles (64km) north–south, and 32 miles (51km) east–west.

By train London Euston to Penrith or to Oxenholme (with a connecting service to Windermere); journey time about 3 hours. From Edinburgh to Carlisle, about 1 hour 30 minutes; tel: 03457-484 950.

By coach National Express from London Victoria to Kendal; journey time about 7 hours 35 minutes; tel: 0871-781 8181.

By car About 5 hours from London via the M40/M6.

By air Manchester Airport, near the M6, is approximately 80 miles (130km) south of Windermere.

Most famous Lakelanders Children's writer Beatrix Potter (1866–1943); the poet William Wordsworth (1770–1850).

For children The World of Beatrix Potter; Grizedale Forest Sculpture; Cumberland Pencil Museum; Brockhole Visitor Centre.

Festivals Appleby Horse Fair (June); Ambleside Rushbearing Festival (July); Kendal Mountain Festival (Nov).

Tourist information Coniston, tel: 01539-441 533; Hawkshead, tel: 01539-436 946; Kendal, tel: 01539-735 891; Keswick, tel: 0845-901 0845; Windermere, tel: 01539-446 499.

AROUND WINDERMERE

The A591 runs from Kendal to the town of **Windermere** ❻ and the lake of the same name. It's a Victorian town, which really came into being when the railway arrived. In a pretty lakeside setting is a striking new complex: the **Windermere Jetty, Museum of Boats, Steam and Stories** (www.windermerejetty.org; Mar–Oct 10am–5pm, Nov–Feb 10.30am–4pm), which opened in 2017 and displays a boat collection of national importance, all built in the Lake District over the past 200 years. Visitors can view yachts, ferry boats, rowing boats (look out for Beatrix Potter's home-made wooden rowing boat), speedboats and canoes, plus motor boats from the 1920s to 1950s, and can take heritage boat trips too (book in advance). It's absorbing, even for non-boaties; kids will love the ancient steamboat rescued from the bottom of Ullswater by divers, while adults will enjoy the stories and people behind each watercraft. For more on children's writer Beatrix Potter (1866–1943), who based many of her novels in the Lake District, **The World of Beatrix Potter** (www.hop-skip-jump. com; daily Apr–Sept 10am–5.30pm, Oct–Mar 10am–4.30pm) in the Old Laundry at Crag Brow recreates her characters in a lively exhibition. You can walk down Lakes Road to **Bowness-on-Windermere** ❼, the most popular resort, which has a very attractive centre but is almost always too crowded for comfort

Visitors can also take a car ferry to Near Sawrey and Beatrix Potter's home, **Hill Top** (www.nationaltrust.org.uk/hilltop; mid-Feb–Oct Sat–Thu 10am–3.30pm, June–Aug daily until 5pm, with exceptions), a fine example of a 17th-century Lakeland farmhouse, with a traditional cottage garden. To the south of Bowness just off the A507 is **Blackwell** (www.blackwell.org.uk; daily 10.30am 5pm, until 4pm Nov–Feb), the distinctive Arts and Crafts house designed by M.H. Baillie Scott for a wealthy Manchester brewery owner. The design is asymmetrical and the light-filled main living areas face south, away from the lake. Two of the upstairs bedrooms have been converted into galleries, where exhibitions are held.

Hill Top, Beatrix Potter's home.

Ambleside.

Kendal, famous for Kendal Mint Cake.

A ferry on Lake Windermere.

In Main Street, in nearby **Hawkshead** ⑧ on the west side of the lake, is the **Beatrix Potter Gallery** (www.national trust.org.uk/beatrix-potter-gallery; Apr–Oct daily 10.30am–4pm, mid-Feb–Mar Sat–Thu 10.30am–3.30pm), housed in the office of her solicitor husband. It has changing displays of many of her original drawings and watercolours from her famous children's books.

William Wordsworth (1770–1850; see box, page 318) attended the **Grammar School** at Hawkshead (www. hawksheadgrammar.org.uk; Apr–Sept Mon–Sat 10.30am–1pm, 1.30–5pm). Downstairs, it suggests little of the excellence of its teaching in the 1780s when the Wordsworth brothers studied there. But upstairs is a superb library with books dating from the foundation of the ancient school by Archbishop Sandys in 1585. **St Michael's Church** preserves wall paintings of scriptural texts. From beneath its east window you can take in the view of this tiny, whitewashed town.

West of Hawkshead stands the medieval arched **Courthouse**, all that remains of a group of 15th-century manorial buildings constructed when the Cistercian monks from Cartmel ruled much of the area. Further west, just off the B5285, is **Tarn Hows**, considered by many to be the prettiest lake in the district. Only a half-mile (800 metres) long, it was originally three smaller lakes but joined after a dam was built. There are adequate National Trust car parks (including designated parking close to the lake for disabled people) and a good footpath right round the tarn, and it takes about an hour to walk all the way around.

You can continue on the west side of the lake towards Ambleside, but if you take the A591 from Windermere you will also be able to visit **Troutbeck**, a delightful village that has several roadside wells dedicated to various saints; a church with a Pre-Raphaelite east window (the combined work of Edward Burne-Jones, William Morris and Ford Maddox Brown); and an atmospheric 17th-century farmhouse, **Townend** (www.nationaltrust.org.uk/townend; mid-Mar–Oct Wed–Sun 1–5pm), built by

⊘ TAKING TO THE WATER

Looking at lakes, in scenery such as this, is wonderful, but at some point most people actually want to get on the water, whether to get from one point to another, to view the fells from a different perspective or simply to feel at one with the water.

Ullswater Steamers are the best way to enjoy the lake and the mountains around it. Boats sail all year every day between Glenridding, Howtown and Pooley Bridge, check for sailing times to Aira Force. You can take a one-way trip and walk back if you prefer that option. Tel: 01768-482 229 (Glenridding Pier); www.ullswater-steamers.co.uk.

Windermere Lake Cruises operates a fleet of launches and steamers year-round between Ambleside, Bowness and Lakeside, with connections for the Lakeside and Haverthwaite Steam Railway, Lakeland Motor Museum, the Brockhole Visitor Centre and the Aquarium of the Lakes. Steamers have licensed bars and coffee shops and are heated in the winter. Tel: 01539-443 360. www.windermere-lakecruises.co.uk.

Coniston Water has the National Trust steam-powered yacht, the renovated *Gondola*, launched in 1859, which takes visitors on memorable cruises, tel: 01539-432 733. The *Gondola* sails from Coniston Pier (half a mile from Coniston village) daily from April to October.

yeoman George Browne, which has a wonderful collection of carved woodwork and domestic implements.

The Browne family collected over 1,500 books between the 16th and 20th centuries, and the existence of this lovingly preserved library is historically significant.

Ambleside ❾ is a Victorian town of splendid slate buildings. If you arrive by boat during peak tourist times you can take the horse-drawn carriage that runs between Waterhead pier and Ambleside town centre (1 mile/1.5km). Spanning the beck beside Rydal Road, the tiny **House on the Bridge** is administered by the National Trust (external view only).

CONISTON TO GRASMERE

Instead of continuing north from here, you could make a diversion on the A593 to **Coniston Water** ❿, where the **Old Man of Coniston** (2,635ft/803 metres) can be climbed via a well-marked route from the village. In St Andrew's Church, John Ruskin (1819–1900), the art historian and critic, is buried. The **Ruskin**

Museum (www.ruskinmuseum.com; Mar–mid-Nov daily 10am–5.30pm, mid-Nov–Easter Wed–Sun 10.30am–4pm) is a few minutes' walk from the church. The museum also features a special wing, dedicated to speed ace Donald Campbell (1921–67) who died on Coniston Water. Ruskin lived at **Brantwood** (www.brantwood.org.uk; mid-Mar–mid-Nov daily 10.30am–5pm, mid-Nov–mid-Mar closed Mon and Tue), on the northeast shore of Coniston Water. Many of his paintings are preserved, and the house remains much as he left it. It's accessible by road (B5285) or by the renovated Victorian steam yacht *Gondola* from Coniston Pier, which is operating once more after lying wrecked in Nibthwaite Bay for many years. To the east of Coniston lies **Grizedale Forest Park** ⓫, a large tract of land the Forestry Commission has imaginatively given over to nature trails, modern sculptures and Go Ape (www.goape.co.uk) activity and tree-top adventure.

Get back on the A593 now to Ambleside, then pick up the road towards Keswick. You'll soon come to **Rydal**

John Ruskin, the art historian, is buried in Coniston.

View of Keswick and Derwent Water.

Lodore Falls.

Dove Cottage in Grasmere.

Mount (www.rydalmount.co.uk; Apr–Oct daily 9.30am–5pm, Nov–Dec, Feb Wed–Sun 11am–4pm), which was the home of the Wordsworth family from 1813 until William's death in 1850. The house (still owned by a descendant) contains portraits and family mementos; the grounds were landscaped by Wordsworth and retain their original form. **Rydal Water** is a small reedy lake with a population of waterfowl, and red squirrels in the larches round the edge.

Two miles (3km) north is **Grasmere** ⑫, a pleasant village on the lake of the same name: "the prettiest spot that man has ever found", according to Wordsworth. **St Oswald's Church** with its ancient timber roof is worth a visit in its own right, not just to see the Wordsworthian graves. The display of manuscripts and portraits of the poet's family and friends in the **Wordsworth Museum** (www.wordsworth.org.uk; Mar–Oct daily 9.30am–5.30pm, Nov–Dec, Feb 10am–4.30pm; the Reimagining Wordsworth redevelopment project will be taking place throughout 2019 and early 2020; check the website for what's open and when) brings home the magnitude of the poetry that was written here and the importance that Wordsworth and his friend Samuel Coleridge held in the cultural life of their day. Entrance to the museum also gives access to whitewashed **Dove Cottage,** from which William, his wife Mary and his sister Dorothy had a view over Grasmere to the fells, although it's now hemmed in by later buildings. When the regeneration project is complete, due spring 2020, the museum will be expanded and Dove Cottage renovated, along with new galleries and events space, plus a redesigned café and additional outdoor spaces.

KESWICK TO COCKERMOUTH

The 17-mile (28km) journey to Keswick on the A591 passes **Thirlmere** ⑬, a reservoir created from two smaller lakes in 1890 to supply the water needs of Manchester. **Helvellyn**, the third-highest mountain in England (3,120ft/950 metres), rises steeply to the right. Close to Keswick you could turn off right to **Castlerigg Stone Circle**, an

Ø THE LAKE POETS

There's no getting away from the Lake Poets – not that anyone really wants to. They were the first generation of English Romantics, united by their love of poetry, free thought, progressive causes and natural beauty.

William Wordsworth (1770–1850) was the focus. Born in Cockermouth, he lived most of his adult life in the district, accompanied by his wife Mary and his sister Dorothy (1771–1855), whose journals provided inspiration for her brother's work. His line "I wandered lonely as a cloud…" must be one of the few that every English person knows. Samuel Taylor Coleridge (1772–1834) joined them in 1800, living in Greta Hall, Keswick, and continuing the intense friendship begun a few years earlier. It ended in an irrevocable quarrel 10 years later, by which time he was addicted to opium. Robert Southey (1774–1843) joined the group shortly afterwards; he took over Greta Hall and lived there for 40 years. He was appointed Poet Laureate in 1813. Thomas de Quincey (1785–1859) was more of a journalist than a poet, but closely associated with the group. He settled for a while in Grasmere, at Dove Cottage, previously occupied by the Wordsworths, and made his name in 1821 with *The Confessions of an English Opium Eater* – a subject on which he was well qualified to write.

ancient monument that Victorian tourists associated with the Druids. The views from here are tremendous.

Keswick ⑭ is a Victorian town with a much older centre, which has been popular with visitors since the 1760s. It has a **Moot Hall** (market hall), grand as a church, which now houses a helpful information centre. The town came to prominence through the manufacture of pencils, using graphite mined in Borrowdale. The factory is now the **Cumberland Pencil Museum** (www. pencilmuseum.co.uk; daily 9.30am–5pm) – pencil-making can be traced to the discovery of graphite in the 16th century; local shepherds soon began to use it to mark their sheep. **Keswick Museum** (www.keswickmuseum.org.uk; daily 10am–4pm) has mementos and manuscripts of Samuel Coleridge, Robert Southey and Hugh Walpole, who all lived nearby.

Lovely **Borrowdale Valley** has long been a favourite with both artists and walkers. The B5289 south from Keswick skirts **Derwentwater ⑮**, which mirrors a range of splendid fells. To the left of the road are the **Lodore Falls** "receding and speeding, / And shocking and rocking..." as Robert Southey wrote. Where the valley narrows to form the Jaws of Borrowdale (best seen from Friars Crag on the right as you leave Keswick) lies the pretty village of Grange, reached over a narrow bridge. A mile to the west is **Brackenburn** (private), the home of Hugh Walpole, who set *The Herries Chronicle* (1930–33) in the region. From Grange you can walk beside the waters of the Derwent and through the oak woods.

Stay on the B5289 and you'll pass Rosthwaite and Seatoller. Between the two is **Johnny Wood**, with a nature trail. The road continues through **Honister Pass**, where fell-walkers park their cars and make the relatively easy climb to the summit of **Great Gable** (2,949ft/899 metres). From here the road drops down to **Buttermere ⑯** at the foot of Fleetwith Pike (2,126ft/648 metres). You can walk round Buttermere (which is quieter than the other lakes), then stop at the **Fish Inn** in the village, where

Dacre Church, with carved stone bear effigies.

Boats moored at Ambleside.

> **Tip**

At Dacre you can go bear-hunting. In the corners of the graveyard are eroded stone effigies known as "the bears", which may indeed have adorned the castle or, as some believe, marked the corner boundaries of a much older burial ground.

the strength of the ale was recommended back in the 18th century. In **Buttermere Church** there's a plaque to Alfred Wainwright (1907–91), most famous of the fell walkers. Through the window (on a clear day) you can see **Haystacks Fell**, where his ashes were scattered.

Back on the road, turn left at the junction of the B5292 for **Cockermouth** ⑰, a pleasant market town of red sandstone, which is mostly visited by those keen to see **Wordsworth House and Garden** (www.nationaltrust.org.uk/wordsworth-house; mid-Mar–Oct Sat–Thu 11am–5pm). Recreated as it would have been when Wordsworth and his sister were children, the experience is bought to life by costumed characters and hands-on activities.

The A595 leads straight to Carlisle from here, but our tour takes the A66, which skirts **Bassenthwaite Lake** for a while then passes Keswick, with Skiddaw Forest to the left. **Skiddaw** (3,053ft/931 metres) and **Blencathra**, also known as Saddleback (2,847ft/868 metres), are the dominant fells. At the foot of Skiddaw lies the home of scholar James Spedding (1808–81), **Mirehouse**, (www.mirehouse.com; Apr–Oct, house: Sun, Wed, Thu 1.30–4.30pm, grounds: Apr–Oct daily 10am–5pm). Children will delight in roaming the estate's four woodland adventure playgrounds.

FROM ULLSWATER TO CARLISLE

It's only a 15-mile (24km) drive from Keswick to the old town of Penrith, but there are a few interesting diversions to be made en route. You could incorporate a visit to **Dacre**, a few miles before the town on the right. It has a largely Norman church, even earlier carvings and views of 14th-century **Dacre Castle**. Nearby is **Dalemain** (www.dalemain.com; mid-Apr–mid-Oct Sun–Thu 10.30am–3.30pm; Oct until 3pm; guided tours only all day Sun and Mon–Wed until 2.30pm), a former manor house that dates back to the 14th century and is essentially unaltered since 1750, with fine interiors (including a Chinese drawing room

The Lake District offers walks for everyone.

> WALKING THE FELLS

Walking is the most popular activity in the Lake District. The travel shelves of local bookshops are crammed with books, most of which describe circular and not-too-arduous routes. The Lake District National Park organises walks, and details are given in their free leaflets, which are available from any information centre (www.lakedistrict.gov.uk).

For more experienced walkers – those who believe there is no substitute for the fell-walking books written and illustrated by Alfred Wainwright – there are some great challenges: a circuit taking in the Langdale Pikes, beginning and ending at the Dungeon Ghyll car park at the head of Great Langdale, is one of the most popular. In the east of the region, the summit of Helvellyn can be approached from either Thirlmere or Ullswater – one route from the latter being up the magnificent Striding Edge. In Central Lakeland, Great Gable can be climbed from Honister Pass, while Wasdale Head is the most popular starting point for those wishing to conquer Scafell Pike. The southern fells are dominated by the Old Man of Coniston, while Skiddaw looms (3,053ft/931 metres) above Bassenthwaite Lake.

Information centres stock local maps showing walks suitable for people with disabilities. The Wainwright Society, based in Kendal, organises memorial lectures and walks in honour of the great Lakeland walker Alfred Wainwright: www.wainwright.org.uk.

with 18th-century wallpaper), paintings and a pleasant garden.

Dalemain lies just off the A592, which leads past **Ullswater** ⑱ and over the Kirkstone Pass to Ambleside. Ullswater is the second-largest lake after Windermere, and it was here that the Wordworths saw the dancing daffodils. There are steamers on the lake from which one can enjoy magnificent views of Helvellyn and other surrounding mountains. **Aira Force**, on the north shore beneath **Gowbarrow Fell**, is one of the most impressive waterfalls in the Lake District, tumbling 65ft (20 metres) in a gorge flanked by trees. The fell, a former deer park, is a good place to wander, enjoying magnificent views without too much strenuous effort.

Heading north now on the A592, **The Rheged Centre** (www.rheged.com; daily 10am–5.30pm) lies at the junction with the A66. Housed in Europe's largest grass-covered building, this innovative attraction incorporates a cinema, shops, cafés, children's activities and special events.

After this diversion, it's on to **Penrith** ⑲, a sturdy working town of red sandstone buildings, where the 14th-century castle is a picturesque stump in a park near the station, and a collection of ancient stones, known as the Giant's Grave, stands in the churchyard of 18th-century St Andrew's. **Brougham Castle**, just southeast of Penrith, is a Norman structure built on the foundations of a Roman fort. The ruins are impressive: the top gallery of the keep has fine views and is worth the effort of climbing. During the 9th and 10th centuries, Penrith was the capital of Cumbria, a semi-independent region that was once considered part of Scotland.

Just north of the town, at Little Salkeld, stands an impressive Bronze Age stone circle known as **Long Meg and Her Daughters**. On the B5305 is a stately home worth a visit:

Hutton-in-the-Forest (www.hutton-in-the-forest.co.uk; Apr–Sept Wed, Thu, Sun 11.30am–4pm). It's a rambling building, with a 14th-century tower and a splendid 17th-century Long Gallery, a walled garden and pleasant woodlands.

Carlisle ⑳, 21 miles (34km) north of Penrith on the M6, is our last stop. It's also the last city before the Scottish border on the northwestern side of the country. Now the capital of Cumbria, it has suffered numerous attacks over the centuries, and the Norman **Castle** obtained its unusual outline when its roof was strengthened to carry cannons. From the castle take the footbridge or underground walkway to **Tullie House Museum and Art Gallery** (www.tulliehouse.co.uk; Apr–Oct Mon–Sat 10am–5pm, Sun 11am–5pm, until 4pm Nov–Mar), containing an eclectic collection of Roman artefacts, wildlife displays and Pre-Raphaelite paintings. Carlisle is a good starting point for Hadrian's Wall (see page 350). Contact the Carlisle Tourist Information Centre for details of public transport (tel: 01228-598 596).

Aira Force, Ullswater.

Ashness Bridge and Skiddaw

YORK

This venerable city of the north, easily explored on foot, has a vast Minster and strong links with the Romans, Vikings and the golden age of railways.

England's most ancient northern city lies on the River Ouse in the centre of the Vale of York between the Yorkshire Dales and the North York Moors. It was once the principal town of Yorkshire, and it remains the see of the Archbishop of York, Primate of England, second to the Archbishop of Canterbury in the hierarchy of the Church of England. Its streets, walls and buildings mark the pageant of its history, from Roman and Viking ancestry to medieval heart and Georgian elegance. A child-friendly city, its Viking, Castle and Railway museums have plenty to engage young people as well as adults.

THE NORTH SIDE OF THE OLD TOWN

The starting point of any visit is **York Minster Ⓐ** (www.yorkminster.org; Mon–Sat 9am–4.30pm, Sun 12.30–3pm), England's largest medieval church, which dominates the city. Beside the cathedral is the half-timbered **St William's College**, founded in 1461 as the home of the chantry priests who sang Masses for the souls of the founder. Today it is used for conferences and receptions. In Dean's Park on the north side of the minster is the **Minster Library**. The Archbishop's Palace once covered this area, and the library, which is the largest cathedral library in the country, is in its former

chapel. To the right of the chapel is the **Treasurer's House** (www.nationaltrust.org.uk/treasurers-house-york; Mar–Oct, house and garden daily 11am–4.30pm). Built in 1419, it was fully restored at the end of the 19th century, but ghosts of Roman legionaries are said to still to march through its cellar. The Roman city was walled, but the walls that can be seen today date largely from the 14th century and are the longest remaining medieval walls in Britain. **Monk Bar Ⓑ**, which lies on the north side of the Minster, gives access up on to the Bar Walls. Walking

Main attractions
York Minster
Yorkshire Museum
The Shambles
Jorvik Viking Centre
Micklegate
National Railway Museum

Map on page 324

Roman goddess Minerva sits on the roof of a shop.

round the wall to the left brings you to the city gate of **Bootham Bar** , which once led out to the Forest of Galtres; armed guards used to wait here to protect travellers, it is said, from wolves and robbers in the forest.

From here descend to Exhibition Square, where there is a fountain and statue of the local artist William Etty, whose work can be seen in the nearby **City Art Gallery** (www.yorkartgallery.org.uk; daily 10am–5pm; free), which displays 600 years of British and European paintings and pottery. Behind the gallery, set within the 10-acre (4-hectare) site of Museum Gardens, is the **Yorkshire Museum**  (www.yorkshiremuseum.org.uk; daily 10am–5pm). One of the oldest museums in the country, it has important geology, natural history and archaeology collections, including a marble head of Constantine the Great who was proclaimed Roman Emperor in this city in 306. Of particular interest are the galleries featuring Roman York – Meet the People of the Empire, Capital of the North (Anglian, Viking and Medieval York), and a particularly child-friendly section, featuring fossils, skeletons and animal specimens.

THE MEDIEVAL CITY CENTRE

Cross the street in front of the museum and head straight into the old town to arrive at **Stonegate** , the finest street in York, which follows the route of the Roman Via Praetoria. Elegant shops now use the 15th- and 16th-century houses: No. 52A is the 1180 **Norman House**, the oldest surviving house in the city. Another historic site is Coffee Yard, where coffee houses were once meeting places described by the 19th-century author Laurence Sterne as "chit chat" clubs.

Stonegate leads down towards the River Ouse, where the Guildhall and **Mansion House** (www.mansionhouseyork.com; check for opening details) lie. The Mansion House is the residence of the city's Lord Mayor, the only one outside London to be accorded the title of The Right Honourable; the building was completed in 1730, 10 years before London's Mansion House. The arched passageway alongside this

Walking York Wall.

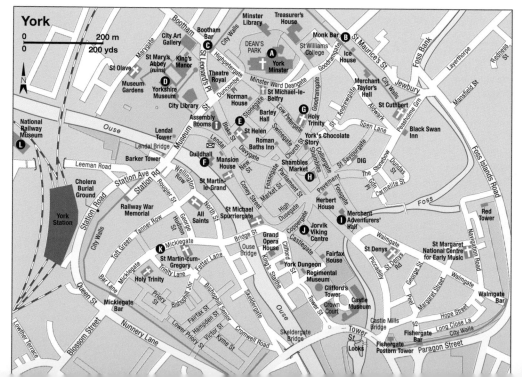

pretty building leads to the **Guildhall ⑥** (open on public occasions and by appointment only). First mentioned in 1256, it was rebuilt in the 15th century, and since 1810 the city's business has been conducted from the council chamber rich with Victorian carved desks and chairs, and with a view over the river. The impressive, oak-beamed Common Hall is a replica: the original was destroyed by German bombs.

Petergate, at the opposite end of Stonegate, leads to **Goodramgate,** where boutiques and antiques shops occupy Tudor buildings. Eleven tenements from the 11th century are known as Lady's Row; opposite is a 1960s error, an eyesore of concrete arches that brought strict controls on subsequent developments.

Halfway down the street is **Holy Trinity ⑥**, one of the most delightful of the city's churches; it has a two-tiered pulpit (1785) and a reredos with the Ten Commandments, Creed and Lord's Prayer.

Goodramgate leads down to **King's Square** and Colliergate, where the shortest street in York has the longest name: Whipmawhopmagate. A plaque suggests this is 16th-century dialect for "What a gate!" King's Square is the place to be in summer: buskers, jugglers and street artists provide some of the best free entertainment in the north of England. Here too is the York's Chocolate Story (www.yorkschocolatestory.com; daily 10am–6pm), where the tasty story of York's famous chocolate manufacturers is told on a guided tour and through interactive exhibits. Leading off the square is **The Shambles ⑥**, York's most famous street and one of the best-preserved medieval streets in all Europe. Once called Fleshammels (the street of the butchers), its broad windowsills served as shelves to display meat. The half-timbered houses lean inwards, and neighbours can shake hands across the street. Three narrow alleyways lead to **Shambles Market**, revamped from the former Newgate Market and open daily from 7am with stalls selling everything from organic foods to books, from fish to fashions. The original main market

The former butchers' quarter, The Shambles.

⊘ FACT FILE

Location 164 miles (264km) from London, 167 miles (269km) from Edinburgh.

By car M1 motorway from London to Leeds, the last 36 miles (60km) on the A1(M) and A64. Allow 3 hours.

By train Direct from London's King's Cross (approximately 2 hours, leaving every 30 minutes) and Edinburgh (2 hours 30 minutes).

Nearest airport Leeds Bradford Intl (www.leedsbradfordairport.co.uk).

Boat trips Cruises on the Ouse include 1-hour trips downstream to the Archbishop's Palace at Bishopthorpe (www.yorkboat.co.uk).

Most famous site The Minster.

Best for Yorkshire high teas Betty's Café Tea Rooms, St Helen's Square.

Festivals Jorvik Viking Festival (February), four-day Ebor Festival at York Racecourse (Knavesmire Road) – "the Ascot of the North" (August).

Historic emblem The white rose: the Wars of the Roses, immortalised in Shakespeare's *Richard III*, were fought between the House of York (white rose) and the House of Lancaster (red rose).

Royal connection The second son of a monarch is traditionally given the title Duke of York.

Tourist information Tel: 01904-550 099; www.visityork.org.

The Jorvik Viking Centre.

Micklegate Bar, the four-storey high gatehouse.

area was on **Pavement**, on the other side of Newgate Market. This was the first paved street in the city, a place of punishment (whipping, pillorying) and execution.

Fossgate, which leads from Pavement down to the River Foss, is where the richest of the city's medieval merchants used to live. Just before the river on the right is a stone portal leading to the **Merchant Adventurers' Hall** ❶ (www.theyorkcompany.co.uk; Sun–Fri 10am–4.30pm, Sun 10am–1.30pm). Still the home of the most powerful of the York guilds, the hall has a massive, timber-framed roof and a 14th-century undercroft used for receptions.

THE SOUTH SIDE OF THE OLD TOWN

The other end of Pavement leads to Coppergate and the **Jorvik Viking Centre** ❶ (www.jorvik-viking-centre.co.uk; daily Apr–Oct 10am–5pm, Nov–Mar until 4pm). The museum is based on an archaeological dig at Coppergate in the 1970s, which revealed wicker houses and shoulder-high walls, the best-preserved

Viking settlement in Britain. Visitors are whisked back to a reconstructed settlement in "time capsules" and immersed in an atmosphere evoking the Viking past. After a major refurbishment in 2017, the museum reopened with new galleries and improved displays featuring ahead-of-the-curve technology. The museum also updated the visitor ride through a new recreation of a Viking city, with more of a focus on the multicultural side to 10th-century York and the role of Viking-era women.

Castlegate behind the Viking Centre ends in a great earth mound topped by **Clifford's Tower**, thrown up by the Normans in their conquest of England. The **Castle Museum** (www.yorkcastlemuseum.org.uk; daily 9.30am–5pm), housed in what were a female and a debtors' prisons, is a folk museum with a reconstruction of a complete Yorkshire street and a glimpse of lost ways of life. There is still evidence of the former prison: the cell of the highway robber Dick Turpin is preserved; in 1739 he was sentenced next door in the Assize Court and hanged on St George's Field. Plans are under way to reimagine the museum, which include creating new temporary exhibition space, adding immersive experiences and displays, and building a riverside walkway.

On the south side of the River Ouse is **Micklegate** ❿, once York's most important street, as it was the road into the city from London. Many fine Georgian houses were built along it. But for a century and a half, visitors have been arriving by rail: York is famous for its railways, personified in George Hudson, the 19th-century "Railway King". The **National Railway Museum** ❶ (www.nrm.org.uk; daily 10am–6pm; free) is one of the greatest in the world. Exhibits include Queen Victoria's favourite travelling "home", a replica of Stephenson's *Rocket*, the Eurostar and the only "bullet train" outside Japan. Visitors can also see *Mallard*, the fastest steam train in the world.

THE MAGNIFICENT MINSTER

With fine medieval stained glass, this is the most elegant building in the north.

The Minster is the largest Gothic cathedral north of the Alps and is both a cathedral – by virtue of its archbishop's throne – and a minster because it has been served since Saxon times by a team of clergy. It has the widest Gothic nave in England, stands 196ft (60 metres) high, is 525ft (160 metres) long and 250ft (76 metres) wide across the transept. The finest stained glass in the country gives an immediate impression of airy lightness. The first church was founded in 627, followed by two Norman cathedrals and the present Gothic one, completed in 1472. Major restoration was needed after two 19th-century fires, and one in 1984, caused by lightning, destroyed the south transept roof.

ARCHITECTURAL FEATURES

The nave is Decorated Gothic in style and was completed in the 1350s. The pulpit on the left has a brass lectern, in use since 1686. The 14th-century West Window, painted in 1338, is known as the "heart of Yorkshire" because of the shape of the ornate tracery. Shields in the nave arches are the arms of nobles who fought against the Scots in the 14th century. The dragon's head peeping out from the upper gallery is a crane used to lift a font cover. To the right of the nave is the Jesse Window of 1310. The north transept is dominated by the Five Sisters' Window from 1260, the oldest complete window in the Minster.

The Chapter House (charge) off the transept was the architectural wonder of its age. It has a beautiful domed roof and fine medieval carvings on the canopied stalls. Beside the entrance to the Chapter House, the astronomical clock commemorates World War II airmen, while 400-year-old figures of Gog and Magog chime the striking clock to the right.

The screen in the crossing is decorated with the statues of 15 kings of England from William I to Henry VI. The magnificently restored Great East Window at the far end of the church has the world's largest area of medieval stained glass, depicting scenes from the Bible. On the south side of the choir, St Cuthbert's Window (1435) shows scenes from the life of the saint. The Norman crypt contains the coffin of the Minster's founder, St William.

The south transept, restored after the 1984 fire, has mirrored tables to see the new carvings, six designed by children. The Rose Window, which commemorates the end of the Wars of the Roses in 1486, escaped destruction in the fire. Walls of the Norman churches and remains of the Roman forum lie beneath the central tower in the Foundations Museum and Treasury.

Visitors who are feeling energetic can climb the 275 steps to the top of the tower, which is lantern-shaped, built in the Perpendicular style, and offers superb views of the city and the surrounding countryside.

The Minster's exterior.

The Victoria Hall in Saltaire.

YORKSHIRE

The Dales and Moors of Yorkshire are as rugged and resolute as their inhabitants. Beyond York are the great former abbeys of Whitby, Fountains and Rievaulx.

Yorkshire is England's 'Big County'. Until 1974 this region north of the River Humber was divided into three Yorkshire "Ridings", from the Old Norse trithing, meaning three administrative parts. North Riding (now largely North Yorkshire) was larger than any other county in England. Characterised by miles of moorland, the three modern counties of Yorkshire extend from the Pennines to the North Sea, and include two national parks – the Yorkshire Dales to the west of York and the North York Moors to the north – separated by the Vale of York, where the A1 follows the old Roman Road heading for Hadrian's Wall.

Limestone, shale and sandstone of the Carboniferous Age shaped the Yorkshire Dales, which are cut through by fast-flowing rivers and douched with waterfalls. The Jurassic limestone of the North York Moors has been used for houses, castles and spectacular abbeys such as Fountains and Rievaulx. To the south, the Yorkshire Wolds are chalk hills rising to 800ft (240 metres), reaching the sea at Flamborough Head. Grouse are the prize of the Moors; trout fill the short, fast rivers and streams of the Pennines and Dales.

Yorkshire is traditionally a sheep-rearing region, and incessant grazing means that, as in the rest of Britain, there is no true wilderness.

An overall pattern of dry-stone walls links the farms, villages and market towns. The buildings, constructed in local slate and stone, are unpretentious in style but perfectly suited to the needs of a pastoral community, from the farmhouse with its big, flagged, ground-floor rooms, to the field barns with just enough space to accommodate young cattle.

The farmers' way of life, evolving in isolation, bred a sturdy, independent type of person, the sort about whom James Herriot, the celebrated Dales

⊙ **Main attractions**
Saltaire
Brontë Parsonage
Yorkshire Dales National Park
Harewood House
Fountains Abbey
North York Moors National Park
Castle Howard
Rievaulx Abbey

Map on page 330

Robin Hood's Bay.

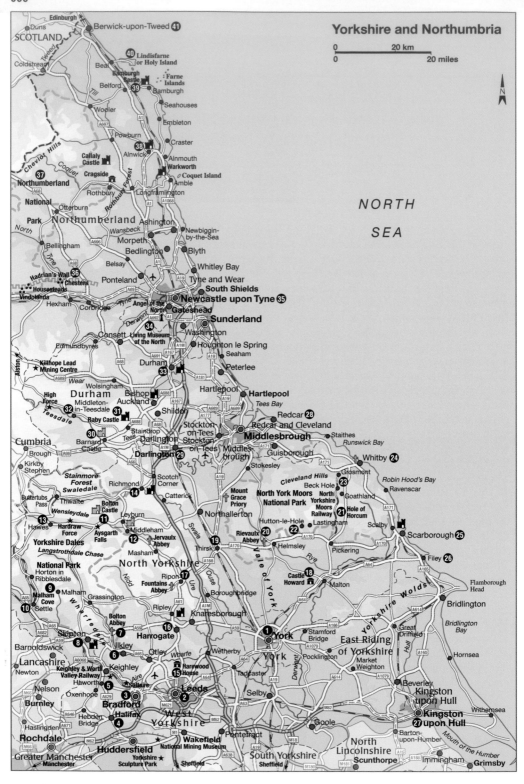

Yorkshire and Northumbria

0   20 km
0   20 miles

NORTH

SEA

SCOTLAND

Edinburgh
Duns
Coldstream
Berwick-upon-Tweed 41
Lindisfarne or Holy Island 40
Beal
Bamburgh Castle 39
Farne Islands
Belford
Bamburgh
Seahouses
Wooler
Embleton
Powburn
Craster
Callaly Castle
Alnwick 38
Almouth
Cragside
Warkworth
Northumberland 37
Coquet Island
Rothbury
Longframlington
Amble
National
Otterburn
Park
Bellingham
Northumberland
Ashington
Newbiggin-by-the-Sea
Wansbeck
Morpeth
Belsay
Bedlington
Blyth
Whitley Bay
Hadrian's Wall 36
Chesters
Ponteland
Tyne and Wear
Housesteads
South Shields
Vindolanda
Hexham
Corbridge
Angel of the North
Newcastle upon Tyne 35
Gateshead
Consett
Living Museum of the North 34
Sunderland
Edmundbyres
Washington
Houghton le Spring
Seaham
Killhope Lead Mining Centre
Durham
Peterlee
Alston
Wear
Wolsingham
Bishop Auckland 33
Durham
Hartlepool
Hartlepool
High Force 32
Middleton-in-Teesdale 31
Shildon
Tees Bay
Raby Castle
Redcar 28
Cumbria
Staindrop
Stockton-on-Tees
Redcar and Cleveland
Brough
Barnard Castle 30
Darlington
Stockton-on-Tees
Middlesbrough
Staithes
Kirkby Stephen
Darlington 29
Middlesbrough
Runswick Bay
Stainmore Forest
Richmond
Scotch Corner
Guisborough
Whitby 24
Swaledale
Catterick
Stokesley
Cleveland Hills
Grosmont
Robin Hood's Bay
Buttertubs Pass
Thwaite
Bolton Castle 14
Leyburn
Mount Grace Priory
North York Moors National Park
Beck Hole 23
Ravenscar
Wensleydale
Northallerton
North Yorkshire Moors Railway 21
Goathland
Hardraw Force 13
Aysgarth Falls
Jervaulx Abbey 12
Middleham
Hutton-le-Hole
Lastingham
Hole of Horcum
Hawes
Masham
Rievaulx Abbey 20
22
Scalby
Yorkshire Dales
Langstrothdale Chase
North Yorkshire
Thirsk 19
Helmsley
Pickering
Scarborough 25
National Park
Ripon 17
Boroughbridge
Rye
Filey 26
Horton in Ribblesdale
Fountains Abbey
Malton
Flamborough Head
Malham Cove 9
Grassington
Knaresborough
Castle Howard 18
Bridlington
Settle 10
Ripley
Bolton Abbey
Harrogate 16
Wetherby
York 1
Stamford Bridge
East Riding of Yorkshire
Bridlington Bay
Skipton 7
Ilkley
Otley
Wharfe
York
Pocklington
Great Driffield
Barnoldswick 8
Keighley & Worth Valley Railway
Keighley
Harewood House 15
Tadcaster
Market Weighton
Hornsea
Lancashire
Newton
Haworth
Saltaire
Leeds
Selby
Beverley
Nelson
Oxenhope 5
Bradford 3
2
Kingston upon Hull
Burnley
Hebden Bridge
Halifax
West Yorkshire
Goole
Kingston upon Hull 27
Withernsea
Rochdale
4
Wakefield
Pontefract
North Lincolnshire
Mouth of the Humber
Greater Manchester
Huddersfield
National Mining Museum
Barton-upon-Humber
Manchester
Yorkshire Sculpture Park
Sheffield
South Yorkshire
Scunthorpe
Immingham
Grimsby
Sheffield

vet (whose real name was Alf Wight), wrote in his bestselling books.

THE WOOL TOWNS

From Yorkshire sheep grew a wool trade that enriched the monasteries and the town of **York ❶** (see page 323). After the Industrial Revolution, however, cloth manufacturing was centred on towns to the south of the Dales. England's third-largest and Yorkshire's main city, **Leeds ❷**, is one place to go to see the region's industrial heritage. **The Armley Mills Museum** (tel: 0113-378 3173; Tue–Sat 10am–5pm, Sun 1–5pm), on the northwest side of this lively university city, was once the world's largest woollen mill and still demonstrates the machinery that once helped to make Britain the richest nation.

The Royal Armouries Museum (www.royalarmouries.org; daily 10am–5pm; free), beside the River Aire at Clarence Dock, contains an impressive collection of arms and armour organised around five themes: war (with a section on peace, too), tournament, self-defence, hunting and the Orient. There is also the Jester's Yard play area, a crossbow range and a tiltyard, where you can watch demonstrations of jousting.

The Leeds Art Gallery (www.leeds.gov.uk/artgallery; Tue–Fri, Sat 10am–5pm, Sun 11am–3pm) has works by Courbet and Sisley as well as Atkinson Grimshaw (1836–93), a local artist and one of the best painters of Victorian towns, and the great landscape painter John Sell Cotman (1782–1842). Contemporary crafts can be bought at the adjoining Craft Centre and Design Gallery (Tue–Sat 10am–5pm). The sculptor Henry Moore, who was born not far away in Castleford in 1898, studied in Leeds, and the Henry Moore Institute, with sculpture galleries, was added in 1995. His work is also to be seen at the **Yorkshire Sculpture Park** (www.ysp.co.uk; daily 10am–5pm; free, charge for car park), south of Leeds near Wakefield, where the sculptor Barbara Hepworth was born in 1903. This self-proclaimed "gallery without walls" also hosts temporary exhibitions; past commissions have included Damian Hirst and Ai Weiwei. A £3.6million visitor centre – The

The cobbled streets of Haworth.

⊘ FACT FILE

Main cities Leeds, York.

Car The A1 goes through the Vale of York. Alternative transport is strongly encouraged within the National Parks.

Bus There is a network of services including extra Moorsbus and Dales Bus (www.dalesbus.org) bus services in summer.

Train The Settle–Carlisle line and two steam railways: the North Yorkshire Moors Railway, from Pickering to Whitby, and the Embsay and Bolton Abbey Steam Railway.

Local words Many of Old Norse origin: fell (hill), scar (cliff face), dale (valley), gate (street), happen (maybe).

National Parks North York Moors (www.northyorkmoors.org.uk); Yorkshire Dales (www.yorkshiredales.org.uk).

Best stately home Castle Howard.

Most famous family The Brontës.

Food and drink Wensleydale cheese, Yorkshire pudding, mushy peas, Yorkshire curd tart, Theakston's beer.

Tourist information Leeds, tel: 0113-242 5242; Harrogate, tel: 01423-537 300; www.yorkshire.com; Scarborough, tel: 01723-383 636; www.discoveryorkshirecoast.com.

THE BRONTËS OF HAWORTH

The reputation of Yorkshire's most talented literary family brings thousands of visitors to their moorland home every year.

It has long been a matter of fascination that one family should produce not just one, but three writers of real genius. The Brontë girls – Charlotte, Emily and Anne – authored novels that are widely seen as the most powerful and enduring expressions of the English Romantic imagination. Indeed, Emily's *Wuthering Heights* is often considered for the accolade of greatest English novel of all time.

Their father, Patrick (1777–1861), was a poor boy from Emdale in County Down who made good. Patrick married Maria Branwell, from Penzance in Cornwall. She bore him six children but died of cancer in 1821 when they were all still young, leaving them in the care of their distraught father.

Patrick was to outlive all of his children, whose short, sad lives give the Brontë story a particular

Haworth, the Brontës' moor.

poignancy. The family moved to Haworth in 1820 after Patrick was appointed curate for life. His two oldest children, Maria and Elizabeth, died in 1825. The other four, often left to their own devices, created a fantasy world, writing tiny books with minuscule script. In 1846, using pseudonyms, the three girls wrote and published a book of poems, which sold just two copies.

LITERARY SUCCESS

Success came the following year with the publication of Charlotte's *Jane Eyre*. Ferndean Manor, described in the book, was probably the 16th-century home of the Cunliffes in Wycoller, reached by a 9-mile (15km) footpath from Haworth called the Brontë Way.

Charlotte's success was followed by Emily's *Wuthering Heights* and Anne's *Agnes Grey*. Charlotte had written: "Speak of the North – a lonely moor, silent and still and trackless lies." But it was Emily who most vividly described the atmosphere of Haworth's moors, which she saw as wild and savage. She used the landscape when portraying Heathcliffe in *Wuthering Heights*; he was described by Catherine, the object of his passion, as "an unreclaimed creature, without refinement, without cultivation; an arid wilderness of furze and whinstone".

Charlotte became a literary celebrity. In 1854 she married the Rev. Arthur Bell Nicholls. Both Emily and her brother Branwell died in 1848, aged 30 and 31. Branwell had become addicted to alcohol and opium, his health compromised, leaving him easy prey to tuberculosis, the disease that also killed Emily. Anne died of the same disease a year later, aged 29, and Charlotte in 1855, aged 38 and pregnant. Patrick – the last of the Brontës – died in 1861, aged 84. The parson's body was lowered into the vault within the altar rails and placed beside the coffin of Charlotte.

All the Brontës except Anne, who was buried in Scarborough, lie in the family vault near to where the Brontës' pew stood in the old church of St Michael and All Angels.

Still very visible is the congestion of old tombstones in the burial ground, recalling mid-19th-century conditions here, when average life expectancy was 28 and the town was racked with typhus and cholera.

Weston – opened in 2019, home to an indoor gallery, restaurant and shop. In Wakefield itself, a stylish public gallery, **The Hepworth** (www.hepworthwakefield. org; daily 10am–5pm; free), showcases modern British art. The gallery also branched outside in 2019 with its new Riverside Gallery Garden – one of the UK's biggest free gardens.

These three venues – the "Yorkshire sculpture triangle" – hosted the inaugural Yorkshire Sculpture International, a festival of exhibitions and events running from June to September 2019, curated by sculptor Phyllida Barlow. The festival will take place every three years (next event in 2022).

Bradford ❸ proudly celebrates its most famous artistic son, David Hockney, who was born in this mill town in 1935. Many of his paintings are on the walls of the **1853 Gallery** (www. saltsmill.org.uk; Mon–Fri 10am–5.30pm, Sat–Sun 10am–6pm; free) in Salts Mill, **Saltaire**. This well-preserved "model" village, founded by 19th-century wool baron Titus Salt, was designated a Unesco World Heritage Site in 2001.

Its design was influential in the "garden city" movement and illustrates the philanthropic paternalism of the time: Salt enshrined his ideals in a mill, hospital, school, library, church and almshouses, but religiously excluded pubs.

Two other famous sons are the composer Frederick Delius (1862–1934), who inspires regular festivals, and the writer J.B. Priestley (1894–1984), who wrote prolifically and with an acute eye for Yorkshire characters. Bradford also has the **National Media Museum** (www. scienceandmediamuseum.org.uk; daily 10am–6pm; free), which has one of the best photographic collections in the country, as well as hands-on film fun.

In the 1950s, immigrants from the Indian Subcontinent were encouraged to work in Bradford's mills, and today over 30 percent of the city's population is Muslim. In mid-June each year, Bradford Mela (www.bradfordfestival.org. uk), a one-day festival (now part of the bigger three-day Bradford Festival) held in City Park, celebrates this community's roots with music, dance, street theatre and crafts.

⊙ **Kids**

A great place for children is Eureka! The National Children's Museum, located in Discovery Road, Halifax. This is England's first "hands-on" museum designed especially to inspire children to learn about the world surrounding them. It is open Tue–Fri 10am–4pm, Sat–Sun until 5pm, daily 10am–5pm during school holidays (www.eureka.org.uk).

Yorkshire Sculpture Park.

Halifax ❹, west of Bradford, was another important wool town, noted for its carpets and yarns. Its 18th-century Piece Hall, set amid stunning scenery, is the only remaining cloth hall in Yorkshire. Cottage weavers sold their "pieces" in 315 small rooms in the colonnaded galleries that are now central to the impressive £19-million redevelopment project featuring the Heritage Interpretation Centre, independent shops and restaurants, as well as hosting concerts and festivals. To the southwest of Halifax lie the attractive Pennine woollen mill towns of **Hebden Bridge** and **Heptonstall**, both good bases for Pennine walks. A little further north is another Pennine mill village, **Haworth** ❺, the second-most popular literary shrine in England after Shakespeare's Stratford. The Brontës moved to Haworth in 1820, and today more than 1 million visitors arrive each year to see the fine Georgian **Parsonage** (www.bronte.org.uk; daily Apr–Oct 10am–5.30pm, Nov–Mar 10am–5pm), restored to look as it did when it was the writers' home. The main street of this hillside village was surfaced with stone setts, to provide horses with a good grip as they drew laden carts. The flanking gritstone houses were built right up to the edge of the street. Houses with a third storey and long, narrow windows were both the home and workplace of handloom weavers – in the time of the Brontës more than 1,200 looms were chattering in the village. The parish church has a Brontë memorial chapel, and an admirer from the USA paid for the stained-glass window on which Charlotte is commemorated. The walk to Top Withens, the inspiration for *Wuthering Heights*, is about 5 miles (8km). Haworth Station is the headquarters of the working steam railway, and the **Keighley and Worth Valley Railway Preservation Society** (www.kwvr.co.uk; July–Aug daily, tel: 01535-645 214 for hours rest of year).

A dozen miles north of Haworth is **Ilkley** ❻, a Victorian inland spa for the prosperous burghers of Leeds and Bradford. Ilkley has immortalised its rugged climate in the Yorkshire anthem *On Ilkla Moor baht 'at*, which, translated,

The ruins of Bolton Abbey.

tells you that it is not prudent to venture forth on Ilkley Moor without a hat.

THE DALES

To the north of Ilkley lies the 680-sq mile (1,762-sq km) **Yorkshire Dales National Park** (www.yorkshiredales.org.uk), characterised by dry-stone walls (each dale has its own distinctive pattern of dry-stoning) bustling market towns, lonely farmhouses and cathedral-like caverns. Dales are valleys, and they take their name from the rivers that created them – Ribblesdale, Wensleydale, Swaledale. Motorists should look out for cyclists and animals on the narrow winding roads or, better still, use the train and bus services within the park. The easiest excursion from Ilkley takes you into surrounding Wharfedale, an alluring mix of water, wood, crag and castle. **Bolton Abbey ❼** (www.boltonabbey.com; daily mid-Oct–mid-Mar 9am–6pm, mid-Mar–May, Sept–mid-Oct 9am–7pm, June–Aug 9am–9pm, last entry two/three hours before closing), 5 miles (8km) northwest of Ilkley, dates from the 12th century. Its picturesque ruins, surrounding footpaths and stunning location by the River Wharf have long made it a major attraction, and it can be reached by steam train from Embsay Station.

West of Ilkley is the market town of **Skipton ❽**, "the gateway to the Dales". Its position on the Leeds–Liverpool canal brought it great prosperity during the Industrial Revolution. Many of the warehouses still stand, and so does the much older **Skipton Castle** (www.skiptoncastle.co.uk; Apr–Sept Mon–Sat 10am–5pm, Sun 11am–5pm, Oct–Mar until 4pm), home of the powerful Clifford family from the 14th to the 17th century. Skipton provides easy access to **Malham Cove ❾**, one of the great wonders of the Yorkshire Dales. Knee-cracking steps lead to the tip of this immense cliff where limestone pavement with clints (blocks of worn limestone with crevices known as "grykes") form a pattern like the whorls of a brain. The view from here is magnificent. It is possible to continue walking north along the Pennine Way. **Gordale Scar**, 1.6 miles (2km) east of Malham, has 16ft (5-metre) overhanging cliffs described by the poet William Wordsworth as a lair "where young lions crouch".

To the west of Malham is the small market town of **Settle ❿**, separated from **Giggleswick** by the River Ribble. Beside Market Place, which comes alive on Tuesday, is The Shambles, which, like York's, were once a butchers' domain. Ye Olde Naked Man Café got its name when it was an inn and fashion was deemed to be needlessly flamboyant. Settle is an excellent point from which to explore Ribblesdale or begin a circular tour of the flat-topped Ingleborough Hill, taking in the magnificent Ribblehead Viaduct, built from 1870 to 1875 to carry the Settle–Carlisle railway across Batty Moss. This trans-Pennine line has the highest mainline station in England, 1,150ft (350 metres) up, at **Dent**.

To the north, **Wensleydale** is broad and wooded and seems serene until

The Settle to Carlisle line.

Wensleydale, the best-known cheese in Yorkshire.

The Moors at Sutton Bank.

the eye catches the forbidding **Bolton Castle** ⓫ (www.boltoncastle.co.uk; mid-Feb–Oct daily 10am–5pm, Feb–Mar, Oct until 4pm) perched on a hillside. Tradition has it that the mortar was mixed with ox blood to strengthen the building. Wander through the stables area into the open courtyard that was once the Great Hall and you can easily imagine yourself transported back to 1568 when Mary, Queen of Scots was imprisoned here. The building was fortified in the 14th century by Richard le Scrope, chancellor to Richard II. He was a friend of Chaucer, and the poet used him as the model for his *Knight's Tale*. Nearby are the impressive **Aysgarth Falls**, where there is a National Park Centre and well-signposted spectacular walks. At the bottom of the dale is the town of **Middleham** ⓬, famous for its racehorse stables and **castle** (www.english-heritage.org.uk; Apr–Sept daily 10am–6pm, Oct daily 10am–4pm, Nov–Mar Sat–Sun 10am–4pm), childhood home of Richard III. As Duke of Gloucester, he came to Middleham to be tutored by the Earl of Warwick, and he married

the earl's daughter, Anne. His death in 1485 at Bosworth (near Leicester), the final battle in the Wars of the Roses, ended the 24-year reign of the House of York. The castle remains include a 12th-century keep, 13th-century chapel, and 14th-century gatehouse.

Near the head of the dale and in the heart of the Yorkshire Dales National Park is the excellent **Dales Countryside Museum** (www.dalescountrysidemu seum.org.uk; Feb–Oct daily 10am–5pm, Nov–Dec until 4.30pm) at **Hawes** ⓭ (from *haus*, a mountain pass). On view is a traditional dales kitchen and displays relating to dairy farming, industry, local crafts and community life. Nearby, approached through the Green Dragon Inn, is the impressive **Hardraw Force**, England's highest unbroken waterfall.

In neighbouring Gayle is the **Wensleydale Creamery Visitor Centre** (www.wensleydale.co.uk; daily 10am–4pm), incorporating the Yorkshire Wensleydale Cheese Experience, where visitors can watch the production of Wensleydale cheese and taste the results, as well as take part in activities for all the family.

Buttertubs Pass, at 1,726ft (526 metres) above sea level, links Wensleydale with **Swaledale** to the northeast ("buttertubs" are deep limestone shafts). Swaledale is steep and rocky, noted for its intricate patterns of drystone walls and field barns. It also has **Richmond** ⑭, a market town with a cobbled square, impressive Norman **castle** (www.english-heritage.org.uk; Apr–Sept daily 10am–6pm, Oct daily 10am–5pm, Nov–Mar Sat–Sun 10am–4pm) and the splendidly restored Georgian Theatre Royal (tel: 01748-825 252).

NORTH FROM LEEDS

There are other ways to leave Leeds than via Ilkley. Strike north on the A61 and, after 9 miles (14km), you reach the richly ornate **Harewood House** ⑮ (www.harewood.org; Apr–Oct daily grounds: 10am–6pm, state rooms: 11am–4pm). Its interiors are by Robert Adam, furniture by Thomas Chippendale and gardens by "Capability" Brown. It also has a remarkable bird park. Built in the 1760s by Edwin Lascelles, whose fortune derived from plantations in the West Indies, the house is now the home of the Earl and Countess of Harewood.

Eight miles (13km) further along the A61 is **Harrogate** ⑯, where the **Royal Pump Room** stands over the famous sulphur wells and still serves the strongest sulphur water in Europe. The **museum** (tel: 01423-556 188; Mon–Sat 10am–4pm, Sun noon–4pm) has displays recalling Harrogate's heyday as the Queen of Inland Spas, while the **Mercer Art Gallery** (same hours; free) is particularly strong on the art of the Victorian period.

Being on a hilltop and a late starter among Yorkshire towns, Harrogate was able to develop gracefully. Many 19th-century buildings have their original cast-iron canopies. The protected 200-acre (90-hectare) Stray gives the town a spacious appearance, added to by a number of gardens. **Harlow Carr Botanical Gardens** (www.rhs.org.uk; daily Mar–Oct 9.30am–6pm, Nov–Feb

until 4pm), sustained by the Northern Horticultural Society, is comprehensive, with a spectacular Streamside Garden and ornamental gardens. The woodland, arboretum and wild-flower meadow are home to birds, squirrels, stoat and roe deer. Harrogate promotes a spring flower show and has the permanent ground for the three-day Great Yorkshire Show in July, the largest agricultural show in the north of England. The prestigious Harrogate Fine Art and Antiques fairs are held twice a year, in the spring and autumn.

Neighbouring **Knaresborough** is celebrated for **Mother Shipton's Cave** (www.mothershipton.co.uk; Apr–Oct Mon–Fri 10am–4.30pm, weekends and school holidays until 5.30pm, Mar Sat–Sun 10am–5.30pm), birthplace and home of England's most famous prophet. She foretold the Great Fire of London, the defeat of the Spanish Armada, the coming of the motor car, and her own death in 1561. In Castle Grounds are **Knaresborough Castle** and the **Old Court House Museum** (tel: 01423-556 188; Apr–Oct daily 11am–4pm). Take

Tempting eats at Betty's Café Tea Rooms, Harrogate.

⊙ Eat

Betty's Café Tea Rooms is the best place for cakes and pastries in Harrogate. This Yorkshire institution was founded by Frederick Belmont, a young Swiss confectioner, in 1919. Now, over 90 years later, you will also find Betty's in York and the market towns of Northallerton and Ilkley.

Swaledale near Keld.

the castle tour and then try a game of medieval putting or bowling.

Four miles (6.5km) to the north, **Ripley** is a village conceived in the style of Alsace in France with a town hall labelled "Hôtel de Ville"; Sir William Amcotts Ingilby and his wife, who were largely responsible for rebuilding the town in the 1820s, were great Francophiles. **Ripley Castle** (www.ripleycastle.co.uk; available to view by guided tour only; check website for details) has been the home of the Ingleby family for 700 years. Take the time to explore the Castle Gardens, deer park and tearooms.

Further along the A61, **Ripon** ⑰ developed around the sombre Saxon cathedral founded by St Wilfrid in the 7th century. The massive seven-light east window, 51ft (16 metres) high and half as wide, dates from the 14th century, but the most special feature is the crypt under the central tower, dating from 672, which is redolent of Saxon times. Nearby is **Newby Hall** (www.newbyhall.co.uk; Apr–Sept Tue–Sun, July–Aug also Mon, house: guided tours noon–3pm with exceptions, grounds: 11am–5pm), an Adam house set in 25 acres (10 hectares) of splendid garden.

Four miles (6km) to the west are the atmospheric remains of *Sancta Maria Fonctibus*, **Fountains Abbey** (www.fountainsabbey.org.uk; Apr–Sept 10am–6pm, Oct–Mar 10am–5pm), which was once Britain's richest Cistercian monastery. In 1132 monks first arrived in Skelldale, "thick-set with thorns, fit rather to be the lair of wild beasts than the home of human beings". Kitchens and dormitories survive, a tribute to old craftsmanship, giving today's visitor an unusually clear idea of medieval monastic life. In the 18th century the estate was landscaped with the 400-acre (160-hectare) deer park and the elegant **Studley Royal Water Garden** with ornamental lakes, temples and statues.

NORTH YORK MOORS

The North York Moors are a place apart. The most sharply defined of Britain's 15 national parks, they are bounded on two sides by steeply plunging escarpments and on a third by towering cliffs that defy the North Sea. Only where neighbouring farmland slopes up gradually from the Vale of Pickering do the Moors lack an obvious frontier. Within their 553 sq miles (1,380 sq km) they embrace the largest unbroken expanse of heather moorland in England. In summer the heather flings a coat of regal purple across the full width of the Moors, from the Vale of York to the sea. Other seasons have colours, too: the bright green of bilberries in spring, russet bracken in autumn and in winter subdued greys and browns.

The Moors can be approached directly from York or from the A1. On the eastern side of the Vale of York, on the A64, is **Castle Howard** ⑱ (www.castlehoward.co.uk; mid-Mar–Oct daily 10.30am–3pm, then guided tour only at 3.30pm and 4pm, gardens open all year 10am–6pm). The first building to be designed by Sir John Vanburgh

(1664–1726), it inspired 20th-century poet John Betjeman to write: "Hail Castle Howard! Hail Vanburgh's noble dome, Where Yorkshire in her splendour rivals Rome!" The centrepiece of the entire house is the marble-floored hall, which rises up to the magnificent 70ft (21-metre) dome, across which charge great "Horses of the Sun". The principal rooms contain paintings by Gainsborough, Reynolds and Rubens and furniture by Sheraton and Chippendale. The Pre-Raphaelite chapel has stained glass by Edward Burne-Jones. The west wing, a Palladian addition, has a magnificent Long Gallery. The stunning gardens and grounds include a walled rose garden, lakes, fountains, statues and woodland. There is also a plant centre and adjacent holiday park in Coneysthorpe village.

Just off the A1 is the thriving market town of **Thirsk** ⑲, now famous as the "Darrowby" of James Herriot's vet books, which translated into the successful 1980s television series *All Creatures Great and Small*. **The World of James Herriot** (www.worldofjamesherriot.

com; daily 10am–5pm, Nov–Feb until 4pm), located in the vet's former home and surgery, is an award-winning museum devoted to the author.

RIEVAULX ABBEY

Approaching the Moors from this southwesterly direction, most visitors will arrive in **Helmsley**, whose quaint shops give it a distinctly "Cotswolds" feel. Nearby, tucked amid hanging woods and placid pastures deep in the Rye Valley, are the breathtaking ruins of **Rievaulx Abbey** ⑳ (www.english-heritage.org.uk; Apr–Sept daily 10am–6pm, Oct daily 10am–5pm, Nov–Mar Sat–Sun 10am–4pm), an extensive Cistercian monastery founded in the 12th century. The now supremely beautiful setting was viewed as "a place of horror and waste" by the abbey's 12 founder monks, who arrived directly from France in 1132. Larger than Fountains Abbey, Rievaulx was both the first and biggest Cistercian abbey in the north of England. At its 13th-century peak it housed 150 monks and 500 lay brothers "so that the church

⊙ Fact

Fountains Abbey has been linked with some folklore about the fugitive Robin Hood. Friar Tuck, Robin Hood's partner in crime, is said to have been a monk at Fountains Abbey, who joined their band of "merry men" after challenging Robin to a sword fight. It is also thought that Robin's bow was once kept at the abbey.

Castle Howard.

swarmed with them, like a hive with bees". Because of the abbey's narrow site, between steep banks of the Rye, the church was aligned north–south. Its greatest glory is its chancel, from around 1230. Standing to its full height, with two tiers of lancet windows above cluster-column arches, it is a majestic example of the Early English style.

Northwest of Rievaulx, by the A19, is another romantic ruin, **Mount Grace Priory** (www.english-heritage.org.uk; Apr–Sept daily 10am–6pm, Oct daily 10am–5pm, Nov–Mar Sat–Sun 10am–4pm). This is the best preserved of Britain's 10 Carthusian monasteries. A monk's cell has been restored and an exhibition is housed in a handsome Jacobean mansion converted from the priory's gatehouse.

Ryedale is just one among a network of dales penetrating the great dome of moorland. In some places they create dramatic natural features, such as the **Hole of Horcum** ㉑ above the Vale of Pickering; elsewhere they enfold villages and farmhouses built mainly of warm, honey-coloured sandstone.

Rievaulx Abbey.

The prettiest villages include **Hutton-le-Hole** ㉒ in Farndale, with a broad green, and 17th- and 18th-century limestone cottages built by Quaker weavers. The **Ryedale Folk Museum** here (www.ryedalefolkmuseum.co.uk; daily Apr–Sep 10am–5pm, mid-Feb–Mar, Oct–Nov 10am–4pm) is the premier museum of moorland life. There are a number of vernacular buildings in the grounds, an Iron Age roundhouse and displays of traditional craft making, as well as an art gallery. Nearby Lastingham has a splendid Norman crypt.

On the northern flanks, above Eskdale, are **Goathland** and **Beck Hole** ㉓, the former the setting for the TV series *Heartbeat*, the latter a delightful hamlet with an arc of cottages facing a green. Quoits is played here, inquests afterwards being conducted in the Birch Hall Inn, where beer is served through a hatch in a flagstone bar adorned with quoiting pictures. **The Moors Centre** (www.northyorkmoors.org.uk; daily mid-Feb–Mar, Nov–Dec 10.30am–4pm, Apr–July, Sept–Oct 10am–5pm, Aug 9.30am–5.30pm; free), a showcase for

⊘ THE END OF THE MONASTERIES

When Henry VIII issued the Suppression Act in April 1536 there were 800 monasteries, nunneries and friaries in England and Wales populated by 10,000 monks, canons, nuns and friars. The Act was ostensibly in response to a six-month survey by a team of royal visitors that found "manifest sin, vicious, carnal and abominable living daily used and committed amongst the little and small abbeys". But this was a smokescreen: Henry wanted the religious houses' wealth to replenish his own treasury. Most had agreed to acknowledge Henry as Head of the new Church of England after his acrimonious break with the Catholic Church of Rome over his divorce arrangements. Only the smaller establishments were at first dissolved, but the manner of their repression led to a rebellion, known as The Pilgrimage of Grace, as the dissolved houses were defiantly re-inhabited, often with the support of the larger houses. The king retaliated, forcing the surrender of the larger monasteries. Four years after the Act was passed not a single monastery, nunnery or friary remained.

By the end of Henry's reign, two-thirds had been sold off, saving the king from bankruptcy. Their grandeur and wealth can be glimpsed at Fountains and Rievaulx, which are among the best preserved of Henry's ruins.

the **National Park** and starting point for waymarked walks, is at **Danby**, 12 miles (18km) west.

Heading north across the Moors to the sea, from **Pickering** to **Whitby**, is the steam-powered **North Yorkshire Moors Railway** (www.nymr.co.uk; Easter–Nov; talking timetable on 01751-472 508, ext 1). A stop in Pickering should include a visit to the Beck Isle Museum of Rural Life (www.beckislemuseum.org.uk; Apr–Sept 10am–4pm, Feb–Mar, Oct–Nov daily until 4pm), where the photography of Sydney Smith (1884–1956) is a beautiful record of rural England in the first half of the 20th century. The most dramatic section of the railway journey is Newton Dale, with sheer cliffs 400ft (120 metres) high. For the more energetic, there is the 42-mile (68km) Lyke Wake Walk, which crosses the Moors between Osmotherley and Robin Hood's Bay.

COASTAL HIGHLIGHTS

The Moors end at the east coast, where breaks in the precipitous cliffs provide space for pretty villages and the occasional town. **Whitby** ⑭ is a picturesque fishing port with a jumble of pantile-roof cottages climbing from the harbour. On East Cliff are the 13th-century remains of **Whitby Abbey** (www.english-heritage.org.uk; Apr–Sept daily 10am–6pm, Oct daily 10am–5pm, Nov–Mar Sat–Sun 10am–4pm), on which site a 7th-century monk wrote the *Song of Creation*, considered to mark the start of English literature. The ruins are said to have inspired Bram Stoker, author of *Dracula*. The Sutcliffe Gallery in Flowergate exhibits and sells the evocative Victorian photographs of Whitby and its hinterland by Frank Sutcliffe (1853–1941). The Antarctic and Pacific explorer Captain Cook (1728–79) lived in this former whaling port – a whale's jawbone still acts as an arch to remind people of the town's former trade. **Captain Cook Memorial Museum** (www.cookmuseumwhitby.co.uk; daily Apr–Oct 9.45am–5pm, mid-Feb–Mar 11am–3pm) in Grape Lane is the focal point of a heritage trail tracing his life throughout the region. To the north of Whitby, steep roads lead down to **Runswick Bay**, a self-consciously pretty

Whitby harbour and abbey.

Captain Cook, the Pacific explorer and Whitby's famous son.

The cobbled streets of Robin Hood's Bay.

assortment of fishermen's cottages, and Staithes, where the young Cook was briefly and unhappily apprenticed to a grocer. To the south, seekers after solitude can divert from the coastal road to find **Ravenscar** – "the resort that never was". It has fine walks, but never developed economically beyond one rather imposing cliff-top hotel.

Robin Hood's Bay, a popular resort close by, once offered sanctuary to the benign outlaw and was a haunt of smugglers. Off its main street run the snickets (narrow lanes) that, together with the diminutive dock, give Robin Hood's Bay its Toytown character. Time should be spent exploring the intimate network, full of odd corners and sunny squares.

Further south stands **Scarborough** ㉕, whose origins as a posh watering hole are exemplified by the imposing frontage of the Grand Hotel, among the handsomest in Europe when it opened in 1867.

The 12th-century **castle** (www.english-heritage.org.uk; Apr–Sept daily 10am–6pm, Oct daily 10am–5pm, Nov–Mar Sat–Sun 10am–4pm) is worth seeing. Anne Brontë – who, like so many invalids, came for the bracing air – is buried in the graveyard of St Mary's. The town also has an enviable theatrical reputation built around Alan Ayckbourn, the local-born playwright, who premieres most of his plays at the Stephen Joseph Theatre.

Filey ㉖ offers unpretentious delights, with amusement arcades, a splendid beach and Filey Brigg, the breakwater at the north end of the bay. Filey Brigg is also the finishing (or starting) point of the 110-mile (177km) Cleveland Way (www.nationaltrail.co.uk), which takes hardier walkers up the coast as far as Saltburn before heading inland right down to Rievaulx and Helmsley.

THE YORKSHIRE WOLDS

To the south of Filey, the dramatic 400ft (130-metre) cliffs of Flamborough Head are where the chalk ridge of the Yorkshire Wolds meets the sea. Further south, and a little inland, is **Beverley**, a picture-postcard mix of medieval and Georgian streets. The town's main attractions are the Gothic minster and its former chapel, St Mary's, which between them contain one of the largest collections of carvings in the world. The minster dates from 1220, and among its wood and stone carvings are 68 misericords and the elegant Percy tomb of the 14th century.

At **Kingston upon Hull** ㉗, usually referred to simply as Hull, on the River Humber, **The Deep** (www.thedeep.co.uk; daily 10am–6pm), a spectacular aquarium, has sharks and other sea creatures, including simulations of those species now extinct, seen from Europe's deepest viewing tunnel and the world's only underwater lift.

The house where William Wilberforce was born in 1758 is now a museum (tel: 01482-300 300; Mon–Sat 10am–4.30pm, Sun 11am–4pm; free), covering the history of slave trade that Wilberforce helped to outlaw.

WILDLIFE ON MOOR AND DALE

The wildness of the Yorkshire landscape attracts a variety of birds and encourages carpets of springtime flowers.

Among the region's varied wildlife, the red grouse, target of the sporting shooters, holds pride of place. A bird that is endemic to Britain, it is also the only bird that remains on the open moor in winter. Its coarse yet cheerful call, uttered as it flies over the heather and often written as "go-back, go-back, go-back", is the archetypal sound of the North York Moors.

In spring the grouse is joined by snipe, plover and golden plover. The Moors are also home to England's largest, though modest, populations of merlins. The Swainby moors are one of the strongholds of this small, darting hawk. Also seen on occasion is the hen harrier, a truly magnificent bird with an enormous wingspan that hunts by flying low over the heather and suddenly swooping sideways. Upland waders – curlews, redshanks, dunlins – fare best on the well-maintained grouse moors.

The Dales support a good population of dippers, with some kingfishers and, in spring and summer, grey wagtails and sandpipers. Mature woodland is home to green and greater spotted woodpeckers and flycatchers, while in the forest plantations of the Moors are crossbills and nightjars.

Roe deer and, to a lesser extent, red and fallow deer can be found where there is woodland cover, and there are sika deer in Studley Royal, part of Fountains Abbey estate. Mink, introduced via Lancashire fur farms, have spread through the area, but in the rivers, otters are scarce, their numbers only slowly beginning to recover. Crow Wood, home of the Moors Centre, has a bird hide and feeding station where visitors can observe woodland species such as goldfinches, nuthatches and green woodpeckers.

FLORA

Several flower species reach their northern or southern limit on the Moors. On Levisham Moor are two arctic-alpine species at the edge of their range – chickweed wintergreen and dwarf cornel, a kind of miniature dogwood. The early purple orchid shows up against the limestone of the Dales, and the yellow mountain pansy is found in many areas. In the moist wooded ravines, such as Gunnerside Gill in Swaledale, are the star-shaped flowers of the spring sandwort.

The rare Lady's Slipper orchid, too, can rear its pretty head, if you are lucky enough to see one. But while other more common species, such as globeflower and bird's-eye primrose, are also found, it is perhaps the more familiar flowers that give most delight. The Farndale daffodils are famous, and there are carpets of bluebells at Glaisdale, Hasty Bank near Stokesley and other places. Nowhere are snowdrops prettier than on the banks of Mulgrave Old Castle, Sandsend. And on early spring walks in the Forge Valley, or through the woods at Sunnington, popular flowers such as wood anemone, wood sorrel, violet and primrose, as well as shyer species such as early purple orchid, brush the boots at almost every step.

Red grouse.

Lindisfarne Castle, Holy Island.

THE NORTHEAST

The lands of the northeast are wild, wide-open spaces, littered with evidence of a turbulent past. Newcastle is its cultural capital, and Durham its most historic city.

History is everywhere in these bleak northern hills – the last flourish of the Pennines before they cross the borders into Scotland. It was a grim posting for Roman soldiers stationed along Hadrian's Wall, but it appealed to the Christians, who chose lonely Lindisfarne on the wild, sandy Northumbrian shore as a bastion and exemplar of the early church. Incursions came from the Vikings, who left their language in such local dialect names as *stell* (sheepfold) and *beck* (stream): the local "Geordie" dialect is the strongest in England.

The Normans came next, ravaging Northumbria, as it was then known, in their pitiless "harrying of the North"; but they were builders, too, and they raised the mighty cathedral at Durham. The Scottish border was always a volatile place and, for some 300 years until the early 17th century, rustic gangsters called "reivers" ruled the roost.

Coal mining put the area in the forefront of the Industrial Revolution, and in the 20th century Britain's major shipbuilding yards grew up along the Tyne and Wear rivers, but those times are now passed.

The farming community, raising both sheep and cattle, is finding life as hard as anywhere in Britain. A tourism campaign has dubbed the north Pennines "England's last wilderness" and at Kielder, the largest man-made forest has proved a great attraction.

TEESDALE AND THE PENNINES

Redcar , the first beach resort in this region, is a lively playground with a sandy beach that serves the former industrial centres of **Middlesbrough**, **Stockton-on-Tees** and **Darlington** ㉙. The region boomed in the 19th century as coal and iron were discovered and the railways pioneered an undreamed-of prosperity. George Stephenson's *Locomotion No. 1,*

⊙ Main attractions
Bowes Museum
Durham Cathedral
Living Museum of the North
Newcastle quayside
Hadrian's Wall
Alnwick Castle
Bamburgh Castle
Lindisfarne

⊙ Maps on pages
330, 347, 350

George Stephenson's Locomotion No 1.

⊙ Fact

The Quakers who ran the London Lead Company built the model town of Nenthead in Cumbria, where they introduced compulsory schooling for their employees and inaugurated the country's first free library. Founded in 1753, with its headquarters at Middleton-in-Teesdale, the company's Quaker origins meant that it tried to provide for its workers who suffered appalling conditions underground working with the lead.

built in 1825, is displayed at **Head of Steam** (www.head-of-steam.co.uk; Apr–Sept Tue–Sun 10am–4pm, Oct–Mar Wed–Sun 11am–3.30pm), Darlington's railway museum. The locomotive ran on the world's first railway line, from Darlington to Stockton.

Sixteen miles (25km) to the west on the River Tees is **Barnard Castle** ㉚, capital of Teesdale. Wednesday is market day on "the cobbles" of Butter Market, and the first Saturday of the month the town is crowded with farmers bringing their produce to be sold. The **Castle** (www.english-heritage.org.uk; Apr–Sept daily 10am–6pm, Oct daily 10am–5pm, Nov–Mar Sat–Sun 10am–4pm) stands on a bluff above the River Tees, with two towers and the remains of a 15th-century great chamber. Follow Newgate out of Barnard Castle to reach the extraordinary **Josephine and John Bowes Museum** (www.thebowesmuseum. org.uk; daily 10am–5pm). Looking like a grand French château, its outstanding collection of French and Spanish paintings include El Grecos and Goyas. There are also tapestries, ceramics and lace

exhibits. The highlight of the museum is the extraordinary, life-size, silver swan automaton, made in the late 18th century and still in working order. Every day at 2pm, visitors can watch as it dips its head and plucks a fish from the "water".

Just outside Barnard Castle is **Raby Castle** ㉛ (www.rabycastle.com; May–June, Sept Sun–Wed, July–Aug Sun–Fri, castle: 1–4.30pm, gardens: 11am–5pm), a fine medieval fortification set in a 200-acre (80-hectare) deer park. It has decorated period rooms, a 14th-century kitchen and stables full of period carriages. **Cotherstone**, just west of Barnard Castle, is many people's favourite Teesdale village, but **Middleton-in-Teesdale** ㉜ is the real centre for Upper Teesdale. A staging post on the Pennine Way, here the moors start to crowd in on the river, making it a superb centre for exploring such sites as **High Force**, a few miles to the west. This is the greatest waterfall in England, which crashes 70ft (21 metres). Continue on the B6277 to **Alston** in the valley of the River South Tyne, where the **South Tynedale Railway** (www.south-tynedale-railway.org.

Durham Cathedral on the River Wear.

⊙ FACT FILE

Main towns Newcastle, Durham.
By Rail 3 hours from London King's Cross; 2 hours from Edinburgh.
By Road A1 and M1 from London, about 4 hours.
By Ferry From North Shields to the Netherlands (overnight 15/16 hours).
Airports Newcastle International (www. newcastleairport.com).
Best wildlife The Farne Islands.
Most historic places Holy Island; Hadrian's Wall, Hexham Abbey.
Best for children Roman Army Museum; Discovery Museum; Living Museum of the North at Beamish.
Tourist information Northumberland, www.visitnortheastengland.com; Durham, tel: 03000-262 626, www.thisisdurham.com; Newcastle, tel: 0191-440 5720, www.new castlegateshead.com.

uk; closed in winter) runs steam- and diesel-hauled passenger trips beside the river. Another local experience is the **Killhope Lead Mining Centre** (www.killhope.org.uk; Apr–Oct daily 10.30am–5pm) to the east along the A689, where visitors can see the workings of the lead mines and go underground.

Between Barnard Castle and Durham at Bishop Auckland is **Auckland Castle** (www.aucklandcastle.org; closed until end of 2019 for refurbishment, check website for opening times; Bishop's Deer Park: daily throughout the year 7am–dusk), residence of Durham's bishops since Norman times. Its throne room, state rooms and the largest private chapel in Europe are open to the public. The castle is run by the Auckland Castle Trust and plans to restore and regenerate the castle are in motion.

DURHAM CITY

The cathedral and castle of **Durham ㉝**, caught in a loop in the River Wear, are both Unesco World Heritage sites. To tour this compact and friendly university town, start at the tourist information point in Millennium Place next to the market place. On the north side are **St Nicholas' Church Ⓐ**, once part of the city walls, and **Guildhall Ⓑ**, with a Tudor doorway and balconies. South of the square, Saddler Street and Owen Gate lead to **Palace Green Ⓒ**. From here there is a grand view of the city's finest buildings, including the cathedral and legacies of a 17th-century benefactor, Bishop Cosin. On the left is the elegant 17th-century red-brick **Bishop Cosin's Hall Ⓓ**, and, bearing right, **Bishop Cosin's Library Ⓔ**, a favourite backdrop for photographs of students who have just graduated. Adjoining is the Palace Green Library home to the Museum of Archaeology (tel: 0191-334 2932; Mon noon–5pm, Tue–Sun 10am–5pm; free), which explores 10,000 years of life in Durham. A gateway to the right of Bishop Cosin's Library leads to University College in **Durham Castle Ⓕ** (tel: 0191-334 2932; guided tours only: phone for times). One of the finest Norman palaces in Britain, it was the domain of the powerful Prince Bishops of Durham, who had their own parliament, laws, coinage and army.

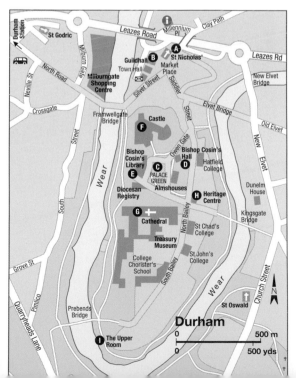

Bowes Museum, Barnard Castle.

Quote

"Half church of God, half castle 'gainst the Scot"

Sir Walter Scott on Durham Cathedral

Across the Green is the **Cathedral** (www.durhamcathedral.co.uk; Mon–Sat 7.30am–6pm, Sun 7.45am–5.30pm, mid-July–Aug until 8pm; donation), once voted Britain's favourite building. Inside, massive columns stride down the nave like a petrified forest; boldly incised with spirals, lozenges, zigzags and flutings, their impact is stunning. Largely completed by 1133, it was the first major English church to be covered entirely by stone vaulting and is the finest example of early Norman architecture. Its outstanding features include the Galilee Chapel, with a tomb of England's first great historian, the Venerable Bede (died 735) and the Chapel of the Nine Altars, which contains the remains of St Cuthbert (see page 355). The **Open Treasure** route, leading from the Monk's Dormitory to the Great Kitchen and passing through the hidden places of the cathedral, is lined with treasures from the collection.

Turn right outside the cathedral down Dun Cow Lane to the **Durham Heritage Centre** (www.durhamheritagecentre.org.uk; Apr–May, Oct Sat–Sun 11am–4.30pm, June daily 11am–4.30pm, July–Sept daily 11am–4.30pm), which has exhibitions and audiovisual displays of the city. From here, descend to the Riverside Walk, a pleasant path beside the river that leads to **The Upper Room**, a sculpture of The Last Supper carved from 11 elm trees by Colin Wilbourn. Cross Prebends Bridge (1777) for a classic view of the cathedral.

COUNTY DURHAM AND THE NORTH PENNINES

Durham's proud industrial legacy can be seen at the award-winning **Living Museum of the North** at **Beamish** between Chester-le-Street and Stanley on the A693 (www.beamish.org.uk; daily Apr–Oct 10am–5pm, Nov–Mar 10am–4pm, closed Mon and Fri Jan–mid-Feb). One of the leading attractions in Northeast England, it vividly recreates the past with reconstructed buildings and shopkeepers and workers in period dress. There is an early 1900s town, with cobbled streets, shops, a pub, stables, a park and railway station with a

Newcastle quayside at night.

replica of George Stephenson's *Locomotion*, the first passenger-carrying steam train in the world. There is a farm with rare breeds and a colliery and engine house with the steam winder built in 1855 for the Beamish colliery. Nearby stand the mine and pit cottages where the miners originally lived.

NEWCASTLE UPON TYNE

Nine miles (15km) from the mouth of the Tyne, **Newcastle upon Tyne** ③⑤ is the hub in a conurbation formed with Tynemouth, South Shields, Wallsend, Jarrow and Gateshead. A centre of coal mining and shipbuilding, industrial England never got grittier than this. But the grim working-class conditions that the popular novelist Catherine Cookson described can no longer be seen in this lively university town, which has a bright nightlife and well-supported football club, plus some of the best shopping in the north of England. The Quayside development has put the city into another league.

The old town, known as the Chares, is a small area of narrow streets and steep lanes on the north side of the river; around here are the **Custom House** (1766), **Guildhall** (1658) and **Castle Keep** (www.newcastlecastle.co.uk; daily 10am–5pm). Constructed by the son of William the Conqueror on the site of a Roman fort, this was the "new castle" that gave the city its name. "New castle" by name, but it was the new technology of the steam train that defined the city's character, and much of the castle was demolished in the 19th century to make way for the railway. The keep and the Black Gate remain and here you can learn about life in the castle throughout the ages, including its time as a gruesome dungeon and a filthy slum. Climb the keep's 99 steps for fantastic views of the city and **Gateshead Quayside**.

Just beyond is **St Nicholas' Cathedral** (www.stnicholascathedral.co.uk; Mon–Fri 7am–6.30pm, Sat 8am–4pm, Sun 7.30am–5.30pm; donation), crowned by its distinctive Lantern Tower, a city landmark for over 500 years. It has a fine altar screen depicting Northumbria's many saints. Several museums are worth seeking out. On New Bridge Street, the **Laing Art Gallery** (www.twmuseums.org.uk; Mon–Sat 10am–4.30pm; free) has permanent 18th- and 19th-century collections and major contemporary exhibitions.

On Blandford Square, the **Discovery Museum** (Mon–Fri 10am–4pm, Sat–Sun 11am–4pm; free) celebrates history and scientific innovation on Tyneside. One of the biggest free museums in the Northeast, it is bursting with interactives for adults and children alike. Joseph Swan's early lightbulbs feature, the first to be produced in the country and made in Tyneside. Another popular attraction is the **Great North Museum: Hancock** (Mon–Fri 10am–5pm, Sat–Sun 11am–4pm; free) at Barras Bridge, a few minutes' walk from Haymarket Metro Station. Its collections include antiquities from ancient Greece and Egypt, as well as family-friendly displays of fossils, a living planet gallery concerning

○ Tip

To the southeast of Newcastle is the Old Hall in Washington village, ancestral home of George Washington, now run by the National Trust. The stone manor house was originally built in the 12th century and holds an incredible collection of Washington memorabilia, and the pretty formal gardens are ideal for a stroll. A special event here celebrates Independence Day.

At the Living Museum of the North at Beamish.

⊙ Where

Northwest of Newcastle, at Belsay on the A696, is **Belsay Hall** (www.english-heritage.org.uk; Apr–Sept daily 10am–6pm, Oct daily 10am–4pm, Nov–Mar Sat–Sun 10am–4pm), with striking gardens filled with exotic species and superb views from the castle tower.

wildlife and habitats and a large-scale interactive model of Hadrian's Wall.

For contemporary art, craft and design check out **The Biscuit Factory** (www.thebiscuitfactory.com; Mon–Fri 10am–5pm, Sat 10am–4pm, Sun 11am–4pm) in Stoddart Street. Housed in a former Victorian warehouse in the heart of Newcastle's cultural quarter, four exhibitions a year are held in two spacious galleries, representing some 250 quality craftspeople, whose work is also on sale.

An impressive collection of bridges spans the River Tyne quayside: the High Level Bridge built by George Stephenson, who inaugurated the railway industry here; the Swing Bridge, where the Roman bridge stood; and the **Tyne Bridge**, which when built in 1928 was the largest single span in the world. The latest addition is the **Gateshead Millennium Bridge**, the world's first tilting bridge. It has received a host of awards for architecture, design, innovation, and for the dramatic night lighting that creates a stunning reflection in the river. Cross on foot to Gateshead and the **Baltic Centre for Contemporary Art** (www.balticmill.com; daily 10am–6pm; free), one of

the biggest art spaces in Europe, with constantly changing exhibitions. Dominating Gateshead Quays is the **Sage Gateshead** (www.sagegateshead.com), a music venue contained within a shell-like building designed by Sir Norman Foster. The concert schedule attracts international names in a variety of musical genres.

Approaching Gateshead by the A1 or A167, a 66ft (20-metre) tall steel giant marks the entry into Tyneside. The *Angel of the North* stands on the site of a former coal mine and was created by Antony Gormley, partly in tribute to the coal miners who worked in darkness beneath its feet.

HADRIAN'S WALL

Built by order of the Emperor Hadrian in AD 122 to consolidate the northern boundary of the Roman Empire, **Hadrian's Wall ㊱** was 15ft (4.5 metres) high and ran 73 miles (117km), coast to coast, from the Solway to the Tyne: it was effectively an enormous customs post, controlling the flow of goods and people between the north and south. Thriving civilian settlements, known as *vici*, spread out to the south behind the protection of the wall, with houses, temples,

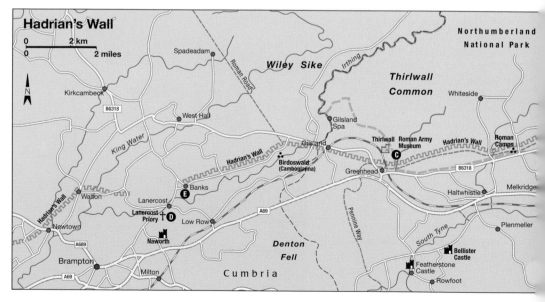

shops and theatres, serving the needs of both the local Britons and the 10,000 auxiliary soldiers from all over the Roman Empire who were stationed here. In 1987 the Hadrian's Wall Military Zone was designated a World Heritage Site by Unesco, becoming part of the Frontiers of the Roman Empire category in 2005. The Hadrian's Wall Path National Trail is an 84-mile (135km) waymarked walking route, from Wallsend in the east to Bowness on Solway in the west. The walk can be broken into day-long stages. If you prefer to visit Roman military sites by car, this suggested route will take a full day. It starts at the historic market town of **Hexham A** and ends at **Housesteads Fort and Museum**. **Hexham Abbey** (www.hexhamabbey.org.uk; daily 9.30am–5pm, services permitting; donation) was founded by Wilfrid c.674. The Saxon crypt (from 11am and 3.30pm) and apse still remain, but the present abbey is 12th-century.

Across the market place stands **Hexham Old Gaol** (www.hexhamoldgaol.org.uk; Apr–Sept Wed–Sun 11am–4pm, Oct–Nov, Feb–Mar Tue, Sat 11am–4.30pm, also July–Aug Mon, which was constructed in 1333, the earliest documented purpose-built prison in England. Inside there are four floors of excellent, interactive displays, which include the life and times of the Border Reivers and exhibits of weaponry and armour. You can also take a trip down to the dismal dungeon in the company of the gaoler. From Hexham take the A69 west through **Haydon Bridge B** and Haltwhistle and turn off at Greenhead for the **Roman Army Museum C** (www.vindolanda.com; daily Apr–Sept 10am–6pm, Oct–mid-Nov, mid-Feb–Mar 10am–5pm, check for winter opening). The museum brings to life Roman frontier history with a variety of multimedia exhibits.

The A69 continues towards the busy little market town of Brampton, and 1 mile (1.6km) beforehand a minor road leads to the 12th-century Augustinian **Lanercost Priory D** (www.lanercostpriory.org.uk; daily 10am–6pm, winter Sat–Sun 10am–4pm; donation). Continue down this road to cross the vallum of the wall at **Banks E**. Follow it eastwards through Gisland to the ruined 14th-century Thirlwall Castle, built with masonry from the wall.

From here follow the B6318, the military road about 8 miles (13km) and turn right to follow the Roman

Hadrian's Wall is marked by a National Trail footpath which follows the line of the wall from Wallsend on the east coast to Bowness-on-Solway on the west.

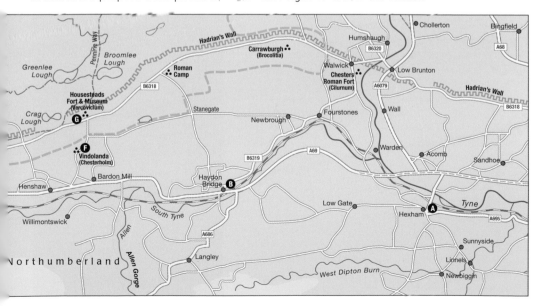

Ancient marble bust of the Roman emperor Hadrian.

Kielder Water is a man-made lake.

Stanegate (literally "stone road") 1 mile (1.6km) to **Vindolanda Fort and Museum** N (www.vindolanda.com; daily Apr–Sept 10am–6pm, Oct–mid-Nov, mid-Feb–Mar 10am–5pm, check for winter opening). This has a full-sized reconstruction of part of the wall and a turret, plus replica Roman temple, house and shop with various artefacts.

The most complete Roman fort in Britain is 2 miles (3km) away on the wall at **Housesteads** N (www.english-heritage.org.uk; Apr–Sept daily 10am–6pm, Oct daily 10am–5pm, Nov–Mar 10am–4pm). There are extensive remains of barracks, plus a bathhouse, hospital and granary. Also on the site, is a museum exploring life during the Roman Empire.

NORTHUMBERLAND NATIONAL PARK AND THE CHEVIOTS

The **Cheviot Hills**, shared by England and Scotland, are quite distinct from the Durham Dales and the North Pennines. Rounded and covered in rough grass, they reach 2,000ft (610 metres), and their cloying blanket of peat is notorious to exhausted Pennine Way-farers on the final leg of their 268-mile (429km) marathon from Edale in Derbyshire. **The Northumberland National Park** N (www.northumberland nationalpark.org.uk) covers 405 sq miles (1,049 sq km) between Hadrian's Wall and the Cheviots. There is a visitor centre for the park on Church Street in the pretty market town of **Rothbury**, the capital of Coquetdale, and the town offers many opportunities for good walks. Just outside town is **Cragside House** (www.nationaltrust.org.uk/cragside; Mar–Oct daily 11am–5pm), a fantastic mock-Tudor, mock-medieval building created by the inventor and arms manufacturer Lord Armstrong and the first house in the world to be lit by hydroelectricity. The stunning setting is enhanced by splendid gardens of extraordinary scale and variety.

There is an important Iron Age hill-fort at **Lordenshaws**, built around 350 BC, and there are good walks along the **Simonside Ridge** from here. The views north towards the Cheviots are among the finest in Northumberland.

KIELDER, MAN-MADE WILDERNESS

Kielder, in its own, entirely artificial way, is a unique landscape. Situated between Hadrian's Wall and the Scottish border on the west of the Northumberland National Park, it has the largest man-made forest in Europe, covering 300 sq miles (777 sq km), complemented by Kielder Water, Europe's largest man-made lake, opened in 1982, with a 27-mile (43km) shoreline (www.visitkielder.com).

This artificial landscape, criss-crossed by hundreds of miles of track, has proved immensely popular with walkers, horse riders and cyclists, especially for visitors from nearby Tyneside. The Lakeside Way allows visitors to walk all around the shore of the enormous lake. The Tower Knowe Visitor Centre (tel: 01434-246 436) near Falstone is the gateway visitor centre for the area, with a café, shop and history displays. Visitors can take the Osprey ferry from here to explore the water.

There are self-catering lodges and a bird of prey centre at Leaplish Waterside Park (tel: 01434-251 000) as well as sporting activities and a café. Kielder Village is a 1950s forestry community that is now the head-quarters of the Forestry Commission's Border Forest operations, based in Kielder Castle, the late 18th-century castellated shooting lodge of the Duke of Northumberland that today has a Visitor Centre. It is the starting point for various mountain bike trails and where bikes are for hire.

To the northwest is the delightful village of **Holystone** and the **Lady's** or **St Ninian's Well**. Set in a copse a short walk north of the village, it is a tranquil rectangular pool of clear water fed by a never-failing sparkling spring. A Celtic cross in the pool is a reminder that, on Easter Day in 627, 3,000 pagan Northumbrians were apparently baptised here by St Paulinus, a Roman missionary from Kent.

THE COAST, LINDISFARNE AND THE FARNE ISLANDS

The Northumbrian coast has some of Britain's finest and least spoilt beaches, and the 40 miles (65km) from **Amble** to the Scottish border has been designated an Area of Outstanding Natural Beauty. Just north of Amble is **Warkworth Castle** (www.english-heritage. org.uk; Apr–Sept daily 10am–6pm, Oct daily 10am–5pm, Nov–Mar Sat–Sun 10am–4pm), a masterpiece of late medieval architecture. Southwest of Morpeth, at Belsay on the A696, is **Belsay Hall** (www.english-heritage.org. uk; Apr–Sept daily 10am–6pm, Oct daily 10am–5pm, Nov–Mar Sat–Sun 10am–4pm), with striking gardens, filled with exotic species.

Inland from Alnmouth further north is the ancient town of **Alnwick** ㊳, and the stupendous **Alnwick Castle** (www. alnwickcastle.com; Apr–Oct daily 10am–5.30pm, state rooms: 10.30am–4.30pm). After Windsor, this is the largest inhabited castle in England and has been home to the Percys, Earls and Dukes of Northumberland, since 1309. The **Garden** (www.alnwickgarden.com; daily, summer 10am–6pm, winter 10am–4pm) has been ambitiously redesigned with features including a "Grand Cascade", a maze, a poison garden and a huge, higgledy-piggledy **tree house** – actually a magical complex of furnished buildings linked by suspended walkways and one of the world's largest.

In the picturesque fishing village of **Craster**, the world-famous Craster kippers can be bought from Robson & Sons (herring smokers for four generations) or sampled in their restaurant during summer. A 30-minute coastal path leads to **Dunstanburgh Castle**, one of the most romantically sited

Bamburgh Castle.

⊙ **Fact**

Northumbrian festivals involve a conflation of fire and music. The fires date back to Celtic, perhaps Viking times. Its musical small-pipes are like Scottish bagpipes inflated by an arm action. Some songs were collected by Sir Walter Scott in Minstrelsy of the Scottish Border (1803).

ruins in Britain. Beyond is the busy little harbour town of **Seahouses**, where, from Easter to September, boats take visitors the 2–5 miles (3–8km) to the **Farne Islands** (www.farne-islands.com). Protected by the National Trust, the rich wildlife includes over 20 species of seabirds and a large colony of seals. Beyond Seahouses, atop a basalt outcrop overlooking the Farne Islands, is **Bamburgh Castle** ㊴ (www.bamburghcastle.com; mid-Feb–Oct daily 10am–5pm, Nov–mid-Feb Sat–Sun 11am–4.30pm), said to be the finest castle in England. It has a Norman keep but was largely remodelled in the 19th and 20th centuries. As well as a fine armoury collection there are aviation and engineering artefacts and memorabilia.

To reach **Holy Island**, or **Lindisfarne** ㊵, it is necessary to turn inland and take the A1 for 6 miles (9km) to Beal. Before crossing the 3-mile (5km) causeway, check the tide tables (to plan ahead, tel: 01289-330 733) and never try to beat the treacherous tide. The island is cut off for about five hours a day. The 4-sq mile (10-sq km) island is a nature

reserve, and birdwatchers flock to the islands' breeding grounds. The romantic remains of **Lindisfarne Priory** (www.english-heritage.org.uk; Apr–Sept daily 10am–6pm, Oct daily 10am–5pm, Nov–Mar Sat–Sun 10am–4pm) date from 1083. The adjacent museum displays Saxon carvings from the site, and the adjoining church of St Mary's, which stands on the site of the original monastery founded by St Aidan in AD 635, contains copies of the famous Lindisfarne Gospels, beautiful illuminated manuscripts. **Lindisfarne Castle** (www.nationaltrust.org.uk/lindisfarne-castle; mid-Mar–Oct Tue–Sun, times vary with tides: 10am–3pm or noon–5pm) is a 16th-century miniature castle transformed into an Edwardian country house by Edwin Lutyens, with a charming walled garden by Gertrude Jekyll (daily all year 10am–dusk).

Berwick-upon-Tweed ㊶, the last town in England before Scotland, has changed allegiance between England and Scotland 11 times. Its most impressive feature is its perfectly intact Elizabethan walls and ramparts, built in 1558.

One of the world's largest tree houses, in Alnwick Castle Garden.

ST CUTHBERT, THE "FIRE OF THE NORTH"

From the Holy Island of Lindisfarne, this legendary local monk and animal-lover inspired the spiritual life of the northeast.

Lindisfarne became a holy place in the 7th century AD, when King Oswald of Northumbria sent for St Aidan from the holy island of Iona in Scotland to spread Christianity through his kingdom. Aidan and 12 companions founded the first monastery at Lindisfarne, a tiny rocky island, cut off by the tides from the mainland twice each day. This was to become the cradle of Christianity in Northeast England and ultimately for the rest of Europe. After Aidan died in 651, he was succeeded by Cuthbert.

Cuthbert, greatest of the northern saints, was born in the Scottish borders in 625. While tending sheep in the Lammermuir Hills he saw a vision of a great light and angels in the sky, and, taking this as a sign that he should spread the Christian message, he became a monk.

Cuthbert, the "Fire of the North", ignited the Christian flame in the region. News of his gift for healing spread far and wide, and he was frequently called to other monasteries to preach and to heal. However, Cuthbert preferred solitude and often withdrew to live the life of a hermit in a tiny cell on the rocky island of Inner Farne.

There are many legends associated with St Cuthbert, mostly related by the Venerable Bede, who wrote the first history of the English people (Historia Ecclesiastica Gentis Anglorum) up to the time of his death in 735 from his monk's cell in the monastery of Jarrow, near Newcastle. Bede said Cuthbert was "unassumingly patient, devoted to unceasing prayer". One of the tales he told was of the sea otters drying Cuthbert's feet and warming him with their breath after he had spent a night praying in the cold North Sea. His love of animals was characteristic, and the eider ducks still found around the Farne Islands are known as St Cuthbert's ducks, or Cuddy's, because he had managed to tame them.

CUTHBERT LAID TO REST

Cuthbert died in 687 and was buried on Lindisfarne. Shortly afterwards, an unknown monk began work on the famous Lindisfarne Gospels, a beautifully illuminated manuscript now in the British Museum. Cuthbert's body was not destined to stay on his beloved Lindisfarne. After a series of Viking raids on the coast, monks removed it, first to Chester-le-Street and later to Ripon, before it eventually arrived, in 995, on a peninsula on the River Wear known as Dunholme (which became today's city of Durham).

Today the remains of the famous Celtic saint reside in the recently excavated Great Kitchen of Durham's Norman cathedral, while those of his great chronicler, Bede can be found in the Galilee Chapel. There is a waymarked walk, the St Cuthbert's Way, which runs from Melrose in the Scottish Borders to Lindisfarne. Stretching 62.5 miles (100km), it can be broken into shorter sections.

A stained-glass window in the chapel on the Farne Islands, depicting Saint Cuthbert.

Walkers on the Cotswold Way, Coaley Park.

ENGLAND

TRAVEL TIPS

TRANSPORT

GETTING THERE

By air

Britain's two major international airports are Heathrow (mainly scheduled flights), which is 15 miles (24km) to the west of London, and Gatwick (scheduled and charter flights), which is 24 miles (40km) south of the capital. An increasing number of international flights now arrive at the regional airports of Birmingham, Manchester, Liverpool, Glasgow, Prestwick and Cardiff, and London's other airports, Stansted and Luton. The small London City Airport, a few miles from London's financial heart, is used by small aircraft to fly to UK and European cities.

London airports

The Airport Travel Line, tel: 08705-747 777, gives information on coaches into Central London and between Heathrow, Gatwick and Stansted airports. Sky Shuttle runs a door-to-door bus service from Heathrow airport to hotels in central areas of London. Booking is essential, tel: 0845-481 0960; www.skyshuttle.co.uk.

National Express also runs coach services connecting Heathrow, Gatwick, Stansted and Luton airports, and the first three airports with Victoria Coach Station in Central London. For enquiries, tel: 08717-818 181; www.nationalexpress.com.

Heathrow Airport (www.heathrow airport.com) is a sprawling airport with five terminals.

There is a fast rail link, the Heathrow Express, between Heathrow and Paddington Station. It runs every 15 minutes from 5.10am–11.25pm and takes about 15 minutes. Fares are £25 single at peak times (£22 off-peak) single and £37 return. Paddington is on the District, Circle, Bakerloo and Hammersmith

and City Underground train lines, tel: 0345-600 1515; www.heathrowex press.com.

The cheapest way into Central London is by the Underground (known as the Tube), which takes about 60 minutes to the West End. The Piccadilly Line goes from Heathrow directly to central areas such as Kensington, Piccadilly and Covent Garden. The single fare is £6 (£5.10 with an Oyster Card 6.30–9.30am, £3.10 at other times) –see page 361). Keep your ticket: you'll need it to exit the Underground system. For all London Transport enquiries, tel: 0343-222 1234; www.tfl.gov.uk.

Heathrow is also well served by taxis. A ride into town in a London black cab will cost £45–85, depending on your destination and whether you have booked a minicab or simply hailed a black cab.

Gatwick Airport (www.gatwickair port.com) isn't on the Underground network, but has train and coach services into London and to other large cities. Gatwick Express trains leaves every 15 minutes from 5.59am until 11.11pm (fewer trains after 8.45pm), and take 30 minutes to London's Victoria Station. For information, tel: 0345-850 1530; www.gatwickexpress. com. First Capital trains to Victoria and Southern Trains to London Bridge Station are much cheaper and take only a little longer, but can be very crowded at peak hours with general commuter traffic.

A taxi into Central London costs around £80.

Luton Airport (www.london-luton. co.uk) has a regular express train service from Luton Airport Parkway (take the shuttle bus) to St Pancras Station, City Thameslink, Blackfriars and London Bridge, taking 25 minutes minimum. Alternatively, Green Line 757 coaches to London's Victoria Station take about an hour, tel: 0344-801 7261; www.greenline.

co.uk, or easyBus coaches (up to 1 hour 40 minutes during peak times; www.easybus.co.uk).

Stansted Airport (www.stan stedairport.com) has the Stansted Express train service to London's Liverpool Street Station. A frequent service operates 5.30am–12.30am and takes about 50 minutes, tel: 0845-850 0150; www.stanstedexpress. com. A non-stop coach service to London Victoria is run by Terravision (www.terravision.eu), and National Express has services to Stratford (East London), Liverpool Street and Victoria.

For those heading elsewhere in Britain other than London, there are regular National Express bus links to nearby British Rail stations.

London City Airport's major strength is its proximity to the city centre (10 miles/16km; www.london cityairport.com). There is a London City Airport DLR station (about 50yds/metres from the airport terminal), and the service from here connects with the Jubilee Line (at Canning Town) and Northern, Central, Circle and Waterloo and City lines (at Bank). The Transport for London website (www.tfl.gov.uk) can be used to help plan your journey.

A London black cab into Central London should cost £30–45.

☉ Children's fares

Airlines Infants (under 2 years) either travel free or for about 10 percent of adult fare. Ages 2–12 years qualify for a child's fare, usually 80 percent of adult fare. These terms may differ with the budget airlines.

Trains Under 5s free on your knee, aged 5–15 half-price most tickets.

Coaches Under-3s free on your knee, 3–15s about half-price.

English regional airports

Manchester Airport (www.manchester-airport.co.uk) is 10 miles (16km) south of the city. Frequent rail services run to Piccadilly Station (20 minutes) in Central Manchester, from where there are regular InterCity trains to London and other major cities. Alternatives are local buses or a taxi (approximately £20–30).

Birmingham International Airport (www.birminghamairport.co.uk) is 8 miles (13km) southeast of Birmingham. The free Air-Rail Link shuttle connects the airport with Birmingham International Station, from where trains run every 10–15 minutes to New Street Station in the city centre (about 15 minutes). InterCity trains from New Street to London Euston run every 20 minutes (about 1 hour 25 minutes).

Newcastle Airport (www.new castleairport.com) is 6 miles (9km) northwest of Newcastle city centre on the A696 at Woolsington. The airport is a main station for the Metro underground system, which takes 23 minutes to Central Station, where regular InterCity trains run to London (3 hours) and Edinburgh (1 hour 30 minutes).

Liverpool John Lennon Airport (www.liverpoolairport.com) is 9 miles (15km) southeast of the city centre. The Arriva Airport Express 500 bus runs to the city centre and takes 25 minutes. Taxis charge about £17 for the 20-minute journey.

Channel Tunnel

Eurostar's regular passenger trains link France, Brussels and Amsterdam with Britain. Services run from Paris Gare du Nord (2 hours 15 minutes), Brussels Midi (2 hours) and Amsterdam (3 hr 40 mins) to London's St Pancras International; some trains stop at Ebbsfleet, Kent.

Booking is not essential, but there are offers on tickets bought in advance. For UK bookings, tel: 03432-186 186. From outside the UK, tel: +44 1233-617 575, or visit www.eurostar.com.

By car

Eurotunnel trains travel through the tunnel from Nord-Pas de Calais in France to Folkestone in Kent. At least two departures every hour during the day, with a reduced service overnight (journey time 35 minutes).

Booking is not essential – just turn up and take the next service. Crossings are priced on a single-leg basis and prices vary according to the level of demand; the further ahead you book, the cheaper the ticket. For UK reservations tel: 08443-353 535 and information, tel: 08444-630 000; www.eurotunnel.com.

By coach

The "Le Shuttle" trains have also facilitated direct coach routes from Continental Europe to London's Victoria Coach Station. Services are run from major cities all over Europe via Eurolines, a network of cooperating national bus companies, offering integrated ticketing and extensive connections. The British part of the operation is run by National Express. For enquiries, tel: 08717-818 177; www.eurolines.co.uk.

Sea transport

Sea services operate between 12 British ports and more than 20 Continental ones. Major ferries have full eating, sleeping and entertainment facilities. The shortest crossing is from Calais in France to Dover in Britain, which takes about 90 minutes by ferry.

Brittany Ferries sail from Plymouth, Poole and Portsmouth to St Malo, Caen, Cherbourg, Le Havre and Roscoff in France and to Santander and Bilbao in Spain. Within UK tel: 0330-159 7000; +44 330-159 7000 in France and Spain; www.brittany-ferries.co.uk.

P&O Ferries run from Calais, France, to Dover, and from Rotterdam, Holland, and Zeebrugge, Belgium, over the North Sea to Hull on England's east coast. In the UK tel: 0871-664 6464; www.poferries.com.

Stena Line sails from Hook of Holland to Harwich, England. In the UK tel: 08447-707 070; www.stenaline.co.uk.

DFDS Seaways operates between Dover and Dunkirk (approx 1 hour 45 minutes). In the UK, tel: 0871-574 7235; www.dfdsseaways.co.uk.

If you plan to bring a vehicle over by ferry it is advisable to book, particularly during peak holiday periods. If travelling by night on a long journey it is also recommended that you book a sleeping cabin.

From the US you could arrive in style on Cunard's *Queen Mary 2* in

Southampton. Operating between April and December, it takes six nights to cross the Atlantic. For information in the UK, tel: 0873-374 2224; from the US call 1-800-728 6273; www.cunard.com.

GETTING AROUND

Driving

In Britain you must drive on the left-hand side of the road and observe speed limits. It is illegal to use a mobile phone when driving. Penalties for drink-driving are severe. Drivers and passengers, in both front and back seats, must wear seat belts where fitted; failure to do so can result in a fine. For further information, consult a copy of the *Highway Code* published by the Department for Transport, and widely available in bookshops. Prepare in advance by visiting www.direct.gov.uk.

If you are bringing your own car into Britain you will need a valid driving licence or International Driving Permit, plus insurance coverage and documents proving the vehicle is licensed and registered in your country and that you are resident outside the UK.

Parking

Road congestion is a problem in most town and city centres, and parking is generally restricted. Never leave your car parked on a double yellow or red line, in a place marked for *permit holders only*, within a white zigzag line close to a pedestrian crossing, or in a control zone. Also, don't park on a single yellow line when restrictions are in force, usually 8.30am–6.30pm

Speed limits

Unless otherwise stated on signs:
30mph (50kph) in built-up areas.
60mph (100kph) on normal roads away from built-up areas.
70mph (112kph) on motorways and dual carriageways (divided highways).
Camping vans or **cars towing a caravan** are restricted to 50mph (80kph) on normal roads and 60mph (100kph) on dual carriageways.

Mon–Fri (consult signs on the kerb; if no days are shown, restrictions are in force daily). These are offences for which you can face a fine. Either use a meter or a car park (distinguished by a white P on a blue background).

If you park illegally you may be given a Penalty Charge Notice, which is issued by local authorities and Transport for London. You usually have 28 days to pay the charge; although the fine will be halved if you pay within 14 days.

Breakdown

The following motoring organisations operate 24-hour breakdown assistance. They have reciprocal arrangements with other national motoring clubs. All calls to these numbers are free.

AA tel: 0800-887 766, or visit www.theaa.com

Britannia Rescue tel: 0800-929 111, or visit www.britanniarescue.com

Green Flag tel: 0800-051 0636, or visit www.greenflag.com

rac tel: 0800-828 282, or visit www.rac.co.uk

Car hire/rental

To hire a car in Britain you must be over 21 years old (over 23 for most companies) and have held a valid full driving licence for more than one year. The cost of hiring a car usually includes third-party insurance, mileage and road tax. Depending on the company, it might also incorporate insurance cover for accidental damage to the car's interior, wheels and tyres. However, it does not include insurance for other drivers without prior arrangement.

Some companies offer special weekend and holiday rates, so shop around. International companies (such as those listed below) are keen to encourage visitors to book in advance before they leave home and may offer holiday packages with discounts of up to 40 percent on advance bookings through travel agents or branches in your own country. Many hire firms provide child seats and luggage racks for a small charge.

Avis tel: 0808-284 0014; www.avis.co.uk

Hertz tel: 0843-309 3099; www.hertz.co.uk

Budget tel: 0808-284 4444; www.budget.co.uk

Enterprise tel: 0800-800 227; www.enterprise.co.uk

Public transport

Domestic flights

From the major international airports there are frequent shuttle services to Britain's many domestic airports. These give quick and easy access to many cities and offshore islands. Airlines providing domestic services include:

British Airways (the country's largest airline), reservations and general enquiries, tel: 0344-493 0787 (from the UK); flight arrival and departure information, tel: 0344-493 0777 (from the UK, daily agents available 6am–8pm, automated out of hours); from the US tel: 1-800-airways; www.britishairways.com.

EasyJet, tel: 0330-365 5000; www.easyjet.com

Ryanair, tel: 0871-246 0000 (from within UK only); www.ryanair.com

Major domestic airports

Bristol tel: 0871-334 4344; www.bristolairport.co.uk

East Midlands tel: 0871-271 0711; www.eastmidlandsairport.com

Leeds-Bradford tel: 0871-288 2288; www.leedsbradfordairport.co.uk

Liverpool John Lennon tel: 0871-521 8484; www.liverpoolairport.com

Newcastle upon Tyne tel: 0871-882 1121; www.newcastleairport.com

Newquay tel: 01637-860 600; www.newquaycornwallairport.com

Norwich tel: 01603-411 923; www.norwichairport.co.uk

Southampton tel: 0844-481 7777; www.southamptonairport.com

Trains

Railways are run by about two-dozen private regional operating companies. They are not known for punctuality, so if your arrival time is critical allow for possible delays. Avoid rush-hour travel in and out of big cities.

There are many money-saving deals, such as cheap-day returns, available. It can be difficult to find out about special offers, so if in doubt, ask again. Generally, tickets bought at least two weeks in advance are vastly cheaper than standard rates, but they sell out fast. Some saver tickets are available only if purchased abroad before arriving.

It is not usually necessary to buy tickets until the day you travel (except to get these special offers), or to make seat reservations, except

over the Christmas and summer holiday period when InterCity trains are fully booked well in advance.

Many trains have first-class carriages with tickets up to twice the price of standard seats. It is sometimes possible to upgrade to first class at weekends for an extra payment once you board.

On long distances overnight, it may be worth having a sleeping compartment. Available on InterCity trains, these have basic but comfortable sleeping arrangements and must be booked in advance. Information available by calling 03457-484 950, or +44 (0)20-7278 5240 from abroad; National Rail Enquiries can then give you the phone number to book with the relevant train operator. Tickets can also be booked online at www.thetrainline.com or via www.nationalrail.co.uk.

Train enquiries

National Rail Enquiry Service For train times, cancellations and advance bookings by credit card, tel: 03457-484 950 or visit www.nationalrail.co.uk.

Rail Europe For services from Britain, tel: 08448-484 064; www.raileurope.com.

Coaches and local buses

National Express operates a large network of long-distance bus services with comfortable coaches running on long journeys, equipped with washrooms and disabled facilities. Fares are (usually) considerably cheaper than the equivalent journey by train, although you must book your seat in advance. For enquiries and bookings, tel: 08717-818 181; www.nationalexpress.com.

National Express provides scheduled day trips to cities of interest such as Bath and Stratford-upon-Avon, as well as transport to music festivals and Wembley and Twickenham stadiums. **Green Line**, tel: 0344-801 7261; www.greenline.co.uk, runs to Legoland and Windsor, among other destinations.

Towns are generally well served by buses, often owned by private companies; rural communities often have very inadequate services.

Ferries

To reach the Isles of Scilly, visitors can travel by the Scillonian ferry from Penzance or by the Skybus small aircraft from Land's End, Newquay or Exeter, tel: 01736-334 220; www.islesofscilly-travel.co.uk. You can also visit Scilly for the day by boat (from Penzance) or plane (from Land's End or Newquay).

Ferries to the Isle of Wight operate from Portsmouth and Lymington, tel: 0333-999 7333; www.wightlink. co.uk. Red Funnel Ferries, tel: 0844-844 9988; www.redfunnel.co.uk, also run ferries to the island, starting from Southampton.

Taxis

Outside London and large cities and away from taxi ranks at stations, ports and airports you will usually have to telephone for a cab rather than expect to hail one in the street. By law cabs must be licensed and display charges on a meter. Add about 10 percent for a tip.

London "black cab" drivers are famous for their extensive knowledge of the city's streets: they aren't cheap, especially at night, but are generally worth the extra. Minicabs (unlicensed taxis, which look like private cars) are not allowed to compete with black cabs on the street and have to be hired by telephone or from a kiosk. If hiring a minicab, agree to a fee beforehand and don't expect drivers to know precise destinations. Never pick up an unsolicited minicab in the street.

If you have a complaint, make a note of the driver's licence number and contact the Public Carriage Office, tel: 0343-222 4444.

Alternatively, book a cab or share a ride by using the smartphone apps mytaxi or Uber.

Travelling around London

If you are staying in London for a while it is worth investing in an *A–Z* street guide, which gives detailed information of the capital's confusing complex of streets and post codes.

The Underground (Tube) is the quickest way to get across London. Although one of the most comprehensive systems of its kind in the world, it's also the oldest. Apart from some central stations, which have been revamped, and the East London line redevelopment work that was performed in preparation for the 2012 Olympics, many remain largely unchanged since the 1930s.

The Tube service starts at 5.30am and runs until around midnight. It gets packed in the rush hours (7–9.30am and 4–7pm). Make sure that you have a valid ticket, as it is illegal to travel without one, and you may be fined. Smoking is prohibited. Fares are based on a zone system with a flat fare in the central zone. Night trains on the network throughout Friday and Saturday nights commenced in summer 2016 with five lines operating a 24-hour service (Victoria, Central, Jubilee, Northern and Piccadilly).

A ride on the Docklands Light Railway is an excellent way to see the redevelopment of London's old dock area. This fully automated system has two branches connecting with the Underground network. It operates in the same way as the Tube, with similar fares.

London buses provide a comprehensive service throughout Greater London and have their route and number clearly displayed on the front. Some buses run hourly throughout the night, with services to many parts of London departing from Trafalgar Square. Smoking is prohibited on buses. Cash is no longer accepted on London buses. You can pay by Oyster, Travelcard, or with a contactless debit or credit card.

Either pay for single journeys on London Transport (expensive, see box) or buy a one-day or seven-day Travelcard or prepay Oyster Card. The Oyster Card is a prepaid card for the Tube and buses. Simply touch the card on the reader in Tube stations and buses. Visitor Oyster Cards cost £5 and you choose how much credit you want. For a guideline for two days in London choose £20 credit, for four days £40 on a pay-as-you-go basis. They can be topped up at Oyster Tickets Stops available at hundreds of newsagents and shops throughout London, as well as stations and Visitor Centres. You can get any credit refunded at a ticket machine at the station or at a Visitor Centre. Buy online at www.tfl. gov.uk. Paying cash for a single journey on the tube within zones 1 and 5 costs £4.90 (£2.40 with Oyster Card). There are no longer manned ticket offices in Underground stations, only machines.

There is a flat fare of £1.50 for any bus journey, regardless if you use a contactless card or Oyster prepay. Buy tickets before boarding from machines at bus stops (a few stops do not yet have machines).

A bus pass (valid in all zones) will cost £5 for one day. Travelcards may be used on Tube, bus, DLR and National Rail services. Prices vary according to zones covered and duration. Family travelcards also available.

Call Transport for London on 0343-222 1234 or visit www.tfl.gov.uk.

Driving in London

If you're staying only for a short time in the Greater London area, and are unfamiliar with the geography of the capital, don't hire a car. Central London is more than ever a nightmare to drive in, with its web of one-way streets, bad signposting, the congestion and ULEZ charges and impatient drivers.

Parking is also a major problem in busy Central London. Meters are slightly cheaper than NCP car parks, but usually allow parking for a maximum of only two or four hours. If parking at a meter, do not leave your car a moment longer than your time allows or insert more money once your time has run out. For either infringement you can be fined up to £130. Some meter parking is free after 6.30pm and all day Sunday, but check the details on the meter. Many parking meters can now be paid for on smartphone apps such as PayByPhone and ParkRight.

⊙ Steam railways

Many steam rail lines have been restored by enthusiasts UK Heritage Railways (www.heritage-railways.com). Among the most notable are:
Bluebell Railway, Sheffield Park Station, Nr Uckfield, E. Sussex TN22 3QL; tel: 01825-720 800; www.bluebell-railway.co.uk. Britain's most famous line.
Watercress Line, Alresford, Hampshire SO24 9JG; tel: 01962-733 810; www.watercressline.co.uk. Runs through beautiful country over steeply graded track.
Severn Valley Railway, Bewdley, Worcestershire DY12 1BG; tel: 01562-757 900; www.svr.co.uk. Spectacular views.
Great Central Railway, Loughborough, Leics. LE11 1RW; tel: 01509-632 323; www.gcrailway.co.uk. One of the most evocative restorations of the steam age.

Lakeside and Haverthwaite Railway, Nr Ulverston, Cumbria LA12 8AL; tel: 01539-531 594; www.lakesiderailway.co.uk. Steep ride, with connections to boats on the lake.
North Yorkshire Moors Railway, Pickering Station, YO18 7AJ; tel: 01751-472 508; www.nymr.co.uk. An 18-mile (30km) line through picturesque moorland.
Paignton and Dartmouth Steam Railway, Queen's Park Station, Torbay Road, Paignton, Devon TQ4 6AF; tel: 01803-555 872; www.dartmouthrailriver.co.uk. Beautiful coastal line, with superb views.
Gloucestershire–Warwickshire Railway, Toddington, Glos. GL54 5DT; tel: 01242-621 405; www.gwsr.com. A 20-mile (32km) round trip through the Cotswolds from Toddington to Cheltenham Racecourse.

Boats can be boarded at Richmond, Kew, London Eye, Westminster, Embankment, London Bridge, Tower and Greenwich piers.

Circular cruises between St Katharine's and Westminster Pier are available from: **Crown River Cruises**, Blackfriars Pier; tel: 020-7936 2033; www.crownrivercruise.co.uk.

Scheduled services are run by:
Thames River Services, Westminster Pier to Thames Barrier (Apr–Oct) and Greenwich (year-round), tel: 020-7930 4097; www.thamesriverservices.co.uk.

City Cruises Departures from Westminster, London Eye, Tower and Greenwich piers, tel: 020-7740 0400; www.citycruises.com.

British waterways

Britain has over 2,000 miles (3,200km) of rivers and canals, the latter a legacy of the Industrial Revolution and now extensively restored. There is a wide choice of vessels to hire. Possibilities include exploring the canals, from the Grand Union in the Midlands to the Caledonian, which stretches from coast to coast in Scotland, or taking a pleasure cruiser along major rivers such as the Thames, Avon or the Severn, or around the Norfolk Broads.

For information, contact:
Canal & River Trust, Head Office, First Floor North, Station House, 500 Elder Gate, Milton Keynes MK9 1BB; tel: 0303-040 4040; www.canalrivertrust.org.uk.

The Inland Waterways Association is a voluntary body that fights for the restoration and maintenance of Britain's waterway network. It has saved many waterways that would otherwise have disappeared. Contact the association at: Island House, Moor Road, Chesham, HP5 1WA; tel: 01494-783 453; www.waterways.org.uk.

You are liable to a £11.50 daily congestion charge if you drive in the central zone between 7am and 6pm Mon–Fri. You can pay by ringing 0343-222 2222, visiting www.tfl.gov.uk/roadusers/congestioncharging, or at many small shops. All vehicles that do not meet ULEZ (Ultra Low Emission Zone) standards are also now liable to a £12.50 daily charge in the ULEZ zone, which covers the same area as the congestion charge (see TfL website for details).

Cycling in London

A bicycle-lending scheme has been set up whereby members of the public can borrow a bike from one of dozens of docking stations all over central London, and then afterwards leave it at any other docking station. Previously called "Boris Bikes" (after the former Mayor of London, Boris Johnson), Santander Cycles, as they are now known, are a familiar sight on the streets of London. There is no need to sign up first: just pay the access fee and usage charge at the docking station with a credit or debit card. See www.tfl.gov.uk for a map of docking station locations. For more conventional bike hire, contact the London Bicycle Company, tel: 020-7928 6838; www.londonbicycle.com.

To encourage more people to cycle in the capital, more and more dedicated cycle lanes are being

established. See www.cycle-route.com for details of routes across the capital (and elsewhere in England).

A new breed of dockless "smart sharing bikes", such as Mobike and YoBike in London and some other major cities is also evolving, whereby users can unlock them using their smartphones and leave them wherever they wish.

River travel and tours

London

Riverboats are an excellent way to see many major London sights whose history is intertwined with the river. During the summer these are plentiful, but there are limited winter services. Some of London Transport's travel passes allow a third off the cost of travel on scheduled Riverboat services.

⊙ Rover tickets

Coach
National Express, tel: 08717-818 181; www.nationalexpress.com, offers a Brit Xplorer pass, which entitles you to unlimited travel on their coaches for specified periods.
Train
For UK residents there are several passes, including a Family

& Friends, Senior and 16–25s Railcard, valid for one year. They cost a fraction of a long-distance InterCity trip and allow you a third off the full journey fare on off-peak trains. The BritRail ticket (from European travel agents and online in US at www.britrail.com) gives you unlimited travel in Great Britain for specified periods.

A

Accommodation

England has a huge variety of accommodation for visitors, from smart luxury hotels in stately homes and castles to bed-and-breakfast (B&B) accommodation in private family homes or country farmhouses.

By international standards, hotels in Britain are expensive, so if you are holidaying on a tight budget you should consider staying in B&B (bed and breakfast) accommodation or youth hostels, which take people of all ages. Wherever you go, always be sure to look at a room before accepting it. Short-term home rental companies like Airbnb (www.airbnb.co.uk) and HomeAway (www.homeaway.com) can also be a cheap way to stay in excellent locations.

Not all hotels include breakfast in their rates, and they may add a service charge of 10-15 percent. However, all charges should be clearly displayed on the tariff.

It is advisable to book in advance, particularly at Christmas, Easter and in July and August. During the rest of the year there is generally little difficulty in finding somewhere to stay. You can book a room through a travel agent, directly with a hotel or via www.visitbritain.com, the national tourist agency and www.visitlondon.com, the capital's tourist agency.

Hotel awards The VisitEngland Quality Rose is the mark of England's nationwide quality assessment scheme, whose ratings (1–5 stars) assess accommodation standards in different categories (eg hotels are in a separate category to B&Bs, which come under Guest Accommodation), informing you what each category has to offer.

The AA (Automobile Association) provides a simple scheme awarding between one star (basic) and five stars (luxury). See www.theaa.com.

A Michelin award is the accolade for which the most notable of hoteliers strive.

VisitEngland (www.visitengland.com) has lists dealing with every type of accommodation in Britain, from farms, B&Bs and pet-friendly accommodation to camping and self-catering boating holidays. To be listed, an establishment first has to pay to be inspected and then pay to be given an enhanced listing – so the guides are not totally impartial.

Stately homes Britain has many grand stately homes and castles that have been converted into luxury country-house hotels (saving many historic buildings from dereliction).

Hotel chains

Hotels belonging to big chains tend to offer a reliable, if at times impersonal, standard of service. The business traveller on an expense account is increasingly well catered for, in both urban and country areas, where there are many hotels offering large conference rooms and health and leisure facilities in addition to internet and secretarial services. The following groups have hotels in most parts of the country:

Premier Travel Inn
Tel: 0871 527 9222; www.premierinn.com. Simple but smart budget hotels in cities and towns.

Travelodge
Tel: 0871-984 8484; www.travelodge.co.uk. Budget hotels often located on the outskirts of town near major roads.

Holiday Inn Hotels
Tel: 0871 423 4896; www.holidayinn.com. Range of hotels in prime locations.

Accor Hotels
Tel: 0871-663 0624; www.accorhotels.com. Brands include Novotel (budget end), Mercure (mid-range) and Sofitel (upper-range).

Stepping back in history

It is possible to stay in restored old buildings, from a medieval castle to a lighthouse. Many such properties have been beautifully restored and are maintained by the Landmark Trust and the National Trust.

The Landmark Trust is a private charity, set up in 1965 to rescue historic buildings. It now has more than 180 properties to let, ranging from castles and manor houses to mills, lighthouses, forts and follies, all restored and furnished in keeping with the original character. A handbook of detailed information is available by post. The book's price is refunded against bookings. Tel: 01628-825 925; www.landmarktrust.org.uk.

The National Trust has more than 400 cottages and smaller houses of historical interest to let, from a romantic cabin hideaway overlooking a Cornish creek to an apartment in York with clear views of the Minster. The National Trust, PO Box 536, Melksham, Wiltshire SN12 8SX; tel: 0344-800 2070; www.nationaltrustholidays.org.uk.

Youth hostels

There are more than 200 youth hostels in England and Wales, ranging from townhouses to beach chalets. Facilities and accommodation are basic but cheap, usually comprising shared dormitories of bunk beds.

Some provide a full meals service, while others have self-catering kitchens, but hostels are only for those who don't mind mucking in, communal living and a shortage of creature comforts. The maximum length of stay is usually 10–14 days. You must be a national or international member to stay at a hostel – although anyone of any age can join the association, overseas or in the UK.

Youth Hostel Association (YHA)
Trevelyan House, Dimple Road, Matlock, Derbyshire DE4 3YH

Tel: 01629-592 700
www.yha.org.uk

London hostels

Earl's Court
38 Bolton Gardens, SW5 0AQ
Tel: 0845-371 9114
Oxford Street
14 Noel Street, W1F 8GJ
Tel: 0845-371 9132
St Paul's
36–38 Carter Lane, EC4V 5AB
Tel: 0845-371 9012
Thameside
20 Salter Road, SE16 5PR
Tel: 0845-371 9756

B&Bs and guesthouses

B&Bs tend to be good value, and it is always advisable to book in advance during the peak seasons. B&B accommodation is also available in many farmhouses, which provide rural accommodation. Contact local tourist offices for lists of recommended accommodation, or consult the annual guide published by the AA (available from most good bookshops) that lists more than 4,000 inspected B&Bs. See also www. theaa.com.

Agencies that specialise in B&Bs include:

Bed & Breakfast Nationwide
Tel: 01255-831 235
www.bedandbreakfastnationwide.com
London Bed & Breakfast Agency
Tel: 020-7586 2768
www.londonbb.com
Wolsey Lodges
Tel: 01473-822 058
www.wolseylodges.com

Camping

Despite Britain's reputation for rainy weather (only partially justified!), camping is once again increasing in popularity. Facilities have been improved at campsites, the retro image of camping is appealing to many, and the development of "glamping" (glamorous camping) is convincing others that it can be a comfortable experience after all.

There are hundreds of campsites across the country, ranging from camping resorts with excellent facilities (sometimes including swimming pools and children's clubs) to a small field behind a country pub. Websites such as www.ukcampsite.co.uk and www. campinguk.com provide listings. The Forestry Commission also runs a large number of campsites around Britain, some with rustic cabins. Tel:

03330-110 495; www.forestholidays.co.uk for details.

The fashionable concept of "glamping" involves staying in yurts, cabins, tepees and bell tents in picturesque locations. Your accommodation usually has standing room, a proper bed, a stove and maybe even a sofa. Sites tend to be very small and have good facilities. See http:// goglamping.net/ for a wide selection of quirky places to stay.

Admission charges

The major national museums and galleries, such as the British Museum, National Gallery, Imperial War Museum and the various Tate galleries, offer free admission. Some municipal museums are free; others make a charge. A comprehensive website for museums is www.culture24.org.uk.

If you're planning to visit a lot of attractions in the capital, it's worth looking at www.londonpass.com; prices start at £75 (adult) or £55 (child) for one day, but six-day passes are better value. Note that they don't cover some of the more expensive attractions such as Madame Tussauds and the London Eye.

If you are interested in visiting a number of stately homes, then membership of the National Trust (www.nationaltrust.org.uk) may be a worthwhile consideration. One year's membership costs £72 (adult) or £36 (child), while family membership is £126. Membership entitles you to free entry to all of the trust's properties. English Heritage (www.english-heritage. org.uk) offers a similar membership scheme, which allows free admission to all the historic sites it manages. A year's membership costs £60 (adult) or £48 (students and under-19s).

B

Budgeting for your trip

Prices for many goods and services can seem expensive to visitors, though much does of course depend on exchange rates. Public transport, for example, is expensive compared to most countries, though admission to museums and galleries is either free or at least reasonably priced. Central London is, unsurprisingly, likely to have the highest prices, but even

there, daily costs such as restaurant meals are kept at moderate levels by the pressure of competition. Be aware that hotels and restaurants in more far-flung places, such as Cornwall, can sometimes be expensive, as overheads have to be covered during a relatively short tourist season.

Average costs guide

Pint of beer: £5
Glass of house wine: £4.10
Main course at a budget restaurant: £8
Main course at a moderately priced restaurant: £14
Main course at an expensive restaurant: £25
Bed and breakfast at a cheap hotel: £70
Bed and breakfast at a moderately priced hotel: £130
Bed and breakfast at a deluxe hotel: £250
Taxi from Heathrow to Central London: £40 pre-booked, otherwise £80

C

Children

Accommodation. Some hotels do not accept children under a certain age, so be sure to check when you book. Many of the more upmarket hotels in England provide travel cots for no extra charge, though they will charge for babysitting services.

Restaurants. Most restaurants accept well-behaved children, but only those that want to encourage families have children's menus, highchairs and nappy-changing facilities. Publicans, like restaurateurs, reserve the right to refuse entry.

Public transport. Up to four children aged 10 or under can travel free on London's Underground if accompanied by a ticket-holding adult. Eleven to 15-year-olds can get half adult fare rate for up to 14 days with Young Visitor discount if travelling with an electronic Oyster or Visitor Oyster card-holding adult; 11–15-year-olds can also apply for a Zip Oyster photocard for longer stays for free travel.

Buses are free for all children under 11, but 11–15-year-olds have same concessions as for the Underground. Buses can take up to two unfolded pushchairs (buggies) at one time (they must be parked in a special area halfway down the bus). Note that wheelchairs take precedence over pushchairs. Any further pushchairs must be folded.

Discounts. Reduced rates for children are usually available for admission charges to museums and other visitor attractions.

Climate

In a word, unpredictable! In a few words, temperate and generally mild. It is unusual for any area in England to have a dry spell for more than three weeks, even in the summer months from June to September. However, it rains most frequently in the hillier areas of the north, where temperatures are also cooler.

In summer, the average maximum temperature in England is in the high 60s Fahrenheit (20°C), although over 80°F (27°C) is not unusual, and sometimes the norm on the south coast and in London. During winter (November to February), the majority of England, with the exception of mountainous regions in the north, tends to be cold and damp rather than snowy. The average maximum temperature at this time is around 45°F (7°C).

The peak holiday season in England is July and August. While these months generally have the greatest number of hours of sunshine, they do also coincide with the school holidays and are very busy. Visiting in May, June or September is therefore preferable. During the winter, attractions such as stately homes are generally closed. Likewise, in more remote regions, such as the Lake District or Cornwall, some hotels and many attractions close over the winter period when the weather is poor.

For recorded weather information, tel: 0370-900 0100 or visit www. metoffice.gov.uk.

What to wear

Temperatures can fluctuate considerably from day to day, so come prepared with suitable warm- and wet-weather clothing whatever the season. Generally, short sleeves and a jacket are fine for summer, but a warm coat and woollens are recommended for winter.

On the whole the British tend to dress casually, and with a few exceptions formal dress is not essential, although a jacket and tie is required by smart hotels, restaurants and clubs.

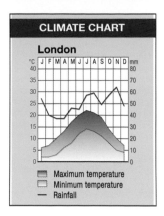

The young are generally style-conscious and as a consequence there is a strong presence of trendy street fashion in Britain's cities. At the other end of the scale, the British reputation for conservative and traditional clothing such as waxed jackets, tweeds, woollen jumpers, cords and brogues is still evident, especially in rural areas.

Crime and safety

Serious crime is low, but in big cities the Dickensian tradition of pickpocketing is alive and well. Hold on tightly to purses, do not put wallets in back pockets, and do not place handbags on the ground or the backs of chairs in busy restaurants. Gangs of professional thieves target the Underground in London.

In a genuine emergency, dial 999 from any telephone (no cash required). Report routine thefts to a police station (address under Police in a telephone directory). The threat of terrorism has led to an increase in police patrols and heightened security at airports and major train stations, so don't hesitate to report any suspicious packages.

Customs regulations

If you enter the UK directly from another European Union (EU) country, you no longer need to exit Customs through a red or green channel; use the special EU blue channel, as you are not required to declare any goods you have brought in for personal use – however, customs are likely to be dependent on the deal struck between the UK and EU post-Brexit. However, if you bring in large amounts of goods such as

alcohol, tobacco or perfume, you may be asked to verify that they are not intended for resale.

Visitors entering the UK from non-EU countries should use the green Customs channel if they do not exceed the following allowances for goods obtained outside the EU, or purchased duty-free in the EU, or on board ship or aircraft:

Tobacco 200 cigarettes *or* 100 cigarillos *or* 50 cigars *or* 250g of tobacco.

Alcohol 4 litres still table wine *plus* 1 litre spirits (over 22 percent by volume) *or* 2 litres fortified wine, sparkling wine or other liqueurs.

Perfume 60ml of perfume plus 250ml of toilet water.

Gifts £390 worth of gifts, souvenirs or other goods, including perfume.

It is illegal to bring animals, certain drugs, firearms, obscene material and anything likely to threaten health or the environment without prior arrangement. Any amount of currency can be brought in.

Consult the HM Revenue & Customs website for further details: www.hmrc.gov.uk.

D

Disabled travellers

Details of transport access for disabled people can be found on a government website, www.gov.uk/transport-disabled.

Inclusive London (www.inclusivelondon.com), Motability (www.motability.co.uk) and AccessAble (www.accessable.co.uk) are free information services, listing the access provisions and disabled facilities for hotels, shops, attractions and arts and entertainment venues across the capital and beyond.

Toilets: Britain has a system of keys to open many of the public toilets available for disabled people. To obtain a key tel: 020-7250 8191. There is a charge of £5.40 for the key and £8.90 for a key and one regional guide. Both prices include UK postal delivery.

E

Eating out

A generation of talented modern British chefs has injected new life into traditional recipes, combining them with French and international influences, to produce lighter, more delicately flavoured meals using the finest ingredients grown on British soil. These days in England it is not difficult to find Michelin-starred restaurants, fashionable gastropubs and cool cafés wherever you travel. Many pubs and restaurants make a point of featuring seasonal local produce on their menus, so look out for these.

The sheer range of ethnic food available is extraordinary – especially in London, where it is possible to sample the world's cuisine in one city. England is one of the best places for vegetarian diners, too, with many places offering increasingly imaginative choices on their menus.

Sunday lunch is a solid English tradition and always worth sampling. Traditional weekly feasts feature a roast meat with trimmings, such as Yorkshire pudding and horseradish sauce with beef, or stuffing and apple sauce with pork. **Pies** are an English staple. Among the nation's favourite savouries are steak and kidney, and Melton Mowbray pork pies. **Fish and chips** is the most characteristic of British dishes, and is best enjoyed on a sunny seafront. However, **curry** is probably the nation's favourite dish today, with particularly good restaurants in London and the area in and around Birmingham.

High-end restaurants

In recent years, dining out has become fashionable and popular across the country. Michelin-starred restaurants are scattered around the country, and have raised expectations of what restaurants should be offering. Some of England's most famous restaurants require booking weeks, perhaps months, in advance. Beware also, if the restaurant takes your credit card details when you book, you may be charged anyway if you do not then show up.

Pubs

Many pubs now serve food at lunch and dinner times. Often it is very simple fare. So-called gastropubs, however, can produce high-quality cooking, on a par with most restaurants. Traditional pub cuisine is a distinctive cuisine in itself; classic dishes include steak-and-kidney pudding, meat loaf, Lancashire hotpot, shepherd's pie, sausage and mash and the traditional Sunday roast.

Ethnic restaurants

Another mainstay of Britain's culinary heritage is the huge variety of ethnic restaurants, especially Indian, Chinese, Japanese, Vietnamese and Thai. In London, visit the Kingsland Road and Mare Street in the East End for Vietnamese, Whitechapel and Brick Lane in the East End or Tooting (South London) for Indian and Mayfair for (mostly upmarket) Japanese establishments. Manchester is renowned for its curry mile along Wilmslow Road, Birmingham boasts its 'Balti Triangle' and Leicester has many excellent Indian restaurants. Liverpool's Chinatown is home to the oldest Chinese community in Europe, and is a good place for dining out.

Chains

England has ever more chain restaurants, more indeed than most other European countries. Some are reasonably good (Carluccio's or the Gourmet Burger Kitchen, for example), others are disappointing, with food microwaved from frozen. Some chains (eg Giraffe) are helpfully child-friendly, offering children's menus, highchairs and nappy-changing facilities.

Drinking notes

Traditionally, beer was to Britain what wine was to France. It comes in various forms, from lager (now the most popular form in Britain) to ale (brewed using only top-fermenting yeasts; sweeter and fuller bodied) and stout (creamy, almost coffee-like beer made from roasted malts or roast barley), of which the most famous brand is probably Guinness. Pubs generally serve beer either "draught" or from the cask.

The popularity of wine-drinking in Britain has increased dramatically over the last few decades. Britain is now the largest importer of wine in the world. Supermarkets stock a wide selection of bottles and have now largely squeezed out mainstream wine merchants from the high street, though many small convenience grocery stores do sell alcohol.

A longer-established English tipple is cider, produced in Southwest England since before the Romans arrived. Made from the fermented juice of apples, it is also known as "scrumpy" (windfalls are "scrumps"). The pear equivalent is

☉ Electricity

230 volts, 50 Hertz. Square, three-pin plugs are used, and virtually all visitors will need adaptors if planning to plug in their own equipment.

called "perry". Beer and cider festivals are popular throughout England and a good place to try the different brews (www.camra.org.uk; www.foodfestivalfinder.co.uk).

The minimum age at which you are allowed to purchase alcohol in a pub or off-licence (store or supermarket) is 18. It is legal, however, for people aged 16 or 17 to drink wine, beer or cider on licensed premises when it is ordered with a meal – though it must be an adult who orders.

Embassies and consulates

Most countries have diplomatic representation in London. Others can be found through the *Yellow Pages* or by calling Directory Enquiries.
Australia, Australia House, Strand, London WC2 4LA; tel: 020-7379 4334; www.uk.embassy.gov.au.
Canada, Canada House, Trafalgar Square, SW1Y 5BJ, tel: 020-7004 6000, www.canadainternational.gc.ca.
India, India House, Aldwych, London WC2 4NA; tel: 020-8629 5950; www.hcilondon.in.
New Zealand, 80 Haymarket, London SW1Y 4TQ; tel: 020-7930 8422; www.nzembassy.com.
South Africa, South Africa House, Trafalgar Square, London WC2N 5DP; tel: 020-7451 7299; www.southafricahouseuk.com.
United States, 33 Nine Elms Lane, SW11 7US; tel: 020-7499 9000; https://uk.usembassy.gov.

Emergencies

Only in an absolute emergency call 999 for fire, ambulance or police. In the case of a minor accident or illness, take a taxi to the nearest casualty department of a hospital. For non-urgent calls to the police in London, dial 0300-123 1212; outside the capital, ask Directory Enquiries (see page 370) for the number of the nearest police station. They will also be able to give you the telephone number of your country's embassy or consulate if needed.

H

Health and medical care

If you fall ill and are a national of the EU, you are entitled to free medical treatment – though this may change depending on the terms of the Brexit deal that is eventually agreed. Many other countries also have reciprocal arrangements for free treatment. Most other visitors have to pay for medical and dental treatment and should ensure they have adequate health insurance.

In the case of minor accidents, your hotel will know the location of the nearest hospital with a casualty department. Self-catering accommodation should have this information, plus the number of the local GP, on a notice in the house.

Treatment: Seriously ill visitors are eligible for free emergency treatment in the Accident and Emergency departments of National Health Service hospitals. However, if they are admitted to hospital as an in-patient, even from the accident and emergency department, or referred to an out-patient clinic, they will be asked to pay unless they fall into the above exempted categories.

Walk-in clinics: There are many National Health Service walk-in centres across the country, usually open seven days a week from early morning to late evening, 365 days a year. A charge may be made to non-EU nationals; again EU citizens should check post-Brexit.

Pharmacies (chemists): Boots is the largest chain of chemists, with many branches around the country. As well as selling over-the-counter medicines, they make up prescriptions. If you need medications outside normal business hours in London, visit Zafash 24-hour Pharmacy (233–235 Old Brompton Road; tel: 020-7373 2798).

Supplies for children: Infant formula and nappies (diapers) can be purchased from pharmacies and supermarkets.

L

LGBTQ travellers

With Europe's largest gay and lesbian population, London has an abundance of bars, restaurants and clubs to cater for most tastes. Many of them will make space for one or more of London's free gay weekly magazines, *Boyz* and *QX*. Monthly magazines on sale at newsstands include *Gay Times*, *Diva* and *Attitude*.

Two established websites for meeting other gay people in London are www.gaydar.co.uk and the female version, www.gaydargirls.com. Other websites reflecting Britain's gay scene include www.gaydio.co.uk and www.outuk.com.

Useful telephone contacts for advice include **London Lesbian and Gay Switchboard** (tel: 0300-330 0630; www.switchboard.lgbt) and **London Friend** (tel: 020-7837 1674; www.londonfriend.org.uk).

Lost property

If you have lost your passport, you must get in touch with your embassy as quickly as possible.

For possessions lost on trains you must contact the station where the train on which you were travelling ended its journey. The same applies if you leave something on a coach. For anything lost on public transport in London, contact Transport for London, tel: 0343-222 1234; www.tfl.gov.uk; Mon–Fri 8.30am–4pm.

M

Maps

Insight Guides' best-selling *FlexiMaps* are laminated for durability and easy folding and contain clear cartography as well as practical information. There is a map of Great Britain and Ireland, and one for London.

In London, map-lovers should head for Stanfords (12–14 Long Acre, in the Covent Garden area), one of the world's top map and guidebook stores.

Tourist information centres can often provide visitors with a free basic map of the area in which they are situated.

Media

Newspapers

With more than 100 daily and Sunday newspapers published nationwide, there's no lack of choice in Britain. Although free from state control and financially independent of political parties, many nationals do have pronounced political leanings. Of the quality dailies *The Times* and *the Daily Telegraph* are on the right and the *Guardian* centre-left. On Sunday the *Observer* also leans slightly left of centre and the *Sunday Times* and *Sunday Telegraph* are on the right.

The Financial Times is renowned for the clearest, most unbiased headlines in its general news pages, plus exhaustive financial coverage.

The mass-market papers are a less formal, easy read. *The Sun* and *the Daily Star* are on the right and obsessed with the royal family, soap operas and sex. *The Mirror*, *Sunday Mirror* and *Sunday People* are slightly left. In the mid-market sector, the *Daily Mail* and *Mail on Sunday* are slightly more upscale equivalents of the *Express* and *Sunday Express*, and espouse a generally right-wing viewpoint.

Some cities have free newspapers, paid for by advertising and often handed out at railway stations.

Listing magazines

To find out what's on in London, the long-established weekly *Time Out* (handed out free in tube stations on Tuesdays) is supreme. But Saturday's *Guardian* includes a good free supplement previewing the week ahead, and there are daily listings in the *Evening Standard*, which is also free and often handed out at tube stations.

For details of events elsewhere, the quality daily newspapers have a limited listings section, but your best port of call is a Tourist Information Centre. Many local papers have a weekly section on Fridays with details of places to visit and things to do in their area. Two websites to try are www.timeout.com and www.bbc.co.uk.

Foreign newspapers

These can usually be found in large newsagents and railway stations nationwide. Branches of W.H. Smith, in larger towns, usually have a reasonable selection.

Television

There are five main national terrestrial channels: BBC1, BBC2, ITV, Channel 4 and Channel Five. Both the BBC (British Broadcasting Corporation) and ITV (Independent Television) have regional stations that broadcast local news and varying programme schedules between links with the national networks based in London (see local newspapers for listings). The BBC is financed by compulsory annual television licence fees and therefore does not rely on advertising for funding. The independent channels, ITV, Channel 4 and Channel Five are funded entirely by commercials.

BBC1, ITV and Five broadcast programmes aimed at mainstream audiences, while BBC2 and Channel 4 cater more for cultural and minority interests. However, the advent of cable and satellite channels has forced terrestrial stations to fight for audiences with a higher incidence of programmes such as soap operas and game shows. The BBC, ITV and Channel 4 also broadcast additional channels dedicated to news (BBC News 24), culture (BBC4), films (Film4) or repeats (More4). The BBC and ITV also operate satellite channels. Digital terrestrial broadcasting replaced the old analogue signals in England in 2012.

There are hundreds of cable and satellite channels on offer, ranging from sport and films to cartoons and music. Pricier hotel rooms often offer a choice of cable stations, including CNN and BBC News Channel.

Radio stations

In addition to the national services listed below, there are many local radio stations that can be useful for traffic reports. Note that the frequencies quoted below may vary in different parts of the country.

BBC Radio 1 98.8FM
Britain's most popular radio station, which broadcasts mainstream pop.
BBC Radio 2 89.2FM
Easy-listening music and chat shows.
BBC Radio 3 91.3FM
24-hour classical music, plus some drama.
BBC Radio 4 93.5FM
News, current affairs, plays.
BBC Radio Five Live 909MW
Rolling news and sport.
BBC World Service Digital only but same frequency as Radio 4 1am–5.20am
International news.
Classic FM 100.9FM
24-hour classical and movie music unpretentiously presented.

While BBC Radio 1 is the main station for the latest pop releases, music fans might also tune into Absolute Radio (105.8FM) for middle-of-the-road rock music, Kiss (FM 100FM) for 24-hour dance tracks, and the digital-only radio station, BBC Radio 6 Music (DAB: 12B), for "alternative" music, including indie, punk, funk, soul and hip-hop.

Money

Currency: Pounds, divided into 100 pence. Scotland issues its own notes, which are not technically legal tender in England and Wales, though banks and most shops accept them. Exchange rates against the US dollar and the euro can fluctuate significantly.
Euros: A few shops, services, attractions and hotels accept euro notes, but give change in sterling. Most will charge a commission.
ATMs: The majority of bank branches have automatic teller machines (ATMs) where international credit or cashpoint cards can be used, in conjunction with a personal number, to withdraw cash. ATMs can also be found at many supermarkets, in shopping centres and petrol stations.
Credit cards: International credit cards are accepted in most shops, hotels and restaurants.
Exchanging money: The major banks offer similar exchange rates, so it's worth shopping around only if you have large amounts of money to change. Banks charge no commission on travellers' cheques presented in sterling. If a bank is affiliated to your own bank at home, it will make no charge for cheques in other currencies either. But there is a charge for changing cash into British currency. Some high-street travel agents, such as Thomas Cook, operate bureaux de change at comparable rates. There are also many privately run bureaux de change (some of which are open 24 hours a day), where exchange rates can be low but commissions high.
Export procedures: VAT (Value Added Tax) is a sales tax of 20 percent that is added to nearly all goods except food (excluding restaurants), books and children's clothes. It is generally included in the price marked on the item. Most large department stores and smaller gift shops operate a scheme to refund this tax to non-European visitors (Retail Export Scheme), but often require that more than a minimum amount (usually £50) is spent.

For a refund you need to fill in a form from the store, have it stamped by Customs on leaving the country and post it back to the store or hand it in to a cash refund booth at the airport. If you leave the country with the goods within three months of purchase you will be refunded the tax minus an administration fee.
Tipping: Most hotels and restaurants automatically add a 10–15 percent service charge to your meal bill. It's your right to deduct this amount if you're not happy with the service. Sometimes when service has been added, the final total on a credit-card slip is still left blank, the implication being that a further tip is expected: most people do not pay this unless the service has been exceptional. You don't tip in pubs, cinemas or theatres, but it is customary to give hairdressers, sightseeing guides and cab drivers a tip of around 10 percent.

O

Opening hours

Town-centre shops generally open 9am–5.30pm Mon–Sat, although a few smaller shops may close for lunch in rural areas. Many small towns and villages have a half-day closing one day in the week, and shopping centres in towns and cities are likely to have at least one evening of late-night shopping (often Thursday evening). Increasing numbers of shops are open on Sunday, usually 10am–4pm.

Supermarkets tend to be open 8 or 8.30am–8 to 10pm Mon–Sat and 10 or 11am–4pm Sun, and some branches of the larger stores are experimenting with all-night opening on certain days of the week (often Thursday or Friday night). Some local corner shops and off-licences (shops licensed to sell alcohol to be consumed off the premises) stay open until 10pm.

Most banks open between 9.30am and 4.30pm Mon–Fri, with Saturday morning banking common in shopping areas.

Most offices operate 9am–5.30pm Mon–Fri with an hour for lunch.

British pubs' opening hours vary due to flexible closing times granted by an extended opening hours licence. Some have a 24-hour opening licence. Some

⏺ Public holidays

Compared to most of Europe, the UK has few public holidays:
January: New Year's Day (1)
March/April: Good Friday, Easter Monday
May: May Day (first Monday of the month), Spring Bank Holiday (last Monday)
August: Summer Bank Holiday (last Monday)
December: Christmas Day (25), Boxing Day (26).

On public holidays, banks and offices are closed, though some supermarkets and newsagents are open. Roads can be heavily congested as people head for the coast or the countryside or to see relatives.

may close for periods during the day, while others may just apply for the extended opening hours licence for special events such as New Year's Eve. However, most pubs will still take last orders at 11pm (and then close at 11.30pm) from Monday to Saturday, and at 10.30pm on Sundays.

P

Postal services

Post offices are open 9am–5.30pm Mon–Fri, 9am–12.30pm Sat. London's main post office is in Trafalgar Square, behind the church of St Martin-in-the-Fields. It is open Mon–Fri until 6.30pm, until 5.30pm Sat. The branch at 11 Lower Regent Street also opens Sun noon–4pm.

Stamps are sold at post offices, selected shops and newsagents, some supermarkets and from machines outside larger post offices. There is a two-tier service for mail within the UK: first class should reach its destination the next day, and second class will take a day longer.

R

Religious services

Although Christians, according to census returns, constitute about 71 percent of the population, half never attend church, so visitors will have no trouble finding a place in a pew. All the major varieties of Christianity are represented. Britain is a multi-faith society and other main religions, including Buddhism, Hinduism, Judaism, Islam and Sikhism, are freely practised. About 23 percent of Britons follow no particular religion.

S

Shopping

If you are looking for something typically British to take back home, there's a remarkably wide choice.
Cloth and wool An important centre for the cloth and wool industry is Bradford, through which 90 percent of the wool trade passed in the 19th century. The area's many mill shops are a bargain-hunter's paradise, where lengths of fabric, fine yarns and fleeces from the Yorkshire Dales can be bought. Some mills give guided tours.
Suits The flagship of Britain's bespoke tailoring industry is Savile Row in London, where gentlemen come from all over to have their suits crafted. Other outlets for traditional British attire are Burberry (for raincoats as well as more cutting-edge fashion), Aquascutum and Austin Reed, which have branches on or close to Regent Street in London and in many department stores in other cities.
Fashion Britain has a thriving fashion market, with its heart in London. Its top designers (including Henry Holland, Sarah Burton, Christopher Bailey, Katharine Hamnett, Stella McCartney, Paul Smith, Phoebe Philo and Vivienne Westwood) are at the pinnacle of the industry and world-famous. Many top international designers can also be found in London's Knightsbridge and Mayfair, and to a lesser extent in department stores nationwide. For quality everyday clothing Marks & Spencer's stores retain their popularity. For affordable fashions with a little more edge, Topshop, H&M and Zara provide up-to-date fashion with high-street prices and have branches nationwide. Mulberry is famous for its leather accessories,

from personal organisers to weekend bags, all embossed with the classic tree logo and a high price tag.
China and porcelain Top-price china, glass and silver items can be found in Regent Street and Mayfair in London at exclusive shops such as Thomas Goode, Asprey and Garrard. Stoke-on-Trent (in "the Potteries", Staffordshire) was the home of the great china and porcelain houses, including Wedgwood and Royal Doulton, Minton, Spode and Royal Stafford (www.visitstoke.co.uk/potteries). Wedgwood still exists, and has a visitor centre where you can often pick up some real bargains. You can also visit Dartington Crystal at Great Torrington in Devon.
Jewellery The centre for British jewellery production is in Hockley, Birmingham, an industry that developed here in the 18th century along with other forms of metal working such as brass-founding and gun-smithing. Today hundreds of jewellery manufacturers and silversmiths are based here, and it is known as Birmingham's jewellery quarter (www.jewelleryquarter.net). London's jewellery quarter can be found at Hatton Garden on the edge of the City (www.hatton-garden.net).
Perfumes English flower perfumes make a delightful gift. The most exclusive of these come from Floris in Jermyn Street, and Penhaligon's in Covent Garden, London. The Cotswold Perfumery in the

In Looe, Cornwall.

picturesque village of Bourton-on-the-Water, Gloucestershire, makes its own perfumes.

Antiques If you are coming to Britain to look for antiques it is worth getting in touch with the London and Provincial Antique Dealers' Association (LAPADA), 535 King's Road, London, SW10; tel: 020-7823 3511; www.lapada.org. It runs a computer information service on the antiques situation throughout the country. A number of antiques fairs are held nationwide throughout the year, and many towns, such as Bath, Harrogate and Brighton, have antique centres and markets. Good places to start in London are the market and stalls around Portobello Road in London's Notting Hill (main market day is Saturday) and the indoor Alfies Antique Market on Church Street, Marylebone (Tue–Sat).

Consumables British delights that are easy to take home include Twinings or Jacksons tea and numerous brands of chocolate. Charbonnel et Walker (www.charbonnel.co.uk) is a famous British chocolatier, established in 1875. Its beautifully packaged products are available at its exquisite shop in the historic Royal Arcade on Old Bond Street, London. More widely available brands include Bendicks, famous for its after-dinner mints, while, on a more popular level, Cadbury is a national favourite.

Britain is particularly proud of its conserves, jams, honeys, pickles and mustards (not least the famous anchovy spread, Gentleman's Relish). Local delicatessens and farm shops nationwide are often worth exploring for edible gifts. Some regional specialities to look out for include: Cornish pasties and saffron buns, Bakewell tarts (correctly termed puddings), Eccles cakes, Kendal Mint Cake and Yorkshire parkin, a type of gingerbread.

For Britain's food at its finest, visit Fortnum & Mason, 181 Piccadilly, London W1, an Aladdin's cave of mouth-watering goodies.

Crafts Almost every town has a weekly street market where cheap clothes and domestic ware can be bought and there may also be a good presence of local crafts. There are many workshops in rural areas of Britain where potters, woodturners, leather workers, candle makers

and other craftspeople can be seen producing their wares. The Crafts Council, 44a Pentonville Road, London N1; tel: 020-7806 2500; www.craftscouncil.org.uk, produces a pdf digital Shops & Galleries guide annually and you can also access their directory of crafts people.

Books London's Charing Cross Road has long been the centre for second-hand and specialist bookshops, though there are fewer these days than there used to be. Cecil Court, just off Charing Cross Road, remains a haven for antiquarian dealers. Waterstones branches nationwide are popular, and Foyles in London has five crammed floors.

Outside London, university towns are the best places for books. Blackwell's in Oxford and Heffers in Cambridge are equally good for publications in English and most prominent foreign languages. Serious book-lovers should head for Hay-on-Wye, on the border of England and Wales; it has around 25 bookshops and also hosts a lively literary festival, with top-notch guests, in late May (www.hayfestival.com).

Gifts Some of the best places to seek out tasteful presents to take home are museum gift shops (especially the ones at the Victoria and Albert Museum and Tate Modern) and the shops on National Trust properties.

Smoking

Smoking is banned in all enclosed public spaces, including pubs, clubs and bars (though not in outside beer gardens).

Student travellers

International students can obtain various discounts at attractions, on travel services (including Eurostar) and in some shops by showing a valid ISIC card; www.isiccard.com.

T

Telephones

It is usually cheaper to use public phones or even your own mobile (cell-) phone than those in hotel rooms, as hotels make high profits out of this service.

British Telecom (BT) is the main telephone operating company for

landlines and provides public telephone kiosks. Some public phones take coins only (minimum charge 60p), some and/or credit/debit cards (charged at a higher rate).

Public telephone boxes are not as numerous as they used to be. Now that so many people have mobile phones, they are not as widely used. Stations and shopping centres in particular are good places to look. In country areas, try a pub.

The most expensive time to use the telephone is 8am–6pm weekdays, while the cheapest is after 6pm on weekdays and all weekend. Call charges are related to distance, so a long-distance conversation on a weekday morning can eat up coins or card payments in a phone box.

Numbers beginning with the prefixes 0800, 0500 or 0808 are freephone lines. Those prefixed by 03, 0300, 0343, 0345 are charged at local rates irrespective of distance. Those starting with 0843/4/5 and 0870/1/2/3 are charged at a slightly higher rate and those starting with 09 are costly premium-rate numbers.

The Directory Enquiries service, once exclusively a BT money-earner, was opened up to competition from other companies and the result was a confusing variety of expensive numbers such as 118 500. A better bet is to use British Telecom's online service, www.192.com.

Mobile phones: You can buy pay-as-you-go SIM cards from most mobile-phone retailers and many electrical stores. If your mobile phone accepts SIM cards from companies other than the one you usually use it with, you should be able to register the SIM and use it during your trip.

Useful numbers

Operator 100
Directory Enquiries (UK) 118 500, 118 888 or 118 811
International Directory Enquiries 118 505 or 118 118
International Operator 155
International dialling code for the UK: +44

City dialling codes

Central London: 0207
Outer London: 0208
Edinburgh: 0131
Cardiff: 029
Bristol: 0117
Manchester: 0161
Newcastle: 0191

International dialling codes
Australia: +61
Canada: +1
New Zealand: +64
South Africa: +27

Tourist information

Tourist information in London
Visit London (www.visitlondon.com) has two main tourist information centres in London. The City of London Information Centre, St Paul's Churchyard, London EC4M 8BX and the Greenwich Tourist Information Centre, Pepys House, 2 Cutty Sark Gardens, London DE10 9LW, both of which provide a wide range of maps, guides and books about London and the UK. You can also purchase transport, theatre and sightseeing tickets. There is also an information kiosk outside Holborn Underground station.
Transport for London Travel Information (TfL) publishes various maps and guides for visitors, as well as transport information and tickets for attractions – available from Heathrow and Piccadilly Underground stations, and Victoria, Euston, Kings Cross, Liverpool Street and Paddington mainline stations. For further information, tel: 0343-222 1234; www.tfl.gov.uk.

Information centres
There are more than 800 Tourist Information Centres (TICs) throughout Britain, which provide free information and advice on local sights, activities and accommodation. Most are open office hours, which are extended to include weekends and evenings in high season or in areas where there is a high volume of visitors year-round. Some close from October to March. TICs are generally well-signposted and denoted by a distinctive "i" symbol. The website www.visitbritain.com can be used to access information from

☉ Time zone
Greenwich Mean Time (GMT) is 1 hour behind Continental European Time, 5 hours ahead of Eastern Seaboard Time, and 9 hours behind Sydney, Australia. British Summer Time (GMT + 1 hour) runs from late March to late October.

regional tourist boards; just click on the relevant area of the map.

The following are offices for different regions with links to the individual tourist offices for information.
Visit East Anglia, www.visiteastofengland.com.
Tourism South East, www.visitsoutheastengland.com.
South West Tourism, www.visitsouthwest.co.uk.
Yorkshire Tourist Board, www.yorkshire.com.
North East England Tourism, www.visitnortheastengland.com.
Cumbria Tourism, www.cumbriatourism.org.
Visit Manchester, www.visitmanchester.com.
Visit Liverpool, www.visitliverpool.com.

Tour operators and travel agents

The Association of Independent Tour Operators and Travel Agents (AITO) represents Britain's main specialist tour operators, who operate to a code of practice. For details of their members and their specialities contact AITO, 18 Bridle Lane, Twickenham; tel: 020-8744 9280; www.aito.com.

Sightseeing tours
All British cities of historical interest have special double-decker buses that tour the sites. Some are open-topped, and many have a commentary in several languages.

The Original Tour is the first and biggest London sightseeing operator. Hop on and hop off at over 80 different stops. With commentary in a wide choice of languages and a Kids' Club for 5–11 year olds. Buy tickets on bus or in advance. Operates year-round. Tel: 020-8877 1722; www.theoriginaltour.com.

Original London Walks organises more than 200 walks, including Along the Thames Pub Walk, Famous Square Mile, Hidden London, Hampstead, Beatles' London, Olympic London and Ghost walks. Under-15s can tag along free with an adult. Tel: 020-7624 3987; www.walks.com.

Footprints Tours offers guided cycle rides of Oxford and the surrounding countryside. Cycle hire is available for the tour and the rest of the day, and children over 12 are welcome. Walking tours are also available. Tel: 020-7558 8706; www.footprints-tours.com.

Windermere Lake Cruises runs vintage and modern cruisers, which offer trips to various attractions around this famous lake. Tel: 015394-43360; www.windermere-lakecruises.co.uk.

V

Visas and passports

To enter the UK you need a valid passport (or any form of official identification if you are an EU citizen, up until the Brexit date when it may change; check current). Visas are not needed if you are an American, Commonwealth citizen or EU national (or come from most other European or South American countries). Health certificates are not required unless you have arrived from Asia, Africa or South America.

If you wish to stay for a protracted period or apply to work in Great Britain, contact the **Immigration and Nationality Directorate**. First look at the website: www.ind.homeoffice.gov.uk.

W

Weights and measures

It's a mess, reflecting Britain's ambivalence about whether it prefers its Imperial past or its European present. So you will fill up a car with litres of fuel (which may be as well since, confusingly, an Imperial gallon is larger than a US gallon), but road signs will direct you to your destination in miles. You buy beer by the pint in a pub. A supermarket will sell you a pint of milk, but most other drinks are packaged as litres. In a few controversial cases, greengrocers have been fined for selling vegetables by the pound instead of by the kilo. The main conversions are:
Kilometres and miles
1 mile = 1.609 kilometres
1 kilometre = 0.621 miles
Litres and gallons
1 gallon = 4.546 litres
1 litre = 0.220 gallons
Kilos and pounds
1 pound = 0.453 kilos
1 kilo = 2.204 pounds

FURTHER READING

HISTORY

The Concise Pepys by Samuel Pepys. A first-hand account of the Great Fire of London and daily life in 17th-century England.
A History of Britain by Simon Schama. Enjoyable and richly-illustrated romp through British history.
Living Back to Back by Chris Upton. Absorbing portrait of domestic life in the working-class industrial Midlands.

LITERATURE

The Adventures of Sherlock Holmes by Sir Arthur Conan Doyle. The Sherlock Holmes stories are evocative portraits of the London of the late 19th century.
Canterbury Tales by Geoffrey Chaucer. Written at the end of the 14th century, these stories provide a warm yet penetrating portrait of English society at the time.
Cider with Rosie by Laurie Lee. Spellbinding memoir of an idyllic youth in rural Gloucestershire in the 1920s.
The Mayor of Casterbridge by Thomas Hardy. Rural life and tragedy in the Wessex countryside.
Oliver Twist by Charles Dickens. The classic tale of Victorian pickpockets in London's East End.
Pride and Prejudice by Jane Austen. Genteel society at the turn of the 19th century provided wonderful material for the wit and psychological insight of Jane Austen.
Wuthering Heights by Emily Brontë. Passion and repression on the brooding Yorkshire Moors.

TRAVEL WRITING

Literary London by Ed Glinert. A detailed, street-by-street guide to the literary lives of London.
Mail Obsession: A Journey Round Britain by Postcode by Mark Mason.

A unique insight into Britain through its 124 postcode areas, full of humour.
Vanishing Cornwall by Daphne du Maurier. A perceptive view of the changing face of Cornwall.
Wild Swimming: 300 Hidden Dips in the Rivers, Lakes and Waterfalls of Britain by Daniel Start. A wonderful compendium of places to swim.

IMAGES OF ENGLAND

England Observed: John Gay (1909–99) by Andrew Sargent (ed.). John Gay's photographs capture the essence of ordinary life in England in the 20th century.
Homes Fit for Heroes by Bill Brandt. Taken during 1939–43, the extraordinary photographs in this beautifully designed book compare the living conditions of ordinary British people.
London Interiors: From the Archives of Country Life by John Cornforth. Sumptuous volume packed with detailed photographs of domestic interiors that have long since disappeared.
London's Disused Underground Stations by J.E.Connor. This intriguing account of the "ghost" stations of London's Tube network is accompanied by stunning photographs.
The Photography of Bedford Lemere & Co.: An Age of Confidence by Nicholas Cooper. Beautifully-produced English Heritage publication on the foremost architectural photography firm in the late 19th and early 20th centuries.

ART AND ARCHITECTURE

Betjeman's Best British Churches by Sir John Betjeman and Richard Surman. Classic work on the country's rich ecclesiastical heritage, written with style and wit.
Blimey! – From Bohemia to Britpop by Matthew Collings. Funny, readable

and copiously illustrated account of the London art world of the last few decades.
A Companion to British Art 1600 to the Present edited by Dana Arnold and David Peters Corbett. Essays providing a comprehensive introduction to British art history.
A Little History of the English Country Church by Sir Roy Strong. A fascinating homage to the English country church.
The Regency Country House by John Martin Robinson. Beautiful photographs and lively text bring to life the world of the Prince Regent and his architects.

OTHER INSIGHT GUIDES

The **Insight Guides** series includes books on *Great Britain, Scotland* and *Ireland*. The **Great Breaks** series include books on London, Edinburgh, Oxford and other regions of the UK.
Explore London has 20 self-guided walks and tours, and a fold-out map.
Insight Fleximaps *London*, *Edinburgh*, *Jersey* and *Guernsey* combine clear, detailed cartography with a durable laminated finish.

⊙ Send us your thoughts

We do our best to ensure the information in our books is as accurate and up-to-date as possible. The books are updated on a regular basis using local contacts, who painstakingly add, amend and correct as required. However, some details (such as telephone numbers and opening times) are liable to change, and we are ultimately reliant on our readers to put us in the picture.

We welcome your feedback, especially your experience of using the book "on the road". Maybe you came across a great bar or new attraction we missed.

We will acknowledge all contributions, and we'll offer an Insight Guide to the best letters received.

Please write to us at:
Insight Guides
PO Box 7910
London SE1 1WE

Or email us at:
hello@insightguides.com

CREDITS

Alamy 150B, 230, 280BR, 345
Alnwick Castle 354
AP/Shutterstock 28B
AWL Images 7ML
Bigstock.com 33, 47BL, 55, 63ML, 63BR, 87B, 135, 136, 141T, 164, 166, 167, 182, 193, 214, 224B, 226, 232, 245, 268, 300, 303, 329, 341, 346, 348, 352T, 353
British Tourist Authority 218BR, 218BL, 279B, 362/363
Chester Cathedral 269T
Corbis 50, 138, 280BL
Corrie Wingate/Apa Publications 7BR, 18, 79B, 134, 139T, 149, 150T, 181, 184T, 185, 186, 187, 188, 192, 202, 203B, 204, 209B, 217, 235, 237, 239B, 240, 241B, 247B, 336T
Country Life 143ML, 219ML
David Beatty/Apa Publications 286T, 292T, 318T
Derby Cathedral 273
Dreamstime 8T, 22, 63TR, 123B, 139B, 141B, 201, 219BL, 252B, 283, 286B, 288, 295B, 305B, 305T, 306, 334, 339, 343, 349
Finn Beales 269B
Fotolia 153, 170, 198, 287, 294, 301
Frank Noon/Apa Publications 17B, 144, 145, 146, 147T, 148B, 148T, 151
Geoff Moore/Shutterstock 238B
Getty Images 1, 4, 10/11, 12/13, 14/15, 27T, 28T, 32R, 41, 42, 45, 48/49, 51, 62BR, 62BL, 63BL, 66, 67, 68, 69, 70, 71, 72/73, 74/75, 76/77, 78, 94, 124, 142/143T, 142BR, 143BR, 143BL, 152, 190/191, 206, 220, 265, 280/281T, 282, 308, 313B, 319B, 336B
Glyn Genin/Apa Publications 195T, 200T, 203T, 223T
Historic Royal Palaces 8B
Imperial War Museum 95B
iStock 6ML, 7TL, 26, 31, 32L, 35, 46BL, 47ML, 47TR, 47BR, 93B, 113, 165, 171, 195B, 197B, 199, 213, 219BR,

262/263, 291, 293B, 311, 317B, 321B, 351, 355, 372
Jaap Oepkes/The River & Rowing Museum 140
Leigh Simpson/Glyndebourne 207B
Lincoln Cathedral 276T
Lincolnshire Tourism 277T
Lydia Evans/Apa Publications 6MR, 6B, 7B, 9TR, 20, 84, 85, 86, 87T, 88T, 88B, 97T, 97B, 98T, 99B, 100T, 101B, 103, 104, 105, 108, 109B, 112, 114, 121T, 123T, 128, 130, 131, 154, 157T, 161, 162T, 163T, 163B, 221, 223B, 224T, 225T, 225B, 227T, 227B, 228, 229, 231T, 231B, 233, 234, 236, 238T, 239T, 241T, 242, 243, 246T, 246B, 247T, 248, 249B, 251, 252T, 253T, 253B, 254, 255B, 256B, 257T, 257B, 258, 259, 260, 369
Mark Read/Apa Publications 255T, 256T
Mary Evans Picture Library 212, 219TR, 281ML
Merlin Entertainments Group 169B, 270T
Ming Tang-Evans/Apa Publications 9B, 23, 59R, 59L, 60, 89, 90, 91T, 92T, 92B, 93T, 95T, 96, 98B, 99T, 102T, 102B, 106, 107B, 109T, 110, 111, 117, 119T, 120B, 120T, 122B, 122T, 125, 127, 129B, 129T, 358
National Maritime Museum 34
National Portrait Gallery 30
NTPL/Joe Cornish 16, 344
NTPL/Penny Tweedie 200B
Phil Wood/Apa Publications 342T
Photoshot 29T, 43, 44, 180, 196, 261, 276B, 281BR, 281BL, 304, 314, 328
Pictures Colour Library 264, 272, 275, 302
Public domain 24/25, 27B, 37, 56, 57, 281TR, 317T
Richard Sowersby/Rex Features 168
Robert Harding 62/63T, 116, 147B
Rupert Hartley/David Hartley/Rex Features 119B

Scala Archives 39, 40
Shutterstock 17T, 26, 29B, 115, 121B, 132/133, 142BL, 143TR, 218/219T, 250/251, 271, 298/299, 323, 332, 333, 335
Sir John Soane's Museum/Martin Charles 101T
Steve Cutner/Apa Publications 205, 207T, 209T, 210, 211, 216
Sylvaine Poitau/Apa Publications 19, 21, 54, 61, 172/173, 174, 175, 176, 177, 179, 184B, 189
Tips Images 7TR
Tom Smyth 91B, 100B, 107T, 215, 249T
Tony Halliday/Apa Publications 155, 157B, 158, 159, 160T, 160B, 162B, 169T, 293T, 313T, 338, 347, 352B
Topham Picturepoint 197T
VisitEngland/Alex Hare 64
VisitEngland/Blenheim Palace/Experience Oxfordshire 46/47T
VisitEngland/Chatsworth House Trust 46BR
VisitEngland/Clive Barda 53
VisitEngland/Cotswolds.com/Nick Turner 356
VisitEngland/Diana Jarvis 277B, 278
VisitEngland/Leicestershire Promotions 279T
VisitEngland/RSC 69
VisitEngland/South West Coast Path/Paul Melling 65
VisitEngland/Visit Stoke on Trent 270B
Wellcome Collection 36, 38
William Shaw/Apa Publications 7MR, 7MR, 9TL, 58, 79T, 285B, 285T, 289B, 289T, 290, 292B, 295T, 296T, 296B, 297, 307, 309T, 309B, 310, 315T, 315B, 316T, 316B, 318B, 319T, 320, 321T, 322, 324, 325, 326T, 326B, 327, 331, 337, 340, 342B

Front cover: Gold Hill, Shaftesbury *Maurizio Rellini/4Corners Images*
Back cover: Tower of London *Lydia Evans/Apa Publications*
Front flap: (from top) Ashness Bridge *iStock*; Statue outside the Sheldonian Theatre in Oxford *Shutterstock*; Stone Henge *Lydia Evans/Apa Publications*; Kynance Cove *iStock*
Back flap: Polperro, Cornwall *Lydia Evans/Apa Publications*

INSIGHT GUIDE CREDITS

Distribution
UK, Ireland and Europe
Apa Publications (UK) Ltd;
sales@insightguides.com
United States and Canada
Ingram Publisher Services;
ips@ingramcontent.com
Australia and New Zealand
Woodslane; info@woodslane.com.au
Southeast Asia
Apa Publications (SN) Pte;
singaporeoffice@insightguides.com
Worldwide
Apa Publications (UK) Ltd;
sales@insightguides.com
Special Sales, Content Licensing and CoPublishing
Insight Guides can be purchased in
bulk quantities at discounted prices.
We can create special editions,
personalised jackets and corporate
imprints tailored to your needs.
sales@insightguides.com
www.insightguides.biz

Printed in China by RR Donnelley Asia Printing Solutions Limited

All Rights Reserved
© 2020 Apa Digital (CH) AG and
Apa Publications (UK) Ltd

First Edition 2000
Fifth Edition 2020

Editors: Helen Fanthorpe and Tatiana
Wilde
Authors: Jackie Staddon, Hilary
Weston and Joanna Reeves
Head of DTP and Pre-Press:
Rebeka Davies
Layout: Aga Bylica
Update Production: Apa Digital
Managing Editor: Carine Tracanelli
Picture Editor: Tom Smyth
Cartography: original cartography
APA, updated by Carte

CONTRIBUTORS

This new edition was comprehensively
updated by **Joanna Reeves**, a London-
based travel writer who loves to explore
the quaint villages and buzzy cities of
England, particularly those with a great
arts scene and excellent restaurants.
The new edition builds on the work of the
contributors including **Jackie Staddon,
Hilary Weston**, **Michael Macaroon,** who
wrote the features on sports, the
monarchy and English cheeses, **Pam
Barrett,** who compiled the essays on

theatre and food, **Roger Williams**, who
contributed the piece on landscape
painting, and **Rebecca Ford**. Other
original contributors include: Susie
Boulton, Roland Collins, Christopher
Catling, Michael Ivory, W.R Mitchell,
John Scott, Harry Mead, Roly Smith,
Andrew Eames, Dorothy Stannard and
Tony Halliday.

Much of the photography was taken by
Ming Tang Evans, Corrie Wingate, Steve
Cutner, Lydia Evans and William Shaw.

ABOUT INSIGHT GUIDES

Insight Guides have more than 45
years' experience of publishing high-
quality, visual travel guides. We
produce 400 full-colour titles, in both
print and digital form, covering more
than 200 destinations across the
globe, in a variety of formats to meet
your different needs.

Insight Guides are written by local
authors, whose expertise is evident in
the extensive historical and cultural

background features. Each destination
is carefully researched by regional
experts to ensure our guides provide
the very latest information. All the
reviews in **Insight Guides** are
independent; we strive to maintain an
impartial view. Our reviews are
carefully selected to guide you to the
best places to visit, so you can be
confident that when we say a place is
special, we really mean it.

Legend

City maps
Freeway/Highway/Motorway
Divided Highway
Main Roads
Minor Roads
Pedestrian Roads
Steps
Footpath
Railway
Funicular Railway
Cable Car
Tunnel
City Wall
Important Building
Built Up Area
Other Land
Transport Hub
Park
Pedestrian Area
Bus Station
Tourist Information
Main Post Office
Cathedral/Church
Mosque
Synagogue
Statue/Monument
Beach
Airport

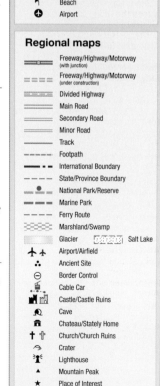

Regional maps
Freeway/Highway/Motorway
(with junction)
Freeway/Highway/Motorway
(under construction)
Divided Highway
Main Road
Secondary Road
Minor Road
Track
Footpath
International Boundary
State/Province Boundary
National Park/Reserve
Marine Park
Ferry Route
Marshland/Swamp
Glacier   Salt Lake
Airport/Airfield
Ancient Site
Border Control
Cable Car
Castle/Castle Ruins
Cave
Chateau/Stately Home
Church/Church Ruins
Crater
Lighthouse
Mountain Peak
Place of Interest
Viewpoint

INDEX

MAIN REFERENCES ARE IN BOLD TYPE

INSIGHT ⊙ GUIDES

OFF THE SHELF

Since 1970, INSIGHT GUIDES has provided a unique perspective on the world's best travel destinations by using specially commissioned photography and illuminating text written by local authors.

Whether you're planning a city break, a walking tour or the journey of a lifetime, our superb range of guidebooks and phrasebooks will inspire you to discover more about your chosen destination.

INSIGHT GUIDES

offer a unique combination of stunning photos, absorbing narrative and detailed maps, providing all the inspiration and information you need.

PHRASEBOOKS & DICTIONARIES

help users to feel at home, when away. Pocket-sized with a free app to download, they go where you do.

CITY GUIDES

pack hundreds of great photos into a smaller format with detailed practical information, so you can navigate the world's top cities with confidence.

EXPLORE GUIDES

feature easy-to-follow walks and itineraries in the world's most exciting destinations, with our choice of the best places to eat and drink along the way.

POCKET GUIDES

combine concise information on where to go and what to do in a handy compact format, ideal on the ground. Includes a full-colour, fold-out map.

EXPERIENCE GUIDES

feature offbeat perspectives and secret gems for experienced travellers, with a collection of over 100 ideas for a memorable stay in a city.

www.insightguides.com

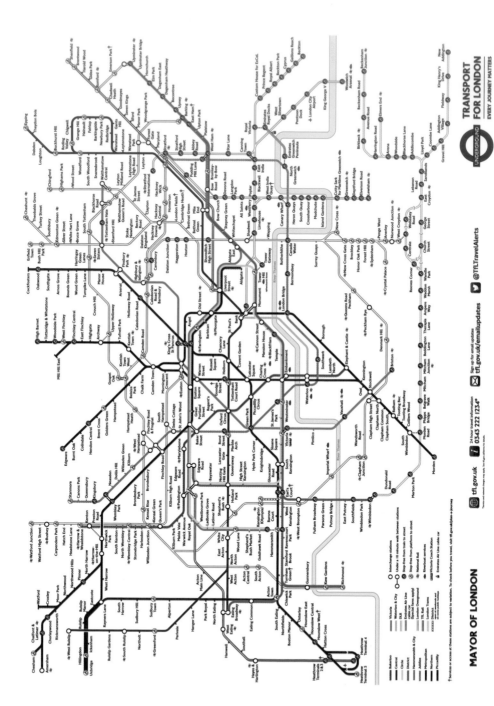